Homer
The Odyssey

Homer
The Odyssey
A Prose Translation

Translated by Charles Underwood

HAMILTON BOOKS
AN IMPRINT OF
ROWMAN & LITTLEFIELD
Lanham • Boulder • New York • London

Published by Hamilton Books
An imprint of The Rowman & Littlefield Publishing Group, Inc.
4501 Forbes Boulevard, Suite 200, Lanham, Maryland 20706
www.rowman.com

86-90 Paul Street, London EC2A 4NE, United Kingdom

British Library Cataloguing in Publication Information Available

Library of Congress Cataloging-in-Publication Data

Names: Homer, author. | Underwood, Charles, 1948– translator.
Title: Homer : the Odyssey : a prose translation / translated by Charles Underwood.
Other titles: Odyssey. English (Underwood) | Odyssey : a prose translation
Description: Lanham : Hamilton Books, 2022. | Includes bibliographical references. | Summary: “This is a complete translation into contemporary English of the ancient Greek epic by Homer. The translation by Charles Underwood is presented in prose to emphasize the distinctive narrative qualities that illustrate Homer’s mastery of stirring language and evocative storytelling”— Provided by publisher.
Identifiers: LCCN 2022039719 (print) | LCCN 2022039720 (ebook) | ISBN 9780761873686 (paperback) | ISBN 9780761873693 (epub)
Subjects: LCSH: Odysseus, King of Ithaca (Mythological character)—Fiction. | Odysseus, King of Ithaca (Mythological character)—Travel—Fiction. | Homecoming—Fiction. | Epic poetry, Greek—Translations into English. | LCGFT: Fiction. | Epic fiction.
Classification: LCC PA4025.A5 U53 2022 (print) | LCC PA4025.A5 (ebook) | DDC 883/.01—dc23/eng/20221006
LC record available at https://lccn.loc.gov/2022039719
LC ebook record available at https://lccn.loc.gov/2022039720>

∞™ The paper used in this publication meets the minimum requirements of American National Standard for Information Sciences—Permanence of Paper for Printed Library Materials, ANSI/NISO Z39.48-1992.

Contents

Acknowledgments

Translation is a collective activity. Although translators work alone for hours, pursuing precise nuances of meaning in multiple languages, we are always drawing on and learning from others' creativity and ideas—both those who have translated the text at hand before and those whose knowledge and experience in various languages and disciplines facilitate the solitary craft of translation. My daughter Alice is both my hardest and most gentle critic. The fact that she has a doctorate in comparative literature, is fluent and knowledgeable in several languages, and has long experience in writing and editing, makes her contribution to my work immeasurable. And the fact that I am continually surprised by the breadth and depth of her knowledge as we work together makes me both joyful and proud.

Others have also contributed greatly to this translation. Richard Martin has encouraged my efforts and provided precise insights for both my previous study of *The Odyssey* and this translation of the epic. Joel Christensen has offered both constructive critique and incisive comments that have made this translation much better than it would have been without his assistance and support. John Paul Russo has contributed invaluable criticism and productive advice, both questioning my choice of words in rendering the subtleties of Homer's narrative and urging me to keep my focus on Homeric style. Michael Nagler offered thoughtful suggestions both on specific passages and on the broad sweep of the narrative. All four of these extraordinary scholars were generous with their time and gracious in scrutinizing drafts of this translation. I am also deeply grateful for the many classical scholars whose cumulative work has vastly expanded and enriched my understanding of Homer's epic narratives.

In addition, I would like to express my profound gratitude to the college professor who first introduced me to *The Odyssey*. Christian Smith was quite simply the best professor—the best teacher—that I ever encountered in over five decades studying and working in educational institutions. He always brought the whole world into our classes on *The Odyssey*—everything from literature to philosophy to explorations of classical antiquity and its relevance for a deeper grasp of contemporary life. With his often droll yet consistently thoughtful guidance, I came to see the enduring significance of *The Odyssey*, both for its earlier audiences and for us today. The passion that Christian Smith brought to the study of ancient Greek language and literature was extremely contagious; I was one among many who caught his sheer enthusiasm, and for me it has lasted unabated into the present moment.

I would also like to offer special thanks to my longtime friend and colleague, Anthony Garcia, whose work as an anthropologist has always been informed by his keen Indigenous sense of time and place and whose calm bearing and persistence has continually stirred my own sense of purpose in this wondrous yet rarely equitable world. It was Anthony who first sparked my interest in Indigenous oral narrative, so that my anthropological work came to be closely linked with my earlier classical studies. Finally, I want to thank my colleagues of many years in the fields of anthropology, sociology, cultural psychology, human development, comparative literature, education, and the institute of hard knocks—including Manuel Aguilar, Mary Ann Aguilar, Diana Arya, Angela Booker, Don Bremme, Betsy Brenner, John Cano, Victor Cary, Michael Cole, Margaret Conkey, Sue Cronmiller, Richard Durán, Chalon Emmons, Manuel Gómez, James Grieshop, Yvette Gullatt, Glynda Hull, Anu Kajamaa, Denise Lambrecht, Regina Langhout, Leslie López, Marcos Matsukama, Jabari Mahiri, Jelani Mahiri, Lara Moammar, Debra McKoy, Zahara Namanda, Marjorie Orellana, Lorraine Orosco, Dirce Pranzetti, Sonia Ritsos, Barbara Rogoff, Lynda Stone, Anna Stetsenko, Tamara Sturak, Cecilia Toloza, Ruth Tringham, Karla Trujillo, Ben Tucker, Judy Underwood, Kelsey Underwood, Sue Lynn Underwood, Wyatt Underwood, Mara Welsh Mahmood, Olga Vásquez, Tom Vogt, and others no less significant but too numerous to mention. The collective work and insight of all these awesome people have contributed mightily to my reading of the human world and of masterful human achievements like *The Odyssey*.

Displaced Voices: Retelling the Mythos of Odysseus's Journey

A Translator's Introduction

The first moment in the Odyssey that lends full depth to the identity of the main character takes place in its nineteenth book, in the story within the story of Odysseus's recognition by his old nurse, Eurykleia. At this crucial moment, the epic poet gives an account of the origin of Odysseus's name. Having journeyed to Ithaka to attend his grandson's naming ritual, Autylokos, the newborn's somewhat crude maternal grandfather, declares:

> τίθεσθ᾽ ὄνομ᾽ ὅττι κεν εἴπω:
> πολλοῖσιν γὰρ ἐγώ γε **ὀδυσσάμενος** τόδ᾽ ἱκάνω,
> ἀνδράσιν ἠδὲ γυναιξὶν ἀνὰ χθόνα πουλυβότειραν:
> τῷ δ᾽ **Ὀδυσεὺς** ὄνομ᾽ ἔστω ἐπώνυμον.
>
> Give him the name I tell you. Since I have come here
> as someone who has been as utterly **odious as** I am
> to so many men and women, all over this teeming earth,
> so call him by the name **Odysseus**.

Autolykos's words in giving the infant his name play on the verb *odússomai*, which, if translated literally, means "to be angry or incensed" or "to be hated, to be the source of others' anger"—that is, denoting the typically antagonistic relationship between Odysseus and others (cf. Stanford 1952; Stewart 1976; Dimock 1989; Kanavou 2015). Although the *mythos* of Odysseus's naming does not take place until the *Odyssey*'s nineteenth book, this kind of verbal play has reverberated throughout the epic since the earliest lines of its first book, when Athena expresses her concern to Zeus for the long-displaced veteran of the Trojan War.

. . . αὐτὰρ Ὀδυσσεύς,
ἱέμενος καὶ καπνὸν ἀποθρῴσκοντα νοῆσαι
ἧς γαίης, θανέειν ἱμείρεται. οὐδέ νυ σοί περ
ἐντρέπεται φίλον ἦτορ, Ὀλύμπιε. οὔ νύ τ᾽ **Ὀδυσσεὺς**
Ἀργείων παρὰ νηυσὶ χαρίζετο ἱερὰ ῥέζων
Τροίῃ ἐν εὐρείῃ; τί νύ οἱ τόσον **ὠδύσαο, Ζεῦ;**

But Odysseus,
longing at least to see the smoke rising up
from his own country, only wants to die.
And yet your own heart is unmoved, Olympian.
Didn't **Odysseus** tactfully please you by preparing
sacrifices beside the Argives' ships on the fields
of Troy? Yet **odious he is** to you now, Zeus. Why?"

This recurrent form of persistent verbal invention and linguistic play is one of the hardest features of the *Odyssey* to capture in contemporary English. The word "odious" is a convenient though not denotatively flawless way to convey in English the rich signification that is at play in the original Greek form of the main character's name (Kanavou 2015), in the same way that other subtle puns and plays on words and names are almost impossible to convey viably and concisely in translation without bringing the narrative to a standstill. Homer (or the Homeric tradition) slips them into the oral narrative adroitly, fleetingly, and the audience (or reader) soon learns to listen for them carefully and comes to recognize that they can easily fly by unnoticed and unappreciated, since this effortlessly casual yet coolly calculated linguistic play on the part of the poet rarely ever calls attention to itself at the expense of story's tempo, or what Arnold (1905) referred to as its narrative quickness. This particular feature of Homeric oral discourse is only one example of the difficulties in translating the epic from archaic Greek to contemporary English. Yet ignoring the omnipresence of this verbal play is one of the greatest hazards to translating the *Odyssey* without reducing the familiar narrative to a superficial shell of its original depth and character.

Christensen (2021) has commented on this difficulty in translating what he aptly calls Homer's poly-symphonic resonances: "Each line has melodies full of resonant meaning that echo differently based on who you are and what you've heard before. When someone tells you that the *Iliad* is about this or the *Odyssey* is about that they are following one repeated series of notes for their movement and resolution, and necessarily leaving others aside" (Christensen 2021). Translating Homer is especially challenging because it is not simply trying to carry meaning across from a book written in one language to a book written in another. Instead, it involves conveying the distinctive rhetorical strategies of an oral performance in one language into the communicative conventions of a written text in the second language. Attempting to take the path of translating Homer is like entering a multidimensional labyrinth that doubles in on itself as one twists and turns and shifts about with the sociolinguistic tropes—the unique turns of speech—at play in both languages.

THE *ODYSSEY* AS ANTHROPOLOGY

Most of us are familiar with the story of Odysseus as legend or folklore before we sit down to read the epic poem, just as Homer's ancient audience must have known the story before hearing any of its epic versions. It is the old story: a man journeys homeward after a long war but is sidetracked by storms and monsters, enemies and lovers, and gods and goddesses, until he finally reaches home and overcomes the suitors besetting his ever-faithful wife. Yet if we know the story so well, why do we keep returning to it, generation after generation? When we first encounter it now, usually as required reading—the translation of a classic text rendered all too often in somewhat antiquated language—some of us find that the agony of the man's journey is one we painfully share as we struggle to read it through to the very end.

Yet when, by some accident of history, we have the chance to read the epic in Greek, somehow the whole story emerges as something very different, with a new density of meaning, a new sense of humor, and a new depth and intensity of feeling, leading us into a previously unimagined human dimension. As we dig further in and around the language and the action, like archeologists unearthing something utterly unexpected, we are struck by the way that Homer's shaping of the epic and its characters forces the audience to recognize—to re-cognize—that the story is as much about characters' inner journeys as it is about their physical movement in the world around them. Many of us are surprised to find that Odysseus has arrived in Ithaka just halfway through the epic, and that much of the remaining part of the story is about his efforts to reclaim his own identity in the home environment from which he has been displaced for so long. We are also surprised by the way in which Homer lucidly sets the scenes for the action of the story. Although the descriptions of the physical settings—the land and the sea, the sun rising and setting, the feel of time passing—are strikingly familiar, there is an utter strangeness, almost a culture shock, as we encounter the vast difference between the imaginary social world of Odysseus and our own contemporary cultural imaginaries.

In this sense, the *Odyssey* is an archeologist's dream come true. It is a cultural document that not only lays out an extensive array of material culture from an ancient society—distinctive everyday objects like double-handled cups, mixing bowls, chairs, clothing, musical instruments, tools, and weapons—but also shows us how they are used in everyday activity. The materiality of the Odyssey is revelatory. Homer does not merely describe these cultural objects; they are intrinsic to the story's action. The passing back and forth of drinking cups and serving bowls displays the intricacy of proper etiquette and is key to the reciprocity of the guest-host relationship in a world where people were continually on the move, either by choice for trade or by necessity as a result of war or other forms of social displacement. The spear held by Athena in the guise of Mentes, politely taken by Telemakhos in greeting, shows the young man's respect for the stranger as a guest and his observance of appropriate ritual protocol in recognition of the host-guest relationship. Penelope's shimmering veil not only hides her face but also suggests her proper social acumen and discretion, insinuating what she is holding back from the inappropriate suitors; in narrative terms, it also evokes Penelope's active inner life of intense emotion and quiet reflection. The description of Eumaios' courtyard reveals how, though enslaved, he has managed to construct a relatively independent life and livelihood for himself. Elpenor's oar is both a tool and ultimately a sign, marking his grave and honoring his unlucky life as a former sailor, "a man of no fortune." The graphic account of the horrid rags that Odysseus wears upon arrival in his own country not only masks his actual identity, but also shows his distance from his former regal past and from a sense of belonging in his own home.

In the *Odyssey*, as in the world around us, cultural objects are signs that both reveal and conceal one's place in the world; they are cues that mediate between oneself and others; they are a call for action—a chair or a cup, for instance, becoming the instigation for certain kinds of action in a specific situation (Keane 2005). They are links between the materiality and immateriality of the social world, between thought and action (Miller 2005). Things are not merely receptacles of thought; we think and act with things. They enter our thoughts and form our thoughts, and they shape our actions (Küchler 2005) in the same way that it can be hard to tell whether people have arranged the furniture or the furniture has arranged the people. The *Odyssey* dramatically depicts this omnipresent materiality as an intimate anthropological process.

As an anthropologist with prior classical training, I have read the *Odyssey* in Greek numerous times since I first studied it as a college student in the late 1960s. I have struggled with various ways of rendering particular passages and wondered at the very different ways that the Greek and English languages construct meaning. I have also read various translations of the *Odyssey* and have liked most of them, since each translator brings out distinctively different aspects of the story, its telling, and the cultural world it describes. As a result, I have come to view translation as an ethnographic process of trying to understand cultural difference through trans-cultural encounter, discovery, and meaning making. It is an interpretive archeological process of excavating and making sense of the cultural remains—in this case, a fragmented ancient text—of a social world very different from our own.

Translation is, in other words, the quixotic act of trying to transcend one's own language and culture—one's own implicit understandings and sense of things and people and what they mean—by grappling with a totally different way of seeing and understanding the world around us. This process can lead us to discover not only how other people in other times and places think about and express their relationships to each other and to the world they inhabit, but also how those other ways of looking at the world have a transformative impact on our own views and perspectives. This reflexive ethnographic approach to translation requires the translator to think critically about language usage and the culturally specific communicative strategies used for narrative effect, in both the original and the target language.

I first read the *Odyssey* as an undergraduate, studying under a professor who was perhaps the most skilled and dynamic teacher I ever had. Every class meeting, he would bring the whole world, and its history and thought—from archaic Greek cosmology, poetics, and epistemologies to German and English philosophy and philology to contemporary theories of translation—into our readings of the *Odyssey*, and in this way he made our reading of the epic narrative as real and compelling as witnessing another place and time, face to face. Later, after being drafted and while serving as a military paramedic, I had to stand numerous interminable (and seemingly eternal) night watches, during which I tried to make time pass by memorizing passages from Homer. In this way, I learned almost the entire eleventh book of the *Odyssey* in Greek by heart. It was at that time that I began to realize how authentic Homer's view of thinking was, linking the intensely emotional, visceral act of wondering and pondering over one's circumstances to the beating of one's heart—at times calm and measured, and at times edgy and uneasy.

I began my career as an anthropologist and ethnographer in a village named Whitehills on the northeast coast of Scotland, where I worked with a community of small-scale fishermen and learned about their use of new technologies and their cultural adaptation to the changes those technologies brought to their community and their sense of the world. Unlike many of the fishermen in adjacent villages, who drove to the nearest city and went out on the huge trawlers that pulled in fish by the ton, fishermen from Whitehills went out in thirty- to forty-foot boats from their own small harbor. They and their families lived in stone houses that kept out the cold, forceful winds off the North Sea.

As I lived and worked with them, I became increasingly interested in how those changing technologies transformed crew relationships and enabled new strategies of information-sharing about fish location and mobility, engendering a dynamic process of distributed learning among multiple boats from a single village. I saw how changing work technologies expanded their sense of the world far beyond their own villages and fishing circuits, and in turn, changed the way they lived their lives, both when at home and out at sea. I also saw how storytelling, jokes, and anecdotes enabled them to communicate a complicit sense of mutual belonging in explicit resistance to the pressures of the outside world. In later years, I had the opportunity to work with Indigenous communities—in particular, studying Lakota narrative styles as evidenced both in traditional cultural narratives and in more contemporary courtroom testimony, and again I came to view the strategic importance of distributed cognition—the collaborative sharing of information and intentions through culturally distinctive communicative practices—to a dispersed community, this time of a historically displaced Indigenous people striving to comprehend and resist their domination by a larger society.

I was subsequently invited to carry out work in educational domains, again to look at rapidly changing digital technologies and what they implied for teaching and learning, both in classrooms and out of school. My colleagues and I have found that changing technologies often entail a kind of social displacement—a restructuring of human relationships—that can be either laboriously repressive or truly innovative in promoting active learning for both students and teachers. Over time, as a result of these experiences, my work has come to focus on the sociocultural context of learning, on social displacement and social agency, and on interinstitutional collaboration as a sociocultural process of distributed learning.

Throughout this time, for over fifty years now, I have continued to read and study ancient Greek, especially focusing on the *Odyssey* and recognizing the ironic position in which I find myself—as an anthropologist who studies human learning in sociocultural context yet who is attempting to interpret an ancient text in which, by some scholars' accounts, no learning takes place. It was Auerbach (1953), in his well-known study of the story of Odysseus's scar, who first argued explicitly that no learning takes place in the Odyssey, an argument that others have since insistently echoed. Yet numerous classical scholars have examined Homer's extraordinarily abundant use of words that convey the cognitive processes of both major and minor characters in the Odyssey—words conveying the processes of thinking, pondering, wondering, and knowing in culturally distinctive terms and expressions.

Such linguistic evidence has led some scholars to suggest that "Auerbach's judgment that 'Odysseus on his return is exactly the same as he was when he left Ithaka two decades earlier' simply ignores all that is actually involved in the full homecoming" (Barnouw 2004, 332). In view of Barnouw's analysis of Odysseus's "visceral thinking," integrating thought and feeling, I have attempted to explore Odysseus's increasingly refined capacity to respond deliberately and agentively to the "tumult of impulse" that he feels and thinks in response to successive instances of dire physical and social displacement—which he faces both in voyaging home to Ithaka and in finding his own place and sense of belonging in that society once he has returned.

From this perspective, I find the *Odyssey* endlessly fascinating as a cultural artifact, a text offering us a glimpse into the imagined life and thought of a very different people in an almost incomprehensible society that is, at the same time, situated in a natural and social world whose day-to-day activities seem strikingly vivid and familiar. In this way, the epic dramatically calls us to take up the anthropological venture to look critically for the familiar in the strange, and the strange in the familiar. This tactic strongly has influenced my approach to translating Homeric Greek into contemporary English.

A QUESTIONABLE MAN

The *Odyssey*, we could well argue, is a narrative about displaced voices—although, of course, this is only one among many of the strands of meaning, or melodic lines, to which the polyphonic narrative speaks (Christensen 2020). It speaks to the pervasive social upheaval in a vast geographical area, the lingering impact of a long, devastating war. It also speaks to people's response to their displacement and to the plight of vast numbers of people—of veterans struggling home from war, then struggling to recover their former sense of belonging in homelands that have profoundly changed; of the families of those absent soldiers; of women who have lost their security and social status in their husbands' absence; of young people who have never known their fathers and whose circumstances have become, at best, precarious; and of enslaved men and women of all ages, wrenched from their homes to live in faraway lands. Yet in speaking to the historical predicament of these imaginary yet seemingly real people, the narrative also gives voice to the vitality and grit they persistently display in response to, and recuperation from, their various circumstances. In this sense, the *Odyssey* is a story about discovery and recovery, not only for many of the characters, but also for the audience (or reader) and undoubtedly for the performer(s) of the narrative as well (Underwood 2018; Christensen 2020).

Accordingly, in this translation, I have tried to keep the focus on social displacement and the agentive struggle of the displaced to find and express their own voices. In *Mythos and Voice: Displacement, Learning and Agency in Odysseus' World*, I explored the kinds of learning that characters in the *Odyssey* either embrace and fulfill (like Odysseus, Telemakhos, and Penelope) or fail to grasp (like Penelope's suitors and Odysseus' companions), in response to their social displacement. Whether or not they even recognize it, the necessity to learn carries significant consequences for all the characters. In this sense, we can approach the *Odyssey* as a study of Homeric cognition in response to the pervasive social displacement that follows an interminable, disastrous war (Underwood 2018). In brief, while the *Iliad* is about the rancor and politics of contentious heroic warriors fighting for a dubious military victory, the *Odyssey* is about the courage of displaced people struggling for an elusive peace in a post-heroic world.

We can already see this dominant theme emerging in the proem of the *Odyssey*. This new translation will, I hope, bring out emphatically what has been formerly implicit or understated. One thing I have learned in reading and re-reading the *Odyssey*, both in Greek and in various English translations, is that the epic poem always bears retelling. Even the ancient performances of this oral epic were retellings, re-experiences for performers and audiences of both the old story and the epic itself (Nagy 1997). Both then and now, the epic rewards every retelling, and so it is always worth our revisiting the epic's opening words, to explore and be yet again surprised at what we discover. Just as the first word of the *Iliad* announces its main theme as *mēnin*, or anger—that is, Akhilles's indignant outrage against Agamemnon—the first word of the Odyssey, *andra*, famously announces its subject: "the man," or perhaps "a man." Just as the *Iliad* is not about Akhilles himself but about his outrage and its consequences (Muellner 2005), the *Odyssey* is not about a god or even about what we usually think of as a hero, but simply about "a man." Yet this subject is in fact the object of the epic's first sentence.

> *Andra moi ennepe, Mousa, polutropon, 'os mala polla*
> *plangthē, epei Troies 'ieron ptoliethron eperse.*

"Man" is in the accusative case—both the object of the Muse's telling and the object of the described action. The man is *polutropon*, which Fagles translates as "the man of twists and turns" instead of the usual, rather stale "man of many turns" or "man of many ways," and thus gives the epic's subject an active participation in the main force of the story. The opening suggests the circumstance in which this man finds himself: he has been "driven about," as the poet says, *mala polla*—"so very much" literally, but with the implication that he has been persistently driven about in both space and time—thus "for so long" or "so far and wide."

Agreeing with the initial word (*andra*), the adjective *polutropon* is also in the accusative, and so implies that the man's action is taken in response to being driven about. We could take Fagles's translation of *polutropon* a bit further and use, instead of the phrase "twisting and turning," something like "shifting, drifting." This would imply, as does the adjective *polutropos*, that the man is not only turned around and about, but that he himself shifts about in response, perhaps with the implication that he is also cunningly "shifty," as he shows himself to be a number of times in the course of the narrative. Yet he is also somewhat passive, even in his active response to being driven about. Again and again, he is like an oar bound within the confines of the *tropos*, the strap that holds the oar in place on the boat's gunnel; that is, he is twisting and turning or shifting within the constrained space that is allowed him, and he at times, as the strap itself twists and turns and stretches, tends to "shift" and "drift" with his circumstances.

He is, in short, "a complicated man," as Wilson (2018) renders *polutropon* in her recent translation. The man in this narrative is certainly complicated, yet *polutropon* implies much more. Homer's beginning refers to "a man" or "the man"—in any case, a deliberately unnamed man who, while being driven about so far and wide, is constantly shifting and drifting. He is thinking and struggling or sometimes, in his exhaustion, merely drifting, going with the flow. Like the oar strapped in the *tropos*, he is again and again, while limited by external constraints, twisting and turning, moving deliberately, driven not only by the winds and waves and gods, but also by his *noos*, his own sense of ultimate purpose, which is focused on his *nostos*, his eventual return home.

So the very first line of the *Odyssey*, in its poetic density, is extraordinarily difficult to translate as a single line in English. As another translator, Robert Fitzgerald, once noted, words are not bricks or stones—and translation cannot be merely the act of building a narrative edifice simply by replacing Greek stones with English bricks. To get the full import of Homer's first line, we might have to go beyond Homer's succinct first line and say something like:

> Tell me, Muse, about a man who was always shifting,
> drifting, driven about so far and wide . . .

In moving to the poet's next line, we find that all this activity occurs within the particular time frame following the Akhaians' war with Troy, a place which Homer characterizes as *ieron ptoliethron*. In one sense, as "the towering stronghold," this wording signifies how formidable an opponent the city had been for the Greek alliance besieging it, while in another sense, as "the holy city," it suggests that the place is a focal point of sacred geography, at least for the Trojans. It also is perhaps "exalted, not only geographically, but also in the sense of its having been the raised to a level of immortality as the prime locus of an earlier epic, the *Iliad*. It is, nonetheless, a "lofty" setting, its recognition as a holy site further exaggerating the power of the final word of the first sentence—'*eperse*—usually translated in English somewhat weakly as "sacked" but in the original Greek having a poetic intensity beyond even the English word, "destroyed."

This man, who is to be the subject of the epic to follow, devastated the city. He "burned and looted" Troy. In the words of this first sentence (*Andra moi énnepe Moūsa, polútropon, 'os mála polla / plágkhthē, epei Troíēs ieron ptoliethron 'eperse*), all the repeated plosives and voiceless consonants impose a blatant expressive force that suggests extreme violence as the primary action for which the unnamed man is said to be known. The fact that this violence is exercised against a city that might be conceived as holy (at least to the Trojans and the gods who favor them) already implicates the dubious moral position in which this man is regarded by both gods and human beings. In this sense, we could say that the focus of this epic is not so much an exemplary hero as a somewhat dubious rogue, or at least a man who does not quite fit the typical conception of an epic hero. So let's read that first sentence again this way:

> Tell me, Muse, about a man who was always shifting,
> drifting, driven about so far and wide,
> after he burned and looted Troy, the holy city.

Already the epic's first sentence leaves us with a feeling of uneasiness and discomfort. We think we know this story, don't we? Already, anyone in Homer's original audience—that is, anyone in the Greek world—would recognize this unnamed man: he is the legendary trickster, the "scourge of cities," as Homer later calls him. But the poet is intent on showing the human side of this questionable man, and thus continues:

> He saw the towns of many peoples, and came to see
> their views, and in his heart he suffered many agonies on the sea,
> struggling for his own life and for his crew's return.

As we read or hear this narrative, already knowing the story, we unavoidably recognize the man's displacement, geographically and socially, as he drifts mysteriously off the historical map into a murky mythical landscape of nebulous lotus eaters, brutal Cyclops, and horrific Laistrygonians. The opening also points to Odysseus's long separation from his homeland and the cultural distance from the peoples he encountered in the other lands he came to, as well as the social distance even from his companions, the Ithakan men who accompanied him on his circuitous journey. We remember the agonies he suffered and his struggles to keep himself and his fellow Ithakans alive, to resolve their postwar displacement and return home. And we also recall—

> . . . he did not bring them back,
> no matter how much he wanted to. Through their own

> recklessness, they perished. The fools—they feasted
> on the cattle of Helios Hyperion, and he took away
> the day of their return.

By now, then, even though the man is not yet named, his identity is obvious to almost anyone, then or now. The proem plays to what we know, or what we think we know—to our assumptions about a legendary journey through a mythic landscape. Even in the time of its first tellings and retellings, and even in the character's own lifetime, the *mythos* of this man and his *kleos*—literally, what was said about and what had been heard about the man—was already in the realm of legend and folklore. As Hartog (2017) has noted, when the man arrives among the Phaiakians as the guest of King Antinoos, he listens to the song of Demodokos, and hears his own story glorified as if he himself were a dead man. Penelope later quips, asking Odysseus (disguised as a beggar) where he came from, or if he simply had "sprung from the oak of old stories, or from some rock"—the irony, of course, being that he, the storied Odysseus, actually *has* sprung from the spreading tree of old stories. Hartog notes how the man is devastated by this realization of being, for all the world, a dead man, or worse, merely the myth of a man. He recognizes himself and his reputation, as a dead man, alive only in what has been said and heard about him.

In the very first lines of the *Odyssey*, the poet gives us this overview of what has been heard about the man—his *kleos*—and what has been said and continues to be said about him—his *mythos*. The poet begins with our conventional understanding of the legend, but already is shaking our confidence in what we think we know. He then says,

> Of all this, beginning at any point,
> Goddess, Daughter of Zeus, tell us once again.

By the end of the proem, then, we know that the epic is about displacement. The man is himself continually displaced, socially and geographically. He is as well largely responsible for the utter displacement of a holy city, an awesome, redoubtable stronghold, and its people. And finally, at the end of the proem, we find that this telling is itself avowedly a *re-telling* of a *mythos* already widely recognized by the audience of its retelling. If we already know the whole story, why keep on listening—why keep on reading? The proem is tantalizing enough to keep us going, and as we read on, we find that what is to make the retelling new and innovative is in fact the *voice* of the poet, inspired by the Muse, rendering the many voices of the displaced audible and powerful.

I say "the voices of the displaced" because, when we speak of the *mythos* of Odysseus, we are also speaking of the *mythos* of other characters who are part and parcel of his story. In *The Language of Heroes*, Martin (1989) has defined *mythos* as the authoritative speech of the powerful (particularly men) in the heroic communicative context of the *Iliad*. In this framework, following Martin, we can define *mythos* in the post-heroic context of the *Odyssey* as culturally persuasive speech, not only by the overtly powerful, but also by those—including women, enslaved persons, and other overtly powerless individuals –who are able to apply their voices in the performance of *mythoi* that constitute acts of assertive self-placement in precarious circumstances (Martin 1989; Underwood 2018). Their stories are integral to Odysseus's (as his is to theirs), and their voices as resonant and powerful as his—particularly those of Penelope, Telemakhos, Eurykleia, Eumaios, and many more. What makes them resound yet again is the integrating "voice" of the poet (or the poetic tradition)—the performance of the *mythos*, the coherent telling of an overarching narrative that consumes and assimilates multiple variants of local legends and folkloric tales and incorporates all of them into a sprawling epic retelling of what everyone has heard before but wants to hear again—the *mythos* of Odysseus.

HOMERIC COGNITION AND RECOGNITION

We have seen how Odysseus's life is characterized by displacement almost from birth; in the story of Odysseus's scar, he is virtually cursed with displacement by his grandfather's naming. Yet the story of Odysseus's naming and how he received his scar is less about Odysseus's relationship with Autolykos than it is about the origin and reawakening of his relationship with Eurykleia, who nursed him in infancy and is the first to recognize him upon his return to his Ithaka. In fact, the story is less about the scar itself—the feature that enables Eurykleia to recognize Odysseus—than about its healing. Contrary to Auerbach's view, Homeric storytelling in this episode is not so much a representation of reality—a *mimesis*—as it is a radical questioning of conventional notions about our experience, individually and collectively, of who we think we really are and what we think reality to be. It is instead a *poiesis*—the making of the self, the act of inventing oneself—the social construction of the person as a visceral becoming, always emerging in the moment of anticipatory encounter with the other. In other words, it is about how one learns to move beyond one's own subjective perception of the world around us to a more inclusive or shared perspective of the natural world and the social world of others.

In its construction, the story of Odysseus's scar is a multilayered narrative. Told in the moment of recognition between Odysseus and Eurykleia, it is, in fact, a moment of *re-cognition* for both of them—a moment of rethinking and reconceptualizing who and where they are in the world. Eurykleia touches the scar with her fingers and, in reaction, drops the man's foot into the metal basin, making it resound in the hall and spill its contents. As this occurs, the two characters are themselves unsettled, and their feelings and perceptions and memories spill over in an expansive, transformative bond that unifies their distinct experiences of the scar in the narrator's retelling of the event—Odysseus's wounding encounter with the wild boar, which Eurykleia could not have witnessed, and Eurykleia's presence at the baby's ritual naming by Autolykos—which, because it took place in the character's early infancy, Odysseus could not have remembered.

The union of their experiences is so subtle in its telling that we, the audience (or we, the readers) hardly notice it. Yet the retelling of the scar story in their unified field of vision—a visionary anticipation of the other, transcending time and place—cunningly reinforces our sense of the mutual re-cognition—the deepening mutual awareness, understanding, and intuitive responsiveness—between these two characters. Although they have been separated for twenty years, they now enter into an implicitly shared view of things—of the situation with the suitors, and approaches and strategies for collaboratively navigating the social world in which they are jointly placed. The accounting of this incident of the scar moves craftily from one historical "present" to another, thus layering the story of the scar through time as it layers the characters' layered experience of the moment.

The story of Odysseus's scar is thus a fascinating entry point to our understanding of Homeric cognition—that is, of how the characters learn to navigate difficulties, how they come to anticipate and put into action the stances and strategies they need to overcome or preserve their circumstances. I have elsewhere discussed Homeric cognition as visceral, integrative, and discursive. It is visceral in that it involves a mental response to a tumult of impulse—an agonizing gut reaction (Barnouw 2004). It is integrative in the sense that it involves a weighing of alternative impulses to work out a course of action (Mead 1934). It is discursive in the sense that it involves the urgent dialogue between voices—the anticipatory reading of each other's status, power, and willingness to transcend social boundaries (Underwood 2018). We begin to recognize this distinctively Homeric view of human learning in the language the poet uses and in the communicative strategies employed in the oral narrative, and it is the task of the translator to try to capture this relational process in a language other than archaic Greek.

In the story of Odysseus's scar, when Penelope calls Eurykleia over to wash the beggar's feet, she calls the older woman *periphron*—"exceptionally thoughtful," which Katz (1991) has translated as "thinking all around," or perhaps, we might say, "thinking [about things] from all angles." It is the epithet usually used for Penelope, to describe her particularly thoughtful or consistently perceptive stance toward the world around her. Penelope's use of the word to describe Eurykleia perhaps also shows the special cognitive affinity or like-mindedness between the two women. Eurykleia emerges in this context as a key character, both because of her shrewdly perceptive intellect and because of her long history and important position within the household. As nurse to both Odysseus and Telemakhos, and as housekeeper to Odysseus and in his absence to Penelope, she has acquired a precise understanding of the workings of the house and the people who live and work within it. In this way, she has taken on the role of primary protector of the household against troublesome outsiders. Her relationship with Penelope is colored both by her status as an older, more experienced woman and by her authority as the keeper of the household (Karydas 1998).

However, when Eurykleia approaches Odysseus to carry out the task of washing his feet, she disparagingly says of herself, "I'm so hopeless" or "I'm so useless," though she nonetheless expresses her willingness to wash the stranger's feet. She goes on to say how upset she is about the mistreatment he has received at the hands of the suitors, which she compares to what Odysseus probably suffered during his journeys. The ambiguity of her language as she addresses the stranger while referring to Odysseus rhetorically is telling:

> No one has ever burned so many luscious thighs
> or so many choice sacrifices as you have offered up
> to thunder-loving Zeus, as you in your appeals to reach
> an easy old age and raise your splendid son.
> But now he's taken away the day of your return.

Her unconscious identification of the beggar with Odysseus signals perhaps that she is already on the verge of recognizing him. She describes Odysseus's displacement aptly, calling the beggar "you" as if she is talking to Odysseus himself, but then adds:

> No doubt the women mocked him too, when he
> came to some great house in some strange place
> far away, just as these bitches here mock you.

Odysseus appears to sense this anticipation, and the next lines show how quickly things are going to move.

> Odysseus sat down beside the fireplace,
> but he hastily turned away toward the darkness.

He sensed within his heart that when she touched him,
she might recognize his scar, and everything
would be revealed. She approached and began
to wash his feet. And right away, she knew the scar . . .

Of course, what happens next is what often distinguishes the storytelling of Homer—what Auerbach (1953) refers to as "the basic impulse of the Homeric style," which is "to represent phenomena in a fully externalized form, visible and palpable in all their parts, and completely fixed in their spatial and temporal relations." In Auerbach's view, Homer could not resist representing the full history of a distinguishing physical feature that has just appeared in the story—representing "this procession of phenomena as necessarily situated in the foreground, "in a local and temporal present which is absolute." As Auerbach notes, the story line moves in mid-sentence from Eurykleia's recognition of the scar to the lengthy stories of Odysseus's naming ceremony and of his coming-of-age rite of passage in the boar hunt, and then back again to the moment when Eurykleia, upon recognizing the scarred leg she is holding in her hands, drops the leg and almost gives away the beggar's identity.

We should by no means underestimate Auerbach's perspective here; it is an eye-opening account of Homeric narrative strategies. Archaic Greek culture is, for Auerbach, a culture in which "Delight in physical existence is everything to them, and their highest aim is to make that delight perceptible to us." In this regard, the digressions in Homer's story of the scar "aren't meant to keep the reader in suspense, but rather to relax the tension." We could well argue, on the contrary, that if relaxing tension was Homer's goal, the narrative fails, because any close reading of this *mythos* reveals it to be, although not overly suspenseful, certainly marked by a sustained narrative tension. We can equally argue that the assertion by Auerbach, never fully developed, that psychological processes are missing or unexpressed in the course of these digressions, does not survive a close reading of the text itself. And Auerbach's more general conclusion that there is no character development in the Odyssey is also a bit curious, if we examine Homer's careful use of language emphasizing characters' internal thinking and the meticulous narrative strategy highlighting the emotional transformation of mutual recognition. Let's look at another key moment in the narrative.

GRASPING THE HEART OF RECOGNITION

With the effortless and quick transition from Eurykleia's moment of recognition to the story of the scar itself, Homer launches the story of Odysseus's naming. The infant is placed in the lap of Odysseus's maternal grandfather, Autolykos, whose very name—meaning "the wolf himself"—suggests a combination of fierce self-centeredness and the potentially menacing wildness of the wolf. It is at this moment that Autolykos says:

> My son-in-law, and you, my daughter, give him the name
> I tell you. Since I have come here as someone who
> has been as utterly odious as I am to so many men and women,
> all across this teeming earth, so call him by the name
> Odysseus.

The story is fast-paced and full of linguistic play. Yet it carries profoundly disturbing undertones with powerful implications for the identity of the infant. Autolykos says, "Since I've come here as someone who has been as odious as I am . . . " and thus projects his own truculence on the life path of the small child. On Autolykos's part, the naming is both a casual, off-the-wall joke and a passing on of his own mythos, his legacy, to the child, with the implication that this tender innocent will in the future have to become as fierce, troublesome, and odious as he is himself.

It is a moment of visceral intensity—Odysseus's naming not only having been based on his grandfather's confrontational stance to the world, rather than any inherent characteristics of the infant, but also having become a nominal scar that Odysseus will have to carry for the rest of his life. But ever intent on persistent narrative movement, Homer presses on to the story of the hunt in which a young Odysseus joins his grandfather. In the welcoming scene prior to the hunt, the hospitable gathering and feasting to welcome the young Odysseus is hardly carried out in a leisurely fashion; instead, it is redolent with intense emotion and both physical and symbolic violence. Then, in the hunt itself, we see the youthful precursor to the mature Odysseus and his cognitive stance toward the world—set up by Homer in this layered narrative context not simply as a precursor to his approach later in life, but also representing yet another instance of Odysseus's tendency to rush into a situation and then back off and carefully reframe his intent—a confirmation of what we as the audience have already witnessed in the epic narrative.

> Odysseus rushed in first, lifting his long spear
> high in his sturdy hand, eager to thrust forward.
> The boar was much too quick for him. It dodged
> and charged in at him from the side, and its tusk
> tore a deep gash in his flesh, but it did not reach
> the bone. Odysseus aimed true and struck the boar
> in the right shoulder. The brilliant point of his spear
> went right through. The boar fell down in the dust

with a yowl, and its life flew away.

Odysseus's initial action is impulsive, almost reckless, and he is seriously wounded as a result. But the youth responds to the immediate crisis with renewed purpose, His *noos*, or purposeful intent, is signaled by Homer's choice of words: *tykhōn* means literally "aiming." The verb *tugkanō* is rich in connotations, suggesting "to strike" or "to thrust home," or "to make good one's aim" or "aim unerringly." Yet it can also mean "to fall to one's lot" or "to have bestowed upon one." In this context, the word suggests that Odysseus's act of stabbing the boar is both a physical and a cognitive act; it is an anticipation of the consequences of the angle at which he holds his long spear and the direction in which he physically drives it into what he thinks may be a vulnerable point in the boar's shoulder.

Odysseus's wound and the remnant scar become the focus of talk, and when he returns home, Odysseus proudly tells his parents the *mythos* of the hunt and his scar. From one line to the next, Homer quickly returns to Eurykleia, who is holding the beggar's scarred leg in her hands.

> He laid it all out to them—how, when he
> had gone to Parnassos with Autolykos and his sons,
> while out hunting, a boar struck him with its white tusk.
> As the old woman took his foot in the flat of her hands,
> she grasped what it was she was feeling. She dropped
> the foot. The leg fell into the basin. The bronze rang out
> as it turned over, and the water spilled on the floor.
> All at once, joy and sorrow clutched at her heart,
> and her eyes filled with tears.

Even with the abrupt shift in location, the lucid description of Eurykleia and Odysseus gives it an almost cinematic clarity and immediacy. And there immediately follows this remarkable phrase: "she grasped what it was she was feeling." The verb *gnō* is, once again, rich in its connotative range. It means" to recognize" or "to realize," or in specific contexts, "to remember," which, in Homer, is often accompanied by the phrase (missing here) "in her heart," suggesting, as Barnouw (2004) comments, the visceral quality of the Homeric process of understanding—the emotionally powerful, anticipatory gut response to a tumult of impulse.

Here, I prefer the translation "she grasped what she was feeling," in that it conveys the visceral character of the woman's moment of recognition as linked directly to holding Odysseus's foot in her hands. Her recognition of the scar involves a shrewd act of insightful observation and interpretation. As she is a person of exceptional *noos*, her noticing of the scar sparks an immediate interpretation of it as a *sema*—that is, as the sign enabling her re-cognition or rethinking of who the beggar really is (Nagy 1990). In recognizing the scar and sensing Odysseus's actual identity, Eurykleia is the only person shrewd enough to recognize Odysseus and outsmart his *mētis*, his scheming, in the process identifying the man overtly before the moment when he himself would have chosen to be identified (Karydas, 1998, 27). In this way, "she is the one person Odysseus does not manage to trick; on the contrary, she is the one who outwits him" (Karydas 1998, 42).

In brief, the foot and the scar she is holding tangibly evoke her memory, which arouses Eurykleia's sudden recognition of the man, with its visceral emotional impact, as "joy and sorrow clutched at her heart." If we the audience find the story touching, it is because the poet has given us the palpable means for experiencing the process of re-cognition through multiple perspectives—that is, through the eyes of several characters—and thus for feeling a powerful compassion for their respective situations, which are, at the same time, one situation that includes them both in their own separate individuality and in their expanding sense of empathetic mutuality.

AN EPIC JOURNEY

As the English language continues to change, new translations of Homer are perhaps both inevitable and necessary. Even the translation of an age-old epic requires the creative work of re-interpretation and re-presentation that Polizzotti (2018) and Rabassa (2006) have noted as key to the process, both to keep the narrative from sounding antiquated and hackneyed and to enable it to offer a live, active impact on the living, evolving language into which it is to be rendered. The etymology of the word "translation" presents it as an act of "carrying across." Grossman (2010) has vividly described the formidable challenge of translation: "The experience of plunging into the maelstrom of signification and intention that whirls and boils between them as we attempt to transfer meaning between two languages, to hear the effects, the rhythms, the artfulness of both simultaneously, can verge on the hallucinatory" (Grossman 2010, 68). In view of this storm of activity, the stance of a translator as an intermediary voice transmitting the original voice of "an inspiring presence," or Muse, or original author, becomes key to the translation process as "a living bridge between two realms of discourse, two realms of experience, and two sets of readers" (Grossman 2010, 69).

In this light, we might suggest that each telling of the Odyssey, even to its original Greek audiences, was already an oral retelling, a re-composition in performance and a re-experience, for both performer and audience, of the old story, inspired by the Muse (Nagy 1997), while each translation of the epic becomes a retelling, inspired by the poetic voice of the epic as it has been passed down in writing. Bellos (2011) notes that as an activity, translation involves a variety of different sociolinguistic tasks that can be understood as a process of discovery: "What translators do is find matches, not equivalences, for the units of which a work is made, in the hope and expectation that their sum will produce a new work that can serve overall as a substitute for the source" (Bellos 2011, 308). Finding a match is always an uncertain, imperfect judgment call, and Bellos cautions that a translation is never the same thing that it attempts to match. If readers want the same thing, they must read the original work (Bellos 2011). And in fact, that is the ultimate goal most translators pursue—to carry the reader across to the source.

Returning to the *Odyssey*, we find that as cultural and historical contexts continue to shift, the significance of this age-old epic still resonates, even in a second language. It continues to reverberate with the world we see around us. As noted above, in an era of ubiquitous social displacement, this new translation presents the *Odyssey* as a narrative that maps the social displacement of its characters and explores both the cognitive consequences of that displacement and the adaptive strategies that various characters employ to resolve their displacement; that is, they learn to make their way through circumstances that are no longer familiar, recognizable, or even livable (Powell 2015; Underwood 2018). The translation attempts to convey this view of Homeric storytelling and to examine Homeric cognition from a sociocultural perspective that draws on the works of Vygotsky (1978), Mead (1934; 1965), Bakhtin (1981), Engeström (2015), Hutchins (1996), and others. I view the *Odyssey* not as a heroic epic, strictly speaking, but as a post-heroic narrative that explicitly marks the passing of the former heroic era depicted in the *Iliad*. It portrays the pervasive social displacement that exists following the devastating Trojan War, and the adaptive response of ordinary human beings, sometimes heroic and sometimes pathetic, to a perplexing world of human, subhuman, and supernatural beings, vying to overcome their own displacement and learn new ways to survive and thrive in the world.

This approach to translation challenges the view of Auerbach (1953) and others that there is no character development in the Odyssey, and instead builds on the work of Barnouw (2004), Felson-Rubin (1994), Heath (2005), Hartog (2001; 2017), Katz (1991), and others in looking closely at how key characters in the epic learn to respond strategically to their social displacement. Of course, social displacement is ubiquitous in the world described in the *Odyssey*. We have seen how Eurykleia, as an enslaved woman in a male-dominated, deeply hierarchical society, is in an especially precarious position, and yet as Homer presents her, she has, over time, positioned herself within Odysseus's and later Penelope's household in a relatively authoritative status, first as nurse to both Odysseus and Telemakhos and ultimately as housekeeper for Penelope. She is depicted as especially articulate and persuasive, authoritative among other enslaved people and a match for others in speaking and thinking. She is given the epithet *periphrōn*, along with Penelope, indicating that the two are equally matched in their perceptive personae, both of them thinking things through from every angle, "thinking around" the masculine mythos that confines and coerces them. Both Penelope and Eurykleia conspire against the masculine *mythoi* of the suitors, not from positions of power or preeminence, but from the urgent necessity to amplify subversively the limited control they each have over their circumstances (Doherty 1995).

The *Odyssey* portrays a world—premised on male-dominance and pervasive slavery—that is so compelling it is easy to forget that it is an imagined world. As such, it represents a cultural imaginary as uncomfortably redolent of the social world in which the epic's audience lived as it is disturbingly evocative of our own. Even for its original audiences, it is explicitly a society of a former time, given a sense of "pretended immediacy" through oral communicative strategies conveyed in a poetic register which serves to distance the narrative present through formulaic expressions that provide for the archaization, exaggeration, and invention of a distant past whose future will be the present moment of the epic performance (Bakker 1997, 2005; Foley 1997, 1999; Franco 2012). The *Odyssey* generally portrays a largely aristocratic perspective on this society, yet in this context, the poet subtly presents alternative, marginalized views through the characters of women and enslaved individuals like Eurykleia and Eumaios, whose speeches and actions at times convey a covertly resistant critique of those who attempt to control their destinies. The poet insists on including the oppressed and disenfranchised as an integral part of the audience. In two consecutive lines at the beginning of Book XIV, introducing the meeting of Odysseus and Eumaios, Homer refers to both master and enslaved man with the same epithet, "brilliant," signifying their inherent equality as distinctively impressive individuals despite their unequal social status, a mere accident of history. Eumaios is also the only character whom the poet addresses directly in the second person, in this way conveying a sense of closeness, affinity, and affiliation between the epic narrator and the keeper of pigs.

Similarly, the poet explicitly recognizes that Eurykleia, despite being enslaved, possesses the capacity for articulate, persuasive speech, or *mythos*. Penelope, too, possesses this quality. Her agency in resisting the dominant masculine mythos of aggressiveness and control may or may not be exceptional. Women in the *Odyssey* take on more active roles and adopt a more agentive stance than those in the *Iliad*, although the poet makes it clear that in the absence of a protective man, a woman's status becomes highly precarious (Franco 2015). Penelope's status in her own household is brought into question both by the aggressive actions of the suitors and by her own son's challenge, demanding that she remove herself from the discourse among men. In this instance, we see how discourse not only reflects differences of status and power; it constructs or intensifies those differences, for instance, as Telemakhos questions Penelope's authority and asserts his own (Minchin 2007).

Interestingly, the *Odyssey* also depicts women of unequal status interacting with each other, enabling us to view both the rebukes by women of higher status against women of lower status, as well as instances of women of lower status reproaching or questioning higher-status women—for example, Eurykleia's rebuke of her mistress, Penelope (Minchin 2007). As Schein has noted,

> the multiplicity and complexity of females represented at making decisions, taking actions, and telling stories challenge listeners and readers to shape views of Odysseus' distinctive heroic identity, evaluate his authority as a narrator, and consider how his interactions with females help constitute both his identity and his authority, even while these representations make problematic any particular interpretation of the hero, the females, and the poem (Schein 1995, 18).

Homer's portrayal of women, both humans and goddesses, in the *Odyssey* may be problematic by contemporary standards, but the poet plainly tells what happens and leaves it to the audience to make judgments on the inequities assiduously portrayed throughout the narrative. Toward the end of the epic, after the killing of the suitors, the hanging of the disloyal enslaved women is described in graphic detail, and the deadpan language of the narrative serves only to deepen the reader's outrage at this excessively violent act. In short, throughout the narrative, the poet quickly and plainly lays out the narrative events—many perhaps drawn from earlier versions of the epic or from folkloric sources—and leaves it to the audience to interpret, judge, and sometimes piece together.

The communicative strategies used to craft the oral epic are distinctively different from those used to produce a long, written narrative. The use of Homeric formulaic expressions in accordance with the grammatical and syntactic conventions of archaic Greek in hexameter lines provided for a coherent, idiomatic manner of speech that reflected contemporary conventions, or communicative strategies, of ordinary conversation, yet articulated them in a special register—that of the Homeric poetic tradition (Foley 1997; 1999). Homeric discourse is in this sense a stylized, elaborate version of everyday speech (Martin 1989; Minchin 2007). It is a distinctive "echoic" context that "brings the lifeblood of generations of poems and performances to the individual performance or text" (Foley 1997, 113). This performative strategy, as mentioned above, established a contrast between an imaginary world of extraordinary heroism and the cultural world of the audience involved in a particular performance, yet also authenticated a continuity of folkloric and epic performances or re-performances across time (Kahane 1997). The voice of the epic poet was in this way polyphonic and inclusive of the various forms of song-making that had come before (Martin 1997; Christensen 2021).

In translating the *Odyssey* from this perspective, I have thus attempted to follow Homer's language and communicative strategies closely and capture both its compassionate representation of human struggles and its profound questioning of what makes a person human. For instance, I have tried to articulate Homeric epithets and other formulaic expressions not merely as static idioms serving a strictly metric function but, in the interest of communicating the true nature of Odyssean *polutropos*, as distinctive tropes—turns of speech that are revelatory of a character's emergent development in the narrative moment. As Knox has suggested, there are many instances of epithets and other formulaic expressions that appear to be contextually meaningful—that is, poetically functional and dramatically pertinent—whether by intensifying the narrative moment, alluding to another comparable moment in the story, or contributing to our interpretation of a particular character's motives. Knox writes, "There are cases where verbal repetition is so poetically effective that it must be the result of poetic design rather than the working of a quasi-mechanical system" (1996, 18). This approach takes into account the audience's participation and involvement in the epic performance, as it recognizes that the formulaic nature of epic discourse is not simply a means to facilitate oral composition, but represents the performer's anticipatory strategies for creating and sustaining the audience's involvement (Bakker 1997).

It is for this reason that, although I originally translated the epic in hexameter lines, I then converted it into a prose narrative. In the first place, I sensed that many contemporary readers are much more familiar with prose narrative than with lengthy poetic narrative, to which ancient Greek audiences were probably very accustomed, but which many present-day readers, including quite a few of my colleagues and students, find to be a formidable barrier to their sustained involvement (that is, their commitment to continue reading). In the second place, in translating epithets and other formulaic expressions in strict accordance with the original metric traditions of archaic Greek, the translator faces the almost impossible task of moving between two distinctly different grammatical and syntactic systems. As an anthropologist trained in sociolinguistic analysis and conversant with the communicative strategies of Indigenous oral narrative, I believe that Homeric epithets and other formulaic expressions represent rhetorically effective discourse strategies in the original context, or traditional register, of Homeric Greek, yet when too literally rendered in contemporary English, they often become rhetorically cumbersome, disrupting and obstructing the epic's narrative flow—which, as Arnold (1905) and others have noted, is ideally rapid, plain, and direct.

For this reason, in moving from Homeric Greek to English discourse, the translator has to be sensitive both to the rhetorical impact of formulaic expressions in both languages and to their often broad connotative range. This transition often means altering the specific grammatical or syntactic feature as it appears in Greek to a feature that is quite different in English. For example, I have not always translated an epithet as an adjective; it may serve as an appositive or even an adverb, modifying and providing the motivational rationale for the character's action. Following this course, for instance, I have rendered Penelope's epithet, *periphrōn*, often translated simply as "wise," as "deep in thought"—a phrase that both defines her usual state of mind and clarifies her situational cognitive response to the immediate circumstance that she is facing. Similarly, Telemakhos's epithet, *pepnuménos*, is often translated as "wise" throughout the epic, thus giving the contemporary reader the false sense, first that the young man is described with the same epithet as his mother, and second, that he is viewed as never really changing throughout the course of the narrative—a sense that is often contradicted by the character's successive actions and understandings, as portrayed by Homer. In contrast, I translate *pepnuménos* by drawing on its derivation from the verb *pneō*, to breathe. Using this approach, as I have discussed at greater length in *Mythos and Voice* (Underwood 2018), the epithet can be translated in a variety of ways, including "having gathered (or gathering) his breath" or "inspired," or in more cognitive terms as "gathering his thoughts," or in some contexts, simply "thoughtful" or "thoughtfully." In these slight variations of the English translation, we can see the broad connotative range that the Greek word has, a range that made it possible for the Greek audience to "read" or "hear" different connotations of the same word in different contexts, and in this way enabled readers to assess for themselves the character's development throughout the narrative.

I believe that these and other interpretive choices open up the narrative for the reader to grasp it as more than a set of static episodes involving stock characters who never quite change or learn anything from the beginning to the end of the story, or who never fully develop in character beyond their initial depictions—a view that many scholars have long held. Instead, following Martin's (1989) view of how Homeric characters learn to develop a more persuasive *mythos*, or persuasive speech, this approach unlocks a surprisingly open narrative that enables audiences or readers to interpret for themselves the emerging emotional and cognitive nature of various characters and their expansive development throughout the narrative.

From this perspective, I have tried to craft a translation of the *Odyssey* that presents the story and its characters as closely as possible to how they appear to be represented in the original Greek text: either as social persons with evolving identities and ever-deepening understandings of their circumstances and of the adaptive strategies they need to meet those circumstances (like Telemakhos, Penelope, and Odysseus), or as individuals who carelessly follow their immediate impulses and fail to adjust their actions in response to others (like the suitors and Odysseus's shipmates). In brief, I have tried to craft a translation that avoids the use of exalted language, on the assumption that the nobility of Homeric storytelling is, as Arnold (1905) wrote, not simply a quality of lofty, formal expression. It is instead, I suggest, equivalent in its narrative intricacy and plainness to the nobility of Chekov, Morrison, or García Márquez, and thus can be as eminently readable, dramatically compelling, cognitively provocative, and profoundly inspiring as it is in the original Greek. Yet again, communicating this not only across languages but also across barely compatible genres of writing and speaking can be a formidable activity, especially given the poly-symphonic character of Homeric discourse. The polyphonic character of Greek epic, as a formulaic practice of making meaning, is charged with multiple implications that often defy interpretation: "the [Homeric] lines of song exist through time and carry many meanings at once. A translator listens to the whole song as it echoes and picks the melodies that ring strongest now" (Christensen 2021).

Homer's verbal play might be described as Joycean, but for the fact that the reverse is true—Joyce's verbal play is distinctively Homeric. Yet conveying this intricate play of language and narrative in translation is no easy task. Rabassa writes, "Even in the best of examples a translation cannot get to the marrow of what has been said in the original. A piece of writing cannot be cloned in another language, only imitated. Like the colors of the spectrum, languages are unique and distinctive; they can approach each other but never reproduce one another" (Rabassa 2005, 20). As a result, every translation is imperfect and unfinished; as Rabassa has commented, the translator never stops wanting to go back and change a word or a phrase or more. Translation is always a work in process, an ongoing act of meaning-making, a *poesis*. It is the translator's challenge to capture in a second language what Homer originally depicted so succinctly and compellingly in Greek. It is a challenge that can never be fully met, yet it is one that is always fruitful in the attempt. In this sense, making or reading a new translation of the *Odyssey* is always a fresh encounter with the other; it is a new opportunity for discovery, an epic journey through the strange to the familiar, and a stirring return to one's sense of being human.

REFERENCES

Arnold, M. (1905). *On translating Homer*. London: John Murray.

Auerbach, M. (1953). *Mimesis: The representation of reality in Western literature*. Princeton: Princeton University Press.

Bakhtin, M. M. (1981). *The dialogical imagination: Four essays by M.H. Bakhtin*. (M. Holquist, ed.; c. Emerson & M. Holquist, trans.). Austin: University of Texas Press.

Bakker, E. (1997). Storytelling in the future: Truth, time, and tense in Homeric epic. In Bakker, E. & Kuhane A. (Eds.) *Written voices, spoken signs: Tradition, performance, & the epic text*. Cambridge: Harvard University Press.

Bakker, E. (1997b). *Poetry in speech: Orality in Homeric Discourse*. Ithaca: Cornell University Press.

Bakker. E. (2005). *Pointing at the past: From formula to performance in Homeric poetics* (Vol. 12). Cambridge: Harvard University Press.

Barnouw, J. (2004). *Odysseus, hero of practical intelligence: Deliberation and signs in Homer's Odyssey*. Lanham, MD: University Press of America.

Bellos, D. (2011). *Is that a fish in your ear: Translation & the meaning of everything*. New York: Faber & Faber.

Christensen, J. (2020). *The Many-minded man: The Odyssey, psychology, & the therapy of epic*. Ithaca: Cornell University Press.

Christensen, J. (2021). Polysymphony: Interpreting and translating Homer. *Sententiae Antiquae*. April 29, 2021. https://sententiaeantiquae.com/2021/04/29/polysymphony-interpreting-and-translating-homer/

Doherty, L. (1995). *Siren Songs: Gender, audiences, and narrators in the Odyssey*. Ann Arbor: University of Michigan Press.

Engeström, Y. (2015). *Learning by expanding: An activity-theoretical approach to developmental research*. Cambridge: Cambridge University Press.

Felsen-Rubin, N. (1994). *Regarding Penelope: From character to poetics*. Princeton: Princeton University Press.

Foley, J. (1997). Traditional signs & Homeric art. In Bakker, E. & Kuhane A. (Eds.) *Written voices, spoken signs: Tradition, performance, & the epic text*. Cambridge: Harvard University Press.

Foley, J. (1999). *Homer's traditional art*. University Park: Pennsylvania State University Press.

Franco, C. (2012). Women in Homer. In James, S. & Dillon S. (Eds.) *A companion to women in the ancient world*. Malden, MA: Wiley Blackwell.

Grossman, E. (2010). *Why translation matters*. New Haven: Yale University Press.

Hartog, F. (2017). *Regimes of historicity: Presentism and experiences of time*. New York: Columbia University Press.

Hartog, F. (2001). *Memories of Odysseus: Frontier tales from ancient Greece*. Chicago: University of Chicago Press.

Heath, J. (2005). *The talking Greeks: Speech, animals and the other in Homer, Aeschylus and Plato*. Cambridge: Cambridge University Press.

Homer. *The Odyssey*. Robert Fagles, trans. New York: Penguin Books.

Homer. *The Odyssey*. Robert Fitzgerald, trans. Garden City, NY: Anchor Books.

Homer. *The Odyssey*. Emily Wilson, trans. New York: W.W. Norton & Co., Inc.

Hutchins, E. (1996). *Cognition in the wild*. Cambridge: MIT Press.

Kahane, A. (1997). Hexameter progression & the Homeric hero's solitary state. In Bakker, E. & Kuhane A. (Eds.) *Written voices, spoken signs: Tradition, performance, & the epic text*. Cambridge: Harvard University Press.

Kanavou, N. (2015). *The names of Homeric heroes: Problems & interpretations*. Berlin: De Gruyter.

Karydas, H. P. (1998). *Eurykleia and her successors: Female figures of authority in Greek poetics*. Lanham, MD: Rowman & Littlefield Publishers, Inc.

Katz, M. A. (1991). *Penelope's renown: Meaning and indeterminacy in the Odyssey*. Princeton: Princeton University Press.

Keane, W. (2005). Signs are not the garb of meaning: Social analysis of material things. In Miller, D. (Ed.) *Materiality*. Durham: Duke University Press.

Knox, B. (1996). "Introduction." In Homer, *The Odyssey*. Robert Fagles, trans. New York: Penguin Books.

Küchler, S. (2005). Materiality & cognition: The changing face of things. In Miller, D. (Ed.) *Materiality*. Durham: Duke University Press.

Martin, R. 1989. *The language of heroes. Speech and performance in the Iliad*. Ithaca: Cornell University Press.

Martin, R. (1997). Similes & performance. In Bakker, E. & Kuhane A. (Eds.) *Written voices, spoken signs: Tradition, performance, & the epic text*. Cambridge: Harvard University Press.

Mead, G. H. (1965). *George Herbert Mead: On social psychology*. A. Strauss, ed. Chicago: University of Chicago Press.

Mead, G. H. (1934). *Mind, self and* society. Chicago: University of Chicago Press.

Miller, D. (2005). Materiality: An introduction. In Miller, D. (Ed.) *Materiality*. Durham: Duke University Press.

Minchin, E. (2007). *Homeric voices: Discourse, memory, gender*. Oxford: Oxford University Press.

Muellner, L. (2005). *The anger of Achilles: Mēnis in Greek epic*. Ithaca: Cornell University Press.

Nagy, G. (1990). *Greek mythology and poetics*. Ithaca: Cornell University Press.

Nagy, G. (1997). Ellipsis in Homer. In Bakker, E. & Kuhane A. (Eds.) *Written voices, spoken signs: Tradition, performance, & the epic text*. Cambridge: Harvard University Press.

Polizzotti, M. (2019). *Sympathy for the traitor: A translation manifesto*. Cambridge: MIT Press.

Powell, K. (2015). *Identity and power in narratives of displacement*. New York: Routledge.

Rabassa, G. (2005). *If this be treason: Translation and its discontents*. New York: New Directions Books.

Schein, S. (1995). Female representations & interpreting the *Odyssey*. In Cohen, B. *The distaff side: Representing the female in Homer's Odyssey*. Oxford: Oxford University Press.

Underwood, C. *Mythos and voice: Displacement, learning and agency in Odysseus' world.* Lanham: Lexington Books.

Vygotsky, L. (1978). *Mind in society: The development of higher psychological processes*. M. Cole, V. John-Steiner, S. Scribner & E. Souberman, eds. Cambridge: Harvard University Press.

I

Uninvited Guests

Tell me, Muse, of a man who was always shifting, drifting, driven about so far and wide, after he burned and looted Troy, the holy city. He saw many peoples' towns, and came to see their views, and in his heart he suffered many agonies on the sea, struggling for his own life and for his crew's return. But he did not bring them back, despite how much he wanted to. They perished, through their own recklessness—the fools. They feasted on the cattle of Hyperion the Sun, and he took away the day of their return. Of all this, beginning at any point, Goddess, Daughter of Zeus, tell us once again.

All of the others who had escaped utter catastrophe were now at home, having survived the war and the sea. He alone, aching for his own return and for his wife, was being held back by Kalypso, a formidable nymph and a stunning goddess, in her yearning for that man to be her husband, there in her hollow caves. But in the turning of the seasons, the year arrived when the gods had agreed he would return home to Ithaka. Even then, he had not escaped his trials. He was not yet among his people. And all the gods pitied him.

Except Poseidon. He would always remain enraged against Odysseus, until he reached his own land. But for now, Poseidon was gone, far away, among the Ethiopians—the most remote of all peoples, who live divided in two, some of them there, where Hyperion sets, and some where he rises—to take part in their ritual offering of a hundred bulls and rams. There, Poseidon was sitting at a feast, enjoying himself. But all the other gods had gathered together inside the halls of Olympian Zeus.

The father of men and gods was first to speak, since he was thinking about the flawless Aigisthos, whom the famous Orestes, Agamemnon's son, had killed. He spoke among the gods about what he was thinking.

"Appalling—how these mortals blame the gods these days! They say misfortunes come from us, but they themselves, through their own recklessness, face hardships beyond their lot in life—just as Aigisthos has, out of all proportion, seduced the legitimate wife of Atreus' son and killed him when he returned, although he knew it was his own utter destruction, since we had already sent Hermes Argeïphontes to tell him not to kill that man or court his wife, because revenge is bound to come from Orestes Atreïdes, once he has grown up and is longing for his own country. Hermes told him for his own good but could not persuade Aigisthos, and now he has had to pay for it all in one stroke."

The goddess Athena, her eyes gleaming, answered.

"Our Father, Son of Kronos, greatest of all rulers, no doubt that man is lying in a ruin that is his due. And so should anyone else who does such things be eliminated. But my heart burns for Odysseus, that unfortunate man who, with fire in his heart, is still enduring torments, far from his loved ones, on an island—the sea's navel, beaten about by waves. An island covered with trees, and on it lives a goddess, the daughter of hardhearted Atlas, who knows the depths of every sea and by himself holds up the towering pillars that keep the earth and sky apart. It is his daughter who now holds back that unlucky, sorrowful man and charms him endlessly with soft, alluring words so that he might somehow forget Ithaka.

"But Odysseus, longing only to see the smoke leaping up from his own country, wants to die. And yet your heart is unmoved, Olympian. Didn't Odysseus please you tactfully, making sacrifices beside the Argives' ships on the fields of Troy? Yet odious he is to you—why, Zeus?"

Gathering dark clouds, Zeus answered her.

"Child, what words have escaped the barrier of your teeth? How could I forget Odysseus, who is like a god? His insight is far beyond all other mortals, and he has given far more to the immortal gods who hold the vast sky. It is Poseidon, who holds the earth in his clutches, who is endlessly, stubbornly angry because of Kyklops, whose eye the man blinded—Polyphemos, like one the gods, whose power is the greatest of all the Kyklops. The nymph Thoosa, daughter of Phorkys, who rules over the restless sea, gave birth to him after scuffling in hollow caves with Poseidon. Since then, Poseidon, the earth shaker, does not kill Odysseus, but only drives him away from his native land. But come, let all of us here think over his return—how he might get home. Poseidon will surely let his anger go, because there is no way he can, on his own, stand up against all of the immortal gods."

The goddess Athena, her eyes gleaming, answered.

"Our Father, Son of Kronos, if it is now agreeable to the blessed gods for Odysseus, with all his ingenuity, to return to his own land, let's send our messenger, Hermes Argeïphontes, off to the island of Ogygia, so he can convey to that lovely haired nymph our firm resolve for sure-hearted Odysseus's return, so he can go home. I will go to Ithaka, to stir up his son even more and place courage in his heart to call the long haired Akhaians to the assembly, to speak before all those courtiers who are continually killing his flocks of sheep and his plodding cattle with their curled horns. I will send him to Sparta and to sandy Pylos, so that he may learn about his dear father's return, and so he'll have a good reputation among men."

As she spoke, she strapped beneath her feet her lovely sandals of pure gold, which carried her over the waters and across vast lands on gusts of wind. She took her thick spear, tipped with sharp bronze—heavy, long, and hard—with which she splits apart the ranks of audacious men with whom she, the daughter of a mighty father, becomes angry. She flew down quickly from the heights of Olympos and there in the land of Ithaka, she stood by the outer gate at the threshold of Odysseus's court. In her hand she held the bronze spear, looking like a stranger, Mentes, leader of the Taphian people.

There she found those brash courtiers, playing games with pebbles to their hearts' content as they sat in front of the doors on the hides of oxen that they had killed themselves. Some of their helpers and attendants were at hand, mixing wine and water in bowls for them while others washed the tables with sponges and set out sumptuous portions of meat for them. Telemakhos, looking like a god himself, was the first to catch sight of her, because he had been sitting among the suitors, troubled in his heart. In his mind he saw his good father coming out of nowhere and scattering the suitors throughout the house, to regain respect for himself and control over his own domain. As he was sitting among the suitors, thinking over these things, Telemakhos saw Athena, and he went straight to the outer gate, because in his heart he was shocked that a stranger might stand at the gates too long. He stood close to her and gripped her right hand and took the bronze spear from her. His words carried like wings to her.

"Cheers, stranger. You'll be well received here, and after you've tasted our meal, tell us what you need."

As he spoke, he led the way, and Pallas Athena followed. When they were inside the enormous house, he carried the spear and set it against a tall pillar in a polished rack, where many others of sturdy Odysseus's spears had been set. He led her across to a beautifully crafted chair, covered with linen, and below it, a stool for her feet. He placed an inlaid chair next to her, away from the others, the suitors, to make sure the stranger would not be disturbed by the noise and as a result dislike the meal because he had come among these overbearing men, and to ask him about his father, who had been away so long.

A slave brought water in a beautiful golden pitcher and poured it over a silver basin for them to wash their hands and drew a polished table beside them. A solemn housekeeper brought out bread and set it in front of them, along with many other delights that she offered generously from what there was at hand. A carver lifted up and set down platters in front of them with all kinds of meat and placed golden cups next to them, and a server kept coming back to them constantly pouring them wine.

Then the lordly courtiers came in. They sat down in rows on couches and high-backed armchairs. Attendants poured water over their hands and women served bread, heaped into baskets before them, and young men filled their bowls to the brim with drink. The courtiers themselves stretched out their hands toward the refreshments that lay ready before them.

After they had put aside their desire for food and drink, they turned their hearts elsewhere, to singing and dancing, the highlights of any feast. And so a server placed a beautiful lyre in the hands of Phemios, who sang among the courtiers against his will. He began to stroke the lyre in prelude to his beautiful song. But Telemakhos, holding his head close so that the others would not hear, said to Athena, her eyes gleaming.

"My dear stranger, will you be angry with me for what I am about to say? These others turn to these things, the lyre and the song, without a care, as they use up another man's resources with impunity, a man whose white bones may well lie, rotting in the rain on a shore somewhere, unless the waves are now rolling them in the surf. If they only saw him returning to Ithaka, they would all pray to be much quicker on their feet, rather than richer in gold and clothing. But now he's lost to some awful fate. And there's no hope for us, if not even one man on the face of the earth can say he will come back. The day of his return is lost.

"But come, tell me this and say it truthfully. Who are you among men? And from where? Where is your city, your parents? On what kind of ship did you come here? How did the sailors bring you to Ithaka? Who did they claim to be? Because I don't think you reached here on foot. And tell me this truthfully, so I will know for sure. Have you just arrived? Are you a stranger here within my father's house? Because so many other men have come here to our house, since he himself also used to wander widely among men."

The goddess Athena, her eyes gleaming, answered.

"And so I will tell you all these things openly. I tell you I am Mentes, Ankhialos' son, a man with fire in his heart. I govern the Taphians, who love the oar. And now, looking for copper, I have come here with my ship and crew while sailing over the sea, dark as wine, toward Temese and to people who speak other tongues. I bring luminous iron. My ship stands out in the country, away from the city, in Reithron Harbor, below the forests of Mount Neion.

"Let's say from the start that we are friends, as our fathers were, if you care to ask that old champion Laertes, who they say no longer comes to town, but endures his sorrows out in the country, attended by an old woman, who sets down his food and drink before him, whenever exhaustion has gripped his limbs, after dragging himself up the slope of his vineyard plot. So now I have come because, they say that he, your father, is back among his people.

"But now it seems the gods are blocking his return, because brilliant Odysseus has not fallen to earth, not yet. He's being held back, somewhere on an island, pounded by the boundless sea, and wild, violent men are somehow holding him there against his will. But I will prophesy for you, since the immortals have put it into my heart, how I think it's going to be, although I'm neither a prophet nor knowledgeable in the signs of birds. He will not be away for long from his native land, not even if iron shackles hold him down. He'll figure out a way to return, because he is always thinking, always scheming.

"But tell me and tell me truthfully, if you are Odysseus's son. It's amazing how much you look like him—in your face, your striking eyes, since we met each other often, before he left for Troy, where others, the Argives' finest, also went in their open ships. But since then, I've not seen Odysseus, nor he me."

Gathering his thoughts, Telemakhos answered.

"Of course, stranger, I'll say openly—my mother tells me I'm his son, but I don't know, since no man ever knew his own parentage by himself. If only I had been the son of a fortunate man whom old age finds among his own belongings. But now, since you ask, they say I was born to the unluckiest of all mortal men."

Her eyes gleaming, the goddess Athena answered him.

"So the gods have by no means granted you a nameless lineage for the future, if Penelope gave birth to such a one as you. But come, tell me and tell me frankly. What feast, what crowd is this? What use is it to you? A celebration, a wedding? Because it's surely no banquet where everyone brings his share, since they all seem to me to be engorging themselves, here in your hall, arrogantly, insolently. Any man of good sense would be incensed, seeing such outrages."

Gathering his thoughts, Telemakhos answered.

"Stranger, since you ask and are questioning me about all these things, this house was at one time known to be rich, untarnished, as long as that man was still among his own people. But now the gods, plotting terrible things, have settled on something else. They have made him, above and beyond all people, unseen and unnoticed, because I would not grieve so much for his death, if he had been cut down among his troops, there in the land of the Trojans, or in the arms of his loved ones, after wrapping up the war.

"Then the Akhaian army would have made him a tomb, and for his son, too, he would have won enormous glory in the time to come. But now the Harpies have snatched him away, without any recognition. He's gone. Unseen, unheard of. And he has left me in torment and tears.

"And I'm not just groaning, grieving for him alone, since the gods have crafted other awful troubles for me, since all the finest men who rule the islands—Dulikhium and Same and forested Zakynthos and those who are ruling rocky Ithaka—all are here, courting my mother and devastating my household. And she neither turns down the bitter marriage nor can she bring this to an end. They keep on feasting, ravaging my household. Soon they'll destroy me too."

Outraged, Pallas Athena answered him.

"Ah, you are at such a loss without Odysseus, who is too far away to lay his hands on these shameless courtiers. If only he would arrive right now and stand at the outer gates of the house, holding a helmet and a shield and two spears, just as he was when I first noticed him at our house, drinking and enjoying himself on his way back from Ilos Mermerides' residence in Ephyre. There, Odysseus had gone in his sleek ship, searching for a deadly drug to spread on the bronze tips of his arrows. But Ilos did not give it to him, fearing the anger of the gods, who live forever. But my father gave it to him because he liked him so much.

"If only Odysseus, as he was back then, would come storming in among these courtiers—they would find a quick end and a bitter marriage. But all this lies in the lap of the gods, whether he'll return and take his revenge this way, or not. You, I suggest, should think about how to drive these courtiers from your hall.

"So come now, pay attention and listen to what I have to say. Tomorrow, call these Akhaian heroes to the assembly and with the gods as witnesses, tell all these suitors to disperse, each to his own place. Then tell your mother, if her heart is driving her to be married once again, to go straight back to her great, powerful father, and they will prepare her wedding and gather many gifts, as many as are fitting to go to a beloved child. And I'll offer you some sound advice, if you'll listen.

"Fit up the very best ship you have with twenty rowers. Go find out about your father, who has been away for so long. First, go over to Pylos and question the extraordinary Nestor, and from there go on to Sparta, to the home of Menelaos the blond, since he was the last of the bronze clad Akhaians to come back. If you hear that your father is alive and about to return, then, however upset you are, you can take another year. But if you hear he is dead and gone forever, then return to your own home country and pile up a burial marker and make funeral offerings, as many as is his due. Then give your mother to another man.

"Then, when you've done these things and carried them to completion, think it over in your heart and soul—how you're going to kill these suitors, here in your halls, whether by deception or out in the open. You have to stop holding on to childish ways, since you are no longer that age. Haven't you heard how brilliant Orestes won his reputation among all people when he killed his father's murderer, that deceitful Aigisthos, who had slain his celebrated father?

"And you, my friend, I see you're very tall and handsome. Be courageous, so anyone of those who are yet to be born will speak well of you. And I will now go down to my ship and my crew, who no doubt are waiting impatiently for me. But you, take care, and think over what I've said."

Gathering his thoughts, Telemakhos answered him.

"Stranger, you have said these things very thoughtfully, like a father to his son, and I will not ever forget them. But come now, stay a while, eager as you are for the road, so that when you've washed and gratified your own heart, you may go to your ship with joy in your heart, holding a valuable and very beautiful gift to be treasured, to you from me, as hosts give to their guests in friendship."

Her eyes gleaming, the goddess Athena answered him.

"Don't hold me back any longer. I'm eager for the road. Whatever gift your own heart urges you to give me, offer it when I come back, to carry home. Pick something beautiful, and you will have its value in return."

As she spoke, Athena, her eyes gleaming, went away, flying up like a bird, but she had placed strength and courage in his heart, and made him think of his father, even more than before. He turned everything over in his mind and he wondered. He thought that this might have been a god. He went back among the suitors, looking like a god himself.

The well-known singer was performing for them and they all sat in silence, listening. He sang about the Akhaians' bitter return from Troy, which Pallas Athena herself had imposed. In the upper room, Ikarios' daughter, Penelope, deep in thought, overheard this marvelous song, and she descended the high stairway from her room, but not alone. Two women slaves went with her. And when the radiant woman reached the suitors, she stood beside the door post of that solidly constructed room, holding over her cheeks her shimmering veil. A loyal slave stood by on each side of her. Her tears streaming down, she spoke out to the singer.

"Phemios, you know many other things to charm us ordinary people, the actions of men and gods that you singers have made famous. Sing one of these as you sit here and they drink their wine in silence. But stop this harsh song, which always tears apart this heart inside my breast, because on me, most of all, has descended a sorrow that never leaves. It reminds me of the face I always yearn for, the man whose fame reaches throughout Hellas and mid-Argos."

Gathering his thoughts, Telemakhos answered her.

"My mother, why do you resent this worthy singer for giving pleasure, however his mind is stirred? It's not the singer's fault. It's Zeus's fault, I guess. He gives, to each one of us people who eat bread, whatever He will. So don't blame this man for raising a song about the Danaans' awful end.

"People praise most the song that's newest to their ears. So harden your heart and soul to listen, because it wasn't Odysseus alone who lost the day of his return at Troy. Many others died too. Go to your room—busy yourself with your own tasks, the loom and distaff, and order your servants to go about their tasks. Speaking out is for men, and especially for me. The power in this house is mine."

In wonder, she went back to her rooms, holding in her heart her son's sharp assertion. She ascended to her upper rooms and there, she cried for Odysseus, her own dear husband, until Athena, her eyes gleaming, shed sweet sleep over her eyelids.

The suitors burst into an uproar throughout the darkening hall, all of them craving to lie beside her in bed. Gathering his thoughts, Telemakhos was the first of them to speak.

"Courtiers of my mother, with all your reckless pride, let's enjoy ourselves feasting, and let there be no disorder, since this is a lovely thing to listen to such a singer and be awed, as he has a voice like the gods. But in the morning, let's all go to the assembly and sit, so that I can publicly declare my affirmation that you leave these halls. Pull together other feasts, where you eat up all your own stores as you go from house to house. But if this seems to be better and more advantageous to you, to use up one man's livelihood, without restitution, eat up! And I will call upon the gods, who live forever, for Zeus to execute some restorative action. Then, without making amends, you would die inside this house."

As he spoke, they all were biting their lips, wondering at Telemakhos for speaking out so forcefully. But Antinoos the son of Eupeithes, answered him.

"Telemakhos, surely the gods must be teaching you to talk such elevated talk, and to say it so audaciously. But may the Son of Kronos never make you king on the island of Ithaka, which is your legacy by birth."

Gathering his thoughts, Telemakhos answered him.

"Antinoos, will you be angry at what I'm about to say? I would be glad to take even this from the hand of Zeus. Do you think that's the worst that can happen to people? No, it's not bad being a king. Right away, your house gets richer, and you become more respected. But there are many other lords, both young and old, on the island of Ithaka. One of these may yet hold this office, since Odysseus has died. But I will be lord over our house and the slaves that brilliant Odysseus took for me."

Eurymakhos, son of Polybos, answered him.

"Telemakhos, certainly these things lie in the laps of the gods—which of the Akhaians will be king on the island of Ithaka. But keep your own belongings and be lord over your own house. Let no man come who would take your possessions away by force, against your will, as long as people live in Ithaka.

"But I'd like, my dear friend, to ask you about that stranger. Where does that man come from? What land does he claim to be from? Where are his family and his home ground? Does he bring some news about your father's coming? Or did he come here to pursue some need of his own? He stood up and then suddenly he was gone. And he did not wait around to become known, although he didn't look so bad to the eye."

Gathering his thoughts, Telemakhos answered him.

"Eurymakhos, my father's return has come to nothing. I myself now place no trust in any news, no matter where it comes from. I pay no attention to prophesies, whatever my mother has drawn out from some fortuneteller she has called into the hall. This stranger was a friend of my father from Taphos. He said he was Mentes, son of Ankhialos, a man with fire in his heart. He rules over the Taphians, lovers of the oar."

Telemakhos said this, but he knew in his heart it had been the immortal goddess. Now they all turned to dancing and lively singing, waiting for evening to come. As they enjoyed themselves, the evening darkness came upon them, and they went out, each one to his own home.

Telemakhos went up to a room built to overlook the courtyard, in an elevated place with an open view. There, he went to bed, mulling over so many things in his heart. With him, carrying flaming torches, went Eurykleia, the loving, watchful daughter of Ops Peisenorides. Laertes had once used all his wealth to buy her, giving up twenty oxen for her when she was still in her first bloom of youth. There in his halls, he gave her the same respect he gave his faithful wife, and he never took her to bed, to avoid his wife's fury. It was she who carried the flaming torches because, of all the slaves, she loved Telemakhos the most dearly, since she had nursed him when he was an infant.

He opened up the doors of the solidly built room and sat down on the bed. He took off his soft tunic and placed it in the hands of the shrewd old woman. She folded the tunic, smoothed it out, and hung it on a hook, next to the carved, open bedstead. Then she left the room. She pulled the door shut by its silver handle, and she threw the bolt across with the strap. And there, the whole night through, covered in a wool fleece, he turned over in his mind the journey Athena had set him on.

II

Disorder in the Court

Very early, as Dawn spread her rosy fingers, Odysseus's son got out of bed and put on his clothes. He slung his sword over his shoulder, tied his splendid sandals around his glistening feet and left his room, looking like a god. He ordered the attendants to lift their clear voices and call the long-haired Akhaians to assembly. They carried out their call, and the others congregated very quickly. And as they met and gathered together, he too, gripping in his hand a bronze spear, left for the agora, but not alone. Two dogs followed him briskly. And Athena shed a wonderful grace about him, and all the people watched in awe as he went by.

He sat down in his father's chair, and the elders deferred to him. Among them, Aegyptios rose to speak—the old, bent-over hero who had by now seen everything. His own son had gone along in those hollow ships with the godlike Odysseus to Ilios, the land of fine horses. But the brutish Kyklops had killed him in his empty cave and made him his latest meal. There were three others. One, Eurynomos, joined up with the suitors, and two endlessly maintained their father's farm. But even so, Aegyptios could not forget the other one and in torment, in sorrow, his tears streaming down, he addressed the assembly.

"Listen to me now, Ithakans, to what I have to say. There has never been an assembly nor any session since Odysseus went away in those hollow ships. Who is calling us here now? To whom has come such need, either among our young men or the older ones? Has he heard of an army's approach and is he going to give us an accurate account, since he is the first to hear of it? Has he some other common concern to speak to us about? He seems fine to me, fortunate. May Zeus bring some good to him, whatever he longs for in his heart."

As he spoke, Odysseus's beloved son rejoiced at these words. He was so intent to speak, he did not sit for long. He stood in the middle of the assembly, and Peisenor, an attendant adept at giving thoughtful advice, placed the staff in his hands. He spoke to the old man first of all.

"Old man, the one who has called the people together is not far, as you will see for yourself. It is to me, most of all, that sorrow has come. I have neither heard any news of an approaching army to tell you openly about, as the first to hear of it, nor is there any other public matter that I have called you here to make known. It is my own need. Twin evils have fallen on my household. I have lost my own honorable father, who once served as king among you, kind as a father. But now, there is something even worse that soon will totally destroy my household and consume my entire livelihood.

"These suitors, the beloved sons of the finest men around, have overwhelmed my mother, against her will. They shudder to go to the house of her father, Ikarios, so that he might himself hand over his daughter's dowry, and give her away to whichever one he wishes—the one who pleases him. Every day, they crowd into our home, slaughtering our oxen, our sheep, and our fat goats, and they feast and drink up our shimmering wine recklessly. And most of it is used up already, since there is no man here like Odysseus to hold off such an onslaught. We cannot hold it off, since we are so miserable and inept in defending ourselves.

"I would defend myself, if only I had the power, since intolerable acts have been taking place and my own house has been devastated beyond what is right. You should be ashamed yourselves, and you should feel shame among the other neighbors who are living around you. You should fear the anger of the gods, or they may turn against you in their fury at these evil actions.

"I beg you, by Olympian Zeus and by Themis, who gathers and disperses the assemblies of men. Desist, my friends, and leave me alone to wear myself out in bitter grief. Unless in some way my father, the honorable Odysseus, has maliciously done you well-equipped Akhaians wrong, and you are only paying me back, doing me wrong in such a cold manner, by urging these men on.

"For me, it would be better if you squandered all of my property and livestock. If you consumed them, then there might be some compensation someday, if we were to go throughout the city, making our appeal to reclaim our resources, until it is all given back. But now the pain you have inflicted upon my heart is beyond any cure."

After he spoke, enraged, he threw the staff onto the ground and burst into tears. Compassion gripped all the people. The suitors were silent, and no one wanted to reply to Telemakhos with angry words. Antinoos alone answered.

"Telemakhos, what an elevated speaker of such intrepid spirit! What are you saying, putting us to shame? You want to fix the blame on us. But it is not we Akhaian courtiers who are to blame. It is your own mother, whose mind is so shrewd. It is already the third year, and the fourth will soon come, that she has been frustrating these hearts inside our Akhaian chests. She offers everyone hope and makes promises to each man, passing them messages, while her mind remains on other things. And she has plotted in her heart this other scheme. She set up an enormous loom here in her halls, and she wove an extensive piece with the very finest thread, and without hesitation she spoke among us.

'Young men, my suitors, since brilliant Odysseus is dead, although you are in a hurry to marry me, be patient, until I finish this robe, so my spinning will not be all for nothing. It is a shroud for the great champion, Laertes, for the time when the cruel finality of unforgiving death will strike him down, or in case some of the Akhaian women in this land may become outraged at me, if he, who had acquired so much, were to lie without a shroud.'

"As she spoke, our eager hearts were persuaded. From then on, every day she'd weave at that enormous loom, and at night, with torches placed beside her, she would unravel it. With this ruse, for three years she swayed the Akhaians, and they did not notice. But when the fourth year came and the seasons rolled around, one of her women, who understood it clearly, told us, and we surprised her as she was unraveling that splendid web. And so she finished it by force, against her will. The suitors answer you in this way, so that you yourself may know in your own heart, and so that all the Akhaians may know.

"Send your mother away and tell her she has to marry whomever her father tells her to, and whoever pleases her. And if she still continues to torment us sons of the Akhaians for much longer, calculating within her heart what Athena has given her especially to know—the exquisite arts, the good sense, the shrewd schemes they never knew, those women of old, all of those fair-haired Akhaian women of antiquity—Tyro, Alkmene, and Mykene with her lovely headband. None of them were equal to Penelope in subtlety. This at least she did not think out properly.

"Because as long as they keep eating away at your livelihood and your property, and as long as she holds onto this idea that the gods have now placed within her heart, she will generate great fame for herself, but for you, only the yearning for your once abundant livelihood. But we will not go back to our former lands or anywhere else, until she marries whichever one of the Akhaians she prefers."

Gathering his thoughts, Telemakhos answered him.

"Antinoos, there is no way that I can throw out of this house, against her will, the very one who gave me life and raised me. And my father is living in some other land, or else he's dead. And also, it would be hard for me to pay back so much to Ikarios, if I sent away my mother willingly. From her father I'd accrue troubles, and some god would send others, since my mother would call on the awful Furies as she left the house. And shame would also come to me from other men.

"So I'm never going to say those words. And you, if you are offended within your heart by these things, then leave my halls and go indulge yourself in some other feast, eating up your own resources, as you go back and forth from house to house. But if it seems better and worth more to you to waste away one man's livelihood without making any kind of compensation, well then, keep on destroying it. But I will call upon the gods, who live forever, so that Zeus may grant some act of revenge to take place. And in compensation, you yourselves will be destroyed within these halls."

As Telemakhos spoke, Zeus, whose vision is vast, sent two eagles flying from high on a mountain peak. For a while they soared up, side by side, their wings extended on the breath of a wind. But as soon as they reached the middle of that clamorous assembly, they both whirled about, wings flapping rapidly, looking down on all their heads, envisioning death. They tore away at each other's cheeks and necks with their claws, then darted away, off to the right, over the houses and above their city.

Seeing this with their own eyes, they all wondered at the birds, and they mulled over in their hearts what might come to be. The old hero, Halitherses Mastorides, who excelled everyone of his age in his knowledge of birds and his sage speech, spoke out among them all, addressing the assembly with good intentions.

"Listen to me now, Ithakans, to what I have to say. And to the suitors especially I am declaring this revelation, since toward them a great misfortune is rolling in, because Odysseus is not going to be away from his loved ones for long. Even now, he is somewhere near, sowing carnage and death for all of them. And to many others of us who live here in sunny Ithaka, he will bring trouble. But long before that, let's think over how to put an end to all this.

"Or let them end it by themselves, since that would be better for them. I'm making this prophecy not as someone who's inexperienced, but as someone who knows for sure. I'm telling you, for that man, everything will be fulfilled as I once put it in plain words to him when the Argives set off for Ilios. And Odysseus, always thinking ahead, went with them. I told him—after suffering many hardships and losing all his fellow soldiers, unknown to everyone, in the twentieth year, he'll come home. And now, all of it is coming to be."

Eurymakhos, the son of Polybos, then answered back.

"Come on, old man. Go home and prophesy to your children, or they may suffer harm sometime in the future. In this, I'm much better at prophesying than you are. Lots of birds go flitting about under the sun's rays, and not all of them are momentous. Odysseus has died, far away, as you yourself should have died too, along with him. Then you wouldn't proclaim your prophecies so much nor stir up Telemakhos's anger, anticipating the gifts that he might bring to your household. And I'll proclaim to you, and this will come to pass. If you, who know so much from being old, delude a younger man and fire up his rage, first, it will be harder for him, and more than that, he will not be able to do a thing, because of all these men here.

"And on you, old man, we'll impose a fine that you in your heart will find grueling to pay. Your sorrow will be bitter. And to Telemakhos, I suggest this. Urge his mother to return, back to her father's house and prepare for the wedding and get many gifts ready, as many as are suitable for a well-loved daughter. Before that, the sons of the Akhaians will not stop their rigorous courtship, since we do not fear anyone anyway, not Telemakhos for all his endless talk, nor do we care about any prophesying that you, old man, utter pointlessly. You will only be despised even more, and his resources will be eaten up spitefully, and there will be no equal compensation, as long as she delays this wedding. We ourselves will go on striving for the sake of her pre-eminence and won't go after any other women who'd be a match for any one of us."

Gathering his thoughts, Telemakhos answered him.

"Eurymakhos, and all you other distinguished courtiers, I will not plead with you any longer about these things, nor even speak of it, since the gods and all the Akhaians know about it already. But come now, give me a fast ship and twenty shipmates to go on a voyage with me here and there. I'll go to Sparta and sandy Pylos, to find out about the return of my father, who has been gone for so long, in case some mortal man might tell me, or I might hear from Zeus, who so often spreads rumors among men. And if I hear my father is alive and on his way back, then, though very distressed, I might endure another year, but if I hear he's dead, no longer alive, I'll return to my native land and pile up a mound to him and offer lavish funeral offerings, as many as are fitting, and I will give my mother away to some man."

After he spoke, he sat down, and Mentor, who had been Odysseus's blameless fellow soldier, stood among them. When he had been leaving on his ships, Odysseus had turned his entire household over to the old man, so they would obey him, and he would keep them all on a sure footing. With every good intention, the man now addressed the assembly.

"Listen to me now, Ithakans, to what I have to say. Never again should any king who holds the scepter be kind and gentle out of his own good will, or look into his own heart for what is right and proper. No, let him be harsh and do evil, since no one whom Odysseus once ruled as a people remembers him. Like a god he was, yet gentle as a father. But I am not objecting to you overbearing suitors, who commit violent actions in the maliciousness of your minds, because you are risking your own heads as you voraciously eat up the resources of Odysseus, who, they say, will never again return. My indignation is for you other people, all of you who sit in silence and do not say a word to castigate these suitors, even though they are so few and you are so many."

Leiokritos Euenorides answered back.

"Mentor, that's harsh. Your mind is wandering. What are you saying, stirring them all up to make us stop? It would be hard even with more men to fight us—and over a meal! Even if Odysseus the Ithakan were to come back himself, eager in his heart to drive out of his halls these noble suitors feasting in his house, his wife would hardly be pleased at his coming, however much she desired it, since he would meet his own distasteful end, if he ever fought against our larger numbers. You chatter away beyond what's right and proper. But come on now, people, scatter away, back to your own business, each of you. Let Mentor and Halitherses urge this fellow on his way. They are friends of his father's household from the old days. But I think Telemakhos will be sitting around a long time, here in Ithaka, listening to gossip, and he will never follow this journey through to the end."

After he spoke, the assembly quickly broke up. They all scattered, each to his own home, except for the suitors, who went back to the house of the legendary Odysseus. But Telemakhos went off, on his own, to the shore of the sea. He washed his hands in the gray surf, and he made his appeal to Athena.

"Listen to me, you who came as a god to our house yesterday and told me to go across the foggy sea in a ship, to hear about my father, who has been gone for so long. The Akhaians are hindering all this, and most of all the suitors in their appalling insolence."

As he said this in prayer, Athena came close to him, looking like Mentor in body and voice. And her words and the sound of her voice flew over to him on the wing.

"Telemakhos, you will not be mean or mindless, if your father's fine spirit was ever instilled in you. Such a man he was to take his actions and words through to the end. And even so, your road is not going to be in vain or unfulfilled. Yet if you are not the offspring of that man and Penelope, then I don't have any hope that you will accomplish what you desire. Few sons are like their fathers. Most are worse. And only a few are better. But since you won't be mean or mindless from now on, and Odysseus's wit has not escaped you, there is hope that you will fulfill this task. Don't think about the suitors' plans and aims. The fools! They are not mindful or reasonable, and they are not thinking of death or the black end that is so close to them—to die, all in one day.

"But you, the road your heart is set on will not be put aside for long. I'm such a friend of your father, I will equip a fast ship for you, and I will go with you myself. But you, go on back to your house and join in that crowd of suitors. Prepare your supplies and stow them all away in vessels, some wine in amphoras, and barley, man's marrow, inside thick skins, while I go back through town to gather a crew of volunteers. There are many ships, new and old, in Ithaka, surrounded by the sea. I will scope out which of these is the best one, and we will ready her and sail out onto the wide sea."

Zeus's daughter, Athena, spoke, and Telemakhos did not stand there for long, after he heard the voice of the goddess. Deeply troubled in his heart, he went back to his house. There in his halls, he found the proud suitors, flaying goats and singeing the bristles off the pigs in the courtyard. Laughing, Antinoos came straight to Telemakhos. He held out his hand and addressed him.

"Telemakhos, what an elevated speaker of such intrepid spirit! Let no more rude words or actions into your heart. Let's all eat and drink, just like before. We Akhaians will no doubt bring all these things together, a ship and some handpicked oarsmen, so you may go on your way with all due speed to sandy Pylos to inquire about your noble father."

Gathering his thoughts, Telemakhos answered him.

"Antinoos, there is no way I could go on eating quietly and enjoying myself without a care before such arrogance as yours. Isn't it enough that in the past you suitors have wasted so many of my fine belongings, when I was only a child? But now, I'm grown and I am learning as I hear what others are saying, my heart surging inside me. I'll find out how to bring you a horrendous death, either by going away to Pylos, or right here in my own native land. I'm going—as a passenger—because that seemed more to your advantage, and I am not the master of either a ship or oarsmen, and the journey I am talking about will not be in vain."

And as he spoke, he casually drew his hand away from Antinoos's hand, as the suitors throughout the hall kept on feasting. They went on mocking him and jeering at him with hard words. And one of those overbearing young men would speak in this way.

"Ah, Telemakhos is plotting our murder for sure! He will bring back bodyguards from sandy Pylos, or maybe even Sparta, he is so dead set on it now. Or else he plans to go to Ephyre, that fertile land, to bring some of those deadly drugs back here and throw them into the wine bowl and kill us all."

And another of the overbearing young men would say, "Who knows? Maybe he'll die, wandering around in his hollow ship, far from his loved ones, exactly like Odysseus. So he'll just make more trouble for us, since we will have to split up his belongings and give his house to his mother and whoever marries her."

As they went on talking, Telemakhos went down to his father's room. It was wide, with a high ceiling. There, gold and bronze lay about in piles, along with clothes in chests and plenty of fragrant olive oil. Large ceramic jars of aged sweet wine, with an unmixed heavenly drink inside, also stood there, arranged in rows along the wall, in case Odysseus ever returned home, after suffering many hardships. The double doors were jammed tight together, and there, both night and day, a woman stood by, guarding it all with the sharpness of her understanding—Eurykleia, daughter of Ops Peisenorides. Telemakhos called her over to the room.

"Nurse, come over here and draw me off some wine into these amphorae, the finest wine there is, except for what you're saving in the hope that that unfortunate one, Odysseus, sprung from Zeus, might come from somewhere, after escaping death and its emissaries. Fill up twelve and top them off with lids. And pour some barley into some of those well-stitched leather skins—a full twenty measures of ground barley meal. Bring everything together, but keep it to yourself. And then, in the evening, when my mother thinks of bed and goes upstairs to her upper room, I will gather them, because I am going to Sparta and sandy Pylos to ask about my father's return, in case I hear something."

As he spoke, his beloved nurse cried out and moaned, her words quavering on the wing in answer to him.

"How, dear child, has this idea come into your mind? Where would you want to go in this great world? You, an only child and so well-loved. He has died, far away, Odysseus, sprung from Zeus—far off in a land known only to strangers. But these men here, when you have gone, will think up awful things for the future—how you'll die through their trickery—and they will divide up all of these things. Stay here. Take charge of what's yours. No need to go off wandering and suffering hardships on the restless sea."

Gathering his thoughts, Telemakhos answered her.

"Take heart, Nurse. This plan is not without the aid of the gods. But swear to me you'll tell none of this to my dear mother before the eleventh or twelfth day arrives, or until she misses me or hears that I've gone, so that she won't harm her lovely skin by crying."

After he said this, the old woman swore a great oath, before the gods. And after she had fully sworn and completed her oath, at once she drew the wine off into jars and poured the barley into well-stitched skins, as Telemakhos went to the hall and re-joined the suitors. Right then, the goddess Athena, her eyes gleaming, had another idea. Looking like Telemakhos, she went around throughout the whole city, and to every man she approached, she had her say, encouraging them to gather at the swift ship that evening. Then she asked Noemon, Phronios's splendid son, for a fast ship, and he promised it sincerely.

The sun set, casting shadows over every road. And she drew the ship into the sea. She installed all the gear that well-benched ships carry. She moored it at the harbor's mouth and all around it a good crew gathered together. And the goddess stirred each one's heart. And then Athena, her eyes gleaming, had another thought. She went back to the house of godlike Odysseus. There, she shed sweet sleep over the suitors and as they drank, they drifted off, and she knocked all the cups out of their hands. They did not sit for long, because sleep was now descending upon their eyelids, and so they roused themselves to go to their beds throughout the city. Athena, her eyes gleaming, in the guise of Mentor in both body and voice, called Telemakhos over to the prominent hall.

"Telemakhos, a well-equipped crew are already sitting at their oars, waiting only for you to make your move. Let's go. Let's not delay the journey."

As she said this, Pallas Athena led the way quickly, and he followed in the footsteps of the goddess. And when they came down to the sea and the ship, they found their long-haired shipmates along the shore, and Telemakhos, his strength renewed, spoke to them.

"Come, friends, let's bring down our supplies, since everything's been gathered together at the great hall. My mother's heard nothing of this, nor have the servants. Only one person has heard what I have told her."

As he spoke, he led the way, and they went with him. They brought everything and they stowed it all below the sturdy benches in the ship, as Odysseus's own son had ordered. Athena boarded first, and she sat down in the ship's stern. Then Telemakhos climbed aboard and sat next to her. The others released the stern cables, and climbed aboard themselves, and sat at their benches. Athena, her gray eyes gleaming, sent behind them a favorable wind—the brisk west wind, roaring over the sea, dark as wine. Telemakhos called out to his crew to grab their tackle, and they all rose up as soon as they heard. And they lifted up the fir mast and stood it inside the open socket. They set it to with forestays, and they heaved up the white sail with tightly twisted ox hide lines.

And the wind filled the middle of the sail, and a dark wave crashed and gleamed about the prow of the ship as it went along. It sped among the waves as it traversed its course. And after they had stored all of their gear away inside the swift black ship, they set out bowls, filled to the brim with wine. They poured out all their offerings to the gods who exist forever, but most of all to Zeus's daughter, her gray eyes gleaming, and all through the night until dawn, the ship went on and on, carving her way through.

III

The Old Horseman

Leaving the lovely surface of the sea, the sun rose into a bronze sky to bring light both to those who never die and those who have to die on earth, the source of grain. They came to Pylos, Neleos's well-built stronghold. Those who were on the seashore were making offerings of black bulls to the dark-haired Earth Shaker. There were nine gatherings, with five hundred men sitting in each, and before each one they held nine bulls. But after they had tasted the entrails, just as they were burning the thigh pieces to the god, the others put in to shore. They hoisted and furled the sail of their trim ship, anchored it, and disembarked. Telemakhos also descended from the ship, with Athena leading the way. The goddess, her gray eyes gleaming, was the first to speak.

"Telemakhos, you no longer need to feel timid, not even a little. It was for this you have sailed the sea, to hear about your father—where the earth has covered him, or whatever end he has met. But come now, go straight to Nestor, the horse tamer. Let us learn what guidance he holds within his breast. Ask him to tell you the truth. He will not speak falsely, because he is very thoughtful."

And thoughtfully, Telemakhos answered her.

"Mentor, how should I go? How should I address him? I'm not yet tested in the subtleties of speech, and besides, it's embarrassing for a young man to talk to an elder."

The goddess Athena, her eyes gleaming, answered him.

"Telemakhos, you will think up some of it in your own heart, and the rest some god will impart, because I do not think you were brought up against the will of the gods."

As she spoke, Pallas Athena led the way quickly, and he followed in the footsteps of the goddess. And so they went up to the gathered groups of men from Pylos. There, Nestor sat with his sons, and all around him, his friends, in preparation for the feast, were roasting some of the meat and piercing other parts on spits. But when they saw the strangers, they all crowded forward.

They shook their hands and encouraged them to sit down. Peisistratos Nestorides was the first one to come close and seize both of their hands, and he told them to sit down for the feast on soft goat skins spread on the sand by the sea, next to his brother Thrasymedes and his father. He gave them portions of entrails and poured them wine in a golden cup. He welcomed them, addressing Pallas Athena, the daughter of Zeus, who holds the aegis, the great shield that drives the winds.

"Stranger, pray to Lord Poseidon now, because you've happened to come here during this feast to him. And after you have poured your offerings and prayed, as is his due, then give this young man the cup of sweet wine to pour, since I think he too prays to those who never die, as every one of us needs the gods. But he is younger, about my own age, so I'm giving the gold cup first to you."

As he spoke, he placed the cup of sweet wine in her hand. Pallas Athena took heart at the man's thoughtfulness and correctness in giving her the golden cup first, and at once she offered a solemn prayer to Lord Poseidon.

"Listen to me, Poseidon, you who clutches the earth. Do not hold back from fulfilling all these things for which we are praying. On Nestor and his sons, first of all, confer your glory. And bestow your gracious compensation for this wonderful hecatomb on all these others, the people of Pylos. And grant that Telemakhos and I return, after we accomplish the mission for which we have come here in our swift black ship."

In this way, she prayed, even as she herself was bringing it all about. She gave the beautiful double-handled cup to Telemakhos, and Odysseus' beloved son prayed in a similar way. When they had roasted the outer meat and removed it, they divided up the portions and they ate the sumptuous feast. But when they had put aside the desire for food and drink, Nestor of Gerenia, the tamer of horses, spoke first among them.

"Now then, it is appropriate to inquire and ask the strangers who they are, since they have enjoyed our food. Strangers, who are you? From where have you sailed in your sea passage? Are you on a mission or are you wandering about aimlessly over the sea, like pirates who drift about, risking their own lives and bringing misfortune to people of other lands?"

Telemakhos took heart. Gathering his thoughts, he answered, because Athena had planted confidence in his heart, so he would ask about his missing father, and so he might have a good standing among men.

"Nestor Neleiades, famed among the Akhaians, you ask where we have come from, and I will tell you. We have come from Ithaka, under Mount Neios. This mission I am sharing is my own, not a public one. I have come so I might hear of any wide-ranging reports about my father, the brilliant, great-hearted Odysseus, who once, they say, fought with you and destroyed the city of the Trojans. Of all the others who warred with the Trojans, we have heard where each one died a miserable death, but the Son of Kronos has left that man's death unreported, so no one can tell for sure where he died, if he was overcome by violent men on the mainland or on the open sea, among the waves of Amphitrite.

"For this reason I have come to your knees, in case you might be willing to inform me about his unfortunate death, whether you saw it somewhere with your own eyes or heard words from some other wanderer, because above all others, his mother bore him to misery. Do not try to soothe me out of sympathy or compassion, but tell me frankly what sights you may have come across. I beg you, if my father, the good Odysseus, ever undertook and carried out any word or action for you in the land of the Trojans, where you Akhaians suffered so much hardship, remember it now for me and tell me the hard truth."

The horseman, Nestor of Gerenia, answered him.

"My friend, you have reminded me of all the misery that we, the Akhaian sons, with our unwavering courage, endured, driven all about on our ships, and hunting loot over the foggy sea, wherever Akhilles led us, and our struggling around Lord Priam's great city—there, where so many of the very finest of us were cut down. There lies Aias, Ares' favorite. And there, Akhilles. There, Patroklos, equal to the gods as an advisor. And there too, my own son, equally strong and without a fault. Antilokhos, the fastest runner, the very best fighter.

"And we suffered many other terrible things. Who among mortal men could tell them all? No, even if you stayed here five or six years and asked about all the horrible things those brilliant Akhaians endured there, you would sooner lose heart and head back to your own native land. For nine years we plotted the worst for them with all kinds of treachery, and the Son of Kronos just barely brought it to an end. There, no one tried to match *him* in intelligence—brilliant Odysseus. He outshined us all by far in all kinds of strategy—your father, if you are in fact his son.

"I am struck with wonder as I look at you. The way you speak is so much like his. You wouldn't think a younger man could speak like this. For the whole time we were there, brilliant Odysseus and I never spoke at odds, either in the assembly or in council. But being of one mind, with alertness and shrewd advice, we both informed the Argives how everything might turn out for the very best.

"But when we had utterly leveled Priam's towering city and had gone away in our ships, and a god had scattered the Akhaians, even then, Zeus planned in his heart a miserable return for the Argives, since we were not all discerning and honorable. Many met a bad end, through the awful anger of that goddess with the gleaming eyes, the daughter of the Brutal One, since she caused discord between the two sons of Atreus, and they called all of the Akhaians to assembly, without any reason or order, and at sunset, the Akhaian sons came, heavy with wine, and they spoke their speeches, the reasons they had gathered the people.

"Menelaos urged all the Akhaians to think of their return over the sea's broad back, but this was not at all pleasing to Agamemnon. He wanted to hold the people back, to make offerings of a hundred oxen, so he might appease the dreaded rage of Athena. The fool! He did not know she was not about to listen, since the minds of the gods who exist forever are not turned around so quickly. The two stood there arguing with harsh words, and the Akhaians, fitted out in their fine shin guards, rose up in a huge furor, and two divergent plans found favor among them. That night we all rested, harboring hard thoughts against each other, because Zeus had set in motion a horrible misfortune.

"In the morning, some of us dragged our ships to the bright sea, and we loaded our goods and our women in their long-draped robes, but at least half of the people held back and remained there with Agamemnon Atreïdes, shepherd of the people. Half of us went on board and rowed away. Very quickly the ships sailed off because a god had calmed the open sea. And when we reached Tenedos, eager to reach home, we made sacrifices to the gods. But Zeus had not yet decided on our return. Stubbornly, he stirred up a terrible dispute for the second time. Some of them were now showing favor to Agamemnon Atreïdes. They turned back their rounded ships and left with that ingenious heart of fire, Lord Odysseus.

"But I fled with the fleet of ships that followed me, since I knew that a god was planning something awful. And Tydeus' son, Ares' favorite, urged on his crews, and they fled too. And later, in our wake, came Menelaos the blond. And he overtook us at Lesbos, as we were arguing over the long voyage, whether to sail above rugged Khios toward the island of Psyria, keeping Khios to our left, or under Khios, past windy Mimas. We asked the god to show us a sign. He showed us, and led us to cut our way across, on a middle course through the sea to Euboeia, so we might most quickly escape danger.

"A shrill wind began to blow. The ships traveled very quickly over the sea, filled with fish. At night, we put in to Geraistos. We offered many bulls' thighs to Poseidon, thankful we had made it across the great sea. It was on the fourth day when the crews of Diomedes Tydeides, the horse tamer, landed their sleek ships in Argos, but I held on for Pylos. And the wind never died down from the moment when the god first set it blowing.

"And so I came, dear child, without hearing a thing, and I know nothing of the others, those among the Akhaians who were saved and those who were lost. All I have heard, sitting here in our halls, you will hear, as is fitting, and I will hide nothing from you. The Myrmidons, who flaunt their spears, and who were led by the famous son of great-hearted Akhilles—they came through fine, they say, and Philoktetes, the illustrious son of Poias. And Idomeneus too brought all of his fellow soldiers back to Krete—those who escaped the war—and the sea took away none of them.

"Of Atreus' son, you yourselves have heard, no matter how far away you may have been, how he came back. And how Aigisthos planned his awful death, but paid miserably for it. And so it's a good thing for a son to be left behind when a man dies, as that one took his revenge on his father's murderer, the deceitful Aigisthos, who had killed his celebrated father. And you, friend, since I see you are handsome and tall, be fearless, so that those who are yet to be born will speak well of you."

Gathering his thoughts, Telemakhos answered him.

"Nestor Neleiades, most esteemed of all the Akhaians, that man truly took his revenge, and the Akhaians will spread his fame widely, so those who are yet to be born may hear of it. If only the gods would wrap me in such power, so I might pay back the suitors for their painful violations, as they insolently think up unpardonable acts against me, but the gods have spun no such satisfaction for me or for my father, and now I simply have to take it."

And the horseman, Nestor of Gerenia, answered.

"Friend, since you have said these things, I am reminded. They say that many of your mother's suitors are plotting horrible things in your halls, against your will. Tell me, are you willingly letting yourself be exploited, or do the people throughout your land hate you, because they are following the voice of some god? Who knows if Odysseus himself might come some day and pay them back for their violence—he alone or all the Akhaians together. If only Athena, with her gleaming eyes, might choose to love you as much as she once cared for the legendary Odysseus, there in the Trojans' country, where we suffered so many miseries, since I have never seen the gods show their love so openly as Athena did, when she was standing there by his side. If she were to love you and care for you in her heart like that, some of them would stop thinking about marriage."

Gathering his thoughts, Telemakhos answered.

"Old man, I don't think this will ever happen, what you're saying—it's far too much. I am amazed. I don't have even the slightest hope that it will happen, even if the gods themselves would wish it to be."

The goddess Athena, her eyes gleaming, said to him.

"Telemakhos, what a word has escaped the barrier of your teeth! Any god who willed it could easily deliver a man safely, even from far away. And I would rather come home and see the day of my return, after suffering many hardships, than be slaughtered at my own hearth, after returning, as Agamemnon was killed by the treachery of Aigisthos and his own wife. But of course, even the gods themselves cannot fend off the utter impartiality of death, even for a man they love, when his own unspeakable share of merciless death cuts him down."

Gathering his thoughts, Telemakhos answered.

"Mentor, as troubled as we are, let's talk about these things no longer. That man's return is no longer realistic. Already, those who never die have arranged his own death, his own black doom. But now, I'd like to inquire and ask Nestor about something else, since he knows what is right and reasonable, above all others. They say he has ruled over three generations of men, just as now he seems to me like an immortal to look upon. Nestor Neleiades, tell me truthfully, how was he killed, Agamemnon Atreïdes, who ruled so far and wide? Where was Menelaos? What death did the deceitful Aigisthos think up for him, since he killed a man far stronger than he was himself? Was Menelaos not in Akhaian Argos, but drifting about among people somewhere else, so Aigisthos took heart and murdered Agamemnon?"

The horseman, Nestor of Gerenia, answered him.

"About this, child, I will tell you the whole truth. You have yourself suggested how all of this would have taken place, if Atreus' son, the blond Menelaos, after he left Troy, had found Aigisthos alive in his halls. They would not have even heaped up the earth in a pile over his dead body. The dogs and birds would have torn away at him as he lay on the plain, far from the city, and not one of the Akhaian women would have wept for him, because the act he thought up was utterly outrageous. But we stayed there at Troy, following our troubles through to the end, while he, in comfort in some corner of Argos, where they raise such fine horses, kept up his charming chatter with Agamemnon's wife.

"At first Klytaimnestre kept herself in denial about the gruesome act, as she had a good mind. With her there was a singer, to whom Atreus' son had emphatically given orders to protect his wife when he had gone away to Troy. But as his destiny from the gods, he was bound to be overcome, and Aigisthos led the singer away to some desolate island and left him there to be the prey and catch of birds. And then he led her, as willing as he was willing, homeward. There he burned many thighs on the gods' sacred altars, and he put up many delightful offerings, gold and woven things, since he had carried out his monumental act, which even his own heart he had never hoped for.

"And we were sailing away from Troy, Atreus' other son and I, in close alliance with each other, but when we reached holy Sunios near the Cape of Athens, Phoibos Apollo attacked with his gentle shafts and killed Menelaos' helmsman as he was holding onto the rudder of the rushing ship—Phrontis' son Onetor, who excelled in the ranks of men in steering ships when the gusts of wind were driving hard. And so they stopped there, though anxious to continue on their way, so they could bury his mate and make funeral offerings over him. But when Menelaos went on in his hollow ships over the sea, dark as wine, and came quickly to the towering heights of Mount Malea, then Zeus, who sees across great distances, envisioned a bitter passage and poured blasts of screaming winds at him. The waves swelled, looming like mountains. And there, he split the ships.

"Some sailed to Krete, where the Kydonians live beside the streams of Iardanos. There is a sheer rock cliff, falling precipitously down to the sea, on the edge of Gortyn, out on the foggy sea. There, the southwest wind heaves a huge wave against the craggy rocks on the west toward Phaistos, and even a small rock will hold back a giant wave. Some of them approached there, and the men barely escaped destruction, but the waves smashed the ships against the reefs. The wind and waters drove five ships with their dark prows onward and brought them to Egypt.

"So Menelaos wandered about there with his ships, gathering provisions and gold among men with strange tongues, while Aigisthos plotted unspeakable things at home. After he killed Atreus' son, the people were oppressed under him. For seven years, he ruled Mykene, but in the eighth year his enemy, Orestes, came back from Athens and killed his father's murderer—the devious Aigisthos, who had killed his celebrated father. After killing him, he gave the Argives a funeral feast for his miserable mother and the spineless Aigisthos. And Menelaos, who was good at shouting his rage, arrived on the same day, bringing many possessions, as much weight as his ship could hold.

"And so, my friend, you must not wander far from home for long, after leaving behind your belongings with such insolent men in your home, or they may use up or divide all your wealth, and you will have gone on a pointless journey. But I encourage and urge you to go to Menelaos, since he has only recently come back from somewhere abroad and a people from whom you would never hope within your heart to return, after the turbulent winds had driven him away, over a sea so vast that even the birds themselves do not come back from there in the same year, it is so vast and dreadful.

"But now, off with you and your ship and your mates, or if you would rather go by foot, here are chariots and horses, and my own sons are here for you. They will be your guides, all the way to bright Lakedaimon, the place where that blond man, Menelaos, lives. Implore him to tell you the whole truth. He will not speak falsely, because he is genuinely thoughtful."

As he was speaking, the sun set and darkness came on, and the goddess Athena, her eyes gleaming, spoke to them.

"Old man, you have described these things fittingly, but come now, cut out the bulls' tongues and mix the wine, so after we have poured out all our offerings to Poseidon and the other immortals, we may think about sleep, for the time is now. The light has already given way to darkness, and it's not right to sit for so long, feasting with the gods, but to go home."

Zeus' daughter spoke, and they all listened to her voice. Attendants poured water over their hands, and young men filled their bowls to the brim with drink. They served them all in equal portions, beginning with the offerings poured in the cups. Then they threw the tongues onto the fire. They stood up and poured out their offerings. And after they poured them out and drank to their hearts' content, right away, Athena and Telemakhos both were anxious to return to their empty ship. But Nestor vigorously held them back, scolding them with these words.

"May Zeus and the other immortal gods keep you from going away from my house to your sleek ship as if from someone completely without clothing—a poor man, without cloaks and plenty of blankets inside his house where neither he nor his guests might sleep comfortably. But I have cloaks and beautiful blankets. Never will the beloved son of this man Odysseus lie down on the deck of his ship while I am still alive and my children after me are left behind in these halls to be hosts to strangers, or anyone who comes here to my home."

The goddess Athena, her eyes gleaming, answered him.

"You have spoken all of this well, old friend, and it is fitting for Telemakhos to listen, since it's far better this way. But while he goes along with you now, to sleep in your halls, I am going to our black ship, so I can lift our shipmates' hearts and tell them everything. Because among them, I alone can claim to be an older man. All the others are younger men who have come along in friendship, all of them close in age to great-hearted Telemakhos. I will lie down there, beside the black ship, only tonight. In the morning, I'll go to the great-hearted Kaukonians, where a debt is owed me, neither recent nor trivial. But since this one here has come to your house, send him on with a chariot and your son, and give him your fastest running horses, the very strongest and best."

After she spoke, the goddess Athena, her eyes gleaming, departed in the form of an eagle. And as they saw it, they were all amazed, and the old man gazed in utter wonder—he had seen it all with his own eyes. He turned and grasped Telemakhos' hand and spoke to him.

"My friend, I don't expect you'll turn out either a bad or a timid man, if the gods now accompany you as your guide, when you are so young. Of those who make their homes up on Olympos, that was no one but Zeus' daughter, Tritogeneia, the most wonderful young woman, who honored your own good father above and beyond all the Argives. Be gracious, Lady, and let me be known as worthy, both me and my sons and my esteemed wife. And to you, I'll sacrifice an untamed yearling cow, one that is wide across its brow and that no man has yet drawn under the yoke. I'll sacrifice it, after overlaying its horns with gold."

As he spoke his prayer, Pallas Athena heard him. And the horseman, Nestor of Gerenia, led his sons and his daughters' husbands across to his beautiful home, and when they reached the king's glorious mansion, they sat down, one after another, on couches and high-backed chairs. As they gathered there, the old man mixed a bowl of sweet wine, which the housekeeper had just opened, after breaking the seal in its eleventh year. It was this the old man mixed, and he prayed aloud as he poured out offerings to Athena, daughter of Zeus, who holds the aegis, the great shield that drives the winds. But after they poured out the offering and drank to their hearts' content, they went off to lie down and sleep, each in his own home.

But the horseman, Nestor of Gerenia, had Telemakhos, Odysseus' own son, who looked like a god himself, lie down and sleep on a cot with holes and interlacing straps in the echoing portico, next to Peisistratos, a good spearman and a leader of men, who alone among his sons in his palace was still unmarried. He himself went off to sleep in the innermost room of the lofty, stately house. There, he and his wife, his dear lady, shared the pleasure of their bedding.

Very early, as Dawn showed her rosy fingers, the horseman, Nestor of Gerenia, rose from bed. He went out and sat down on the polished stones in front of his tall doors. They were white, glistening as if oiled. Neleus, equal to the gods as an advisor, had once sat on them, but by now, overcome by death, he had gone down to Hades. Nestor of Gerenia, protector of the Akhaians, now sat there, holding his staff. His sons came from their rooms and gathered close around him—Ekhephron and Stratios and Perseus and Aretos and Thrasymedes, and among them came a sixth champion—Peisistratos. And they led out Telemakhos, who seemed himself like one of the gods, and they made him sit next to the old man, and the horseman, Nestor of Gerenia, was the first of them to speak.

"Quickly, dear children, fulfill my expectations, so that I may win the support of Athena, first of all the gods, who came to me openly during the sumptuous feast. But come, someone go to the fields for a cow. Bring it quickly and have the cattle herder drive it. Go to the great-hearted Telemakhos' black ship and bring back all his shipmates. Leave only two of them behind. And also, go out and order our goldsmith Laerkes to come here, to plate the cow's horns with gold. The rest of you stay here, all together, and tell all the servants inside to prepare a feast, inside our splendid halls, and bring out some seats and firewood and good, clear water."

As he spoke, they all began to do what he said. The cow arrived from the fields, and from the swift, well-crafted ship, great-hearted Telemakhos' mates. The metallurgist came, carrying in his hands the tools of the bronze worker's trade, the anvil and hammer and the well-made tongs with which he worked the gold. Athena arrived to receive the offering, and the old man,

Nestor, the driver of chariots, offered over his gold. And the smith crafted it to overlay the heifer's horns, so the goddess would be delighted when she saw this treasure.

Stratios and the elegant Ekhephron led the cow over by the horns, and Aretos came out of the inner room, bringing them water for their hands in a basin molded in a florid design. In his other hand, he carried barley in a basket. Thrasymedes, vigorous in battle, stood by, holding a sharp axe in his hands, to bring down the cow, while Perseus held the receptacle to catch the blood. The old man, Nestor, the chariot driver, washed both his hands and scattered the barley, while praying aloud to Athena, and he started the rite by cutting off some hair from the cow's head and throwing it into the fire. After praying and scattering the barley, Thrasymedes, Nestor's son, his heart soaring, stood close and struck.

The axe sliced through the muscles of the neck and the cow began to lose its strength. The daughters and sons' wives and even Nestor's esteemed wife, Eurydike, Klymenos' oldest daughter, ululated. The men lifted up the cow's head and held it high above the earth's broad sweep of roads. And then Peisistratos, a leader among men, cut its throat.

When the black blood had run out and the life had left its bones, they cut everything up in large pieces. Right away, they cut away the thighs in the appropriate manner. They covered them over with a double layer of fat and placed raw pieces on top of them. And then the old man burned them on split pieces of wood and poured shimmering wine over them. Beside him, all the young men were holding forks with five prongs in their hands, and when the thighs and entrails had been fully roasted, they cut up all the rest into small bits and speared them on spits, and they roasted them, holding the pointed spits in their hands.

Meanwhile, the lovely Polycaste, Nestor's youngest daughter, was bathing Telemakhos. After she had washed him and anointed him with oil, and had thrown a tunic and a lovely cloak around him, he emerged from the bath, looking the equal of the gods. He went out and sat down beside Nestor, the shepherd of the people. And when they had roasted the outer meat and taken it off the spits, they sat down and feasted, and men served them skillfully, pouring the wine into gold cups. But when they had put aside the desire for food and drink, Nestor of Gerenia, the tamer of horses, was the first to speak.

"My sons, lead out those horses with the lovely manes, yoked to a chariot, so Telemakhos can finish his journey."

As he spoke, they all listened and promptly obeyed. They placed the fast horses under the chariot's yoke quickly, and the housekeeper placed bread, wine, and sauces—the kinds that kings for whom Zeus cares would eat. Telemakhos climbed onto the stunning chariot and Peisistratos, Nestor's son, a leader of men, climbed onto the chariot next to him and took the reins in his hands. He cracked the whip, and the two men eagerly flew across the plain and left behind the towering stronghold of Pylos.

All day, the horses yanked the yoke about. And the sun set, and all the roads grew dark. They came to Pherae, the home of Diokles, son of Ortilokhos, whom Alpheios raised. There, they spent the night, and their host offered them hospitality. And very early, as Dawn flourished her rosy fingers, they yoked up the horses and climbed onto the inlaid chariot. They drove through the gate and the echoing portico. Peisistratos cracked the whip, and the two men cheerfully flew across the plain, lush with grain. Afterwards, the fast horses carried them along so quickly, they came to their journey's end. And the sun set, and all the roads grew dark.

IV

The Thread of Fortune

They came to the valley of Lakedaimon, full of ravines, and they drove to the household of the famous Menelaos. They found him inside his house, giving his many kin a feast for the weddings of his flawless son and daughter. He was sending her away to the son of Akhilles, the breaker of the ranks, because at Troy, he once had promised and pledged to give her, and the gods had brought the wedding to fruition. He was just about to send her off with horses and chariots to the celebrated city of the Myrmidons, whom her husband-to-be ruled. And he had also brought Alector's daughter from Sparta for the daring Megapenthes, his own son, born of an enslaved woman and now full grown.

The gods had granted Helen no more progeny after she first gave birth to her child, the charming Hermione, who possessed the beauty of golden Aphrodite. And so they were feasting and enjoying themselves, there inside the great hall with its lofty ceilings, the neighbors and family of the illustrious Menelaos. Among them a heavenly singer was playing the lyre, and two acrobats leading the entertainment were whirling about in their midst, when the two, our hero Telemakhos and Nestor's splendid son, stopped at the palace gates. Lord Eteoneus, the eager attendant of the illustrious Menelaos, came forward and saw them and went back through the house to inform the shepherd of the people. He approached and his words quivered like wings. "Two strangers are here, Menelaos, favored by Zeus, two men like the progeny of Zeus Almighty. Tell me, should we unharness their fast horses for them, or send them to someone else who will entertain them?"

Deeply enraged, the blond Menelaos said to him, "You were not a fool before, Eteonos Boethoïdes, but now you're talking utter nonsense like a child. How many times we have eaten other people's food as we journeyed here, hoping Zeus would cut short our own hardship? So release the strangers' horses and lead them through, so they can share our feast."

After he spoke, the attendant hurried through the hall. He ordered the other attendants nearby to follow him. They released the sweating horses from under the yoke and tied them up inside the horse stalls. They threw coarse barley down in front of them and mixed it up with white barley. They leaned the chariot against the gleaming vestibule walls and led the men into the heavenly palace. The two looked around in awe, passing through Menelaos's palace. There was a radiance, as if from the sun or moon, in glorious Menelaos's home with its high ceilings.

After feasting their eyes, observing it all, they entered the well-polished baths and washed. And after the women slaves had washed them and anointed them with olive oil and then had thrown wool cloaks and tunics about them, they sat down beside Menelaos Atreïdes, and an attendant brought water in a lovely golden pitcher to wash their hands. He pulled over a polished table close to them, and then the esteemed housekeeper brought out some bread and placed it next to them, and set down various delicacies in large quantities, offering freely whatever was at hand. A carver took and set before them plates, full of all kinds of meat, and he placed golden cups next to them. And the blond Menelaos welcomed the two.

"Take this food and enjoy it, and after you have eaten supper, we will ask you who you are among men, because the wellspring of your ancestors is not lost in either of you. Yours is a lineage of men who are descended from kings with scepters and favored by Zeus, because no ordinary man could engender the likes of you."

As he spoke, he took in his hands some choice slices of roast beef—the same slices that had just been placed before him as a special honor—and he set them out before the two young men. They reached out their hands to the delicacies that lay before them, and when they had put aside their desire for food and drink, Telemakhos leaned close to Nestor's son, so the others might not hear, and whispered to him.

"Nestorides, you've raised my spirits, but look at all the bronze, gleaming throughout this echoing house, and the gold, the silver, the amber and the ivory. The court of Zeus must look just like this inside, it's so unspeakably rich. I'm struck with awe to look at it."

When he spoke, the blond Menelaos heard him, and his voice carried across to them like wings.

"Dear children, no mortal could ever compete with Zeus—his halls and holdings are infinite, but among men, maybe someone might match me in wealth, or maybe not. Because after wandering and suffering so much, I brought back quite a lot in my ships when I came home in the eighth year. I wandered all over Kypros, Phoenikia and Egyptos, and reached the Aithiopians, the Sidonians, and the Eremboi—all the way to Libya, where the lambs mature quickly, as the sheep all give birth three times in one full turning of the year. There, neither lord nor shepherd goes without cheese or meat or sweet milk, because the flocks are always, without fail, producing milk for their young to suck. And as I wandered around those lands, gathering considerable provisions, another man deviously murdered my unsuspecting brother, through his detestable wife's treachery.

"So there's no joy in being the master of all these belongings. You're likely to have heard this from your fathers, whoever they are, how much I suffered and how I came to lose a very pleasant house that held so many valuable things. But I'd rather be living in my house with only a third portion of it and with those men safe—those who died back then on the open fields of Troy, so far from Argos, this land for raising horses. Often, while I am sitting here inside my halls, crying and aching for all of them, I indulge my heart with mourning for a while; but then I stop, since one quickly has one's fill of the chill of sorrow.

"And yet, I don't mourn so much for all of them, no matter how distressed I am, as for the single person who makes me abhor sleep and sustenance whenever I remember him, because none of the Akhaians worked as hard as Odysseus toiled and struggled. But for him, there was only to be sorrow, and as for me, there is this unforgettable ache for that man—endlessly. He has been gone so long, and no one knows if he is alive or dead. They must be mourning, the old man Laertes, faithful Penelope, and Telemakhos, whom he left behind at home a newborn child."

As he was speaking, he aroused in Telemakhos the desire to weep for his father. And tears fell down from his eyelids onto the ground as he heard his father's name, and with both hands he held his purple cloak up over his eyes. Menelaos noticed him, and wondered in his mind and heart, whether to let him speak about his father on his own or question him first and test him about everything.

And as he was thinking it over in his mind and heart, Helen, looking like Artemis with her golden arrows, emerged from her fragrant room with its high ceilings. Adraste was with her and set down a beautifully crafted chair for her. Alkippe brought a soft, wool rug, and Phylo brought a silver basket given her by Alkandre, the wife of Polybos, who lived in Thebes, Egypt, where so much wealth lies about in homes. Polybos had given Menelaos two silver bath tubs and two tripods and ten gold talents. And his wife offered Helen various exquisite gifts—a golden spindle, and she also offered a silver basket with wheels, its rims overlaid with gold. The slave Phylo brought in this basket and set it down beside her. It was full of finely spun yarn, and at the top, the spindle was wrapped in dark violet wool. Helen sat in the chair, and below it was a stool for her feet. And all at once she began to question her husband about everything.

"Do we know yet, Menelaos, esteemed by Zeus, who these men who've come here to our house claim to be? Should I lie or tell the truth? My heart's driving me on. I have to speak out—I've never seen anyone, man nor woman, who looked so much like someone else. I'm struck with wonder as I look at him, since this man here is like the son of that great heart, Odysseus—Telemakhos, the one that man left behind a newborn child when, due to my own shamelessness, the Akhaians arrived below Troy, eager for brutal violence."

Blond-haired Menelaos answered her and said, "I am noticing it only now, woman, just as you yourself are seeing it. For just like this were that man's feet, and like this his hands, and the shifting of his eyes, and his face and above all, his hair. Just now, I was remembering Odysseus, and talking about the troubles he went through for me, and he let a bitter tear fall from under his brow, and he held his purple cloak before his eyes."

Peisistratos Nestorides answered him.

"Menelaos Atreïdes, favored by Zeus, leader of the people, this is his son, just as you are saying. But he has a cautious mind, and is embarrassed in his heart to show off with self-assured talk when he has just now come before you, whose voice we glory in as like a god's. But the old horseman, Nestor of Gerenia, sent me along with him to be his guide, because he was keen to see you, so that you might plant some word or action in his heart, because a child living at home has many troubles when his father is absent, and there is no one else to be his ally and helper, just as it is now with Telemakhos. His father's gone. There's no one else among his people to hold off misfortune."

Blond-haired Menelaos, answered him.

"Amazing! The son of a man whom I love so dearly, who for my sake endured so many struggles, has come here to my house. And I had thought if *he* came back, that I would welcome him, above and beyond all of the other Argives, if Olympian Zeus, who sees so far, had given both of us our return over the sea in our ships. I'd have given him a whole city and I'd have built him a house to live in, after emptying out one of those cities near here that are ruled by me, and I would have brought him here from Ithaka with all of his possessions and his son and all of his people, and being here close by, we would have socialized and no one would have kept us from loving and enjoying each other, until at last the dark cloud of death gathered around us. But he must have envied us, that god who resolved that that unlucky man alone was never going to return."

As he spoke, it stirred in all of them the urge to cry. The Argive woman, Helen, the child of Zeus, wept, and Telemakhos wept, and Menelaos Atreïdes too. Even the son of Nestor could not hold back his tears, because he remembered the faultless Antilokhos whom the glorious son of shining Dawn had killed. As he thought of him, his words took wing.

"Atreïdes, old Nestor always used to say that you were the most thoughtful of all mortals, whenever it happened that we were questioning each other and thought of you. But for now, if it is at all possible, listen to me, because I find no enjoyment in mourning after supper, and Dawn will soon be here. I find no blame at all in crying over any mortal who has met his end and died. This is surely the least debt we owe our fellow miserable beings who face death—to cut our hair and let the tears flow down our cheeks. My own brother is dead. He was not one of the worst of the Argives, and you are likely to have known him. I never met him or even saw him myself. But they say he was fast at running and fighting above all others."

The blond-haired Menelaos answered him.

"My friend, you've said all that a thoughtful man might say or do, even someone older than you—from such a father—and you yourself speak so thoughtfully. It's easy to recognize a man for whom the Son of Kronos has spun the thread of good fortune, both in marriage and in his children, as now, he has made it possible for Nestor to grow into old age with ease, through all his days in his own halls, and for his sons to become sensible and matchless with the spear, so let us set aside the weeping that just happened, and remember our dinner. Pour some more water over our hands! There is sure to be more time for conversation in the morning, for Telemakhos and me to talk things through with each other."

As he spoke, the famous Menelaos's eager attendant, Asphalion, poured water over their hands, and they reached out their hands to the refreshments before them. But Helen, daughter of Zeus, had something else in mind. She dropped in the wine they were drinking a drug to leave them without sorrow, without anger, and make them forget everything unpleasant. Anyone who swallowed it, after it was mixed in the bowl, would not let a tear fall from his cheeks for a whole day, not even if his mother and father dropped dead, or if someone, right in front of him, killed his brother or his beloved son, and he saw it with his own eyes.

Zeus's daughter had such cunning drugs, really good ones, given to her by Polydamna, Thon's wife, a woman from Egypt, where the earth, our source of grain, brings out the most drugs—many of which, when mixed, are good for healing, though many others are dangerous. There, every man is a healer, more knowledgeable than all other peoples, since they are the descendants of Paieon. And after Helen put in the drug and ordered that the wine be poured, she offered a few words in reply.

"Menelaos Atreïdes, so well endowed by Zeus, and you, the sons of fine men who are with us here—while Zeus gives both good and bad, now to one and now to another, since he is able to do anything he wants—for now, sit here in our halls and feast and enjoy the conversation. And I will tell you something suitable. I cannot tell or describe all the struggles of Odysseus and his tenacious mind. But how much this hardy man accomplished and endured there in the land of the Trojans, where you Akhaians suffered such hardship! His body beaten down with unwelcome blows, he threw some awful tatters over his shoulders, and like a slave, he entered into the broad streets of a city full of violent men, and he disguised himself in the likeness of someone else, a beggar—he, who was no such thing back there, among the ships of the Akhaians. Yet it was like this he entered into the Trojans' city, and all of them were unaware of it.

"I alone recognized him and questioned him firmly, but he shrewdly avoided me. But just as I was bathing him and anointing him with oil, and giving him clothes, after I had sworn a firm oath not to expose him as Odysseus among the Trojans before he again reached the Akhaians' fast ships and huts, then at last he told me the Akhaians' entire strategy. And then, after he had killed many of the Trojans with this long bronze sword, he went back among the Argives and brought them considerable intelligence. The other Trojan women wailed loudly, but my own spirit lifted, since my heart had already turned back to my home, and I groaned over the foolish passion that Aphrodite gave me when she led me away from my native land, leaving my child, my bridal chamber, and my husband, who lacks nothing in brains or looks."

Blond-haired Menelaos answered her.

"Without a doubt, woman, you've recounted all of these things accurately. I've come to know the guidance and strategies of many brave men, and I've wandered all over the wide earth, but I have never seen with my own eyes anyone as tenacious in his mind and heart as Odysseus. How much this powerful man accomplished and endured inside that carved horse from which all the finest of the Argives were about to bring bloodshed and death to the Trojans! It was then that you came there. It had to be that you were called there by some god who intended to bring glory to the Trojans, and Deiphobos, who was like a god himself, followed you as you went.

"Three times you circled that hollow trap, touching it and calling by name the finest of the Danaans and likening your voice to those of all the Argives' wives. I and Tydeus and brilliant Odysseus were sitting in their midst, and we heard you calling out to them, and even we were anxious to stand up and either climb out or answer you back from the inside. But Odysseus held us back. He held us back, eager as we were. Then all the other sons of the Akhaians were quiet. Antiklos alone wanted to speak up and answer, but Odysseus held his jaws tightly shut with his strong hands, and saved all the Akhaians. And he held him like that until at last Pallas Athena led you away."

Gathering his thoughts, Telemakhos answered back.

"Menelaos Atreïdes, esteemed by Zeus, leader of the people, that is even more painful, since this did not hold off his miserable death, not even if his heart inside was made of iron. But come now, send us to bed, so that we can enjoy ourselves in being lulled to sweet sleep."

As he spoke, the Argive Helen told her slaves to set up cots under the portico, toss a few beautiful purple blankets onto them, spread some covers over them, and put wool cloaks on top as well. The slaves went out from the great hall, holding torches in their hands, and prepared the beds, spreading and smoothing them out. An attendant led the guests out. And they slept there on the porch, the brave Telemakhos and the splendid son of Nestor.

But the son of Atreus slept in the innermost room of the house with its high ceilings, and beside him, in her long robe, lay Helen, brilliant among women. And very early, Dawn spread out her rosy fingers. Menelaos, good at shouting orders, rose from his bed and put on his clothing. He threw his sharp sword over his shoulder, bound his beautiful sandals under his feet, and he left the room, his face looking like a god's. He sat down next to Telemakhos and called him by name.

"What necessity has brought you here, Telemakhos, over the broad back of the sea to bright Lakedaimon? Is it something public or private? Tell me the plain truth."

Gathering his thoughts, Telemakhos answered back.

"Menelaos Atreïdes, esteemed by Zeus and leader of the people, I came so that you might offer me some report of my father. My household is being consumed; my rich lands devastated. My house is filled with violent men who are continually killing my flocks of sheep as well as all my cattle with their curled horns and shuffling hooves. These suitors are so overbearing in their insolence toward my mother. So it is for this that I've now arrived at your knees, to see if you'd be willing to tell me of his miserable death, if somehow you might have seen it with your own eyes, or if you have heard some story from some other drifter—because above all others, his mother bore him to misery.

"Don't try to calm me out of sympathy or compassion, but tell me frankly what sights you have come across. I beg you, if ever my father, the good Odysseus, took on and carried out any word or action for you in the country of the Trojans, where you Akhaians suffered so much hardship, remember it now for me and tell me the hard truth."

Deeply outraged, blonde-haired Menelaos spoke to him.

"Clearly these are spineless men who would lie down in the bed of a man with a much greater heart. It's like when a deer has laid her newborn suckling fawns to rest in the lair of a lion and wanders off, grazing over the mountain slopes and grassy meadows, and then the lion returns to its bed and unleashes an unspeakable end on both fawns. That's how Odysseus will unleash an unspeakable end on them.

"Oh, Father Zeus, Athena, and Apollo—if only he would, like that time in orderly Lesbos when he stood up and wrestled with Philomedeides, and threw him down decisively, and all the Akhaians cheered. In the same way, if only Odysseus would come upon the suitors, they would all face a quick death and a bitter marriage. But I will not digress from these things that you are asking and begging from me in order to speak of other things, and I won't mislead you. The old man of the sea told me about those things—and I will not hide or hold back a word.

"Eager as I was to return here, the gods held me in Egypt, because I hadn't performed the complete sacrifices of oxen, and they always advise us to be attentive to their mandates. And so, there is an island in the always surging sea, before you get to Egypt. They say it's called Pharos. It's as far away as a hollow ship can travel in one whole day, when a shrill wind is blowing from behind. There's a harbor there, with good anchorage, from which they launch their well-designed ships into the sea, after they have drawn fresh, deep water aboard.

"The gods held me there for twenty days. And those winds never appeared, the ones that blow over the sea and speed ships over the broad back of the sea. All of my supplies and all the strength of my men would have been used up, if one of the gods had not felt sorry for me and saved me—Eidotheea, the daughter of powerful Proteus, the old man of the sea—as I had stirred her heart most of all. She came upon me as I was drifting about alone, away from my mates, who themselves were always wandering about the island, fishing with bent hooks, because hunger was tearing away at their bellies. She stood very close to me and her voice intoned, 'Are you a fool, stranger? Slow witted? Or have you actually chosen to take leave of all your senses, and you enjoy suffering all this hardship? You've stayed here on this island for so long, that you can find no resolve yourself, and your shipmates' hearts are wasting away.'

"After she spoke, I spoke up and answered her.

"'I will tell you, whichever one of the gods you are, I am not staying here on my own. I must have sinned against the immortals who occupy the vast skies. But tell me, since you gods know everything, which of the gods is detaining me and keeping me back from my journey—and my return? How can I go off across this sea, infested with fish?'

"Right away, the brilliant goddess answered me.

"'Well, for you, stranger, I will answer truthfully. There is someone who comes here very often—the old man of the sea, the immortal Proteus of Egypt, who is always so bluntly truthful and who knows the depth of every sea. He is a servant of Poseidon. And they say that he is the father who brought me into existence. If you could somehow lie in ambush and seize him, he will tell you the way to go and the length of your journey, and all about your return—how to sail away across the sea, filled with fish. And if you wish him to, he'll tell you—you who are so favored by Zeus—everything that has taken place in your halls, the good and the bad, while you've been gone on your long, hard journey.'

"After she spoke, I answered her, 'Can you yourself, right now, think of some plan to ambush the old god? Or else, he might see me somehow, ahead of time, and get away, because it is hard for a mere man to overcome a god.'

"As I was speaking, at once the brilliant goddess answered.

"'Well, for you, stranger, I'll tell you very openly. When the sun has reached its midpoint in the sky, that brutally honest old man of the sea comes out of the surf, on the breath of the west wind, hidden by the dark rippling waters. After he emerges, he lies down to rest in a hollow cave. Around him, the seals, children of the sea's beautiful daughter, come out of the gray water and sleep, all together, and the stench they exhale, from the very depths of the sea, is awful. I will take you there at daybreak, and lay you there in a row, because you will have to select three of your shipmates carefully, the best you have with you on your ship's many benches.

"'I'll tell you all the cunning tricks of that old man. First, he'll go around and count the seals, and when he's tallied them by fives and looked them over, he'll lie down with them, like a shepherd among his flocks of sheep. And when you first see him lie down to rest, find your strength and force and hold him there, no matter how hard he struggles and moves around to escape. He'll try to change into everything that thrashes about on the ground, in the water, or out of the blazing fire. Hold him firmly and grip him even more tightly, but when at last he speaks and asks you in the very same shape he had when you first saw him lie down, then stop forcing him. Let the old man go. Ask him which of the gods is angry and about your return, and how to sail across the sea, full of fish.'

"After saying this, she dove into the surging sea, and I went off to where the ships stood on the sands. My heart was raging over so many things as I went. But when I came down to the sea and my ship, we prepared our supper, and the enchanting night came on. We lay down to rest on the seashore. And very early, as Dawn showed her rosy fingers, I went along the shore of the sea with its infinite courses, praying intently to the gods. And I took the three men I trusted most for any undertaking. Meanwhile, she had plunged under the deep chasm of the sea and brought up the skins of four seals, all freshly flayed.

"And she crafted a plot against her father. She scooped out some beds in the beach sand and sat there waiting. We came up very close to her and she had us lie down in a row, and she threw one of the skins over each of us. There and then, our ambush would have been most horrible, since the utterly awful stench of the seals, born of the sea, was tormenting us—for who can lie down next to a creature from the sea? But she saved us by thinking up a very helpful thing. She brought us some ambrosia, very fragrant, and placed it under each of our noses, and eliminated the creatures' stench.

"All morning we waited with persevering hearts, as the seals came out of the water in droves. They lay down in rows by the seashore, and at midday, the old man emerged from the surf and found the seals well fed. He went along among them all and calculated their numbers. He counted us first among the creatures, and in his heart he did not think there was any trick, so he lay down himself.

"We rushed at him, yelling, and we threw our arms around him, and the old man had not forgotten his own cunning skills. First, he turned into a lion with a full mane, and then into a snake, a leopard, and a huge boar. Then he turned into flowing water, and into a tree, very tall and full of leaves. We held on—with determination in our stubborn hearts. But when at last the old man, so skilled in cunning tricks, grew tired, he questioned me and said these words.

"'Which of the gods, son of Atreus, conspired with you to ambush me against my will? What do you need?'

"After he spoke, I answered him, 'You know, old man. Why are you trying to distract me with this question? How long am I to be held back on this island, without being able to find an end to it? My heart is wasting away. You tell me, since you gods know everything, which of the gods holds me here, keeping me from my journey? And my return—how can I get across the sea, infested with fish?'

"After I spoke, he answered me right away.

"'But of course. You should have made generous offerings to Zeus and the other gods before you went on board, so you'd come as quickly as possible to your native land after sailing the sea, dark as wine. Because it is not your lot to see your loved ones or to reach your well-maintained household and your native land before you go once again to the waters of Egypt, that river powered by Zeus himself, and offer sacred sacrifices of a hundred oxen to the gods who occupy the vast heavens and never die. Only then will the gods open the way you're yearning for.'

"As he spoke, my heart broke deep inside me, because he was urging me across the foggy sea to Egypt, yet again, a long and arduous journey. But even so, I answered him and said these words.

"'All this I'll carry out, old man, exactly as you've ordered. But come now, tell me this and lay it out truthfully. Have all of the Akhaians come back unharmed on their ships, all of those whom Nestor and I left behind when we departed Troy? Did some die a brutal death aboard ship, or in the arms of their loved ones, after slogging through that war?'

"After I had spoken, he answered right away.

"'Atreïdes, why are you asking me these things? You don't need to know or to think about what's in my mind. I don't think you'll be without tears for very long, when you've heard it all. Many of them were killed, and many were left behind. Only two of the Akhaian leaders in their bronze armor perished as they returned home, and of course, you were there for the fighting. Only one, perhaps, is still alive, held back on the open sea. Aias was brought down among his ships, with their long oars. Poseidon at first drove him onto the massive rocks at Gerai, but he saved him from the sea. And the man would have escaped his death, hated as he was by Athena, if he had not tossed out, in his utter blindness, such an arrogant statement. He said he had escaped the great gulf of the sea despite the gods. Poseidon heard him speaking out so smugly, and at once he picked up his trident in his powerful hands. He struck the Rock of Gerai and shattered it apart. One fragment remained there, but the piece that had been broken off, on which Aias had been sitting before in his moment of blindness, plunged into the sea, and it carried him down into the endlessly surging sea. And so he died, swallowing salty water.

"'But your brother escaped somehow on his hollow ships and avoided the brokers of death. The venerable Hera saved him. But as he was about to reach towering Mount Maleia, a blustery wind caught him up and carried him, groaning deeply, across the sea, filled with fish, to that most distant land where Thyestes once lived, and where Aigisthos Thyestiades now lived. But even from there, he was shown a safe return. The gods turned back the wind, and they reached home.

"'Overjoyed, he stepped out onto his native land, and picking up some of his own ground, he kissed it, and many hot tears flowed from his eyes, because his own land was welcome. From his vantage point, a lookout whom the insidious Aigisthos had led up and positioned there, after offering him a reward of two gold talents, saw the arrival for which he had been keeping watch for a year, in case the king arrived unseen and remembered his own irascible power.

"'So the lookout went to the palace to bring the word to the shepherd of the people, and Aigisthos immediately plotted an underhanded scheme. He selected twenty men, the best in the land, and he set them up to wait in ambush and also gave orders to prepare a feast. And then he went out with his horses and his chariots—and with his mind on the unspeakable—to summon Agamemnon, shepherd of the people. Aigisthos led the man inside, unaware of the death that was intended for him, and as soon as they had finished feasting, Aigisthos cut the man down, as you would cut down an ox inside the stables. And out of all those soldiers who had followed the son of Atreus, not even one was left alive, and not even one of Aigisthos' men. They were all cut down there, inside those halls.'

"As he spoke, my heart broke inside, and I wept, sitting there in the sand. Now, my heart no longer wanted to go on living or to see the light of the sun. But when I'd had enough of crying and flailing about, right then, the blunt old man of the sea spoke to me.

"'Son of Atreus, don't keep on weeping for so long without letting up, because we'll find no use in it. As quickly as you can, figure out how to move on to your native land. Either you'll find him alive, or Orestes may have arrived there first and killed him. And you'll be able to take your part at his funeral feast.'

"As he spoke, my heart and soul were again strong inside my chest, although I was still full of sorrow, and as I spoke my words soared to him on the wing.

"'I know about these now, but name the third man, the one who is held back on the open sea, or is dead. I want to hear it, even though I am in anguish.'

"I said this, and he answered immediately.

"'The son of Laertes, who makes his home in Ithaka. I saw him on an island, his hard tears welling and streaming down, in the halls of the nymph, Kalypso, who holds him there by force. He's not able to reach his native land, since he has no ships equipped with oars and no shipmates at hand to take him across the broad back of the sea. But you, Menelaos, favored by Zeus, are not destined to meet your end on Argos, where they raise such horses. The immortals will take you to the Elysian plain and the ends of the earth, where the blond Radamanthus is and where life is the easiest it can be for human beings. No snow, no storms, and it never rains, but Oceanos always sends gusts of the west wind, blowing shrill to keep the people cool. Because you have Helen and in their eyes, you are the husband of Zeus's daughter.'

"Saying this, he plunged into the surging sea. And I went to my ships and my able mates, and my heart brooded over many things as I went. But when I came down to the sea and my ship, and we prepared our supper, and the bracing night came on, we lay down, there on the seashore. Very early, as Dawn showed her rosy fingers, first we hauled our ships down to the gleaming surf. We set the masts and sails on our splendid ships, and the men went on board, sat at their benches, and sitting there all together, they thrashed at the gray sea with their oars.

"I headed the ships back to Egypt, the river fed by Zeus, and carried out the sacrifices perfectly. And after I'd appeased the fury of the gods who live forever, I heaped up a burial mound to Agamemnon, so his memory would be inextinguishable forever. And when I had completed all this, I sailed away, and the gods gave me a fair wind and brought me quickly home.

"But come now, stay here in my halls until the eleventh or twelfth day. Then I'll send you off well, and give you splendid gifts, three horses and a well-polished chariot. And then, on top of that, I will give you a lovely cup, so that whenever you pour your offerings to the immortals, you will always remember me for all your days."

Gathering his thoughts, Telemakhos answered him.

"Atreïdes, don't keep me here for a long time, although I'd be content to sit with you for a year without the least desire for my home or my parents. I enjoy hearing all your stories and accounts heartily, but my shipmates back in holy Pylos must already be aggravated, and you've been keeping me here for quite some time. Whatever you offer me as a gift, let it be just a token. I won't take horses to Ithaka. I'll leave them here for you to enjoy, since you rule over this wide plain, which is so rich in lotus, fragrant grasses, wheat, coarse barleys, and the white barleycorn that grows far and wide. In Ithaka there are neither open courses for running nor meadows. There are only pastures for goats, much more lovely than those for raising horses. Of all those islands that slope sharply into the sea, not even one is useful for driving horses, with nice open meadows, and Ithaka is the worst of all."

As he spoke, Menelaos, so good at shouting orders, merely smiled. He touched him with his hand, and calling him by name, he said these words.

"You are of good blood, my dear child, in speaking like this. And so I'll change these gifts, because I can. Of all the valuable gifts lying around in my house, I'll give you the most beautiful and most precious. I'll give you a mixing bowl, very finely crafted. It's pure silver, and all along its rims, it's overlaid with gold—the work of Hephaistos. Phaidimos, that heroic king of the Sidonians, brought it to me when his household sheltered me as I was coming homeward. And now I'd like to give it to you."

They went on talking to each other, as the guests began to arrive at the palace of the king, who was like a god. They herded along their sheep, and they brought in hearty wine, and their exquisitely veiled wives sent along some bread. In this way, they busied themselves with the feast, while the suitors, in front of Odysseus's great hall, were enjoying themselves, throwing the discus and javelin in a leveled field, as they always had in their arrogance. Antinoos and godlike Eurymakhos, the suitors' leaders and by far the most reputable of them, were sitting there. Noemon, the son of Phronios, approached and asked Antinoos,

"Antinoos, do we know at all when Telemakhos will return from sandy Pylos? Or not? He took a ship of mine and has gone, and I need it now to cross over to spacious Elis, where I have twelve mares and some stout young mules, unbroken and still feeding at the breast. I am going to take one of them and break it in."

As he spoke, they wondered in their hearts, since they did not know he had gone to Pylos, Neleus' home, but thought he was somewhere close by, among his sheep or with his keeper of pigs on his own land. Antinoos, the son of Eupeithes, at once said to him, "Tell me the truth. When did he go away and which of the young men went with him? Were they selected from among the Ithakans here, or were they all his mercenaries and slaves? He could well have managed that. Tell me truthfully, so I'll know. Did he take your black ship away from you by force, against your will, or did you give it to him on your own, because he talked you into it?"

Noemon, the son of Phronios, answered him.

"I gave it to him on my own. What would anyone do, when a man like him, who has so many troubles in his heart, makes such a request? It would be hard to deny the gift. The young men who went along with him are the finest in the land, besides ourselves. I noticed one of them who was going as their leader—Mentor—or a god who was like him in every way. I wondered about that. I saw Mentor here, yesterday at dawn, but by then he had embarked for Pylos."

After saying this, he went away to his father's house. But the smug hearts of the other two were enraged. At once, they told the other suitors to stop their games and sit down. Antinoos, the son of Eupeithes, spoke among them, deeply distressed. His black heart was utterly filled with anger, and his eyes were like fires, blazing.

"Apalling—a great act, this journey, has been arrogantly carried out by Telemakhos, and we all thought he could never bring it about. In spite of all of us, this young man, this child, has gone and launched a ship on his own, after choosing the finest men in the land. He'll soon begin to be trouble. May Zeus undermine his power before he attains a measure of manhood. But come on now, give me a fast ship and twenty shipmates, so I can keep watch and ambush him in the channel between Ithaka and Rocky Samos, so that he will have sailed at a high cost for the sake of his father."

As he spoke, all of them agreed and urged him on. At once, he stood up and went to Odysseus's home. It was not for long that Penelope was uninformed about the plot the suitors were constructing covertly inside their hearts. The attendant Medon told her, right after he had overheard their meeting, since he was outside the courtyard and they were inside, weaving their plan for action. He himself made his way through the house to take the information to Penelope.

As he stepped across the threshold, she spoke to him.

"Attendant, why have those noble suitors sent you? To tell Odysseus's servants to stop their work and prepare a feast for them? As they neither do their courting nor come together anywhere else, let them feast here now for the latest and last time. You who are always crowding in here and wasting so much of our livelihood, Telemakhos's resources, and firing up his mind. When you were only children, long ago you must not have listened to your parents, those who gave you life, when they said what kind of man Odysseus was. He never did or said anything unjust to anyone in the land, as is the way of godlike kings—some men they detest and some they love, but he himself never acted heartlessly with any man. But your hearts and inappropriate actions are very evident. There's no gratitude tomorrow for acting well today."

Medon, carefully gathering his thoughts, answered.

"If only this, my queen, were the most awful thing. The suitors are plotting something much more serious and treacherous now. May Kronos' son never let it happen. They plan to cut Telemakhos down with sharpened bronze as he's returning home, since he's gone to holy Pylos and brilliant Lakedaimon to hear about his father."

As he spoke, both her knees and her heart gave way. She was struck speechless by his words, for a long time. Her eyes filled with tears; her voice was tight and heavy. After a while, she raised her voice and answered him.

"Attendant, why is my son gone? He had no need to board some fast-sailing ship, like a horse for men at sea, crossing over the vast waters. Was it so that not even his very name would be left behind among men?"

Medon, carefully gathering his thoughts, answered.

"I do not know if some god drove him, or if his own heart was aroused to go to Pylos, so he might learn either of his father's return or of what end he has met."

After he spoke, he went away through Odysseus's house. And a heart-crushing sorrow descended over her. She could not even manage to sit down on one of the many chairs in the room, but sat down on the threshold of her beautifully constructed room, moaning inconsolably, and around her, all of the slaves who were in the house, both young and old, wailed. Heaving while she wept, Penelope spoke to them.

"Listen, friends, the Olympian has given me sorrows beyond all the women who were born and raised with me. Already I have lost my lion-hearted husband, who was the ultimate among the Danaans in all good qualities—a worthy man, whose reputation was widespread throughout Hellas and mid-Argos. But now the winds have snatched away my dearly beloved son from these halls, without any account of his going. Cruel! Not one of you even thought to rouse me from my bed, although you knew inside your hearts when he boarded his hollow black ship, because if I had heard he was even thinking about this journey, he would have stayed here, eager as he was for the journey, or he would have left me behind, dead in these halls.

"But someone—quickly—call the old man, Dolios, my servant, whom my father gave me when I was about to come here—the one who keeps my garden, full of so many trees—so that he, as quickly as possible, can get Laertes and tell him all these things. Maybe that old man can weave some scheme in his mind and go out weeping to the people, who now seem so eager to eliminate his and Odysseus's seed."

Her loving nurse, Eurykleia, then answered her.

"Dear girl, you can kill me with merciless bronze or leave me alive, here in your hall. I'm not going to hide what I have to say to you. I knew about all of these things, but I brought him whatever he asked me for, bread and sweet wine. And he obtained a solemn oath from me not to tell you before the twelfth day comes, or until you yourself miss him and hear that he has gone, so you would not spoil your lovely flesh with crying. Now go and bathe yourself. And choose some fresh, clean clothing for your body, and go on up, along with your servants, to your upper room, and pray to Athena, daughter of Zeus, who holds the great shield that drives the winds, because she may truly be able to rescue him from death. But don't go trouble a troubled old man, because I don't think the offspring of Arkeisiades are totally despised by the blissful gods. Surely there'll be someone who'll come to shield this house, with its towering roofs and the fertile fields beyond."

As she spoke, her words put the other's grief to rest and kept her eyes from crying. She bathed. She put some fresh, clean clothing on her body and went up to her upper room, together with her attendant women. And after pouring a few grains of barley into a basket, she prayed to Athena.

"Listen to me, child of Zeus who holds the aegis, you who are never weary. If Odysseus, always thinking ahead, ever burned thick pieces of thighs from oxen or sheep for you in these halls, remember them now for me and save my dear son. Hold off those horrible, egotistical suitors."

After she had spoken, she cried out sharply, and the goddess heard her plea. But the suitors themselves burst into an uproar, there in the shadowy halls, and one of the overbearing young men would say: "Now for sure this queen, who's being courted by so many of us, is preparing for her wedding, without knowing that death is being prepared for her own son."

So one of them would say, but they did not know how everything would turn out in the end. Antinoos addressed the whole gathering.

"Are you touched by some god? Let's avoid these overconfident statements of every kind, or else someone might pass it on, here inside the house. But come on now, let's stand quietly and bring about this plan that has cheered all our hearts."

After he spoke, he chose twenty of the best men, and they went to the seashore and their fast ship. First of all, they dragged the ship into the deep surf. Then they set the mast and sail on the black ship and fitted all the oars to twist and turn within their leather straps, each in order, and then they spread out the white sail. Swaggering attendants brought them their weapons. They anchored the ship in the channel, and then they all climbed out. They had their supper there and waited for evening.

In her upper room, Penelope, thinking it over and over, lay there without touching her food, without tasting either meat or drink, worrying in agony whether her faultless son would escape his death or be overpowered by the contemptuous suitors. As a lion, entrapped within a gathering of men, anxiously broods as they are drawing together their clever circle, all around—she went on worrying, as sweet sleep came over her. She sank back and went to sleep, and all her joints relaxed.

Then the goddess Athena, her eyes gleaming, thought of something else. She created a vision, in the likeness of a woman—Iphthime, the other daughter of the great-hearted Ikarios, whom Eumelos had married and who lived in Pherai. Athena sent it to Odysseus's household, to Penelope while she was sobbing and mourning, to get her to stop crying and shedding tears. It passed through the cord of the latch into the room, and stood there over her head, and said what it had to say to her.

"Are you sleeping, Penelope, worried in your heart? The gods who live at their ease don't want you to cry, because your son is going to return again, since he has not offended the gods in any way."

Deep in thought, Penelope answered her then, as she slept very sweetly at the gates of dreams.

"Why, sister, have you come here? You have not often come before, since you live so far away. And you're telling me to stop my suffering and the many agonies that plague my heart and soul? Already, I have lost my lion-hearted husband, who among the Danaans was the ultimate in every good quality. A worthy man, whose fame was vast throughout Hellas and mid-Argos. And now, again, my most dearly beloved son has left in his hollow ship—the fool. He knows nothing at all about hardship or holding his own in disputation. I grieve for him, even more than for that other one, and I am afraid that something's going to happen to him, either in the land of those to which he has gone, or out there on the sea. Because many enemies are plotting against him and are eager to kill him before he reaches home."

And the shadowy apparition answered, "Take heart, and don't be too terribly afraid in your heart, because such a guide is going with him that other men would have implored to have standing by their side—Pallas Athena, since she has the power, and she empathizes with your suffering. It was she who sent me now to convey these things to you."

Deep in thought, Penelope again answered her.

"If you yourself are some god or if you happened to hear the voice of some other god, then come now—tell me all about that unlucky man, whether he is alive and still can see the sunlight, or if he's already dead and in the house of Hades."

The shimmering shadow answered and said to her, "No, about him I will not speak openly, whether he's alive or dead. There's no use talking idly into the wind."

After these words, the apparition slipped away, through the bolted door and into a breath of wind. The daughter of Ikarios started from her sleep, her heart deeply warmed by so clear a vision flashing before her in the depths of the night.

But the suitors went on board, and they sailed away, tracing a course over the waters and plotting in their minds the blatant murder of Telemakhos. There is a rocky island in the middle of the sea, halfway between Ithaka and rugged Samos—Asteris—not very large, but with inlets open on both sides. There, the Akhaians lingered, waiting to ambush him.

V

The Island

Dawn rose from her bed beside Lord Tithonos to bring light both to those who never die and those who have to die. The gods were sitting down for their assembly, and there among them was Zeus, who thunders from on high and whose power is the greatest. Athena was reminding them all of Odysseus's many troubles and recounting them because it upset her that he was still in the nymph's dwelling.

"Zeus, Father, and all you other carefree gods who live forever. May no generous-minded king who holds the scepter ever again be caring and gentle, with a benevolent heart, or think of what is right. He should be harsh and act unjustly, since no one now remembers how Odysseus, like a god himself, ruled his people—as gentle as any father.

"Yet now he lies on an island, deeply and painfully tormented in the household of that nymph, Kalypso, who is holding him against his will, and he cannot return to his own land, since he has no ships equipped with oars and no crew to transport him over the broad back of the sea. And now, on top of that, they are anxious to kill the son he loves so deeply as he is heading for home, because he has gone away in case he might hear word of his father, in sacred Pylos and bright Lakedaimon."

Zeus, gathering clouds together, answered her.

"What a word has escaped the barrier of your teeth, my child. Didn't you yourself advise this plan, so that Odysseus might come back and take revenge on those men? And Telemakhos? Guide him with your understanding, since you can, so he reaches home, unharmed, and the suitors in their ships head back where they came from, unfulfilled."

And then he called over to Hermes, his own son.

"Hermes, because you are in various other matters our messenger, tell this nymph with the lovely hair our firm ruling: the return of unwavering Odysseus. Tell her that he is to return with the guidance of neither the gods nor men—that on a raft, amply corded together, after suffering through agonies, on the twentieth day he is to come to bountiful Skheria, the land of the

Phaiakians, who are close kin to the gods. That they will wholeheartedly show him respect as a god and send him on a ship to his own land, after giving him plenty of bronze, gold, and clothing—much more than Odysseus ever would have taken from Troy, if he had come back unharmed, with his own proper share of the spoils—because it is his due to see his loved ones and reach his own land, his own home with its high ceilings."

After he had spoken, the runner, Argeïphontes, did not refuse him. At once he strapped about his feet his beautiful sandals, made of utterly resplendent gold, which would carry him far over the waters and over the boundless earth upon the breath of the wind. He picked up his wand, with which he charms the eyes of whomever he wishes to charm, while others he rouses out of their sleep. And holding it firmly in his hand, the powerful Argeïphontes flew away. Over Pieria he left the upper currents of air and swooped down over the sea, rushing over the waves like a sea bird which dampens its thick wings in the salt water as it searches about for fish over the awesome vastness of the restless sea. In this way, Hermes carried himself over the countless waves. But when he had reached the island, which was so remote, he left the blue sea and landed.

From there, he went on until he came to the large cave where lived the nymph with the lovely hair. He found her inside. A large fire was burning on the hearth. The scent of freshly cut cedar and citron spread far across the island as it burned. Inside, she was singing in a beautiful voice as she moved back and forth before her loom, weaving with a golden spindle. A luxuriant forest grew all around the cave—alder and poplar and sweet-scented cypress trees, where birds with long wingspans made their nests—owls, falcons, and sea crows with outstretched tongues that find their calling out on the sea. Around the open cave stretched a flourishing vine, teeming with grapes. Four streams were flowing very close to each other with splashing water, cutting this way and that, and all around, gentle meadows with violets and celery were blossoming. There, even an immortal who happened by would gaze in wonder, savoring it heartily.

There, Argeïphontes the runner stood in awe. But after he had wondered in his heart at everything, he went straight into the open cave, and Kalypso, the radiant goddess, face to face with him, did not fail to recognize him, since the immortals are not unknown to each other, even if one lives in a home far away. But he did not find proud Odysseus inside. He was sitting on the shore in his usual spot, crying, racking his heart with tears, groans, and agonies. There, he let his tears flow as he looked out at the restless sea. And Kalypso, the brilliant goddess, after allowing Hermes to sit down on a brightly shining chair, questioned him.

"Why have you come to me with your golden wand, Hermes—though it is both an honor and a privilege. You have not often come before. Say what you think. My heart urges me to carry it out, if it can be done and is feasible. Now follow me further inside, so that I can set out some refreshment for you."

After voicing these words, she set out a table full of ambrosia and mixed the red nectar, and the runner Argeïphontes began to drink and eat. But after he had eaten and satisfied his heart with sustenance, he answered her and spoke these words.

"When I arrived, you, a goddess, questioned a god, so I will say frankly what I have to say, since you asked. Zeus compelled me to come here against my will. Who, on his own, would rush over such a vast expanse of salty water? There is not even a town nearby with mortals to make exemplary offerings and sacrifices. There is no way for any other god to avoid or deter the will of Zeus, who carries the aegis, the great shield that drives the winds.

"He says that there is a man who is here with you, the most unfortunate of all the men who fought for nine years around the city of Priam, and then, in the tenth, burned and looted it and headed home. But as they were returning, they offended Athena, and she stirred up against them a violent wind and towering waves. There, all the rest of his worthy mates were lost. But the wind and waves carried him and brought him here. Now, Zeus is urging you to send him on his way, as quickly as possible, since it's still his lot to see his loved ones and to reach his own land and his own house, with its high roofs."

As he spoke, the brilliant goddess trembled, and her voice carried her words, quivering like wings.

"You are so cruel, you gods, so utterly envious beyond all other beings. You resent us goddesses who sleep with men openly and make them our lovers. That's how it was back then, when Dawn lay her rosy fingers on Orion. You gods, who live so free and easy, envied her until, there in Ortygia, from her golden throne, innocent Artemis released her gentle arrows and cut him down. And that's how it was when Demeter, with her lovely hair, gave in to her heart and lay with Jason, embracing there in a fresh field, plowed three times. Zeus was not unaware of it for long. He threw a flash of lightning and killed the man. Now, once again, you gods—you envy me for having a mortal man live with me.

"I saved him as he was straddling the keel, alone, for Zeus had struck his swift ship with a flash of lightning and shattered it there in the middle of the sea, dark as wine. There, all the rest of his worthy shipmates were lost. But the wind and the waves carried him on and brought him here. I welcomed him and fed him, and I told him I would enable him never to die or grow old through all his days. But because there's no way to avoid or hold back the will of Zeus, who holds the aegis, let him go across the restless sea, since that one orders and demands it. I won't send him off myself, since I have no ships or oars or shipmates to take him over the broad back of the sea. But I myself will graciously offer him advice, and I'll hold nothing back, so he may reach home unharmed."

Again, the runner Argeïphontes answered her.

"Send him away now and be wary of Zeus's fury, or he will become enraged at you in the time to come."

After he had spoken, the sturdy Argeïphontes departed, and after she had heard Zeus's message, the venerated nymph went to the proud Odysseus. She found him sitting on the rocks, his eyes never dry, because life's sweetness was ebbing away as he ached for his return, since the nymph no longer pleased him. At night, inside her empty cave, he slept beside her against his will, disinterested in her interest, but during the day he would sit outside on the sand and rocks, racking his heart with tears, groans, and agonies. He looked out over the restless sea, his tears flowing. The brilliant goddess came close to him and spoke.

"Unlucky man, don't go on sitting and weeping any longer. Don't let your whole life slip away. I am ready now to send you on your way with a gracious heart. So come now, chop down some long timbers with your bronze and fasten them together to make a large raft, and then tie up some wooden planks to make a deck above it, so it can carry you across the misty sea. And I'll place some bread and water and red wine upon it to brace your spirit and hold back your hunger, and I'll put some clothes on you and send a favorable wind from behind, so you may reach your native land unharmed, if it's the will of the gods who hold the vast heavens, because they are stronger than I am in both their resolution and their execution."

As she spoke, brilliant Odysseus, who had suffered so much, trembled, and his words fluttered like wings.

"Goddess, you're planning something else here, not my passage. You're telling me to cross over the great chasm of the sea. That's frightening and not so easy. Not even quick, well-crafted seafaring ships that revel in a fair wind from Zeus are sure to make their way across. I won't step aboard any raft unless you, Goddess, bring yourself to swear a solemn oath that you will not plan any more troubles against me."

As he spoke, the brilliant goddess Kalypso smiled. She caressed him with her hand and spoke amiably.

"You are truly a scoundrel and obviously no fool, even to think of saying what you've just said. So now, with the earth here and the boundless skies up above as my witnesses, and the plunging waters of the Styx—which is, to the blissful gods, the most powerful and terrible oath—I'll plan no more troubles against you. Instead, I'll think it through, and I will tell you exactly what I would envision for myself, if I encountered such a necessity. My intent is sympathetic. Here within my breast, my heart's not made of iron. It's compassionate."

After she had spoken, the brilliant goddess quickly led the way, and he followed in the footsteps of the goddess. The goddess and the man came back to the empty cave. He sat in the chair from which Hermes had just stood, and the nymph placed in front of him all kinds of food to eat and drink, the kinds of things mere mortals eat. She herself sat across from Odysseus, who was like a god himself, and her servants placed ambrosia and nectar before her. They reached out their hands to the refreshment that lay in front of them, and when they had fully enjoyed their food and drink, Kalypso, brilliant among goddesses, was the first one to speak.

"Odysseus Laertiádes, descendant of Zeus, always thinking ahead—so then, do you really want to go back to your own native land? Even so, fare well. If you only knew in your heart all the troubles it is your fate to go through before you reach home, you would stay here and keep this house with me, and you'd be immortal, even though you desire to see your wife, whom you long for day after day. Surely I can claim to be no worse in form and figure than that woman, since there's no way mortal women can compete with immortals in body or appearance."

Odysseus, always thinking ahead, answered her.

"Great goddess, don't be angry with me about this. I know very well that Penelope, while very thoughtful, is not as tall or beautiful to look at as you are, because she's mortal and you are immortal and never age. Even so, every single day, I wish and long to go home and see the day of my return. And if one of the gods should ever strike at me out on the sea, dark as wine, I will endure, because I have inside my chest a heart that presses on through trouble. Already I've suffered so much and worked so hard through both war and waves. So let all this come about on top of all that."

As he spoke, the sun set and the darkness came on. The two entered into the deepest recesses of the empty cave. They enjoyed making love and stayed beside each other. And very early, as Dawn spread out her rosy fingers, right away Odysseus put on a tunic and a cloak, and the nymph wrapped herself in a long white robe, delightfully thin. She threw a golden belt around her waist and placed a veil over her head. And then she began to plan his departure, heartening Odysseus.

She handed him a large axe, made to fit his hands. It was bronze, and filed sharp on both sides, with a beautiful handle of olive wood, tightly set. She also gave him a polished adze. And she led the way to the island's furthest shores, where the tall trees grew—alder and poplar and fir, reaching up into the sky. Old growth, very dry—they would float lightly. But after she showed him where the tall trees grew, the beautiful goddess, Kalypso, went back to her home, while he took to chopping wood.

He carried out his work very quickly. He brought down twenty trees in all, and trimmed them with the bronze, and smoothed them out expertly, and he lined them all out straight. And Kalypso, the beautiful goddess, brought him some augers. He bored out all the beams and fit them to each other, then hammered them together with wooden pegs and cords. Odysseus made his raft as wide as a man experienced in building marks out the hull of a cargo ship. Then he set the deck planks in place and made them fit into all the close-set braces.

He finished it off with long gunwales and crafted the mast and a yardarm fitted to it. He made a rudder to steer it and closed in the whole thing with willow rushes as a defense against waves, and he packed in lots of brush. Meanwhile, the lovely goddess Kalypso brought him a large piece of cloth to make a sail, and he crafted it skillfully. He tightened all the braces, the halyard lines, and sheets on the craft, and with levers, dragged it down to the gleaming surf. And so the fourth day came, and everything was done.

On the fifth, brilliant Kalypso sent him away from the island, after she had bathed him and dressed him in fragrant clothing. And the goddess placed on board one skin of dark wine and another large one, full of water, and in a knapsack, she put some supplies and many enjoyable treats. She sent a fair wind, warm and easy, and Odysseus spread out his sail joyfully in the wind. Then he sat down and steered skillfully with the rudder, and sleep did not fall upon his eyelids as he looked up to the Pleiades, the Shepherd, which sets so late, and also the Bear, which they also call the Wheel, as it turns around in circles and looks over at Orion, and all alone, holds back and takes no part in bathing in the ocean. Kalypso, brilliant among goddesses, had advised him to keep this star on the left as he was making his way over the sea.

And so for seventeen days he made his passage over the sea, and on the eighteenth, the shadowy mountains of the Phaiakians' land appeared where it was nearest to him. It looked exactly like a shield through the sea mist. But the Earth Shaker saw Odysseus coming into view in the distance, sailing across the sea, as the god himself was heading back from the Ethiopians, from the mountains of the Solymians. He became even more enraged in his black heart. He shook his head and called out to his own spirit.

"Appalling! The other gods must all have changed their minds about Odysseus while I was far away among the Ethiopians. Already he's near the land of the Phaiakians, where it is his due to escape this trap of misery that has come to him. But even so, I think I'll bash him with his fill of the worst there is."

As he spoke, he gathered together the clouds. He grabbed his trident in his hands, and he stirred up the sea, and he tossed up all kinds of wind and covered land and sea alike, and out of the heavens, the night rushed in. The east and the south winds fell upon each other, and the west wind blew hard, and the north wind, starting from high in the atmosphere, rolled in a huge wave.

Odysseus's knees gave way, and his heart melted, and in anguish, he called out to his own great heart.

"How unlucky can I be? What's finally going to happen to me? I fear that everything the goddess said is true when she predicted I'll have had my fill of agonies on the sea before I reach my own land. Now it's all coming to be. Zeus has filled the vast heavens with so many clouds and stirred up the sea, and bursts of all kinds of wind are coming down on me—now my total ruin is here for sure. They were three times blessed—no, four times—those Danaans who died back then in spacious Troy, at the pleasure of the sons of Atreus. If only I too had died and met my end that day when so many Trojans hurled their bronze-tipped shafts at me, around the dead body of Peleus' son. Then at least I would have received a funeral, and the Akhaians would have carried back my fame. Now it's only this miserable death I'm bound to be taken by."

As he spoke, a huge wave struck him from above, rushing over him with crushing force and spinning his raft around. He fell off, far from the raft, and dropped the rudder out of his hands. The mast was broken in half by the fierce bursts of swirling winds that swept against it, and the sail and yardarm fell far away in the sea. He was held under the water for a long time and could not pull himself out right away from the rush of the huge wave. The clothes that brilliant Kalypso had brought him weighed him down. But at long last, he surfaced. He spewed from his mouth the bitter salty brine, which also streamed copiously from his head. Even so, despite how upset he was, he did not forget his raft. He lunged through the waves and grabbed it. He sat down in the middle of it, to avoid the finality of death. And the heavy seas carried it here and there with the current.

As the north wind carries thistles, clinging close to each other, across the plain in the autumn, the winds carried the raft here and there over the sea. For a while, the south wind tossed it over, across to the north wind to carry it on, and then the east wind passed it over to the west wind to speed it along. But Kadmos's daughter, Ino, saw him—Leukothea, who had lovely ankles and once had been a mortal and still spoke as one, even though now, in the depths of the sea, she held her share of respect among the gods. She felt compassion for Odysseus, his wandering and his troubles. She surged up from the waters like a seagull in flight, landed on the sturdily bound raft, and said these words.

"Unlucky man, why has Poseidon, shaker of the earth, viewed you as odious as he has, to keep on making so much trouble for you? Yet surely he will not utterly destroy you, no matter how enraged he is. You don't seem to lack understanding, so do exactly what I say. Strip off these clothes and leave your raft to be driven by the winds. Use your arms to swim and try to reach the Phaiakians' land, where it is your destiny to escape. Here, stretch out this heavenly veil under your chest and have no fear that you are going to suffer or die, and when your hands have touched ground, take it and throw it far from the land, back into the sea, dark as wine, and then, turn away."

As she spoke, the goddess passed him the veil and then dove like a seagull into the sea, and a dark wave folded over her. Odysseus, who had endured so much, deeply distressed, called out to his own heart.

"Oh, me—it must be one of the immortals, weaving a web for me again, urging me to leave my raft. I won't trust her, not yet, because the land I saw—where she said I was to flee—is so far. This is what I'll do—it's what seems best to me. As long as the timbers hold in their bindings, I'll stay here and endure the troubles I have to suffer. When the waves shake up the raft, I'll swim, since there's nothing else that I can think of."

While he was turning this over in his mind and heart, Poseidon, the earth shaker, was gathering yet another huge wave, ominous, forbidding, and curling over, it struck him. As a violent wind whisks away a heap of dry straw and scatters it here and there, it scattered the timbers of the raft. Odysseus straddled a beam, as if riding a horse, and stripped off the clothing that brilliant Kalypso had brought him. Then he stretched out the veil under his chest and threw himself forward into the sea, his arms spread wide, ready to swim. The mighty Earth Shaker saw him, shook his head, and spoke his mind.

"There—after you suffer many more misfortunes, go on wandering over the sea until you find yourself among men favored by Zeus. Even then, I'd bet you're not likely to make light of so much trouble."

After he had spoken, he whipped up his horses with their beautiful manes and went all the way to Aigai, where his glorious home is. But Athena, daughter of Zeus, was thinking of something else. She held back the other winds and ordered them to stop and be at rest. And then she stirred up the rushing north wind and made it break in another direction so that Odysseus, descendant of Zeus, might find himself among the Phaiakians and escape utter extinction. For two nights and two days he was driven about by the looming waves. And many times, his heart foresaw destruction. At last, as Dawn with her lovely hair was bringing into being the third day, the wind stopped. There was a calm on the sea. Quickly he looked around, and as a large wave lifted him up, he could see the land close by.

Like a father's life when he is lying in sickness, feeling sharp pains and wasting away for as long as some angry god keeps strangling him, and then the gods release him from the very worst and his children are heartened—that is how the land and the trees heartened Odysseus. He kept on swimming, eager to step foot on dry land. But when he was as near as a shout will carry, he heard the booming of the sea against the rocks as huge waves roared against the shore, slinging its spray up horribly, and everything was smothered in sea foam. There was no harbor for boats to enter and no pier—only rocks, cliffs, and projecting headlands. Odysseus's knees gave way. His heart melted. Deeply distressed, he called out to his fiercely pounding heart.

"Ah, me. Just when Zeus has allowed me to see land, against all hope, and I've been able to make my way to cut across this gulf, there seems to be no way out of this gray sea. There are sharp crags on the outside and all around them the waves are rushing in, booming, and the rocks running up are sheer. The sea's so deep, even close to shore, and there's no way to stand on both feet and escape the worst. As I move in, a large wave might snatch me up and throw me against the jagged rocks, and all my scurrying about will have been for nothing. But if I keep on swimming further, to find a protected beach or harbor shielded from the sea, I'm afraid the storm winds will snatch me up, yet again, and carry me, groaning deeply, across this fish-infested sea. Or some god might send a great sea beast after me, one of those that the famous Amphitrite breeds, because I know how odious is my name to the one so widely known as the Earth Shaker."

As he turned these things over in his mind and heart, a large wave carried him in toward the rocky shore. There, his skin would have been stripped and his bones shattered, if Athena, her eyes gleaming, had not put a thought in his mind. As he was being swept in, he grabbed a rock with both his hands and, groaning, he held on, until the immense wave surged on past. And so he escaped, but as the wave was pulling back again, rushing at him, it struck him, and tossed him far back into the sea.

As an octopus is dragged out of its hole, with countless pebbles sticking to its suckers, pieces of skin were ripped away from his hands, straining against the rocks, and the huge wave covered him. Odysseus, desperate, would have perished, despite what he deserved, if Athena, her eyes gleaming, had not granted him presence of mind.

He surfaced, out beyond where the waves pitched upon the shore. He swam along, outside the breakers, keeping his eyes on the shore for sheltered beaches or harbors that might be shielded from the sea. And as he was swimming along, he came at last to the mouth of a beautifully flowing river, which seemed the most ideal place, because it was smooth, free of stones, and sheltered from the wind, and he reached what he knew to be the river's outflow. There, he prayed to the river from deep within his heart.

"Listen, Lord, whoever you are. I come to you as to someone deeply longed for, seeking to escape the sea and Poseidon's cruelty. For surely to the immortal gods, worthy of respect is any man who arrives as a wanderer, as I come now to your stream and to your knees, after many hardships. Only show some feeling for me, Lord. I avow I am under your protection."

After he spoke, the river at once paused its current, held back the waves to create a calm before him, and brought him out of danger to the river's mouth. And he let both his knees and his strong arms go slack, because his heart had been overpowered by the sea. His flesh was swollen, and sea water was oozing copiously through his mouth and nostrils. He lay there, breathless and speechless, far too weak to move. Extreme exhaustion had come over him. But when he gasped and came to, and his spirit returned inside his chest, he loosened the goddess' veil and let it drop, into the river flowing toward the sea. A large wave carried it back with the current, and Ino soon received it in her hands. He turned and staggered back, away from the river, and lay down in the reeds. He kissed the earth, the source of grain. Deeply distressed, he called out to his fiercely pounding heart.

"Oh, me! What will I have to go through next? What's going to happen to me after all this? If I keep watch, here beside the river for the whole exhausting night, then the severe frost and heavy dew together may stop my gasping heart, as the wind blows cold before dawn. But if I climb up the slope into the woods' deep shadows, and lie down there in the thick bushes, so that the cold and exhaustion will go away, and sweet sleep comes over me, I fear I might fall prey to wild animals."

As he thought about it, it seemed much better to move on toward the woods, and he found a place near the water, next to a clearing. He crawled inside, under two bushes growing out of the same spot—one full of thorns and the other an olive bush. The force of the damp winds could not blow through, and the sun's blazing rays could not shine through, and the rain could not penetrate through them, because they had grown together so intricately, twisting and turning around each other. Odysseus edged in under them.

With his hands, he pulled together a large bed, since there was a copious mass of leaves, enough to shelter two or three men in the wintertime, even if it were to become extremely harsh. Radiant, Odysseus, who had endured so much, looked it all over, and he was thrilled. He lay down in the middle and heaped masses of leaves over himself. As a man with no friends or neighbors close by buries a firebrand under smoldering black embers, somewhere out in a distant field, to save the seed of fire, so that he will not have to light it up again from some other source. In this way Odysseus buried himself in those leaves. And Athena shed sleep over his eyes, to close his lids and quickly end his onerous fatigue.

VI

Nausikaa

As Odysseus, who had endured so much, was lying there, overcome with sleep and exhaustion, Athena went to the land and city of the Phaiakians. Long before, they had lived in Hypereia, near the Kyklops—brutal men who were much more violent than they themselves were, and who raided them constantly. Nausithoos, who was like a god, had taken them from there and led them away to settle in Skheria, far from people who eat grain. Around the city he had raised a wall, built houses, and designed temples to the gods and divided up the land. But all too soon he was overcome by death, and he went down to the domain of Hades.

Alkinoos now ruled, a man well-versed by the gods in leadership. The goddess Athena, her gray eyes gleaming, went to his house to bring about great-hearted Odysseus's return. She went up to the intricately crafted room where a young girl, like an immortal goddess in figure and appearance, was sleeping—Nausikaa, the daughter of great-hearted Alkinoos. Two slaves, each with the beauty of the Graces, lay near her, one on each side of the doorposts. The polished doors were closed. Athena swept over toward the girl's bed like a breath of wind and stood there over her head. She spoke to her, looking like the daughter of Dymas, known for his ships, a girl of the same age, very dear to Nausikaa's heart. Looking like this girl, her gray eyes gleaming, Athena spoke to her.

"Nausikaa, did your mother raise you to be so oblivious? Your nice bright clothes are lying all around in a mess, but your own wedding day's getting close, so you'll be needing to dress up in nice things yourself, but also to provide for those of us who are going to be your bridesmaids. It's from things like this, you know, that good standing among people comes, and your father and mother will be happy. So come on, let's go and do a wash, as dawn is breaking, and I'll go with you and help you to get ready as fast as possible, because you won't be a virgin much longer. Already they're courting you, the best of all of the Phaiakians in the land—and that's where your family comes from, too—so come on, early this morning, talk your father into getting some mules and a cart ready for you to carry the wraps, robes, and the bright rugs, and it'll be better for you too to go like this and not on foot because those stone wash basins are so far from the city."

After saying all of this, Athena, her eyes gleaming, left for Olympos where, they say, the gods' dwelling is and will always be, neither shaken by the winds nor dampened by the rain, and where snow never falls. The air is clear, without a cloud in any direction, and a white radiance stretches all around it. There, the carefree gods enjoy themselves every day. After speaking with the girl, it was there that Athena returned, her gray eyes gleaming.

And right away, Dawn arrived on her bright throne and awakened Nausikaa, tangled in her lovely robes. She wondered about her dream and went through the house to tell her parents, her dear father and mother, and she found them inside. Her mother was sitting at the hearth with her slaves, spinning a yarn as purple as the sea. She met her father going out to join the grand lords at council, where those august Phaiakians had called him. She stood very close to her father, and she spoke to him.

"Dear Papa, won't you get a wagon ready for me right away—that tall one with the good wheels—so I can take my nice clothes that are lying around dirty, to be washed beside the river? It's for you too—it's only proper, when you're deliberating here before the assembly, to have fresh clean clothes on your body. And you have five sons living here in these halls. Two are married, but three are still unmarried and easygoing, and they always like to have fresh clothes to go out dancing in, and I'm the one who has to think of all these things."

She spoke this way because she was embarrassed to talk to her father about the full blush of getting married. But he understood everything and offered these words.

"I will refuse you neither the mules nor anything else, my child. Go on. The servants will get the wagon ready—that tall one with the good wheels and the chest on top."

After he spoke, he called out to the slaves and they obeyed him. Outside, they prepared the mule wagon with the good wheels, and they led the mules forward under the yoke and rigged them to it. A young girl brought out the bright clothes from Nausikaa's room. She loaded them into the highly polished wagon, and her mother placed all kinds of nourishing food into the chest. She included some cuts of meat and poured some wine into a goatskin container, and then the girl climbed up onto the wagon. Her mother also gave her some smooth olive oil in a golden flask so Nausikaa and her servants could anoint themselves while bathing. Then the girl grabbed the whip and the gleaming reins, and she lashed out. There was a clang and clatter as the mules heaved and strained, hauling the clothing and the girl too, but not by herself. Her slaves went along with her.

And when they arrived at an especially beautiful bend in the flowing river, where there was an abundance of stone wash basins and plenty of clear water that welled up from below and washed over everything, no matter how dirty, they unhitched the mules from the wagon and drove them down beside the swirling river to chomp on the grass. They carried the clothes in their arms into the dark water and tromped on them in the river troughs, competing with each other to get it all done as fast as possible.

But when they had washed and cleaned out all the dirt, they spread the clothes out on the seashore where the waves pounding on the beach would best wash out the pebbles. After they had washed themselves and generously anointed themselves with olive oil, they took their meal on the riverbank and waited for the clothes to dry in the sunlight. And after they enjoyed their food, she and her slaves threw off their veils and played ball, and Nausikaa, her white arms bare, led them as they all played and sang.

As Artemis the archer passes over long, high mountains, Mount Taygetos or Erymanthos, enjoying the wild boar and the speed of the deer; and the nymphs, the daughters of Zeus, who carries the aegis, play together out in the fields; and Leto is joyful in her heart and she holds her head and forehead high above them all, easy to recognize herself—though all of them are lovely—in the same way, the unmarried virgin was conspicuous among her slaves.

But as she was about to fold the clean clothes and yoke the mules to go back home, the goddess Athena, her eyes gleaming, had another plan—for Odysseus to wake up and see the pretty face of the young girl, who would lead him on to the city of the Phaiakian people. Right then, the princess tossed the ball to one of her slaves. The girl missed and knocked it into a deep whirlpool, and they all began to shout loudly.

Odysseus woke up. He sat up straight and began to turn things over in his mind and heart.

"Ah, me, what land and people have I come to now? Are they brutish and savage and without justice, or are they kind to strangers and possess minds that are observant of the gods? I heard the shrieks of young girls somewhere around here, or were they nymphs who live high on the towering mountain peaks, or in the springs close to rivers and grassy meadows? Am I now somewhere among people who can speak? But come on, I'll go and try—and see for myself."

As he spoke, brilliant Odysseus emerged from the bushes, and with his thick hand, he snapped off a leafy sapling from the underbrush, to keep his private matters to himself. He came out like a fierce mountain lion, confident of its power, that moves about through the rain and wind, its eyes blazing, and then closes in on the cattle or wild deer. His belly drives him on to enter even the sturdy pen to go for the sheep. So Odysseus, totally naked, was about to mingle among those young women with their lovely hair, because necessity had now overcome him. To them, he appeared awful, caked with slime. And they fled in fear, one here and another there, along the jutting sand bars.

Only Alkinoos' daughter remained, since Athena filled her heart with courage and took the fear out of her limbs. She stood and faced him. Odysseus wondered whether or not to kneel and grab the knees of this young girl with the lovely face and make his plea, or to stand back on his own, and ask her humbly with charming words if she would be willing to show him the way to the city and offer him some clothes. As he thought it over, it seemed better to stand back and make his appeal with charming words, just in case the young girl's heart might be outraged if he were to clutch her knees. So right away, he voiced a shrewd, endearing speech.

"I come to your knees, madam. Are you a goddess or are you human? If you're a goddess, one of those who dwell high in the heavens, I find you to be most like Artemis, the daughter of almighty Zeus, in your manner, height, and figure. But if you're one of us human beings who lives here on earth, your father and esteemed mother are three times blessed and your brothers also three times blessed. Their hearts must always be warmed with such utter happiness because of you, whenever they happen to see such a budding beauty as you, entering the dance. And that man, whoever succeeds in his courtship and takes you to his home, is also to be the happiest in his heart beyond all others. Because I myself have never seen with my own eyes any person such as you, neither man nor woman. I am struck with wonder as I look at you.

"Only once, in Delos, have I ever seen anything like it—a young sprig of a palm beside the altar to Apollo, since I went there once, and many people followed me on a journey where I was to face terrible hardships—yet when I saw that, I stood in awe for a long time, because such a tree had never before sprung up from the earth. In the same way, young woman, I am taken back and wonder at you, and I am terribly afraid even to touch your knees.

"I am overcome with overflowing sorrow. Yesterday, on the twentieth day, I escaped from the sea, dark as wine. Throughout that time, the waves and the hard winds carried me away from the island of Ogygia, and now some god has thrown me down here, so I'll suffer misfortune yet again, because I don't think it's going to end now. Before that, the gods will bring on many more troubles to come. And so, my lady, take pity because, after suffering many hard times, I have come to you, first of all, and I know no one among the other people who dwell in this land and city.

"Show me the way to your city and give me a tattered rag to throw about myself, if you happen to have some wrap among the clothes you've brought here. And may the gods grant you everything you desire in your heart, a husband and a home and precious harmony of mind and heart, since there is nothing greater or better than when a man and a woman hold their home in a singleness of heart. It's very painful to their enemies and a joy to their friends, and best of all, they themselves realize it."

Her white arms bare, Nausikaa answered him.

"Stranger, since you don't seem to be a mean or a thoughtless man—and as it's Zeus the Olympian himself who allots happiness to human beings, good and bad, to each as he himself is inclined, so he has given this to you for some reason or other—you will just have to endure it. But for now, because you've come here to our city and land, you will lack neither clothing nor anything else among those things one offers to any unfortunate beggar who comes along. And I myself will show you the way to the city and tell you the name of our people. The Phaiakians occupy this city and this country, and I am the daughter of the great-hearted Alkinoos, who himself holds the power and the might of the Phaiakians."

She called to her slaves, with their lovely hair.

"Stand by me, servants. Why are you running away at the sight of a man? Are you really thinking that he's an enemy? There's no mortal man alive, nor will there ever be, who'd come bringing violence here to the land of the Phaiakian people, because we are so dear to the gods. We live so far away over the surging sea, so far that no other mortals come to deal with us. This is some unlucky wanderer who's come here. It's necessary to tend to him now, since all strangers and beggars are from Zeus. Even a small gift is welcome. So come on now, offer the stranger some food and drink and wash him in the river, where there's shelter from the wind."

As she spoke, they stood still and called out to each other, and then they moved Odysseus into shelter, as Nausikaa, great-hearted Alkinoos' daughter, had ordered. They placed a cloak and a tunic beside him and gave him smooth olive oil in a golden vessel, and urged him to wash himself in the river currents. Then brilliant Odysseus spoke up among them.

"Stand over there, servants, so I can wash the slime off my shoulders and massage myself with olive oil. It's been a long time since olive oil was on my skin. But I will not bathe with you here. I'm embarrassed to be naked among young ladies with such lovely hair."

As he spoke, they backed away and spoke to their mistress. With the river water, brilliant Odysseus washed from his skin the salty slime that covered his back and broad shoulders, and he wiped the foam from the choppy sea off his head. When he had washed himself entirely and rubbed himself with oil, and put on the clothes the young innocent had given him, Athena, Zeus's daughter, made him appear much taller and sturdier, and she made his thick hair fall in curls like hyacinth blossoms. As when some resourceful man, whom Hephaistos and Pallas Athena have taught all kinds of craftsmanship, overlays gold with silver, and the work he completes is grace itself, so the goddess shed her grace over his head and shoulders. Then he drew away and sat down on the seashore, gleaming in his good looks and gracefulness. The girl was filled with wonder, and she spoke to the slaves.

"Listen, my servants, with your white arms, to what I am about to say. It's not without the will of all the gods who live on Olympos that this man has arrived among us Phaiakians—we who are so much like the gods ourselves. Before, he seemed to me to be coarse, but now he's like the gods who occupy the vast skies. If only someone like him might be called my husband, and be willing to stay here and live here. But come now, my servants, offer the stranger something to eat and drink."

As she spoke, they very willingly listened and obeyed, and they set some food and drink in front of Odysseus. Radiant, Odysseus, who had endured so much, drank and ate voraciously, since he had been without food for so long. But Nausikaa, her white arms exposed, thought of something else. She folded the clothing and placed it in the beautiful cart. She yoked the mules, with their thick hooves, and then she climbed in herself. She called to Odysseus and spoke these words to him.

"Get yourself ready now, stranger, to go to the city, so I can send you to the house of my judicious father. There, I assure you, you'll come to know the very finest of all the Phaiakians, but do it precisely in this way. You don't seem to be lacking in understanding, so as long as we are going along through the country and the people's fields, go quickly along with the servants behind the mules and wagon, and I will lead the way. But as we near the city, there's a high wall around it, and there's a lovely harbor on each side of the city, and the way in is narrow.

"The curved ships are drawn up to the road, each with its own berth. The assembly yard is there, around the beautiful monument to Poseidon, with huge stones set deep into the ground. There, the Phaiakians tend to their ships' gear, the lines and sails, and they sand and plane their oars, since they do not concern themselves with bow and quiver, but with the masts and oars of sailing ships, and with crafting those ships and delighting in them as they sail across the gray sea. I skirt their odious talk, in case someone might mock me one of these days. There are some very thoughtless people in this land, and some of the more surly, if we encountered them, might say, 'Who's this, tagging along with Nausikaa—this tall, handsome stranger? Where did she find him? He'll soon become her husband. Somehow, she must have picked up some drifter off his ship, from some people far away, because there aren't any nearby. Or else it's some god, long implored and prayed for, who's come down from the skies, and she will have him all her days. Well, then, better she's gone off and found herself a husband from somewhere else, since she spurns us Phaiakians here in this land, where so many honorable men have courted her.'

"So they'd talk, and this would be an insult to me, even as I would blame another woman who would do the same thing, passing time openly with men before her wedding day, against the wishes of both her loving father and mother. Stranger, listen to what I'm saying, so that you may most quickly obtain an escort and your return from my father. You will find a lovely grove of poplars, dedicated to Athena, close to the road. A spring runs right through it and on both sides, there is a meadow. That's my father's estate and his fertile vineyard, as far away from the city as a shout can be heard. Sit there and wait for a while, until we've come to the city and my father's house. As soon as you anticipate that we've surely reached the house, go on yourself into the city and ask for the house of my father, the great-hearted Alkinoos. It's easy to identify. Even a silly child could lead you there, as the Phaiakians' houses are not constructed at all like the palace of Alkinoos, the old hero.

"But as soon as you are well inside the palace and courtyard, go quickly through the great hall until you reach my mother, who is always sitting beside the hearth in the glimmering of the fireplace, leaning against a pillar, spinning her purple yarn—a wonder to observe—and her servants are always sitting behind her. There also, leaning against the same pillar, is my father's throne, where he sits and sips his wine like some immortal. Move on past him and throw your arms around my mother's knees, so that you might soon see the day of your return and rejoice, although you are still so far away. If she, within her heart, is kindly disposed to you, then there's hope that you'll see your own people and reach your country and well-built home."

After she said these words, she lashed out at the mules with her gleaming whip. Quickly, they left the flowing river behind. They tromped along steadily, their hooves clopping along, as she drove them with care, so that her slaves and Odysseus might follow along on foot. She cracked the whip judiciously.

The sun was setting as they came to the well-known grove, sacred to Athena, and so brilliant Odysseus sat down. Right away, he prayed before the daughter of almighty Zeus.

"Hear me, unwavering daughter of Zeus, who holds the aegis. Listen to me now, since you never listened before, when I was cast away as the almighty shaker of the earth wrecked me. Grant that I come before the Phaiakians as someone who's welcomed with compassion."

As he spoke his prayer, Pallas Athena heard him but did not yet appear to him, face to face, out of respect for her father's brother, who would remain furious at Odysseus until he reached his own land.

VII

Among the Phaiakians

Odysseus, who had endured so much, prayed there, while the two intrepid mules carried the young girl to the city. When she reached her father's magnificent palace, she stopped before the outer gates, and her brothers, like immortals, gathered around her. They unhitched the mules from the wagon and carried all the clothing inside. She went to her room, and there, an old Apeiraian woman, Eurymedousa, lit a fire. Long ago, rounded ships had brought her from Apeiraia. They had taken her as a special present for Alkinoos, because he was the ruler over all the Phaiakians, and the people deferred to him as if he were a god. She had raised Nausikaa with her white arms in those halls, and it was she who now stoked the fire for her and prepared her supper within.

It was at that time that Odysseus arose to go into the city, and Athena, thinking to help him, cast a dense mist around him so none of the gregarious Phaiakians would meet him and goad and grill him about who he was. But as he was about to enter into the lovely city, Athena, her eyes gleaming, looking like an innocent young girl carrying an urn, came to him. She stood in front of him, and brilliant Odysseus questioned her.

"Child, would you lead me to the home of this man, Alkinoos, who rules these people? I've just arrived here—a stranger—after coming from far away and enduring many trials, so I don't know any of the people who live in this land and this city."

The goddess Athena, her eyes gleaming, answered him.

"Of course, stranger, father. I'll show you the house you're asking me about. He lives close to my faultless father, but let's go in silence, and I'll lead the way. Don't even glance at anyone or ask any questions, because the people here don't hold with strangers or like them or welcome anyone who comes from somewhere else, as they trust only in the swiftness of their own ships' crossing over the sea's great abyss, since this is what the Earth Shaker has given to them, and their ships are as fast as the flight of wings, or even your own thoughts."

After she had spoken, Pallas Athena led the way quickly, and he followed along in the footsteps of the goddess. The Phaiakians, who were famous for their ships, did not notice him as he moved among them through their city, because Athena, with her lovely hair, yet a goddess much to be feared, did not allow it. She thought fondly of him in her heart, and so she cast a mysterious mist all around him. Odysseus marveled at the harbors, the lovely rounded ships, the agoras where their finest men would meet, and the walls—long, high, and set with watch towers—a wonder to see. When they reached the king's famous palace, the goddess Athena, her eyes gleaming, was the first to speak.

"Here it is, old stranger, sir—the house you asked me to show you, and you will find the king and queen, nurtured by Zeus, enjoying their feast. But go inside and have no fear in your heart, because a man of courage ends up better in everything, even if he's come from somewhere far away, and you'll come first to the queen—Arete is the name by which she is called. She comes from the same lineage as King Alkinoos. Nausithoos was the first to be fathered by the Earth Shaker, Poseidon, and Periboia was the prettiest woman ever and the youngest daughter of the great-hearted Eurymedon, who once ruled over those big-headed giants, but he destroyed his own reckless people and so he was himself destroyed, and then Poseidon slept with Periboia and they had a son, the great-hearted Nausithoos, who ruled the Phaiakians and himself had two sons, Alkinoos and Rhexenor, who Apollo struck down with his silver bow when he had only just been married, with no male heir. And so he left behind only one daughter, Arete, and Alkinoos made her his wife and he has honored her as no other woman on Earth is honored—of those women who now run their households, though under their husbands' keeping. And she is honored so whole-heartedly by her children and by Alkinoos himself and by the people, who look to her as if she were a goddess and point her out and speak of her as she moves around the city, because she no doubt has a sure sense of understanding and she settles disputes for those she thinks well of—even the men—and if she thinks kindly toward you within her heart, then there is still hope for you to see your loved ones and reach your own land and your own house with its overhanging roofs."

After she spoke, Athena, her gray eyes gleaming, made her way over the restless sea. She left lovely Skheria, went to Marathon and Athens with its wide streets, and entered Erekhtheos's well-crafted house, while Odysseus went on to Alkinoos's lovely home. He stood there, and his heart was thinking over so many things before he reached the bronze doorway, because there was a gleam, as from the sun or the moon, that was falling upon the towering rooftops of the palace of the great-hearted Alkinoos.

The walls, which extended all around, from the threshold to the inner rooms, were bronze, and above was a deep blue cornice. The doors were golden and closed securely in this well-constructed house, and the silver doorposts were set in a bronze threshold. The lintel above was silver. The handle was made of gold. On each side of the doorway there were dogs, made of gold and silver, crafted with cunning skill by Hephaistos—deathless, ageless dogs, to guard all their days the home of the great-hearted Alkinoos.

Inside, chairs were attached here and there, all along the walls, from the threshold to the inner rooms, and tossed across them were soft, woven robes, finely crafted by the women. There, the Phaiakian leaders sat, drinking and eating, since they had everything in limitless abundance. Young men with golden hair stood on sturdy pedestals, holding flaming torches in their hands, lighting up the evening for those who were feasting in the house. There were fifty slave women there in the house. Some of them grind the yellow grain on the millstone, while others weave fabric and spin the yarn as they sit, busy as the leaves of a poplar, and liquid olive oil drips down from the finely woven linens hanging there, for as the Phaiakian men are adept beyond all others in driving their fast ships over the sea, the women are expert at the loom, because Athena has granted them beyond all others the craft to generate both exquisite works and open hearts.

Outside the courtyard, near the gates, there is a large, four-acre orchard. A hedge runs around it on all sides, and inside, the trees grow tall and lush—pears, pomegranates, and apple trees with bright fruit, and also sweet fig trees and luxuriant olive trees. Their fruit never fails or falls away, winter or summer. It lasts all year. And as the west wind blows incessantly, some flourish as others grow ripe. Pear upon pear ripens, apple upon apple, grapes upon grapes, fig upon fig. There is also the profuse vineyard—on one side, a sunny patch in a level place for drying grapes in the sun, while in others, the slaves are gathering and treading, but before that, the unripe grapes shed their flowers, while others are darkening, growing purple. And there, by the furthest row of vines, all kinds of tidy gardens grow, brightening into bloom all year. In that orchard there are two streams—one of them flows about throughout the garden, and on the far side, the other flows under the gateway to the courtyard and on—to the towering palace. Here, the populace draws its water. All this was the glorious gift of the gods to Alkinoos's domain.

Odysseus, who had endured so much, stood there and stared. But after wondering deep in his heart at everything, he stepped quickly across the threshold into the house. There, he found the Phaiakians' leaders and advisors, pouring out offerings from their cups to sharp-eyed Argeïphontes, the last god to whom they would pour out their cups, when they began to think of going to bed. Odysseus, who had endured so much, passed through the house within the thick mist that Athena had shed over him, until he reached Arete and King Alkinoos. He threw his arms about the knees of Arete, and right away, the mysterious cloud dropped away from him. Speechless, all those in the room gazed at the man. They stared in utter wonder. And Odysseus implored her.

"Arete, daughter of Rhexenor, who was like a god, I have come to your husband and to your own knees, after suffering many hardships, and to these who are feasting here as well—may the gods grant them good fortune in their lives and may each one pass on to his children both the wealth in his own halls and the honors the people have given them. But send me with an escort to reach my own land, as quickly as possible, because I have been suffering misfortune for such a long time, far from my own people."

After he had spoken, he sat down at the fireplace in the ashes beside the fire. All of them were awed to silence. At last, an old man spoke to them—the heroic Ekheneus, the eldest, skilled in proper speech, with a deep grasp of the old ways. With good intent, he addressed the gathering.

"Alkinoos, this is not the best way possible. It is not fitting that a stranger should sit on the floor, here in the ashes around the hearth, while these others hold back, waiting for what you have to say. Come now, have the stranger stand up and sit here on this silver-studded chair. Tell the attendants to mix the wine, so we can pour our offerings to Zeus, who delights in thunder and walks in the footsteps of estimable petitioners. And have your housekeeper give him supper from whatever she has within."

When the supreme power of Alkinoos heard this, he took the hand of Odysseus, that intricately skilled and cunning man, and lifted him up from the hearth and had him sit down upon a bright chair from which he had asked his son, the easygoing Laodamas, to stand. He would sit next to Alkinoos and was his favorite. A slave brought water in a lovely golden pitcher to pour over Odysseus's hands. She poured it over a silver basin for him to wash, then drew a polished table over to him. Then the cherished housekeeper brought bread and placed it in front of him, along with an abundance of treats, generously sharing what there was at hand. And so Odysseus, who had endured so much, drank and ate.

The power of Alkinoos spoke to the attendant.

"Pontonoos, mix the bowl and serve it to everyone here, so we can pour out all of our offerings to Zeus, who delights in thunder and walks in the footsteps of estimable petitioners."

After he spoke and Pontonoos stirred the wine, like honey to the heart, he passed it all around to everyone—first, pouring a little into the cups. And when they had poured out all their offerings and had drunk as much as their hearts desired, Alkinoos spoke to all of those who were gathered around.

"Listen, you leaders and advisors for the Phaiakians, so that I can tell you what this heart inside my chest urges me to say. Now that you have feasted, go back to your homes to rest. And in the morning, we will call together even more of the elders, and we will host this stranger here in these halls and offer some marvelous sacrifices to the gods. Then we'll think about this escort, so the stranger, without hardship or discomfort, can by means of our transport reach his native land, quickly and joyfully, even if it is far away. But for now, let him suffer neither hardship nor trouble until he steps onto his own home ground. After that, he will face whatever thread of destiny the dreadful Fates have spun for him from the beginning, when his mother gave birth to him.

"And if he is one of the immortals who has come down from the skies, this is something else the gods are instigating, because in the past they have always appeared to us openly, when we make our magnificent sacrifices to them and they sit among us and feast with us. And if one of us meets them face to face, awed, as he is wandering along, they do not hide themselves, since we are close to them, just like the Kyklops and those wild bands of giants."

Odysseus, always thinking ahead, answered him.

"Alkinoos, put that thought aside. I am nothing like the immortals who occupy the vast heavens, either in looks or physique. I'm mortal. Whoever you know of those who suffer the most distress, I am like them in their sorrows. I could tell you more of the hard times that I have endured at the will of the gods. But let me eat, troubled as I am. Nothing is more appalling than one's own abominable belly, which goads you to think of it, however upset or full of grief you are in your heart, as I myself am full of grief in my own heart, and yet it doggedly urges me to eat and drink, and it makes me forget everything I have suffered and nags at me to keep filling it. But at sunrise, let us hurry so that I, unfortunate as I am, can go on to my own native land, after having suffered so much. Then, let life leave me, once I have seen my own things, my slaves, my own house, my own high roofs."

As he spoke, they all approved of what he said and called for the stranger to be sent on, because he had spoken so fittingly. And so, after pouring out their offerings and drinking as much as their hearts desired, they left, each one back to his own house to go to bed and sleep. Odysseus was left behind in the great hall. Beside him sat Arete and Alkinoos, like a god. The slaves cleared away the dishes from the feast. And Arete, her white arms exposed, was first to speak, since she had recognized his cloak and tunic as soon as she had seen the lovely clothes that she herself had made, together with her slaves. When she spoke, her words swept across like wings.

"Stranger, first I will myself ask you this question. Who are you among men and where are you from? Who gave you these clothes? Didn't you say that you had come here, wandering over the sea?"

Always thinking ahead, Odysseus answered her.

"It would be hard, my queen, to tell you all my troubles from beginning to end, because the gods above have given me many. But I will tell you everything you are asking and inquiring about. There is an island that lies far away across the sea—Ogygia. There, Atlas' daughter lives—sly Kalypso with her beautiful hair, but still a goddess much to be feared. No one mixes with her, neither the gods nor ordinary people, except for me. Some god conveyed unlucky me to her hearth, alone, after Zeus had struck my swiftly moving ship with a lightning flash and shattered it in the midst of the sea, dark as this wine. There, all the rest of my fine shipmates perished.

"But I grabbed onto the keel of my rounded ship and I was carried on for nine days. On the tenth black night, the gods brought me to that island, Ogygia, where lived Kalypso, with her beautiful hair, yet still a goddess much to be feared. She took me in and welcomed me with open arms, and she fed me and told me that she'd make me free of death and aging for all my days. But she could never win over this heart inside my chest.

"For seven years I remained there, unmoved, and for that entire time, I dampened the exquisite clothing Kalypso gave me with my tears. But when the eighth year came rolling in its cycle, she called me in and told me to go on home, either because of some message from Zeus, or maybe she just changed her mind. She sent me away on a raft, intricately held together, and gave me many things—bread and sweet liquor—and she dressed me up in exquisite clothing and stirred up a favorable wind, gentle and warm.

"For seventeen days I sailed across the sea, and on the eighteenth day, the shadowy mountain of your land appeared, and my heart was glad, yet unlucky, because I was about to rediscover my immense misfortune, which Poseidon, the Earth Shaker, called upon me. He roused the winds to hinder my way. He stirred up the unfathomable sea. The waves kept my raft from carrying me on, and I moaned deeply. The storm winds shattered it and I swam, carving over the depths of the sea, until the winds and the waters, carrying me on, brought me to your land.

"There, as I was trying to get out, the waves would have slammed me against the shore, throwing me up against the massive rocks in a place without joy. But I pulled back and swam away until I came to a river, which seemed to be the best place—smooth and free of rocks and sheltered from the wind. Once out, I fell, catching my breath as the eternal night came on. I came away from that river, sent from above, and after gathering leaves around me, I fell asleep in the undergrowth. Some god poured infinite sleep over me.

"I slept there in the leaves, although my heart was troubled, throughout the night until morning and midday. The sun was just beginning to set, when sweet sleep loosened its hold on me. I noticed your daughter's servants, playing on the shore. She was there with them, looking like a goddess. I approached her, and she did not fall short in her sure understanding, in a way you don't expect a young person to act when you meet them face to face. Young people are so thoughtless usually, but she offered me lots of bread and some shimmering wine, and they washed me in the river and gave me these clothes. I am telling you all this truthfully, if in agony."

Alkinoos lifted his voice and answered him.

"Stranger, my child was not thinking very sensibly when she did not bring you here with her women servants, since it was she whom you approached first."

Always thinking ahead, Odysseus answered him.

"Sir, don't rebuke your blameless daughter on this account. She had urged me to follow along with her servants, but out of fear and embarrassment, I did not wish to, so that you would not be outraged in your heart when you saw us, since we are suspicious, we ranks of men here on this earth."

Alkinoos again raised his voice and answered him.

"Stranger, the heart inside my chest is not like that—getting angry without reason. It is better to be moderate in all things. Ah, Father Zeus, and Athena and Apollo, if only a man such as you, who thinks so much like me, would take my child and remain here and be called my son. I would give away my house and all my wealth, if you were willing to remain here, but none of us Phaiakians will hold you back against your will, and may that never be what Father Zeus would want.

"As for this escort, just so that you will know for sure, I will arrange that for tomorrow. At that time, you will simply lie down, overcome with sleep, and they will take you over the calm waters of the sea until you reach your own land, your home, or wherever it is that you might want to go, even if it is much farther than Euboeia, which, they say, is the most distant land, those of our people who saw it when they brought the blond-haired Ragamanthus to visit Tityos, the son of Earth, and they went there and even completed the journey without growing tired, and they made the journey back home the very same day. And you will see for yourself how they are the best—my ships and my young men—at pitching the salty sea with the blade of an oar."

As he spoke, Odysseus, who had endured so much, was glad. He prayed, uttering these words.

"Father Zeus, may Lord Alkinoos accomplish all he has said, and may his reputation be inextinguishable throughout the whole earth, the source of grain, and may I reach my own land."

They went on speaking in this way until Arete, her white arms bare, called out for her slaves to set up a bed frame under the portico and to throw on the beautiful purple blankets and to place on top of these some covers and above these, wool cloaks to wear as clothing. And they came out from the great hall with torches in their hands, and after they had swiftly smoothed out the sturdy bed, they came and stood beside Odysseus and urged him on.

"Get up, stranger, and go to sleep. Your bed is made."

As they spoke, it seemed more than welcome to him to lie down and sleep. So Odysseus, who had endured so much, went to sleep, there on the carved and covered bed inside the portico. And up in the inmost room of that imposing house, Alkinoos lay down and close beside him, his wife, his woman, shared the pleasure of their bedding.

VIII

Telling Moments

Very early, Dawn spread out her rosy fingers, and the towering will of Alkinoos arose from his bed, and Zeus's descendant, Odysseus, the scourge of cities, also arose. The towering will of Alkinoos led the way to the Phaiakian agora, which had been built for them beside their ships. They arrived and sat on the polished stones, next to each other, and Pallas Athena, in the guise of a courier from Alkinoos the peace maker, went throughout the city, plotting the return of great-hearted Odysseus. She came up close to each man and said these words.

"Come now, all you Phaiakian leaders and advisors. Let us go to the agora to hear about the stranger who has recently come to honorable Alkinoos's palace—a man who's been driven about all over the sea, yet in his appearance is much like the immortals."

As she spoke, she aroused the heart and passion of each one, and all the assembly seats were quickly filled by those who were gathering. And many wondered at the sight of Laertes' skilled son, as Athena had cast a dazzling grace over his head and shoulders. She made him taller and heavier in appearance, so that he would be welcome and gain deference and respect among the Phaiakians, and so he would come out well in the many contests with which the Phaiakians were to test Odysseus. And when they had all arrived and had gathered together in the agora, Alkinoos addressed the assembly, and spoke out among them.

"Listen, Phaiakian leaders and advisors, so that I can say what this heart inside my chest is urging me to say. This stranger—I do not know who he is—has come here to my home, a wanderer from people to the east or west. He requests transport and prays to be given assurance. Let us, as we have before, facilitate his transport, since no one else who has ever come to my house has stayed here in sorrow for long, lacking means of transport.

"But come now, let's haul a black ship down to the gleaming surf for her maiden voyage, and choose fifty-two young men from among the people—all of those who have been the best before—and when you have all strapped the oars down well beside the benches, disembark and quickly come to my home and enjoy a feast. I'll provide well for everyone. I order those young men to do this, and you others, you sceptered lords, come now to my lovely home, so that we can make this stranger welcome within our halls, and let no one turn away. And call in that heavenly singer, Demodokos, who, above all others, was given by God a voice to delight, however his heart urges him to sing."

After he spoke, he led the way. The sceptered lords went with him, while a messenger went for the singer. The fifty-two young men who had been chosen went as ordered to the shore of the restless sea. And when they had come down to the sea and their ship, they hauled the black ship into the deep water. They set the mast and sail on the black ship and strapped the oars into the leather turns, all in proper order, and they spread out the white sail. They anchored the ship outside the quiet waters of the harbor and went back to the enormous palace of Alkinoos, the peace maker. The porticos and the courtyard and the rooms were filled with all the gathering men. There were many of them, young and old. Alkinoos sacrificed twelve sheep for them, and eight boars with white tusks, and two lumbering oxen. They flayed them and turned and prodded them as they prepared the luscious feast.

The messenger then approached, leading in the celebrated singer, whom the muse loved more than anyone else, having granted him the good together with the bad. She had deprived him of his eyesight but given him the gift of sweet song. Pontonoos placed a silver-studded chair for him in the middle of the feasters. He leaned it against a tall pillar and hung his lyre with its clear tone on a peg just above his head. The messenger showed him how to reach up and find it with his own hands. Beside him he placed a lovely table and a basket, and a cup of wine to drink whenever his heart desired.

And they all reached out their hands to the refreshment that lay before them. But when they had put aside their desire for drinking and eating, the muse moved the singer to sing about men's legendary actions from a song whose fame had reached to the vast heavens—the quarrel between Odysseus and Akhilles, the son of Peleus: how they had once argued at an extravagant feast to the gods, and Agamemnon, lord of men, relished in his heart the fact that the Akhaians' best men were arguing, because Phoibos Apollo, speaking through an oracle, had foretold it, back when he had crossed the stone threshold for consultation at holy Pytho, for that had been the very beginning of the hard times that had swirled in over the Trojans and Danaans alike, through the will of almighty Zeus.

The famous singer went on singing this old song, and Odysseus clutched his great purple cloak tightly in his hands and drew it over his head to hide his handsome face. He was mortified for letting his tears fall from under his eyebrows before the Phaiakians. Whenever the heavenly singer stopped singing, Odysseus would wipe away his tears and draw the cloak down from his head and take the double-handled cup and pour out another offering to the gods. But soon the singer began again, since the Phaiakian lords enjoyed his singing and urged him on to sing again. Once again, Odysseus covered up his head and groaned. He hid the tears he was shedding from all of the others, but Alkinoos noticed him and thought the whole thing over, since he was sitting right beside the man and heard him groaning deeply.

At once he spoke to the Phaiakians, who loved the oar.

"Listen, you leaders and advisors of the Phaiakians—now we have satisfied our hearts, sharing this feast and this lyre, the complement to any delicious repast. But let's go outside now and test each other in all kinds of contests, so this stranger can tell his loved ones, whenever he returns home, how well we outperform everyone else in boxing, in wrestling, in jumping, and in running."

Voicing these words, he led the way, and everyone went with him. The attendant hung up the lyre with its clear tone on the peg and took the hand of Demodokos and guided him outside the hall. He led him along the same road the Phaiakian lords took to enjoy the games. They made their way to the agora, and an immensely large crowd went along with them. Numerous strong, young men stepped forward: Akroneos, Ocyalos, Elatreus, Nauteus, and Prumneus, Ankhialos, Eretmeus, Ponteus, Proreus, Thoon, Anabesineos, Amphialos, the son of Polyneus Tektonidas, and Euryalos, the equal of that killer Ares Naubolidos, who in looks and build was the best of all the Phaiakians, except for Laodamas, a man who had no flaw. And the three sons of faultless Alkinoos—Laodamas, Halios, and Klutoneus, who himself was like a god—they all stood up.

First they ran some pretrials. A course had been set out for them from the mark, and they all ran fast, raising dust above the plain. And flawless Klutoneus was by far the best runner. As wide as the span of a mule team on newly plowed ground, he ran ahead and reached the crowd, leaving the others behind. And then they had contests in vigorous wrestling, and here Elatreus overcame the best of them. And in leaping, Amphialos was the very best of all of them, and in the discus, Elatreus was once again the best of all, and then in boxing, Laodamas, Alkinoos's sturdy son. And when they had filled their hearts enjoying the matches, Laodamas, Alkinoos's son, spoke out.

"Here, my friends, let's ask this stranger if he's ever learned any sports. His build isn't bad—his thighs and calves, and his two arms, his thick neck, and his great strength. He isn't so much past his prime, but he's been broken down by many hardships. Because, I think, there's nothing worse than the sea to bring a man down, no matter how strong he may once have been."

Euryalos, in turn, raised his voice and answered.

"Laodamas, what you say is well spoken. You yourself go challenge him. Put your words out in the open."

When Alkinoos's fine son heard this, he went and stood in the midst of them, and he called over to Odysseus.

"Come here, stranger, father. Come and try out our competitions, if you've ever learned any, and it seems likely that you'd know these contests, as there's no greater distinction for any man, as long as he lives, than what he has been able to do with his own hands and feet. Come on, test yourself, and cast your troubles out of your heart. Your journey won't be delayed for much longer. Your ship is already launched and the crew is ready."

Odysseus, always thinking ahead, answered him.

"Laodamas, why are you calling me out and taunting me? My troubles weigh much more on my heart than sport, because I've suffered so much and I've worked so hard, and now I'm sitting in your agora, longing for my return, as I have implored the king and all of your people."

Euryalos answered in turn and mocked him openly.

"No, stranger. Anyway, you don't look like a man who knows any of these sports that are so common among men, but more like a man who comes and goes on a ship with many benches, a captain of sailors, mere traders, with a mind only for freight and an eye for cargo and easy profits. You don't look like an athlete."

Glowering at the man from under his eyebrows, always thinking ahead, Odysseus answered him.

"Stranger, you speak badly—like a careless man. Undoubtedly, the gods do not give the same qualities to all men, neither in build nor heart nor speaking. One man may be unremarkable in looks, but Zeus has crowned his words with elegance. People enjoy looking at him. He speaks so well without wavering, with gentle humility, and so he is conspicuous in every gathering. And as he moves through the city, people stop and stare at him as if he were a god. And another is in appearance like one of the immortals, but no crown of elegance is placed upon his words. And you—your appearance is remarkable, and not even a god could make it better—and yet, your mind is empty.

"And now you've aroused this heart inside my chest, by speaking so improperly. I'm not so new to sport, as you are saying. I think that I was among the best as long as I could count on my own youth and hands. Now I'm held back by hardship and pain, since I've endured so much, while moving among men at war and amid unsettling waves. But even though I've suffered so much hardship, I'll try out your games, because what you have said cuts deep into my heart. You've thoroughly annoyed me with your words."

He jumped up with his cloak still around him, and grabbed a discus, larger than the rest and much heavier than those the Phaiakians were used to throwing against each other. Spinning around, he flung it away from his thick hand, and the stone hummed. They cowered, down on the ground, the Phaiakians with their long oars, famous for their ships, under the stone's flight. It moved quickly out of his hand, and much farther than all their marks. Athena, in the body of a man, placed the mark and called out to him, uttering these words.

"Even a blind man, stranger, groping about, could place this mark, since it's not in the middle of others. It's the best by far. You can enjoy this turn. None of the Phaiakians will reach it or go beyond it."

As she spoke, Odysseus, who had endured so much, was radiant, glad that he had found a true friend in this contest. With a lighter heart, he spoke among the Phaiakians.

"Now, reach that, young men. Soon I'll toss another, just as far, I think, or even farther. If any of you others have the heart, come and be tested, since you've really angered me. Whether it's boxing or wrestling or even running—I don't care—any of you Phaiakians, except Laodamas himself, since he is my host here.

"Who would confront the one who entertains him? A man is mindless and of no account if he'd challenge the one who has received him in a strange land. He cuts things short for himself. All the rest of you, I won't refuse or disregard anyone. I want to know and be tested against you, because I'm not so bad in all these contests among men. I know well how to handle a nicely polished bow, and I'd be the first to shoot and strike a man in the thick of the enemy, although many of my fellow soldiers stood next to me and were also shooting their bows at those men.

"Philoktetes alone exceeded me with the bow, back when we Akhaians shot our bows on Trojan ground. But I'd say that I'm the best by far of anyone else, any man who is now alive and eating bread here on Earth. But of those men who came before the likes of us, I would not want to compete—with Herakles or Eurytos of Oikhalia, who rivaled even the immortals in shooting the bow. It was for that reason Eurytos died so young, and old age did not come upon him in his halls. Apollo became enraged and struck him down, because the man had challenged him to an archery match. I can also throw the spear farther than anyone else can shoot an arrow. Only in running, I'm afraid that some among you Phaiakians might better me, since I've been badly battered by so many waves, and on my craft there was no way to care for myself, so my limbs have come to be slack and flabby."

After he spoke, they were all utterly silent, speechless. Alkinoos alone was able to answer him.

"Stranger, since you have said these things among us, not without grace, but are eager to show the skill you have, in anger at this man for having insulted you so openly to your face—and since no ordinary man who knows how to speak properly would call you down—come now, listen to what I say, so you can tell some other great man, whenever you are feasting with your wife and children in your halls and remember our skill, these acts Zeus has always enabled us to do since the time of our fathers, up to now. Because we are not flawless boxers or wrestlers, but we run fast in footraces and we are excellent as seamen, and we are really fond of feasting, the lyre and dancing, warm baths, changing clothes, and bedding down.

"But come, you who are the best dancers among us Phaiakians, perform for us now, so the stranger can tell his loved ones, when he has returned home, how much we surpass all others in sailing and running and dancing and singing. One of you, go now and bring Demodokos that lyre with the clear tone—it's lying around in our halls somewhere."

Alkinoos spoke like a god, and the messenger got up to bring back the hollow lyre from the king's palace. Then all nine officials who were chosen by the people to organize everything properly in the games stood up. They leveled and smoothed out an open space for dancing, a lovely, wide arena, as the messenger approached, bringing Demodokos the lyre with the clear tone. He moved into the center, and some young men in the first surge of youth came and stood around him. They were accomplished dancers and beat a divine rhythm with their feet. Odysseus gazed at the blur of their feet with wonder in his heart.

The singer struck a beautiful chord and began to sing about the love of Ares and Aphrodite, covered in flowers—how they first mingled inside Hephaistos's house, in secret, and Ares gave her everything he had and sullied Lord Hephaistos's bed. Right away, Helios came to tell him. He had seen them, clinging together in the act of love. What Hephaistos heard stung his heart. He made his way to his forge, thinking the worst in the very depths of his heart. He set his huge anvil down on the block, and he forged unbreakable shackles that could not be loosened, so they would stay firmly in place. And after crafting this trap, incensed at Ares, he made his way to the room where his bed lay. He wrapped the chains all around the bedposts and he hung many more from the rafters above, fine as a spider's web, so that no one, not even the blissful gods, could see them, they were so cunningly crafted.

When he had spread his trap around the bed, he pretended to go away to Lemnos, that well-built city, which to him is the most beloved of all lands. And Ares, holding his golden reins, was by no means keeping a careless watch when he observed Hephaistos, celebrated for his craft, departing. In his passion to make love with the radiant Kytheria, he made his way to Hephaistos's house. And she had just come back from being with the almighty Son of Kronos. She sat down. Ares went inside the house. He held her hand. He called her by name and said these words to her.

"Come, my love, let's go to bed and enjoy ourselves making love. Hephaistos is not here in this land any longer. He's gone to Lemnos, among those uncouth Sintians."

As he spoke, it seemed delightful to her to lie down and relax. They both went to the bed and lay down. The clever chains that sly Hephaistos had crafted fell around them, and they were not able to move or even lift their limbs, and at last they realized that there was no escape. And Hephaistos, who was famous for his two lame legs, drew near, after turning back before he reached the land of Lemnos, because Helios had kept watch for him and told him the story. He made his way home, his heart troubled. He stood at the gate. A hard anger seized him. Loudly, he called to all the gods.

"Father Zeus, and all you other carefree gods who live forever—come and see something here that's both laughable and intolerable. How Aphrodite, Zeus's daughter, disdains me for being lame and makes love to useless Ares, since he's handsome and quick on his feet, while I was born twisted. For this, there's no one else to blame except my own two parents. If only they had not even given birth to me. But look—how these two have climbed into my bed to lie down and make love. I'm hurt to see it, but I don't expect that they will want to stay much longer, lying around like this, not even for a little while, even if they're really in love. Soon enough, they'll prefer not to be in bed together, but this trap and these chains will hold them down, until her father pays me back for all the wedding gifts I once gave him for his shameless girl, since his daughter is beautiful but out of control."

As he spoke, the gods gathered around near the bronze threshold of his house. Poseidon, the Earth Shaker, came, and Hermes, the helper, and Lord Apollo, who works from far away. The goddesses stayed back, out of embarrassment, each in her own house, but all the male gods, the givers of everything good, stood at the gate. Uncontrollable laughter arose among all the carefree gods as they looked at what Hephaistos, so full of craftiness, had cunningly contrived.

And one of them would glance at another, next to him and say, "Bad actions don't win out. The slow catches the quick, as now Hephaistos, slow as he is, has caught Ares, by far the fastest of all the gods who occupy Olympos. Although lame, he has him by designs. And Ares has to pay for his adultery."

They all went on talking to each other in this way. But Lord Apollo, son of Zeus, said to Hermes, "Hermes, son of Zeus, guide, giver of good things, would you yourself be willing to be tied down with chains, lying next to golden Aphrodite?"

The messenger Argeïphontes answered him.

"If only that would happen, Lord Apollo, you who always hit your mark from far away. If only there were three times those inescapable chains, all around me, holding me down. You and all the goddesses could go on watching as I went on snuggling close to golden Aphrodite."

As he spoke, laughter arose among the immortal gods. But Poseidon did not laugh. He constantly implored Hephaistos, the famous craftsman, to release Ares. He raised his voice, his words rumbling like wings.

"Release him! I promise you, as you demand, here among the immortal gods, he will pay what's right!"

And the well-known god with two lame legs answered.

"Poseidon, you may hold the earth in your hands, but don't ask me for this. A guarantee is something useless, if guaranteed by someone useless. How could I ever put you in chains, in the presence of the immortal gods, if Ares escaped from his chains and his debt and got away?"

Poseidon, the Earth Shaker, spoke to him again.

"Hephaistos, even if Ares were to elude his debt and escape, then I myself will pay you back for this."

And the well-known god with two lame legs replied, "It would not be right to refuse to take you at your word."

After he had spoken, Hephaistos with all his strength ripped away the chains, and the two removed their fetters, powerful as they were, and they jumped up immediately. Ares went off to Thrace, and Aphrodite, who loves to laugh, went to Paphos in Cyprus, where there is a fragrant altar to her. There the Graces bathed her, and they anointed her body with that heavenly oil that graces the skin of the gods who live forever. And they wrapped some lovely clothing about her, a wonder to observe.

The famous singer sang this song, and Odysseus listened and felt joy in his heart, as did all of the Phaiakians, men famous for their ships and long oars. Alkinoos then ordered Halios and Laodamas to dance alone, because no one could match them. After they took in their hands a beautiful purple ball that the ingenious Polybos had made for them, one leaned back and threw it toward the dark clouds, and the other jumped high above the ground and easily caught it before his feet again touched ground, and after they had tested themselves, throwing the ball straight up, they danced around the generous earth, quickly flinging the ball back and forth, and all the other young men stood inside the arena and beat a rhythm on the ground with their feet, raising a loud noise. Radiant, Odysseus spoke at once across to Alkinoos.

"Lord Alkinoos, you are widely known among all peoples, and you've boasted that your dancers are the best, and now your words have been borne out. I am struck with wonder as I look at them."

As he spoke, the towering will of Alkinoos was pleased and called to the oar lovers, the Phaiakians.

"Listen, you leaders and advisors of the Phaiakians—it seems to me this stranger has great presence of mind. So come, let us extend to him our open hospitality, as is fitting, since twelve admirable kings rule our land as leaders, and I am the thirteenth. So now, let each of you offer a freshly washed cloak and tunic and provide a talent of gold in his honor, and let us bring it all together right away, so our guest may go to dinner, holding it in his arms and rejoicing in his heart. And you, Euryalos, settle with him both with your own words and a gift, since the words you spoke were not fitting."

After he had spoken, they all praised everything that he had said and ordered all of it to be done, and each one sent out a messenger to bring back the gifts. And Euryalos in turn made his reply.

"Lord Alkinoos, celebrated among all peoples, I wish to make my peace with the stranger, as you request. I offer him this sword, of solid bronze with a silver hilt, and this scabbard with freshly carved ivory worked about it. May it be something of suitably great value to him."

As he spoke, his voice and words soaring like wings, he placed the sword, crafted in silver, in Odysseus's hands.

"Cheers, stranger, Father. If harsh words have been spoken, may gusts of wind snatch them up and carry them away, and may the gods grant that you see your wife and reach your own land, since you have suffered so many hardships for such a long time, far away from those you love."

Odysseus, always thinking ahead, answered back.

"And cheers to you, my friend. May the gods give you good fortune, and may you never, in the future, yearn for this sword that you have given me with such soft words."

He slung the silver-lined sword over his shoulder. The sun was setting, and the dazzling gifts were brought in. The dignified messengers carried them to Alkinoos's home, and Alkinoos's sons took the lovely gifts and placed them before their esteemed mother. And Alkinoos led the way, in all his exalted power.

They all came in and sat down on elevated chairs, and Alkinoos spoke firmly to Arete.

"My dear, bring over here a special chest, whichever is the best one, and place a freshly washed cloak and a tunic in it, and heat a cauldron on the fire until the water is warm, so that after he has washed and seen the beautiful display of all the gifts that the blameless Phaiakians have brought, he may then take his pleasure, feasting and listening to music. And I will give him this exquisite gold cup, so that he will remember me all his days, whenever he pours offerings in his own halls to Zeus and the other gods."

After he spoke, Arete ordered her slaves to place a large cauldron on the fire as quickly as possible. They placed the wash tub on the blazing fire, poured in the water, and grabbed some pieces of wood and set them to burn. The fire leaped up around the cauldron's belly. The water grew warm while Arete brought out an elegant chest for her guest from an inner chamber, and inside the chest, she placed all the beautiful gifts—the clothes and gold that the Phaiakians had given him. She herself added a cloak and a beautiful tunic. Then she lifted her voice, her words as soft as wings.

"Now see to the lid yourself and quickly draw some twine around it, so no one can steal from you during your journey, if you should happen to fall into a sweet sleep, while traveling on our black ship."

When Odysseus, who had endured so much, heard what she said, he applied the twine quickly in an elaborately tied knot that Kirke had taught him. Then the housekeeper led him away to be bathed, and he saw the warm bath with joy in his heart, because he was no longer accustomed to such attentive care since he had left the home of Kalypso, with her lovely hair, although before, he had always been cared for as if he were a god. After the slaves had washed him, rubbed him down with oil, and had thrown around him a beautiful tunic and cloak, he went out from his bath and joined the men, who were busy drinking wine.

And Nausikaa, in all her natural beauty, was standing beside the doorway of the sturdily constructed hall, and when her eyes caught sight of him, she looked at him in wonder, and she spoke to him, her words soft as wings.

"Goodbye, stranger. When you are back home in your own land, remember me, since it is to me, before all else, that you owe the value of your life."

Odysseus, always thinking ahead, answered her.

"Nausikaa, daughter of that great heart, Alkinoos, may Zeus, Hera's loud, thundering husband, now make it possible for me to go home and see the day of my own return. And there, for all of my days, I will always offer prayers to you as to a goddess, because you, young lady, have given me my life."

He sat down in a chair next to King Alkinoos. They were mixing the wine and serving out portions. An attendant approached, leading in Demodokos, the singer, a man who was revered by the people. The attendant sat him down and leaned him against a tall pillar in the middle of those who were feasting.

Odysseus, always thinking ahead, as he was slicing off a piece from the back of a white-tusked boar, thick with fat on both sides, spoke to the attendant.

"Steward, take this piece of meat and offer it to Demodokos, so he may eat, and I will offer him my respects, troubled as I am, because of all the people who live on earth, singers deserve their special share of admiration and honor, because the muse loves the company of singers and has given to them the spring and sway of music."

After he had spoken, the attendant took the meat and placed it in the hands of the great Demodokos. He accepted it with joy in his heart. And they all reached out their hands for the refreshments that lay before them, and when they had all put aside their desire for food and drink, Odysseus, always thinking ahead, spoke to Demodokos.

"Demodokos, I honor you above all mortals, whether it was the muse, Zeus's daughter, who taught you, or Apollo, since very fittingly you sing about the Akhaians' destiny—all they achieved and suffered, and all the hardships that they went through, as if you yourself were there, or somehow heard it all from someone else. But come now, shift your theme and sing about the stratagem of the wooden horse, which Epeios built, along with Athena—the trick that Odysseus led to that towering city, after loading it up with men to burn and loot Ilios. If you can tell this story accurately, I will declare before everyone that Zeus has generously inspired in you the power for inimitable song."

After he spoke, the singer, moved by the spirit to begin, opened his song, taking up the story when the Argives went aboard the long, well-benched ships and sailed off, after they had set their huts afire, while the others who were with the famous Odysseus were sitting inside the horse in Troy's assembly ground. It was the Trojans themselves who had dragged it there, inside the towering city. And there it stood, and the people kept arguing endlessly, indecisively, as they sat around it. Three plans seemed good to them. Split the hollow wood into pieces with ruthless bronze, or drag it to the heights and throw it down on the rocks, or let it stand as a great offering to placate the gods, as it was to happen, since it was their fate to perish when their city had enclosed the massive wooden horse in which they were all sitting—the best of the Argives, about to bring devastation and death upon the Trojans.

He sang—how the sons of the Akhaians poured out of the horse, leaving behind their hollow hiding place, and he sang—how they burned and looted throughout the city, some here and others there, laying waste to the towering stronghold. And how Odysseus went like Ares to Deiphobos's house with Menelaos, as if he were a god himself. There, they risked a horrible battle and won at last, with the help of Athena's great heart. The famous singer sang this song, and Odysseus's heart melted, and the tears flowed out from under his eyelids down over his cheeks.

Like a woman who cries out and then throws herself upon her beloved husband, who has fallen before his city and its people, trying to hold back the merciless day for his city and his children. She watches him as he is dying, gasping for breath, and she throws herself upon him, shrieking loudly. They beat on her back and shoulders with the shafts of their spears, then lead her away to servitude, to suffer hardship and misery, her cheeks wasting away with the most pitiful grief. In this way, Odysseus let his own mournful tears fall under his brow. He concealed the tears he was shedding from the others. Only Alkinoos noticed, as he observed him, sitting by himself, and heard him groaning. At once he spoke to the Phaiakians, who love their oars.

"Listen, all you leaders and advisors of the Phaiakians, let Demodokos quiet the clear tones of his lyre, because his song is not bringing joy to everyone here. From the moment we started feasting and our heavenly singer began to sing, since then the stranger has not stopped weeping bitterly. Some torment must be closing in on his heart, and so, let us hold off, so that all of us may enjoy ourselves, both host and guest, because it is much better that way. It is for our respected guest that all this is being done, both the escort and the gifts of friendship we give him most freely. A stranger or a petitioner is like a brother to any man whose heart can be touched, even a little bit. So do not hide now, for any self-serving purpose, whatever it is I am about to ask you. Speaking out is always better.

"Tell me the name they call you by, and your mother and father, and the others, all those who live in and about your city. Since no one among all human beings is ever nameless, whether he is of low birth or a man of worth. Once he has been born, parents give one to all of those they have brought to life. So tell me your country, your people, and your city, so our ships may send you there, setting the course on their own. Because we Phaiakians have no pilots and no rudders like those that other ships have. The vessels themselves recognize the minds and hearts of our men. They know the cities and fertile fields of all peoples and make their way quickly across the depths of the sea, hidden in mists and clouds, and there is never any fear of being harmed or lost at sea, although once I overheard my father Nausithoos speaking. He said Poseidon was angry at us for giving safe conduct to everyone. He said one day, as one of the Phaiakians' well-made ships returns from a convoy over the misty sea, he would shatter it and enclose our city behind a mountain. Or so the old man said.

"And Zeus will bring about these things or let them go unfulfilled, whatever his heart's desire may be. But come now, tell me this and tell me truthfully where you have been driven about—what places, pleasant cities, and peoples you have come upon, both those who were hard and brutish or unjust, and those whose minds are god-fearing and welcome strangers. And tell us why you keep on weeping here, with grief in your heart, as you hear about the fate of the Argives and Danaans. The gods made this happen, as they have spun the thread of death for all those men, so there might be a song for those yet to be born. Did one of your relatives die there, before Ilios—a fine brother-in-law or father-in-law—one of those who is the closest to us by blood and birth? Or a friend of yours, a good man, close to your heart? Because nothing less than a brother is an understanding friend."

IX

The Wandering Eye

Odysseus, always thinking ahead, answered him.

"Lord Alkinoos, eminent above all people, there's no doubt that this is a good thing, to listen to a singer such as this, his voice like the gods, because I would say there is nothing more fulfilling than when joy takes hold of everyone, and all those who are feasting inside the house listen to a singer as they sit, side by side, and the tables are filled with bread and meat in front of them, and the steward draws the wine from the bowl and carries it around and pours it into all the cups. This, to my heart, seems to be the most beautiful thing there is.

"But now your heart is distracted to ask me about my dismal troubles, and so I groan and am full of even more sorrow. What, then, should I tell you first, and what last? The gods above have given me so many troubles. So first, I will tell you my name, so that all of you will know it, and so that I, after I have postponed that inescapable day of death, may someday be your host, although my home is far away.

"I am Odysseus Laertiádes, well-known for my cunning. My reputation reaches to the skies. I live in Ithaka, easily seen. There is a mountain on it, Neriton, with its quivering forests, visible from far away, and many islands, close to each other, all around. Dulkhios, Samos, and forested Zakynthos. Ithaka lies low on the horizon, the furthest toward the darkening sky. The others are off toward the dawn and the sun. It is rugged, but it's a good caretaker for raising the young. To me, there cannot be anything sweeter than seeing one's own land.

"Although Kalypso, that radiant goddess, kept me with her in her hollow caves, longing for me to be her husband, and Kirke, the cunning goddess of Aiaia, detained me in her halls, also longing for me to be her husband, they could never deter this heart inside my chest. Nothing is so sweet as one's own land and parents, even if he lives in a wealthy home, far from his parents in another land. But let me tell you about my trouble-filled return home, which Zeus imposed after I left Troy.

"From Ilios, the wind picked up and carried me as far as Ismaros to the Kikones. There, I burned down the city and killed the men. We took their wives and a lot of goods from the city and divided it up, so no man would go away cheated out of his equal share. I strongly advised that we take quick steps to get away, but those great fools would not obey. A lot of wine was drunk. By the shore they slaughtered a lot of sheep and lumbering cattle with curled horns, while those Kikones went and called out their neighboring Kikones, who were more numerous and more daring. They lived inland and knew how to fight, if the need should arise, either with horses or on foot.

"And so they came—as many as all the leaves and flowers that appear in spring. It was a horrible destiny from Zeus himself that came upon us. We were doomed to face many agonies. They took their stand and fought, close to our fast ships. Both sides threw their spears, tipped with bronze, at each other all through the morning, and as that wondrous day progressed, we held on and kept them off, though they outnumbered us. But as the sun moved toward evening, when you unyoke your oxen, the Kikones pushed the Akhaians back. They overcame us. From each ship, six of my well-equipped soldiers were lost. The rest escaped the call of destiny and death.

"We sailed on from there, anguish in our hearts, glad we had escaped death, although we had lost some trustworthy mates. I did not allow our rounded ships to leave until we'd called out three times for each of those unlucky mates who died on the field, cut down by the Kikones. But then, Zeus, gathering the clouds together, stirred up the north wind against our ships in a storm that was beyond belief, and he obscured both land and sea with clouds, and from the heavens the night rushed in. The ships were swept over, leaning sideways, and the force of the wind ripped the sails into three or four shreds. We hauled them in and stored them in the hold, fearing our destruction, and we rowed vigorously toward land. There, for two full days and nights, we lay about, eating out our hearts in weariness and pain.

"But then, when Dawn with her flowing hair brought into being the third day, we set the masts in place, hauled up the white sails, and sat at our benches. The wind and our helmsmen steered, and soon I would have reached my own land unharmed, but rounding Malea, the waves, the current, and the north wind kept on beating against me, and I was driven beyond Kythera. From there, I was carried along by treacherous winds for nine days, over a sea filled with fish.

"On the tenth, we stepped onto the land of the lotus eaters, who eat a flowering fruit. We went ashore and drew on some water, and my shipmates took their meal by the swift ships. And when we had tasted our food and drink, I sent some of my crew to find out what men there were about, of those who eat bread here on earth. I chose two men, and with them, I sent along a third as a messenger. They went off, and at once mingled with those lotus-eating men. The lotus eaters did not even think of killing my shipmates, but merely gave them the lotus to eat. And those who ate the lotus fruit, sweet as honey, no longer wanted to return home or take back news. They only wanted to stay there with the lotus-eating people and feed on the lotus and forget about returning.

"I led them crying, against their will, back to the ships and dragged them into the hollow ships and tied them down, and I called out to the rest of my trusty mates to hurry and board our fast ships, so no one else would eat the lotus and forget about returning home. Right away, they went on board and settled at their benches, and sitting there, all in proper order, they struck the gray sea with their oars. From there we sailed on, with anguish in our hearts.

"We came to the land of the Kyklops. Insolent and unruly, they put all their faith in the immortal gods and neither plow nor plant by hand, yet without planting and without plowing, everything grows—wheat and barley and vines bearing thick clusters of grapes for wine. Rain from Zeus makes them flourish. They don't have either assemblies or councils or any kind of established laws. They live on the mountaintops in hollow caves. Each one makes his own rules for his own children and wives, and they have no use for one another.

"There is a fertile island that juts out cockeyed from the harbor. It's neither close nor very far from the forested land of the Kyklops. On it, there are countless wild goats, because they are not curbed by human care or taste. No hunters go there, enduring hard work in the forests as they head over the mountain tops. It's unoccupied, with neither tended flocks nor plowed fields, and unplanted and untilled, it goes without a human touch, all its days, but it feeds the bleating goats.

"There are no ships with bright red bows among the Kyklops and no ship builders who might build them ships with fine benches to fulfill each need by going off to human cities, in the way so many other people travel across the sea in ships, to trade with each other—or any others who might have built up the island. It is by no means a bad place. It could engender everything in its season. There are meadows near the shores of the gray sea with soft, moist soil, where vines would never die. There are level fields from which they might reap a booming harvest, the under-soil is so fertile. And there is a harbor with good anchorage, where there's no need for moorings, for throwing out stone anchors or for tying up the stern cables. You can simply beach the ship and linger there awhile, until the wind blows fair and the sailors' hearts urge them on. There, at the head of the harbor, a stream of bright water flows from a cave. Dark poplars grow all around it.

"We landed there. Some god was guiding us through that gloomy night. It wasn't light enough to see. The fog was thick, all around the ships. The moon was not shining, up above, but was closed in by clouds. No one was able to catch sight of the island with his eyes, and we did not sight the long waves curling upon the beach until our ships, with their firm benches, drove up onto the shore. After beaching the ships, we lowered all the sails and disembarked onto the seashore. There, waiting for the radiance of Dawn, we fell asleep.

"Very early, as Dawn spread out her rosy fingers, we moved about the island in wonder. The nymphs, daughters of Zeus who holds the aegis, stirred up the mountain goats so that my mates could eat. At once we grabbed our curved bows and long javelins from the ships, and organizing ourselves in three groups, we began throwing our javelins at them, and right away, Zeus gave us a satisfying hunt.

"There were twelve ships following me, and nine goats were allotted to each ship, and the crew picked out ten of them for me alone. All day long, until the sun set, we sat there, feasting on massive amounts of meat and sweet wine, because the red wine on our ships was not yet used up. There was still some of it left, because each crew had drawn plenty of it into their own amphoras when we took the Kikones' towering city. We looked across to the land of the Kyklops, who lived close by. There was smoke, and sheep and goats, and they themselves were bellowing. But the sun set and darkness came on, so we lay down to sleep, there on the seashore, and very early, Dawn spread out her rosy fingers.

"I called for an assembly and spoke to them all.

"'The rest of you stay here for now, my trusty mates. I myself will go with my own ship and crew, and find out about these people—who they are and whether they are violent, unjust and disorderly, or if they welcome strangers and are observant of the gods.'

"After I spoke, I went aboard the ship and told the crew to get aboard themselves and release the stern cables. They went on board right away and settled at their benches, and sitting all in order, they struck the gray waters with their oars. When we had reached the place, which was close by on a point near the sea, we saw a high cave overhung with laurel. There, large flocks of sheep and goats were kept at night. All around it, a towering courtyard was built with stones embedded in the ground and tall pines and lofty oak trees.

"It was the night dwelling of some huge man who shepherded his flocks at a distance, on his own, and who was not used to being with others but was disposed to remain isolated, with no regard for right or wrong. He had been created to be a gigantic wonder, not at all like a man who eats bread, but like some wooded crag among lofty mountains, alone, set off from others. I told the rest of my trustworthy mates to remain close by and guard the ship, and I chose twelve of my very best mates, and we departed.

"I had a goatskin of dark sweet wine that had been given to me by Maro, the son of Evanthes, a priest of Apollo, who kept watch over Ismaros. Out of reverence, we had protected him and his wife and child, since he lived in a wooded grove that was dedicated to Phoibos Apollo, and so he gave me some splendid gifts. He gave me seven talents of crafted gold and a mixing bowl of solid silver. And the wine—sweet, unmixed, heavenly to drink. He poured it into twelve jugs in all, and none of the slaves or personal attendants in his house knew about it, only his beloved wife and only one housekeeper. And when they drank that red wine, sweet as honey, he would fill one cup and pour it into twenty measures of water, and a smell so sweet—beyond words—would rise from the mixing bowl, and no one could bear to hold back.

"I filled up a large goatskin with this wine and I carried it along with other provisions in a pack, since my swelling heart told me that we would soon come upon a man clothed in great strength—a wild man who did not know what's right and just. Quickly we came to the cave, but we didn't find him inside. He was at that time grazing his plump flocks in the fields. We went inside the cave and stared in wonder at everything. There were baskets full of cheeses and corrals loaded with lambs and kids. Each pen was set for separate groups, with one place for the firstborn, another for those who came later, and yet another for all those that were newly born. All the well-built pots, the pails and bowls into which he milked, were full of whey.

"My companions spoke up and begged me to grab some of the cheese and go at once and quickly drive the lambs and kids from their pens down to the ship and sail away over the salty waters. But I did not listen—although that would have been better—so I might see him for what he was, and in case he might give us what guests are due. But then, when he did appear, he was by no means a cheery sight to my shipmates. We kindled a fire and performed a sacrifice, and then we took some of the cheese and ate it, and we sat there and waited for him until he came back, driving his flock.

"He carried inside a heavy load of dry wood to use at mealtime. He threw it all down inside the cave, with a booming noise like thunder. In fear, we drew back into the recesses of the cave. He drove his plump flock, all of those he milked, inside the enormous cave, but he left the males, the rams and goats, outside the door in the deep courtyard. Then he picked up and set a huge, heavy stone to block the door. Twenty-two sturdy wagons with four wheels could not have hauled it away from the ground, it was such an immeasurably massive rock that he set into the doorway.

"He sat down and began to milk the bleating sheep and goats, all of them in their proper order, and under each one of them, he placed her young. Then he curdled half of the white milk and he gathered it into wicker baskets and put it aside. The other half he stood in jugs, so that he could drink some of it and keep the rest for mealtime. But after he had made himself busy getting all of his work done, he rekindled the fire. And then his eye fell upon us, and he questioned us.

"'Strangers, who are you? Where are you sailing from, in your course across the waters? Are you on some mission or are you wandering aimlessly as pirates do, roaming about, risking their lives and bringing trouble to people from other lands?'

"As he spoke, all our hearts were crushed in fear of his deep voice and his gigantic presence. Even so, I managed to speak up and offer him an answer.

"'We have come to you from Troy—we Akhaians, driven about by all the winds over the great chasm of the sea. Heading homeward, we've come by an unfamiliar route, an unfamiliar course. It is perhaps how Zeus wished to plan it out. We claim to be the people of Agamemnon Atreïdes, whose fame is by now the greatest under the heavens, as he destroyed such a great city and killed so many people. But we have happened to come to your knees in supplication, so that you might offer us hospitality and give us what is due us as your guests—in reverence, honored sir, to the gods. We have come here to you as supplicants, since Zeus himself is the avenger of suppliants and strangers, the god of strangers, who walks in the footsteps of proper strangers.'

"As I spoke, at once he answered with a pitiless heart.

"'You're a fool, stranger, or you've come from far away, since you're asking me to be afraid of or shrink from the gods. Us Kyklopses don't care about Zeus or that big shield he carries, or those other gods up high. We're much better than they are. I won't spare you or your friends just to avoid Zeus's anger, unless my heart urges me to. But tell me, where did you put in your good ship whenever it was you got here—over there on the far side, or close by? Just so I'll know.'

"He said this to test me, but he did not fool me. I read him well. I answered with shifty words.

"'Poseidon, Shaker of the Earth, smashed my ship to pieces, by throwing her on the rocks along the coast of your country. The wind drove her in from the sea, and then he brought her up against the headlands. But I, with these men, escaped utter destruction.'

"After I spoke, he did not answer, given his merciless heart. He jumped up and reached out his hands for my mates. He grabbed two of them together and dashed them both against the ground like puppies. Their brains flowed out on the ground and drenched the earth. He cut off their limbs and prepared his meal. Like a mountain lion, he devoured the entrails, the flesh, and the bones with all their marrow, leaving nothing. We watched this vicious act, and we cried out, holding our hands up to Zeus. Helplessness clutched our hearts.

"After the Kyklops had filled his enormous belly by eating human flesh and drinking down pure milk, he lay down inside the cave and stretched himself out among his sheep. My heart bursting, I began to plan a way to get close to him and draw my sharp sword from beside my thigh and plunge it into his chest, where the lungs hold the liver in place, feeling for it with my hand. But I was held back by second thoughts, because all of us as well would have died a horrible death, since we would not have been able to heave back that heavy stone he'd set into that enormous door. And so we groaned and waited for brilliant Dawn.

"Very early, as Dawn spread out her rosy fingers, he rekindled the fire and milked his fine sheep, all of them in good order, and placed under each one her young, and after he had vigorously finished up his work, again he grabbed two men together and prepared his meal.

"After eating, he nimbly removed the great stone and drove his fattened sheep from the cave, then pushed it back into position, as someone might place the lid on a quiver. Whistling noisily, the Kyklops turned his fattened flocks to the mountains, and I was left there, brooding deeply over how to pay him back brutally, with Athena's backing.

"And this strategy seemed in my own heart to be the best. The Kyklops's massive club, which was made of green olive wood that he had recently cut to carry when it dried, lay next to one of the pens. Looking it over, it seemed so long and thick that we reckoned it was as large as the mast of a black ship with twenty oars, a wide trading ship for crossing that great chasm. I stood next to it and cut away a full fathom. I passed it over to my mates and told them to strip it down. They smoothed it out, and I stood next to them and sharpened it to a point. They took it and scorched it hard on the blazing fire. And then I put it carefully away, hiding it under the dung, which was strewn about the cave in numerous huge piles.

"I encouraged the others to cast lots among themselves—which of them would be daring enough to pick up the stake together with me and press it into his eye as soon as delicious sleep had settled upon him. The lots fell to those whom I myself would have wanted to choose. There were four of them, and I myself made five. Toward evening, he came back, herding his flocks with their lovely fleece. At once he drove every one of his fattened flocks into the vast cave, not leaving even one of them out in the deep courtyard.

"Either some hunch or a god was urging him on. But as soon as he had lifted and set the huge stone in place, he sat down and milked the bleating sheep and goats, each in proper order, and under each he placed their young. But after he had busied himself, getting his work done, once again he grabbed two men together and prepared his meal. I then stood closer, holding in my hands a wooden bowl of dark wine, and I spoke to the Kyklops.

"'Kyklops, here, drink some wine, to go along with the human flesh you have eaten, so you'll know what kind of drink our ship holds. I brought it here to you as an offering, so you'd have some mercy and send me back home. But now you've become mad in a way no one can bear. Heartless man, how would any human being ever come to you again in the future, since what you have done is neither right nor proper.'

"As I spoke, he grabbed it and drank it down. He was thrilled to drink the sweet wine and asked for more.

"'Give me more, out of the goodness of your heart and tell me your name now, so I can offer you what a guest deserves, and you'll be delighted. Because the earth, which brings us grain, turns out rich clusters of wine for us Kyklops, and the rain that comes to us from Zeus makes them grow—but this here's a taste from a stream of ambrosia and nectar.'

"After he had spoken, I offered him the shimmering wine again. I brought and gave it to him three times, and three times he drank it down without thinking. And when the wine had overwhelmed the Kyklops's mind, I spoke to him with captivating words.

"'Kyklops, you ask me for my illustrious name and I'll tell you. Then you can offer me what a guest deserves, as you've just promised. No One is my name. They call me No One, my mother and my father and all of my friends.'

"After I spoke, he answered with a callous heart.

"'I'll eat No One last of all, after your shipmates and all those others before. That'll be what you deserve.'

"He staggered and fell on his back and lay there with his neck bent cock-eyed, and sleep, which overcomes everyone, took him in its clutches. Wine surged from his throat, along with bits of human flesh, as he vomited in his drunkenness. Right away, I drove the stake deep into the embers until it grew hot. I encouraged all my shipmates, so nobody would draw back from me in fear. And soon, when the olivewood stake was just about to catch on fire, even though it was still green and glowing fiercely, I brought it out of the fire, close to him. My shipmates stood around me and some god breathed great courage into us. We took the olivewood stake, sharp at its point, and thrust it into his eye. I leaned my weight against it from above and turned the stake around.

"As a man bores a ship's timber with a drill, while those below keep it spinning around with a leather strap they are holding on both sides, and the drill keeps spinning around constantly—that's how we all gripped that smoldering stake, turning and twisting it inside his eye, and the blood was hot and streamed out, all around. The heat from the burning eyeball singed his eyelids and eyebrows, and the roots of the eye crackled in the fire.

"When a blacksmith plunges a large axe or adze into cool water to temper it, and it raises a massive hissing, from which the strength of iron comes about—that's how his eye sizzled around that stake of olive wood. In horror, he cried out, and his cry echoed back from the rocks, all around. In fear, we all drew back. He pulled the stake, rank with foul blood, out of his eye. With both hands, he flung it away, beside himself. And he cried out in a loud voice to all of the Kyklops who lived around him in caves along the windy hilltops. They heard him bawling, and they lumbered in from every direction and stood around the cave, and they asked him what was troubling him.

"'What's this, Polyphemos? Yelling and screaming to us on this heavenly night? It'll make us lose our sleep. Is someone among those mortal men deviously driving off your flocks against your will, or is someone killing you by force or trickery?'

"From inside the cave, the huge Polyphemos answered, 'Friends, No One is killing me by force and trickery!'

"They answered, their words batting about him like wings, 'Well, if no one's hurting you, on your own as you are, there's no avoiding this sickness from almighty Zeus. You've just got to pray to our father, Lord Poseidon.'

"As they said this, they went away, and my heart leaped up inside me. My name and my flawless plan had worked. The Kyklops, groaning now in agony and pain, groped about with his hands and took the stone away from the door. He sat down in the doorway and reached out his hands to catch anyone who tried to go out through the door with the sheep. It seemed he hoped within his heart that I would be that foolish. I thought over how it all might turn out for the best, how I might find a way for my fellow shipmates—and myself—to escape death.

"I interwove all kinds of tricks and schemes, as someone grasping for life itself, since the horror close at hand was huge. And this plan seemed in my own heart to be the best. There were several well-fed rams, fine and large with thick coats of dark wool. In silence, I worked them all together, very skillfully plaiting together the pliable twigs on which the Kyklops, that huge thing with no thought for what was right, used to sleep.

"I picked out three rams at a time—one in the middle to carry a man, and two on each side, going along together, to save my shipmates. Every three rams carried a man. But I—well, there was a ram, by far the very best of the whole flock. I grabbed its back and twisted myself, face up, under his wooly belly. With my hands holding onto his sumptuous wool, I held on with a stubborn heart. Groaning, we waited for radiant Dawn.

"And very early, as Dawn spread out her rosy fingers, the flock's males scurried out for the pasturelands. The females bleated, unmilked in their pens, their udders about to burst. Their master, worn out by awful pain, felt along the backs of the sheep, as they idled by. The fool did not notice how my mates had been bound, under the breasts of his very wooly sheep. The ram, the last one of all the flock, went out through the doorway, encumbered by the weight of his own fleece and my own intricate thinking.

"Feeling along its back, powerful Polyphemos said, 'Little ram, why are you leaving the cave like this, the last of the flock? You've never been left behind by the sheep, but are always the very first to step up high to graze on the fresh grass and flowers, the first to reach the running streams, and the first in your longing to return to the fold at evening time. But now you are the last of them all. You must be sorrowing for your master's eye, which that awful man has blinded, along with his miserable companions,after weakening my heart with wine. But I'm telling you, No One has not yet escaped destruction. If only you could think and talk good like me, so you could tell me where that one is now skulking about to avoid my anger. His brains would be splattered about all over this cave after I thrashed him, and then my heart could calm down from this horror which that no good No One has brought on me.'

"As he spoke, he sent the ram outside and away, and after going a short distance away from the cave and the courtyard, first I freed myself from the ram, and then I released my mates. Quickly we herded and drove those eagerly trodding, thoroughly fattened sheep until we reached the ship. And the appearance of those of us who had escaped death was welcome to our loyal shipmates. But for the others, they started to groan and cry, but I did not let them weep. Raising one eyebrow to each man, I gave them orders to throw on board those fine, wooly sheep and sail out onto the salty waters. They went on board and settled at their benches, and sitting in proper rows, they struck the gray sea with their oars. But as soon as we were out as far as you can make your voice heard, I yelled out to the Kyklops with contemptuous taunts.

"'Kyklops! He was not at all helpless—that man whose shipmates you were going to eat so viciously, there in your empty cave! Your awful acts were sure to come right back on you, you brute! Since you would not hold back from eating your own guests, here in your own home! And so, for this, Zeus and the other gods have taken their revenge on you!'

"As I spoke, he became even more enraged in his heart. He ripped off the top of a huge crag and threw it down, just a little in front of the dark prow of our ship. It just missed the tip of the steering oar. And the sea surged under the rock as it came down, and the swell, like a tidal wave, seized the ship in a backward flow and swept it back onto the shore. I grabbed a long pole in my hands and pushed us away and stirred up my mates, and with a nod of my head, I told them all to throw themselves into their oars so we might escape this horror. They leaned in and rowed. But when we had passed twice as far out at sea, I called out again to the Kyklops. My shipmates, one after another, tried to hold me back with pleading words.

"'You brute, why do you want to enrage this wild man? He just now threw a rock into the sea, and it drove our ship right back to shore, and we thought we were going to be destroyed there! If he'd heard us speaking or uttering a sound, he would have thrown a big jagged stone and smashed our ship's timbers, along with all our heads, he throws with such force!'

"They said all this, but they could not hold back my raging, reckless heart, and I called back at him.

"'Kyklops! If anyone of us mere mortals ever ask you about this rude blinding of that eye of yours, tell them that Odysseus, scourge of cities, the son of Laertes, who makes his home in Ithaka—*he* blinded you!'

"After I spoke, he let out a groan and answered me.

"'Appalling! That old prophecy, told so long ago, has caught up with me. There used to be a seer who lived here, a good, tall man—Telemos Eurymides. He was the best at prophesizing, and he prophesized, and he grew old among us Kyklops. He then told me everything that was to be in the time to come—that I would lose my eyesight because of Odysseus, but I was always looking out for a tall, good-looking man who'd come here, dressed up in the greatness of strength. But now, some little, no-good weakling here has blinded my eye, after weakening me with wine. But come on back, Odysseus, so I can now give you everything a guest deserves. Maybe I'll coax that famous Earth Shaker to give you an escort, since I'm his son, and he claims to be my father. He'll heal me, if he wants to, and no one else, not one of the carefree gods and not some damned human.'

"After he spoke, I called out and answered, 'If only I could rid you of your life and soul and send you down to the house of Hades, since not even the Earth Shaker will heal your eye.'

"After I spoke, he then prayed to Lord Poseidon, stretching his arms up to a sky full of stars.

"'Listen, dark-haired Poseidon, you who hold the earth in your hands, if I am in fact your son, and you claim to be my father, grant me that Odysseus, the scourge of cities, son of Laertes, who makes his home in Ithaka, never reaches home. But if it's his lot to see his people and his nicely built home and his own native land, make him come home delayed and in deep trouble, after losing all his companions—on someone else's ship. And may he find misery in his own house.'

"As he prayed, the dark-haired god heard him, and the Kyklops lifted up an even larger stone and twisting around to gather his great strength, he threw it a little behind the dark stern of our ship. It just missed reaching the tip of the steering oar. The sea surged up under the rock as it came down, and the wave carried the ship further forward, over to the other shore. And when we reached the other island, all of the other ships with their many benches remained together, with our shipmates all around, sitting and waiting for us in sorrow. When we arrived, we beached the ship on the sands and we jumped out onto the shore.

"We unloaded the Kyklops's flocks from the hollow ship and divided them up, so no one might be denied by me his equal share. Yet in allotting the sheep, my well-stocked crew gave the ram especially to me. I burned its thighs and offered it up in sacrifice to Zeus, the Son of Kronos, the Dark Cloud who rules over us all. But he did not acknowledge my sacrifice. By then, he was already pondering how my well-benched ships and all my loyal shipmates were going to be lost. Through that whole day, until sunset, we sat and feasted on massive amounts of meat and sweet wine. When the sun set and darkness came on, at last we lay down to sleep, there on the shore by the sea.

"And very early, as Dawn spread out her rosy fingers, I woke up my mates and ordered them to get on board and release the stern cables. They went aboard at once and settled at their benches, and sitting there in order, they struck the gray sea with their oars. From there, we sailed on, with anguish in our hearts—glad we had escaped from death, but we had lost some precious friends.'

X

Kirke

"We came to Aiolia, the floating island where Aiolos Hippotades, dear to the immortal gods, lived. The cliffs rise up sheer, and all around them is an indestructible bronze wall. Twelve children had been born in his household, six daughters and six sons in their prime of life. Aiolos presented his daughters to his sons in marriage, and now they all feast perpetually with their dear father and caring mother, and delicacies without limit always lie before them. The house is redolent with savory aromas, and the whole courtyard echoes throughout the day. At night, they all go to sleep beside their esteemed wives on corded bed frames with many blankets.

"We came to their city and their lovely palace. For a month he hosted me and questioned me about everything—about Ilios and the Argives' ships, and the Akhaians' return. I laid out the whole thing for him, as was his due. When I asked him to let me go and to send me on my way, he denied me nothing. He organized my passage and offered me a hide that he had flayed from a nine-year-old ox. He tied up the streams of howling wind inside, because Kronos's son had made him keeper of the winds, both to calm them and arouse them, whichever he wished. He tied it all down inside my hollow ship with a bright silver cord, so not even a little would leak out. And he sent a breath of the west wind to blow for me, to carry our ships across, and us as well. But he could not bring this about. We were lost, because of our own thoughtlessness.

"For nine days and nights we sailed and at last, on the tenth, our own land appeared. We were so close, we saw people tending their fires. And just then, worn out from being perpetually on my feet, handling the ship, never giving it over to any of my crew so we might reach our own land as soon as possible, sweet sleep came over me. My mates began talking to each other. They said I was bringing home gold and silver for myself—gifts from Aiolos, the great-hearted son of Hippotas. And one would say, glancing at the man next to him, 'Appalling! That man is so welcome and honored among whatever people whose land and city he comes to. He's bringing back so much lovely treasure from the looting at Troy, while we, who've all carried out the same journey, are coming home empty-handed. And now, Aiolos has given him these gifts so freely, out of friendship. So come on, quickly, let's find out what's here—how much gold and silver's in this skin.'

"As they spoke, the terrible advice of these shipmates won everyone over. They opened up the bag and all the winds came rushing out. The high winds snatched us up at once and carried us out to sea, away from our native land. It was only then that I awoke and brooded over everything in my heart, whether to leap from the ship and be lost under the sea, or to endure in silence and remain among the living. I endured. I remained. I covered myself over and lay down in the boat. And our ships were carried by a horrible stormy wind back to the island of Aiolos.

"My shipmates groaned. We went ashore there and drew on water, and my shipmates took their meal next to our swift ships. But when we had tasted food and drink, I brought one messenger and one shipmate with me to Aiolos' illustrious home. I found him feasting with his wife and children. We approached and sat down on the threshold by the door posts. They were all astounded in their hearts and questioned us.

"'Odysseus, how did you get here? What cruel god has assaulted you? We sent you away in good faith, to reach your own land, or wherever you wished to go.'

"After they spoke, I said to them with anguish in my heart, 'My careless shipmates and cruel sleep have ruined me. But restore us, friends, since it is within your power.'

"But as I spoke, addressing them with modest words, they remained silent. At last, the father answered me.

"'Leave this island right away! You are the most disgraceful of all living beings. It would not be fitting for me to offer help or send on his way a man who is so abhorred by the blissful gods. Leave now—since you have made your way back here as someone who is abhorred by the gods.'

"After he said this, he sent me, groaning deeply, away from his home. From there, we sailed on, our hearts in anguish. My men's spirits were worn down by hard rowing and all our wasted work, because there was no longer a fair wind escorting us. We sailed for six days and nights and on the seventh day, we came to the towering stronghold of Lamos and then on to the Laistrygonian land of Telephos, where one shepherd calls to another as he drives in his herd, and the other one answers as he drives his flock out. There a man who goes without sleep could earn double wages by herding cattle and taking white sheep to pasture, because the roads of night and day run close together.

"When we had come there to that fine harbor, there were towering cliffs looming along both sides, and protruding points jutting out, opposite each other at the mouth. The entrance is very narrow. There, all our rounded ships put in and anchored close together in that empty harbor. Inside it, the waves never swelled, large or small, and there was a gentle calm all around. I alone moored my black ship outside the harbor, at land's end, and I tied the stern cables to the rocks. I climbed up to a rugged lookout point and stood. From there, no sign of cattle or human activity was evident. We only saw smoke, rising from the earth.

"I sent out some of my mates to go out and learn who these people might be among those who eat bread, here on this earth. I chose two men and sent a third as messenger. They went off along a smooth road by which wagons brought wood down from the high mountains to the city. Near the city, they met a girl drawing water, the sturdy daughter of Antiphates the Laistrygonian. She had come down to the beautiful, flowing stream, Artakia, from which they carried water back to town. They drew near and spoke to her. They asked her who was the king of this land and over whom he ruled.

"Right away, she showed them to her father's high-roofed house. When they entered that magnificent house, they found his wife—as massive as a mountain peak. They shuddered with disgust at her. All at once, she called in her husband, the famous Antiphates, from the agora. He plotted a bitter death for them. He seized one of my mates immediately and began to prepare a feast. But the other two jumped up and came back in flight to the ships.

"Antiphates raised an outcry throughout the city and when they heard about it, the hardy Laistrygonians came together from everywhere—thousands—more like giants than men. From the cliffs, they threw down huge boulders, as heavy as any man could lift, and an awful uproar rose from our dying men and the shattering ships. They speared my men like fish and carried them back home for a gruesome meal. While they were killing those within the deep harbor, I drew my sharp sword from my thigh and cut the cables of my ship's dark stern. I stirred up my shipmates and told them to throw themselves into their oars so that we might escape from this danger, and they churned the sea in fear of death. Gratefully, my ship escaped the overhanging cliffs, but the others perished all together in that place.

"From there, we sailed on, our hearts in anguish. We were relieved to be free of death, but had lost our valued companions. And so we came to the island of Aiaia. There lived Kirke, with her lovely flowing hair and human voice, but no less a goddess, much to be feared. She was the sister of Aeetes, with her malicious heart, and both were the offspring of Helios, the Sun, who gives light to mortals, and Perse, their mother, a child of the Ocean. There, we brought our ship in toward the shore, within a harbor deep enough to hold a ship, and some god must have guided us in. We jumped out, and we lay about there for two days and nights, with weariness and sorrow eating at our hearts.

"But as Dawn with her lovely hair brought the third day into its fullness, I grabbed my spear and sharp sword and quickly went away from the ship to a viewpoint so I might observe the activities of men and hear their chatter. I climbed to a rugged lookout point and stood there. I saw rising from the earth and its broad stretch of roads the smoke from Kirke's lodging, which was in among the timberlands and thick brush. Once I had seen the fire and smoke, I mulled it over within my mind and heart, whether I should go and find out about it. And as I thought about it, this appeared to be the better approach—to go first to the ship on the seashore and offer my shipmates their meal, then send them back out to investigate.

"But just as I was getting close to the rounded ship, some god took pity on my isolation and sent a large stag with towering antlers straight into my path. It was heading down from its pasture in the woods toward the river to drink, since the power of the sun had seized it. As it came out, I struck it in the spine at mid-back, and my bronze spear passed right through. Crying out, it fell in the dust, and its spirit flew away. I placed my foot on it and drew my bronze-tipped spear out of the wound.

"I left it there, lying on the ground. I pulled out some twigs and vines, at least a fathom long, and I twisted them around each other to plait them into a rope. I tied that massive creature's legs all together, and slinging it across my back and leaning on my spear, I headed back to the black ship. There was no way I could hold him on my shoulder with just one hand, since he was such a large beast. I threw it down before the ship and standing before each man, I encouraged my mates with gentle words.

"'Friends, no matter how deeply troubled we are, we won't go down to the house of Hades yet, not before our day of destiny comes upon us. But come now, while there's still some food and drink on our fast ship, let's turn our thoughts to eating and not let ourselves waste away with hunger.'

"I said this, and they at once listened to my words. Uncovering their heads, there beside the shore of the restless sea, they stared in wonder at the stag, it was such a large animal. But when they had satisfied their eyes with looking it over, they washed their hands and prepared a marvelous feast. So all day long until the sun was setting, we sat there and feasted on massive amounts of meat and sweet wine. But then, as the sun set and darkness came on, we lay down to sleep, there on the seashore. And very early, as Dawn spread out her rosy fingers, I called them to gather all together, and I spoke to all of them.

"'Listen to what I have to say, my friends, you who've suffered so much. We don't know where darkness is or where the sun goes under the earth, or where it rises, to shed light on all of us who have to die. But let's quickly consider whether there's some strategy open to us. I don't think there is, because I've climbed up to a rocky lookout point and looked out over the island. The endless ocean stretches all around it like a crown. The island lies low and halfway across, my eyes saw smoke rising from the woods and thick underbrush.'

"As I was speaking, their hearts were breaking inside them, because they remembered the actions of Antiphates, the Laistrygonian, and the brutality of the Kyklops, whose heart was large and yet he ate human beings. They cried aloud, the hard tears welling and streaming down. But their weeping was futile. I counted off my well-equipped shipmates into two groups, and I chose a leader for each one. I led one, and the extraordinary Eurylokhos the other. We quickly shook lots in a bronze helmet, and the lot of great-hearted Eurylokhos jumped out. And so he went away with twenty-two weeping shipmates and left us there in sorrow.

"In a glen, they came upon Kirke's house, built with well-polished stone, in a spot where one could see all around. Lying about were wolves and mountain lions that Kirke had dulled by giving them strong drugs. They did not rush at my men. Instead, they stood and moved about meekly, wagging their long tails. As dogs wag their tails about their master when he comes out after a meal, because he has always offered them sweet morsels to delight their hearts, those wolves and lions, with their sharp claws, wagged their tails about, but the men were afraid when they caught sight of these terrifying beasts. And so they stood there at the gates of that goddess with the lovely hair, and they heard Kirke singing with a sweet voice as she went about, back and forth, before a weaving of unearthly size, as intricate and delightfully delicate as the work of goddesses is.

"Polites, a leader among men, the dearest and most trustworthy of my shipmates, said to the others, 'Friends, inside there's someone going back and forth in front of a large loom and singing sweetly, some goddess or a woman, so the whole floor keeps echoing. Let's call out to her right now.'

"After he spoke, they shouted and called out to her. She came and opened the brilliant doors, and she called them in. In their innocence, they followed her inside. Only Eurylokhos stayed behind, because he thought it was a trap. She led the others inside and prepared a stew made of cheese, barley, yellow honey, and Pramnian wine. But in this dish she mixed some noxious drug to make them utterly forget their native land. And after she had offered it to them and they had drunk it down, she touched them with her wand and shut them into her pigsties.

"They had the heads, the utterance, bristles, and bodies of pigs, but their minds were the same as they had been before. And so, penned in, they squealed, as Kirke tossed out in front of them some mush, acorns, bark, and rotten fruit for them all to eat, such stuff as wallowing pigs always feed on. Eurylokhos at once came back to the swift black ship to tell us the news of his mates and their rude fate. He could not get out a word, no matter how much he wanted to, his heart was wracked with such utter torment. His eyes were filled with tears, his heart with anguish. But as we questioned him in our wonder, he finally described the loss of the other shipmates.

"'As you had told us to, esteemed Odysseus, we went into the brush, and in a glade, we found a beautiful palace made of polished stone in a place where you can see all around. There, someone was going back and forth in front of a huge loom, singing clearly, some goddess or a woman, and they shouted and called to her. At once she came out and opened the bright doors and called them in. And in their innocence, they all followed her in, but I stayed behind, thinking it was a trap. Then, they just disappeared, all together. Not a single one of them ever appeared again, although I sat there and watched for a long time.'

"As he spoke, I slung my long bronze sword, studded with silver, over my shoulder, and arranged my bow around me. I urged him to lead the way back at once, but he grabbed me with both hands and at my knees, he begged and sobbed, his words trembling like wings.

"'Don't lead me there against my will—you yourself are favored by Zeus, but leave me here. Because I know that you will neither come back yourself, nor will you bring back any of your mates. Let's get away quickly with those of us who are here, so that we might yet escape this horrible day.'

"After he spoke, I answered him and said, 'Eurylokhos, of course, stay here, eating and sleeping here in this place, beside our empty black ship. But I'm going. A powerful urge compels me.'

"After saying this, I climbed away from the sea and our ship. But as I entered the sacred glade and was approaching at the enormous home of Kirke, who herself possessed so many charms, Hermes with his golden wand came upon me. Looking like a young man of that most captivating age, with the very first hint of a beard, he took me by the hand and called to me.

"'Where are you going now through these hills, alone again, you unlucky man, without knowing anything about this place? Your shipmates are being kept like pigs in cramped pigsties. Are you coming here to release them? I'm telling you, you will not return but will remain there yourself, like the others. But come on, I'll keep you safe from harm. Take this powerful antidote and go on to Kirke's house. It will keep your head from having an awful day. And I'll tell you all about Kirke's deadly arts.

"'She will make you a mixed drink and throw some drugs into the food. But she will not be able to cast a spell on you, because this powerful antidote I'm giving you will not allow it. And I'll tell you everything. When Kirke strikes you with her long wand, draw your sharp sword from beside your thigh. Leap at her as if you're planning to kill her. She'll be overcome with fear and she'll ask you to go to bed with her. There and then, do not turn down the goddess' bed, so that she will release your mates and offer you hospitality. But first of all, order her to swear, before the carefree gods, a solemn oath that she will not contrive any other troubles for you, so that when she strips you down, she will not strip away your honor and your manhood also.'

"As he spoke, Argeïphontes pulled up a plant from the ground. He gave it to me, and he showed me its properties. It was black at the roots, and yet its blossom was like milk. The gods call it Moly. It is hard for mortal men to dig it up, but the gods are able to do anything. Hermes then went away through the island's forests and off to the heights of Olympos. But I proceeded to Kirke's house, and my heart brooded darkly over many things. I stood there, in front of the gates of that goddess with the beautiful hair. I stood there and shouted, and the goddess heard my voice.

"Right away she opened the bright doors, and she came out and called to me. I followed her inside, my heart aching. She led me to a silver-studded chair. It was beautifully crafted, with a stool for the feet below. She prepared the mixture in a golden cup so that I would drink it, after she had poured in the drug with foul intent in her heart. But when she had given it to me and I drank it down and was not spellbound, she struck me with her wand, and then she called to me and uttered these words.

"'Get off to your sty now and lie there with the others.'

"I drew out my sharp sword from along my thigh and rushed at Kirke, as if planning to kill her. She screamed loudly and ducked, grabbing my knees, and wailed, her words trembling like wings.

"'Who are you among men? Where are you from? Where are your city and your parents? I'm shocked you drank this drug and were not at all charmed! No other man has ever withstood this drug, once he's taken it and it has passed the barrier of his teeth. The resolve you carry in your chest is not vulnerable to charm. You must be Odysseus, always shifting, drifting. Hermes Argeïphontes, with his golden wand, told me that you would come here, heading home from Troy on your swift black ship. But come now, put that sword of yours back inside its sheath and let us both climb into bed, so we can come to trust each other, lolling about and making love.'

"After she spoke, I answered her back and said, 'Kirke, how can you ask me to be gentle to you? You've turned my shipmates into pigs here in your own halls, and now you're holding me here and are asking me with treacherous intent to go to your room and climb into bed with you, so you can strip me of my honor and my manhood. But I would never want to climb into your bed unless you are willing to swear a solemn oath that you will plan no further harm against me.'

"After I spoke, she at once swore she would not, as I had ordered. But when she had sworn her oath completely to its end, I went up to her exquisite bed. And her servants busied themselves inside her halls—four of them who did the domestic work and who had emerged out of the streams and groves, and from the sacred rivers that flowed down to the sea. One of them threw some beautiful purple rugs onto the chairs, after spreading linen underneath. Another drew tables in front of the chairs and set golden baskets on them. The third mixed sweet wine, like honey to the heart, in a silver bowl, and set out golden cups. The fourth brought water and kindled a big fire under a huge pot, and the water warmed.

"And when it had boiled inside the gleaming bronze, she set me in a tub and tempered it to my heart's desire. She poured water from a huge cauldron over my head and shoulders, until she had taken the heart-numbing weariness away from my limbs. After she had washed me and anointed me with luxurious oils, and had thrown a fine cloak and tunic around me, she brought me into the hall, and led me to sit in a silver-lined chair, beautifully crafted, with a stool for the feet below.

"One of them brought water for my hands in a lovely gold pitcher and poured it over a silver basin for me to wash. She drew a polished table close to me. The esteemed housekeeper brought in some bread and set it down before me, along with plenty of meat, offering generously from what there was at hand. She urged me to eat, but I was aggravated in my heart. I sat there, thinking of other things, my heart suspecting the worst. And Kirke noticed I was sitting in this way—I did not reach my hands out to the food, and I was overcome with extreme sorrow. She stood close to me, and her words came whispering like wings.

"'Odysseus, why are you sitting here this way, like someone who's unable to speak, like something's eating away at your heart, so that you're not touching either food or drink? Do you suspect some other trick? You need not fear. I have already sworn a solemn oath.'

"After she had spoken, I answered her and said, 'Kirke, what man who knows what's right and good would allow himself to taste his food and drink before his friends were released, and he had seen them with his own eyes? If you are saying what you mean when you ask me to drink and eat, then release them, so that I can see my worthy mates with my own eyes.'

"After I spoke, Kirke went out through the hall with her wand in her hand. She opened up the gates of the pigsty and she drove them all out, looking like nine-year-old pigs. They stood in front of her, and she went among them and rubbed another drug on each one. The bristles that the horrible drug had made them grow when Kirke had given it to them before now fell away, and they became men once again—even younger, taller and more handsome to look at than before. They recognized me, and they all grasped my hands, each one of them, and an intense sobbing came over all of them. It echoed inharmoniously around the house, and the goddess herself was moved to compassion. The radiant goddess stood close to me and spoke.

"'Odysseus, son of Laertes, always thinking ahead, go now to the seashore and your swift ship, and first of all, haul it all the way up onto the shore.

Store all your provisions and tackle in the caves. Then come back with your loyal mates.'

"As she spoke, my brash heart was persuaded. I made my way down to the seashore and my ship. There, I found my earnest mates beside the fast ship, weeping bitterly, their hard tears welling and streaming down. Like calves in the barnyard who are free of their pens and frolick about a herd of cattle as it returns to the farm yard after getting its fill of grazing, and they low constantly as they romp about their mothers—that's how those men, when they saw me with their own eyes, gathered around me, shedding their tears. It seemed as though within their hearts they had made it back to their own land and their own city in rugged Ithaka where they'd been born and raised, and weeping, they cried out loud, their words trembling like wings.

"'Your return, descendant of Zeus, lightens our hearts—it's as if we've already reached our native land. But come, tell us about the death of the others, our shipmates.'

"After they spoke, I answered them with gentle words.

"'First, let's haul the ship all the way up on land and store our provisions and gear inside those caves. Then all of you rouse yourselves to come with me and see your mates drinking and eating in Kirke's towering halls, since they have endless quantities.'

"As I spoke, they quickly responded to my words. Eurylokhos alone tried to hold back all of my crew. He spoke out, his words trembling like wings.

"'Fools, why are we going there? Why are you so taken with these awful things—to go down into the halls of Kirke, who will turn us all into pigs or wolves or lions, to guard her great palace against our will? The same way the Kyklops did, when Odysseus spoke so boldly, and our shipmates went inside his cave—it was because of this man's recklessness that they died!'

"As he spoke, I pondered in my heart whether to draw out my thick, sharp sword from beside my thigh and cut off his head and let it fall to the ground, although he was my kin by marriage, but my mates, one after another, spoke to me with convincing words.

"'Child of Zeus, if you say so, let him remain here to guard the ship, but lead us on to Kirke's sacred house.'

"Having said this, they went up from the ship and the sea, but Eurylokhos was not left beside our empty ship. He went with us, because he feared my harsh rebuke. Within her halls, Kirke had bathed my other shipmates, anointed them with luxuriant oils, and threw woolen cloaks and tunics around them. We found them feasting well in those halls. And when they all saw each other, they broke down crying, calling out to each other as they sat down. The house rumbled all around us, and that radiant goddess drew close to me and spoke.

"'Child of Zeus, Odysseus Laertiádes, always thinking ahead, don't raise this outcry any longer. I know the troubles you've suffered out at sea, filled with fish, and all the harm violent men have done to you on land. But come, eat this food and drink this wine until you bring the spirit back into your hearts again, as it was back when you first left your home, rugged Ithaka, long ago. Now you're worn out, with no heart, always thinking about your arduous wanderings, your hearts without joy, because you've suffered so much.'

"As she spoke, our brash hearts agreed. And so we sat there, feasting on massive amounts of meat and sweet wine, day after day, fulfilling one whole turn of the seasons. But as the year went on, and the seasons rolled around, the months waning, and the long days turning about, at last my trusty shipmates called me out and said, 'You are possessed by some god! But now, at last, remember your own country, if it's your fate to be saved and to reach your home with its towering roofs—your own land!'

"As they spoke, my heart, though stubborn, agreed. So all day long until sunset, we sat there, feasting on massive amounts of meat and sweet wine, and when the sun set and darkness came on, they lay down to sleep in the shadows of the hall. But I went up to Kirke's lovely bed and I prayed at her knees, and the goddess heard my voice as I spoke to her, my words lifting like wings.

"'Kirke, fulfill the promise you gave me—to send me home. My own heart is eager to go, as are those of my shipmates, who are wearing out my heart as they sit about, mourning, when you're not there.'

"When I spoke, the goddess answered me at once.

"'Descendant of Zeus, Odysseus Laertiádes, always anticipating, don't stay in my house any longer, if you're not willing. But first you'll have to complete another journey, all the way to the house of Hades and formidable Persephone. There you are to consult the spirit of that blind mystic, whose mind continues to be unimpaired, Teiresias the Theban. To him Persephone has given presence of mind, even in death, while all the rest are nothing but mere shadows of themselves, flitting all about.'

"As she spoke, my heart broke down inside me. I sat on the bed and wept. My heart no longer wanted to live and see the sunlight. But after I had had my fill of twisting, turning, and crying, I answered her and spoke these words.

"'Kirke, who will guide me on this journey? No one has ever gone to Hades in a black ship.'

"After I spoke, the brilliant goddess answered.

"'Descendant of Zeus, Odysseus Laertiádes, always anticipating, don't worry yourself about how your ship will be guided. Set your mast and spread your white sails, and then sit back. A breath from the North Wind will carry your ship on. But when at last you've crossed over the ocean, there's a jut of shore overgrown with brush and the groves of Persephone, with tall poplars and willows shedding their fruit. Beach your ship there beside the deeply churning waters of the ocean and go by yourself to Hades' steamy domicile. There, two rivers, the Burning and the Agony, flow into the Sorrow, a tributary flowing from the waters of the River Styx. And where those two roaring rivers merge, there is a rock.

"'There and then—be brave—draw in close, just as I am telling you, and dig a hole as long as your forearm, and pour all around it an offering to all the dead—first, with honey, and then, sweet wine, and third, some water. And last, scatter some white barley meal over it all. Then make a vow to those shadows' powerless heads that once you reach Ithaka, you will sacrifice an ox that's not yet calved, the best you have, and fill the sacrificial pyre with valuable things, and to Teiresias himself, sacrifice a sheep, all black, the very finest of all your flocks.

"'But when you have offered up your prayers to all the honored nations of the dead, then sacrifice a ram and a black ewe, twisting them around to face Erebos, while you are turning to look over at the flowing river. Then, the souls of many of those who have died will come forward. Right then, call up your crew and order them to flay and burn all the sheep lying there, killed by your pitiless bronze, and pray to the gods, to almighty Hades and to formidable Persephone. Draw your sword from beside your thigh and sit down there, but do not allow any of those powerless heads of the dead to come near that blood until you have asked all your questions of Teiresias. The seer, that leader of the people, will then and there approach you, and he will tell you all about the course and scale of your return journey—how to make your way across the sea, with all its fish.'

"As she spoke, Dawn arrived on her golden throne. The nymph threw a tunic and a cloak and some other clothing to wear around me, and she herself put on a long, shimmering robe, very lovely and fine, and threw around her waist a beautiful golden belt, and placed a veil over her head. I went through her halls, and I came up close to each one of my mates, and I roused them with calming words.

"'No more sleeping and lolling about in the fleece of sweet sleep! Let's go! I have Kirke's word.'

"As I spoke, their hearts, always proud, agreed. But I was not able to lead my men away unharmed, not even from there. There was one of them, Elpenor, the youngest of us all. He was not especially brave in battle or particularly steady in his mind. And weighed down with wine, he went looking for a cool breeze, and he lay down, apart from his mates, there on top of Kirke's towering house. But he heard the noise and uproar of his mates moving about, and he jumped up suddenly and his mind forgot to go over to the long ladder to come down. He fell from the roof. His neck broke away from his spine, and his soul went down to Hades.

And now, as the others moved about, I spoke these words.

"'So you think you are going to your beloved home, your native land. But Kirke has laid down another course for us—to the domain of Hades and the formidable Persephone, to consult the soul of Teiresias the Theban.'

"As I spoke, their hearts broke. They sat down right there and started to weep and tear at their hair. But all their crying was of no use—for while we were making our way to the shore of the sea and our sleek ship, in anguish, our tears welling and streaming down, Kirke had gone to tie down a ram and a black ewe alongside our black ship. She slipped past us very easily—for whose eyes can see a goddess moving here or there without her willingness?"

XI

Shadows

"Then we went down to the sea and our ship. First, we dragged the boat into the gleaming surf, and we hoisted the mast and sail above the black ship. Then we loaded the sheep and went on board ourselves, deep in anguish, our tears welling and streaming down. And Kirke, with her lovely hair and human voice, no less a goddess, much to be feared, sent behind the dark stained prow of our ship a favorable wind, swelling the sail—a good friend to have.

"After stashing all our gear away, we sat down, and the wind and our helmsman kept us right on course. All day long, the sail stretched full as we crossed the sea. The sun set, darkening every course, as our ship reached the edge of the ocean's unfathomable stream. There, the land and the city of the Kimmerians is always cloaked in fog and clouds. The sun never sheds its light on them, neither when it climbs up into a sky filled with stars, nor when it returns to earth. Only monotonous night shrouds those miserable people.

"Arriving there, we beached the ship. We unloaded the sheep and headed up river from the sea to the place that Kirke had told us about. There, Perimedes and Eurylokhos held down the animals for sacrifice. I drew my sharpened sword from my hip and dug a hole, as long as my forearm on each side, and all around it, I poured out an offering to all the dead, first of all with milk and honey, then with sweet wine, and third with water, and on top of that I spread white barley. For a long time, then, I implored the hopeless dead—that whenever I reached Ithaka, I would kill a cow, my best one, and heap up precious goods on a fire within the halls of my own palace. And besides that, for Teiresias himself I would kill a ram, a black one, the very best of all my sheep. But after I had made all of my pleas, with promises and prayers to the nations of the dead, I held the sheep down, and I cut their throats.

"The dark blood flowed. And all the souls of the dead began to gather together from Erebos. New brides, unmarried youths, and old men, torn apart by so many troubles, young virgins, still fresh to sorrow, and so many of those who were wounded by bronze spear points, and men killed in battle, still wearing their blood-stained armor. From all sides, this huge horde swarmed all around the pit with an ungodly roar, and ashen fear took hold of me. But I aroused my companions and gave them orders to cut up and burn the sheep that were now lying there, killed by cold bronze, and to appeal to the gods, to all-powerful Hades and chilling Persephone.

"And I myself drew out my sword from my hip, and I sat down there, not allowing the heads of those dead souls to push closer and draw near, until I had heard from Teiresias what I had to know. But first, the spirit of my comrade stepped forward—Elpenor—because he was yet to be buried, down here, below the wide sweep of the earth's surface. We had left his dead body behind in Kirke's palace—unmourned and unburied, because this other undertaking was now spurring us on.

"Seeing him, I cried. I felt a deep sorrow in my heart for him. But then I found my voice and my words trembled like wings.

"'Elpenor, how did *you* get here below in this shadowy darkness—you were on foot, and yet, here you are ahead of me, and I came here in my black ship!'

"As I spoke, he cried out and answered in these words.

"'Son of Laertes, favored by Zeus, shrewd Odysseus, a horrible misfortune sent by some god has been my downfall—that and an awful lot of wine. When I lay down to get some sleep at Kirke's place, I didn't think to take the long ladder to go down, and I fell, head over heels, down from the roof. The bones in my neck broke apart, and my soul came down here to Hades. Now—I'm begging you—for all of those we left behind and are not here—for your wife and your father who cared for you when you were a little boy, and Telemakhos, whom you left at home, your only child—because I know when you go away from this house of Hades, you and your sturdy ship will come to that island.

"'There and then—I beg you, my lord—remember me. Don't go away and leave me behind, unburied or unmourned. Don't turn your back on me in disgust, or I might become the impetus for the gods' anger against you. Instead, burn me with all my armor on, and all that is mine, and then pile up a marker for me somewhere along the shore of the gray sea—*To a man of no fortune*—so that those who are yet to be may know of me. Do all this for me and then jab into the stone cairn the oar I rowed with, while I was still alive with all my shipmates.'

"After he had spoken, I offered him my answer.

"'For you, my unlucky friend, I'll carry it all out to the very end and get the whole thing done.'

"Both of us sat there and we exchanged raw words with each other, I on one side holding my sword over the blood, and on the other, the unreal image of my fellow soldier. We went on talking there and remembering. Then the soul of my dead mother came forward—the daughter of the great

Autolykos—Antikleia—I had left her alive when I went to Ilios. I saw her, and I broke down. I cried, and I felt sorry for her, but I would not let her get near the blood, though overcome with sorrow, before I had been heard by Teiresias. And it came, the soul of Teiresias the Theban, holding his golden staff. He recognized me and spoke.

"'Son of Laertes, favored by the gods, shrewd Odysseus. What is this? You unlucky man—why have you come away from the sunlight to see the dead, here in such a joyless place? Step back from the pit and keep your sword down, so that I can drink this blood and speak openly.'

"That's what he said, and I gave way, and I thrust my silver studded sword back into its sheath. And when he had drunk the dark blood, and only then, the keen visionary spoke these words to me.

"'You are about to ask me of your honey-sweet return, illustrious Odysseus, but a god is going to make it hard to bring about, since I do not think you will elude the Earthshaker, who still harbors outrage in his heart for you. He is fuming, ever since you blinded his son. But even so, you may get there, though only aftergoing through some hard times, and only if you can rein in your own heart, and those of your companions. When you first draw your sturdy ship in, close to the island of Thrinacia, after escaping the turbulent seas, you will find the cattle and plump sheep that belong to the Sun, who looks down upon everything and listens to everything. If you leave them unharmed and if you keep your mind on our return home, you may well get back to Ithaka, though only after going through some hard times.

"'But if you harm them, then I foresee total destruction of your ship and crew. And even if you yourself escape, you will get home with difficulty, and only after a long stretch of time, after losing all of your companions, and in someone else's ship. And you'll find many troubles in your own household—arrogant men who are using up your resources, courting your wife and offering her wedding gifts. But when you get there, you will exact your revenge against their violations.

"'And when you have killed the suitors with sharp bronze, there in your house, whether by deception or out in the open, then it will be time for you to take up an oar, finely crafted, and go away, until you come to a people who have no knowledge of the sea, who do not eat their food seasoned with salt, and don't know anything about ships with red prows or finely crafted oars that are like wings for ships.

"'And here is an unmistakable sign—you can't miss it. When some other traveler that you happen to meet says it's odd to see you carrying a winnowing shovel upon your broad shoulder, then sink that straight oar into the earth, and make your generous offerings to Lord Poseidon—a ram, a bull, and a lusty boar—then head back home to offer more sacred offerings of a hundred oxen to the gods, one after another, to all of them who make their home up there in the boundless sky and who never die. And Death will come to you, worn out with age, gently, imperceptibly, out of the sea, and the people around you will live on, in good fortune. I'm telling you truly what is to be.'

"That is what he said, and I answered back and said, 'Teiresias, the gods themselves have spun the thread of all this. But come, tell me this, and tell me frankly. I see the soul of my dead mother. She sits in silence, close to the blood, but she does not have the heart to look at her son, face to face, or to talk with me. Tell me, sir, how can she get to know her son again?'

"After I spoke, he answered back at once and said,

"'Easy, these words I am going to tell you—place them within your heart. Of all these shadows—these dead—whoever you allow to come closer to the blood, they will talk to you truthfully, and whoever you turn away, they will go back where they came from.'

"After he had spoken and laid out everything that he was given to say, the soul of Lord Teiresias turned back into the house of Hades. But I held my ground, until my mother came and drank the black blood. At once she recognized me, and she cried out loud and spoke these words, quavering like wings.

"'My boy, how did you get here, under the shadows and darkness, and still alive! It's hard for the living to see all this. Between us, there are mighty rivers and dangerous waters—first of all, there's the ocean. There is no way anyone can cross it on foot, but only with a sturdy ship. So now you have come—all the way from Troy, after wandering around for such a long time in the ship with all your mates? You have not reached Ithaka yet? Or seen your wife at home?'

"That is what she said, and I offered her my answer.

"'Mother, mother, necessity has brought me down to Hades to get advice from the soul of Teiresias the Theban. I haven't come anywhere near the coast of Achaia, or set foot in my own land. I've been wandering in sorrow, endlessly, since the first day I went off with Agamemnon to Troy, the land of horses, to fight the Trojans.

"'But come, tell me this, and tell me frankly. What horrible death claimed you? Was it a long illness? Or did Artemis the archer attack and bring you down with her painless arrows? And tell me about my father and about the son I left behind. Does my reputation still hold with them, or does some other man have it now, and do they say that I will never return? And tell me about my wife—how is her thoughtfulness and her determination? Does she still care for her own son and watch over everything, or has someone else, the very best of the Achaians, already married her?'

"After I spoke, my dear mother answered at once.

"'Without a doubt, she has kept her uncomplaining heart there in your home—endlessly, her miserable nights and days waste away with her tears streaming down. No one yet holds your proper claim, since Telemakhos himself keeps your estate intact and takes a suitable part in every feast, much like a man who dispenses justice, since everyone wants his company.

"'But your father waits, out in the country, and does not come to town. He goes without bed and bedding, blankets, or colorful throws, but throughout the winter he goes to sleep in the house where the slaves sleep, there in the dirt and ashes, lying next to the fire, and he now wears rough clothing against his flesh. But when summer and the abundance of autumn arrive, then he beds down among scatterings of fallen leaves, anywhere along the sunny slope of his vineyard. There he lies about in anguish, harboring his great sorrow and longing for your return. And the weight of old age has come to him.

"'And I too have had to face my lot. I died. It was not the keen eyed archer who struck me down and killed me with her painless arrows, and no disease came over me, as happens so often, when an awful wasting away takes the spirit out of your limbs. No, it was my longing for you—and your guidance, my shining Odysseus, and for your gentle nature—that took away my own life, sweeter than honey.'

"She said all this, and I turned it over in my mind to take hold of my dead mother's soul. Three times my heart impelled me to hold her, and I moved forward. Three times she slipped from my arms like a shadow or a dream, and the pain became sharper in my heart. I found my voice and made these words take wing.

"'Mother, why won't you stay? I want to hug you, so that the two of us, here in the house of Hades, might throw our arms around each other with love and find solace in our coldest grief? Is this some hallucination that her grace Persephone has sent me, to make me cry out and groan even more?'

"After I spoke, my dear mother answered at once.

"'Ah, me, my boy, you're the most miserable of all men. Persephone, daughter of Zeus, is not deceiving you. This is the way it goes with us mortals, when we die. Our muscles no longer hold our flesh and bones together. The powerful heat of a roaring fire reduces them, and the soul flutters away and flies about like a dream. But hurry—get back to the light—and keep all these things in mind, so that you can tell them later to your wife.'

"And so we shared a few words, but then the women came. Gracious Persephone had sent them forward—all the wives and daughters of our best men. They came, gathering together in a swarm around the black blood, and I considered about how I might question each of them, and in my heart it seemed to me that the best strategy was this—I drew my long sword from my hip and did not let them drink the dark blood, all at the same time. And so they approached, one after the other, and each one confirmed who she was.

"I questioned them all. The first one I saw was the aristocrat, Tyro, who said she was the offspring of the impeccable Salmoneos, And she said that she was the wife of Kretheos, who was the son of Aeolos. She fell in love with the river, the divine Enipeos—by far the most beautiful of rivers that flow on earth. She liked to frequent the fair waters of Enipeos. But he who clutches the earth and makes it shudder assumed the other's form and lay with her at the mouth of the river. There, a wave loomed, dark as a mountain, and curled over them, hiding the god and the woman. He loosened her protective belt and shed sleep over her. And when the god had finished with the act of love, he took her hand and called her by name and spoke.

"'Take heart, woman, in our making love. In the turning of time, you will give birth to striking children, because to sleep with gods is never fruitless. Look after them. But right now, go home and hold your tongue. I am Poseidon, he who pounds the earth with his waves.'

"After he had spoken, he plunged into the surging sea. And she conceived and gave birth to Pelias and Neleos, and they both grew up to be powerful attendants for almighty Zeus. Pelias lived in airy Iolkos and was rich in sheep. The other lived in sandy Pylos. And Tyro herself, a queen among women, bore other children to Kretheos—Aeson, Pheres, and Amythaon—who fought on horseback.

"And then I saw Antiope, the daughter of Asopos, who claimed she had slept, wrapped in the arms of Zeus, and she gave birth to two sons, Amphion and Zethos, who founded the site of Thebes and built its wall with its seven gates, because they could not hold their own in an open place like Thebes without walls, no matter how strong they were. And then I saw Alemene, the wife of Amphitryon. She gave birth to Herakles, that force of nature, with the heart of a lion, after she grappled and tussled, wrapped in the arms of almighty Zeus. And Megara, the high and mighty daughter of Kreon, whom the son of Amphitryon, always so dogged in his passion, took for his wife.

"And I saw Oidipos's mother, beautiful Epicaste, who unknowingly carried out the appalling act of marrying her own son. And he, after killing his father, had married her. Right away, the gods made this known to everyone, and although Oidipos went on ruling over the Kadmeans in lovely Thebes, he suffered deeply from the harsh will of the gods. She herself went down to the house of Hades, the formidable keeper of souls, after she tied a noose to the high beam—she was so overcome by sorrow. But for him, she left a world of trouble, all those things that the Furies work to bring about to avenge a mother.

"And I saw the very beautiful Khloris. Long ago, Neleos married her for her beauty and brought her thousands of wedding gifts. She was the youngest daughter of Amphion, the son of Iasos, who ruled as lord over the Minyai during that time. She herself was the queen of Pylos and bore several striking children—Nestor, Khromios and Perklymenos, and Pero. She was a wonder to look at. Every man who lived anywhere nearby wanted to marry her, but

Neleos would not give her away, except to the man who would drive the great Iphicles' screw horned, stiff necked cattle that were so hard to manage, all the way from Phylake.

"The impeccable visionary himself swore that he would deliver this herd by himself. Just one catch, conferred by the gods, held him back—herdsmen and chains, hard to overcome. Yet when at last the days and months came to fruition and the seasons passed by, and the year rolled around, then the great Iphikles let him go—but only after he had spoken all his visions, fulfilling Zeus's will.

"And I saw Lede, Tydareos's wife. She bore him sons—Kastor, the tamer of horses, and the boxer, Polydeukes. The earth, the giver of life, holds them both, down below, and yet alive—honored by Zeus in the underworld. In turn, each one lives, every other day, and then is dead the next day. And they are admired in honor like the gods.

"After her I saw Iphimedeia, the wife of Aloēos, who claimed that she, too, had mingled with Poseidon. And she gave birth to two sons, both of whom lived only for a short time, Otos, who was like a god, and the legendary Ephialtes. The earth, our source of grain, engendered them to be the tallest and most handsome of anyone but Orion. By the time they were nine years of age, they were already nine cubits across the shoulders and nine fathoms tall, and they swore to wage a reckless war against the immortals. They planned to pile up both Mount Ossa and Mount Pelion, with its leaves trembling, on top of Mount Olympos, to climb up to the heavens, and they would have managed to carry it out, if only they had grown to full manhood, but Zeus's son by Leto, who had such lovely hair, killed both of them, before the fuzz below their temples sprouted and grew into full beards on their jaws.

"And I saw Phaidra, Prokris and the lovely Ariadne, the daughter of hateful Minos—the girl whom Theseus had planned to carry off to mighty Athens, but he had no joy with her. Before he had the chance, Artemis killed her on Dia Island, after Dionysus told her what had happened. And Maera and also Klymene, I saw them too, and Eriphyle, who was so evil, she traded away her man's life for just a speck of gold.

"But I cannot name or tell about them all—I saw so many—before night passed away. But now it's time to sleep—either when I have gone off to your fast ship and its crew, or right here. My departure is in your care, and in the gods."

After he had spoken, they were all speechless—charmed to silence in the shadows of the great hall. Arete, raising her white arms, was the first to speak.

"Phaiakians, how does this man here appear to you in bearing and distinction, and in his own inner spirit? He is, after all, my guest, although each of you shares this honor. So don't be in any hurry to send him off, nor curb your gifts to anyone who is so much in need, since so much wealth is lying inside your homes by the will of the gods."

The aged hero, Ekheneos, who was an elder spokesman among the Phaiakians, said to them, "Friends, our very thoughtful queen is by no means speaking off the mark from our own views. So listen, let's agree with her. Of course, the final word and judgment are in the hands of Alkinoos."

And Alkinoos answered him with these words.

"What she has said is what is to be, as surely as I am alive and rule the Phaiakians—we lovers of the oar. But let this stranger, anxious as he is to return, stay with us until tomorrow—that is, until I am able to finish collecting all of our gifts. Let his passage become everyone's concern, but mostly mine, since the power in this land is mine."

Then Odysseos, astute as always, answered him.

"Lord Alkinoos, eminent among all peoples, if you urge me to remain here, even for a year, and smooth my passage and give me wonderful gifts, I'd agree to that. Far better it would be for me to return to my own dear country with more in hand, since I'd receive much more respect and love from everyone who'd see me, upon my return to Ithaka."

Alkinoos lifted his voice and answered him again.

"Odysseus, when we look at you, there is no way that we think we are seeing a deceiver or a cheat, and there are so many men across this dark earth who shape artifice out of what no one can see. But there is a grace in your words and there is goodness in your heart, and you have strung out your yarn like a storyteller who knows what he is doing—a story of all the Argives' devastating troubles, and your own. But come now, tell me this, and lay it out exactly, if you saw any of your splendid comrades who went with you to Ilios and came to their end. The night is ever so long, and still unspoken for, And it is not yet time for sleep, not in this palace, so tell me more of these wonders. I could stay here until the light of dawn, if you could bring yourself to tell us, here in my palace, about your sufferings."

And so Odysseus, always thinking ahead, answered.

"Lord Alkinoos, eminent among all peoples, there's a time for many words, and there's a time for sleep, but if you are still so eager to listen, I will not hesitate to tell you all about some even more unfortunate sufferings that my fellow soldiers went through—all those who escaped the Trojans' gut wrenching battle cry, only to be killed when they returned, due to the schemes of a horrible woman.

"And so it was, when Persephone scattered apart that swarm of women's souls in every direction, Agamemnon Atreïdes came forward in anguish, and around him gathered all the others who had met their end and were killed along with him, there in Aigisthos's house. He knew me right away. And when he had drunk the dark blood, he cried out, his tears flowing, and anxiously he reached out to me with his hands, but he no longer had his old strength and steadiness. When I saw him, I burst into tears. I felt a deep sorrow inside my heart. But then, I found my voice and I said these words, trembling like wings, to him.

"'Most honored son of Atreus, Agamemnon, lord of men, what horrible death has brought you down? Did Poseidon strike you down while on your ships by stirring up a punishing blast of unfavorable wind? Or did violent enemies wound you on dry land, as you were surrounding their cattle and good flocks of sheep, or battling them to take their town or women.'

"I said this and right away he answered with these words.

"'Zeus's descendant, shrewd Odysseus Laertiádes, Poseidon did not bring me down while on my ship by stirring up a punishing blast of unfavorable wind, and violent men did not wound me on dry land. It was Aigisthos who arranged my end, and killed me with the aid of my abominable wife, after inviting me into his house for a feast, just as one butchers an ox in the barn. So I died a horrible death. And around me, all my fellow soldiers were deliberately murdered, like pigs butchered in the house of a wealthy man of great power, for a wedding feast, a formal banquet or an extravagant drinking bout. I know that you have witnessed the death of many men, killed in single combat or in battle formation.

"'But you yourself would have been deeply moved if you had seen us lying there in the hall, around the full tables and the mixing bowl for wine, and the floor ran with blood. But the saddest cry I heard came from Kassandra, Priam's daughter. The scheming Clytemnestra killed her, right next to me. I threw my hands up around the sword, then let them drop to the ground. Without a blush of shame—that bitch—she turned her back on me. And though I was already on my way down to the house of Hades, she did not even lower herself to close my eyelids with her hands or compose my mouth. There's nothing more horrible or lacking in shame than a woman who throws her heart into such acts. She herself conspired to execute this vicious act—to bring about her legitimate husband's death. I had thought that I would return home, welcome to my children and slaves. But she has shed disgrace not only upon herself but on all women yet to be, and even on those whose do what is only right.'

"After he had spoken, I answered him. I said, 'My god! From the very first, Zeus, whose voice reaches so far, has treated the offspring of Atreus poorly through the machinations of women. It was for Helen so many of us once died, and now, Clytemnestra has crafted this plot while you were so far away.'

"After I had spoken, he answered me at once,

"'So now, because of that, in the time to come, it's best to keep a gentle, quiet eye on your wife. Don't tell her everything you're thinking. Only tell her part of it—keep the rest to yourself. But for you, Odysseus, death is not to come from your wife . . . because Penelope is so thoughtful, so astute, so sharp. Back when we all went to war, we left her behind, a new bride with a child at her breast—so delicate—but now I bet he is sitting around with all the men, confident because he knows that his dear father will see him when he comes, and he will embrace his father, as is only right.

"'But my own wife did not even let me feast my eyes on my son, before she murdered me. Me! And I'll tell you something else—place it deep inside your heart—when you are back there in your own beloved country, make sure that you beach your ship covertly, and not out in the open. Because you cannot trust any woman any more. But come. Tell me—and lay it all out truthfully. Have you, by chance, heard if my son is still alive, maybe in Orkhomenos or in sandy Pylos, or maybe with Menelaos on the plains of Sparta, because brilliant Orestes has not yet lost his life on earth.'

"He said all this, and I answered with these words.

"'Son of Atreus, why are you asking this of me? I do not know whether he is alive or has been killed. It's no good, airing all this idle talk.'

"And yet we both stood there, talking our bitter talk in anguish, our tears welling and streaming down. And then the soul of Akhilles Peleïades, came forward and also the souls of Patroklos, Antilokhos, and Aias, all without equal, the best in appearance and physique of all the Greeks, except for the faultless son of Peleos. The spirit of the great runner, Aiakos' grandson, recognized me, and in tears, he threw out words that beat the air like wings.

"'Son of Laertes, engendered by Zeus, Odysseus, always so shrewd, so stubborn—what mischief could you have thought up better than this? How did *you* manage to come down here to Hades, where all the brainless dead come, all of us shadows of men and women who have worn themselves out?'

"After he had spoken, I answered him.

"'Akhilles, Peleos's son, the greatest by far of all the Akhaians, I have come here because I had to. I had to see if maybe Teiresias could tell me how to reach my rugged Ithaka. Because I have never yet come close to Akhaia, or touched shore there in my own native land. Instead, I'm always having trouble. But you, Akhilles—no one has ever been more fortunate than you before, nor will anyone ever be. When you were alive, all of us Argives honored you as someone equal to the gods, and now you are here, you still rule magnificently over the dead, so do not mourn because you're dead, Akhilles.'

"After I had spoken, right away he answered back.

"'Don't talk around the fact that I, in fact, am dead, charming Odysseus. I'd rather work as a hired hand for someone else, some man without a speck of land and very little means, than be the ruler over all these lifeless dead. But come, tell me about my fine son, whether or not he has gone to war and is a leader. And tell me of Peleus, who has no equal, if you've heard anything. Does he still maintain his honor among the Myrmidon people, or do they now dishonor him throughout Hellas and Phthia, because old age is holding him down, hand and foot, since I am not up there, under the sun's rays, to protect him, as I was before when I was fighting for the Argives and killed the very best of the others on the Trojan plains. If only I could go back up to my father's home, even for a short time, I would make all those who work against him and his honor cower under the strength of my invincible hands.'

"After he had spoken, I answered him.

"'I have not heard anything about your matchless father, but as for your son, Neoptolemos, I'll tell you the whole truth, since you asked me. I myself brought him in my hollow ship from Skyros to be there among the well-equipped Akhaians. And whenever we were working out our plans there, around the city of Troy, he was always the very first to speak, and when he spoke, his words never missed their target. Only Nestor, who's like a god, and I surpassed him. And whenever we were wielding the bronze, out there on the Trojan plains, he never held back in the thick of the ranks, but always dashed forward, far to the front, with all his might. He yielded to no one, and he killed many men there in the horror of battle.

"'I could not recount them all or tell you all their names, all the troops he killed while he was defending the Argives, but one was Eurypylos, Telephos's son—what a fighter—he ran him through with his bronze. And all around him, there were so many other Ceteian troops who died, all because of one woman who desired a few gifts. In fact, your son was the very finest looking one I saw, except the brilliant Memnon. And when we, the Argives' very best, were about to enter the horse that Epeos had made and I found myself in charge, and was about to pull back and shut the thick door of our hiding place, then the other Danaan leaders and advisors wiped away their tears, and their limbs trembled under them—but I never saw him turn pale or wipe any tears from his cheeks. Again and again, he begged me to let him jump out of the horse, and he kept fingering the handle of his sword, anxious to do the Trojans harm.

"'But after we had ransacked Priam's city, though it was perched on sheer cliffs, he went aboard his ship with his share of precious spoils—and he was unscathed. He was neither jabbed by the bronze point of a spear nor wounded by a thrust in hand to hand combat, as happens so often in war, for Ares' rage is haphazard.'

"After I spoke, swiftly, with long strides, the soul of Aiakos's grandson, the fast runner, walked away, across the fields of asphodel, pleased that I had said his son was so pre-eminent. The other souls of the lifeless dead stood around in sorrow, and each one asked about his own loved ones. Only Aias, Telamon's son, stood apart, still furious about my triumph over him when I won the contest there beside the ships for the arms of Akhilles, whose revered mother had settled on the prize. The sons of the Trojans, as well as Pallas

Athena, had made that decision. If only I'd never triumphed in that competition! The earth then closed over this man's head—Aias, whose face and power had risen above all the other Danaans, except for Peleus's son, who had no match. And so, to him I voiced these soft, conciliatory words.

"'Aias, son of Telamon, you who had no match, are you never going to forget your anger at me over those damned arms? The gods themselves must have sent them as a curse on the Argives, such a tower of strength was lost to us. For you, and your death, even as much as for the life of Akhilles, Peleus's son, our sorrow never ends. No one but Zeus is to blame. He hated the army of Danaan spearsmen deeply, and it was he who brought about your destiny. But come here, my Lord, so you can hear my words, everything that I have to say, and calm down your rage and your magnificent spirit . . . '

"He did not answer me. He went away to Erebos, to be with the other dead souls. Even then, he might have spoken to me, or I to him, as furious as he was, but the heart pounding inside my chest wanted to see those other souls who had died.

"And so it was I saw Minos, the famous son of Zeus, holding his golden scepter, passing judgment on the dead. They crowded through the wide gates of the house of Hades, and they drew close around the Lord and pressed their own cases. After him, I noticed Orion, immense, driving across the fields of asphodel the wild beasts that he himself had killed, high up in the desolate mountains. He was holding in his hands a club, totally bronze, unbreakable. And I saw Tityos, the son of the radiant Gaia. He was lying on the ground, nine miles long, and a vulture on each side of him was biting at his liver and groping deep into his intestines, and he could not keep them away with his hands. He had attacked Leto, the famous wife of Zeus, as she was going toward Pytho, through the lovely grasses of Panopeos.

"I saw Tantalos in awful agony, standing in a pool, the water splashing up to his chin. He seemed thirsty. But he could not drink. Whenever the old man bent down to drink, the water was swallowed up and evaporated, and black earth appeared around his feet. Some god had made it dry. And there were tall trees, full of leaves, and fruit hanging down over his head—pomegranate, pear, and apple trees, growing in profusion. But when he reached up to clutch one in his hand, the wind blew them away into the shadowy clouds.

"And I saw Sisyphos in awful agony, trying to heave a huge stone with both hands. He leaned into it and pushed it with both his hands and feet, rolling the stone up toward the top of the hill. But just as he was about to shove it over the ridge, the force of its own weight made it fall back down, and the inconsiderate stone rolled down below. But he gathered together all his strength to push it back up. The sweat poured from his limbs, and the dust rose above his head.

"And after him I noticed the powerful Herakles—or rather, his shadow. All around him rose a huge outcry, like birds flying all about in terror, and he, dark as night, with a bow in his hand and an arrow on the bowstring, was glancing around at everyone with a hideous look, like someone about to shoot. The belt across his chest was stunning. His quiver was golden, created with amazing craft, with bears, wild boars, and lions with burning eyes, and fighting, battles, murders, and human carnage. If only the man who gathered all his craft to design that belt had never made it, or at least if he would never make another like it. Herakles recognized me. He moaned loudly and said,

"'Odysseus Laertiádes, descendant of Zeus, you shrewd, miserable man, do you also have to slog out a lousy destiny, as I once had to, up there under the sun's rays? I was the son of Zeus, and he was Kronos's son, and even so I had endless trouble, because I was bound to a man much worse than me. He forced some hard labors on me. One time he even sent me down here, to catch the hound of Hades. He couldn't think of any other task greater than this, and so I caught it and fetched it away, and then escaped from Hades. Hermes led me, and also Athena, her eyes gleaming.'

"After he spoke, he went his way, back inside the house of Hades. And I myself, for a little while, stood my ground there stubbornly—just in case someone else might come, one of those heroic men who had died so long ago.

"And I would have liked to have seen many others—Theseus and Peirithoos, the illustrious children of gods, but at that moment, all the innumerable dead started to swarm forward with an unearthly roar, and pale fear took hold of me—the fear that imperious Persephone herself might send at me the huge, hideous head of Gorgon from the depths of Hades.

"And so at once I went down to the ship and ordered the crew to get on board themselves—and release the stern cables. They boarded quickly and sat down at their benches, and the ship was carried downstream by the surging current to the ocean, where at first we had to row—and then the wind was good."

XII

Hazards

"So we left behind the current of the river Okeanos and came to the surging, open sea—and to Aiaia, the island where Dawn lives and performs her dance with every rising of the sun. We arrived, landed our ship on the sands, and walked along the surf. There, waiting for the light of Dawn, we fell asleep. And very early, as Dawn's rosy fingers appeared, I sent my crew to Kirke, to collect Elpenor's dead body. Without delay, we hacked apart some pieces of wood, and there, where a headland jutted out into the sea, at the very furthest point, we held the burial rites in sorrow, our tears welling and streaming down.

"But when the body and its armor had burned away, we piled up a mound and hauled a pillar onto it, and at the very top, we planted his well-balanced oar. While we were all attending to these tasks, Kirke herself was not blind to our return from Hades. She prepared herself and came down very quickly, and her attendants brought plenty of bread, meat, and sparkling red wine. The brilliant goddess stood there among us and spoke.

"'So headstrong—you go down to the house of Hades while you're still alive, face to face with death two times, while all other men die only once. But come now, eat some food and drink some wine today. And when Dawn appears, you can set sail. I'll tell you the way, and I'll point out everything you need to know, so you won't have to go through needless pain because of some horrible blunder.'

"As she spoke, though our hearts were brash, we listened. And so, for the whole day until sunset, we gorged ourselves on copious servings of meat and sweet wine. And when the sun had gone down and darkness came, we lay down to sleep beside the ship's stern moorings. But she took my hand and sat me down, away from my own companions. She lay down beside me and she probed at me over everything. And I acquitted myself in due order. And afterward, the esteemed Kirke said these words.

"'So everything's come down to this—listen to what I'm telling you, and some god will himself remind you. First of all, you are going to come to the Sirens, who work their charm on all men, whoever comes to them. And whoever, in his innocence, draws close enough to hear their voices, will never return home, and his wife and little children will never again stand joyfully beside him. The Sirens charm him with their clear song as they sit on a bluff, and all around them lies a huge pile of the bones of men, rotting, the strips of skin about their bones shriveling.

"'But you, keep rowing past them, and knead some wax and work it into the ears of your crew, so none of them will hear. But if you want to hear them, let yourself be tied up tightly, hand and foot, to the mast of your ship, so you can enjoy listening to the Sirens—and if you order or even beg your crew to release you, have them tie you up with even more ropes. But when your crew has rowed past all this trouble, beyond that, I am not going to tell you which way your course should be, all the way through. No, turn it over in your heart. And I will tell you about both ways.

"'On one side are overhanging cliffs, and enormous waves from dark-eyed Amphitrite pound against them. The carefree gods call them the Shifting Rocks. Not even birds are able to make it past them—not even the wild doves that bring ambrosia to Father Zeus. The sheer rock always takes one of them down, and our father sends another in its place. And not a single ship that has drawn close to these rocks has ever escaped those waves, nor the hot blasts from the terrible fires that toss about the planks of ships and the dead bodies. Only one seagoing ship, the Argo, has sailed past, on its way from Aietes, as everybody knows. And the waves would have hurled even that one against the massive rocks, but Hera sent it through, because she loved Jason.

"'And on the other course, there are two cliffs. One reaches up to the endless sky with its sharp peak, and a dark cloud wraps around it and never pulls away. There is no clear sky around that peak, either in summer or in the fall. No mortal man could ever climb it or reach the top, even if he had twenty hands and feet. The rock is smooth, as if highly polished. And in the middle of the cliff is a dark cave, facing toward the gloom of the setting sun, toward Erebos—that's the way, without a doubt, illustrious Odysseus, for you to steer your hollow ship. But not even the most powerful man could shoot an arrow from his ship to carry all the way into that open cave.

"'That is where Skylla lives, always squealing horribly. Her voice is something like a newborn pup's, but she herself is a massive, repulsive thing that no one would ever want to see. She has twelve feet, all deformed, and six necks, extremely long, and on each one a menacing head with three rows of teeth, thick and close and full of black death. Up to her waist she squirms inside the deep cave, but she holds all her heads outside, over the frightening chasm, rummaging all around the rocky crags, fishing about for dolphins and seals—whatever she might catch of the larger creatures that groaning Amphitrite raises by the thousands. There is not one sailor who can brag that he has escaped her unscathed, because with each head, she will snatch a man from his ship's black deck and carry him away.

"'And the other cliff, you'll see, is not so high, Odysseus. They are close to each other. You could shoot an arrow across. And on top of it is a large fig tree, full of leaves. But down below, Kharybdis everlastingly sucks at the black water. Three times a day she vomits it all back up, and three times she sucks it down again, unspeakably. Don't happen to be there when she's sucking it down. No one could pull you out—not the Earth-shaker himself. So keep close to Skylla's cliff and sail past quickly. Far better to mourn six of your men than all of them.'

"After she had spoken, I answered her and said, 'Come, goddess, tell me this and tell me truthfully—is it possible to get away from the awful Kharybdis and fight her off when she strikes out at my crew?'

"After I spoke, the brilliant goddess answered at once.

"'Still so headstrong—filling up your mind with acts of war and force. Will you never give an inch even to us gods, who never have to face death? Skylla herself will never die, but though immortal, she's hideous, vicious, much to be feared. She's feral, not to be tangled with. There is no defense. Your only option is to flee. And if you hang back to prepare yourself to fight, I fear that she will be aroused to strike out yet again with all her heads and take as many men as before. No, pull hard on your oars for all you're worth and call for help from Krataiis, Skylla's mother, who gave birth to her to be a curse on all of you mortals. She'll hold her daughter back from attacking you again.

"'And then you will come to the island of Thrinakia. It is there that Helios' numerous cattle and stout sheep graze—seven herds of cattle and as many flocks of sheep, fifty in each. They bear no offspring and never die, and are tended by goddesses, nymphs with lovely hair, Phaithusa and Lampetie, whom the brilliant Neaira bore to Helios. After their esteemed mother had raised them, she sent them off to live far away on the island of Thrinakia, to protect their father's sheep and cattle. If you leave them unharmed and think only of your return, you may yet reach Ithaka, though only after suffering hard times. But if you harm them, I'm telling you, then your ship and all your crew will be destroyed, and even if you yourself escape, you will return home, but only after a long time, and in trouble, after losing all your mates.'

"After she spoke, Dawn appeared, enthroned in gold. The brilliant goddess left me and made her way inland. And I went back to the ship and roused the crew to get themselves on board and release the stern cables. They got in at once and sat down at their benches, and settling in, they thrashed the sea with their oars, and Kirke, with her lovely hair and human voice, but no less a goddess, much to be feared—sent behind our ship's dark hull a steady wind to swell the sails, a good friend to have. And when we had stored away all our gear, we sat down, and the wind and our helmsman kept us right on course. I spoke then to the crew, their hearts filled with anguish.

"'My friends, it's not right for only one or two of us to know the warnings that Kirke, the radiant goddess, gave me, and so I am going to tell you. That way we'll all know, so we'll all either die together or avoid our deaths and get through all this together. First, she said to steer clear of the unearthly Sirens and their flowery bluff. She urged that only I should listen to them, and you should tie me up with rope, strong and tight, so I'll be held there securely, standing at the foot of the mast. Tie both ends to the mast itself, and if I give you orders or even if I beg you to let me go, then tie me up even tighter with extra ropes.'

"That's how I made these things known to my crew. And our sturdy ship came swiftly to the Sirens' island, as a favorable wind carried her on. But soon the wind dropped into a deadly calm, as if some god had stilled the waves. The crew got up, furled the sail, and set it down in the hollow ship, and then they sat back and churned the sea white with their oars of polished fir.

"And I cut a large slab of wax into little pieces with my sharp sword. I kneaded it with my thickset hands and soon the wax warmed up from the force and light of the sun. I pressed it into the ears of all my crew, each in turn, and they tied me up, hand and foot, standing straight against the mast, and tied the ends of the rope tight to the mast, and then they thrashed at the gray sea with their oars. We moved along in a hurry, and when we had come close enough that anyone could hear or be heard shouting, the Sirens did not overlook our swift ship as it drew near, nor let it slip by. They chanted their melodious song.

"'Come closer, dearest Odysseus, the most famous of the Akhaians—send your ship in nearer to the shore so you may listen to our voices more closely, since no one's ever sailed his ship past this place before hearing our voices pass sweetly from our lips. And yes, each person finds such satisfaction from us, and then goes on his way so much the wiser. We sympathize with all the sorrows the Argives and the Trojans suffered in spacious Troy, through the will of the gods, as well as what is still to surface in this bounteous world.'

"They sang their exquisite harmony, and deep in my heart I wanted to keep listening. I ordered the crew to loosen the ropes, pointing and nodding at all of them with my head and my eyebrows. But they leaned into their oars and rowed. And Perimedes and Eurylokhos quickly stood and tied me even tighter with more ropes. And when we had sailed on past, and could no longer hear their voices or their song, then at once my worthy comrades removed the wax that I had plugged into their ears, and they untied the ropes.

"But soon after we had left that island, I saw some smoke and a huge wave and I heard its roar, and the oars flew out of the hands of the crew in their panic and splashed into the swirling sea. The ship held still because they were no longer pulling on the sharp oars with their hands. So I went throughout the ship to boost the crew's spirits with gentle words, standing beside each man in turn.

"'Friends, up to now, we've not at all been unacquainted with hardships, and this here is hardly worse than when the Kyklops held us inside his sunken cave with brute force. And yet we escaped, even from there, through nerve, planning, and hard thinking, and I think, someday, we will remember this. But come now, do as I say, all of you. Keep to your benches and dig your oars deep in the surf, so Zeus may let us get away from this hazard. And you, helmsman, I'm telling you—drive it deep into your heart—when you grip the rudder, work the ship away from the smoke and waves and hold us close to the cliff, or else, if you let it slip, the boat will veer away into something far worse.'

"I said all this, and they quickly responded to my words. But I did not tell them anything more about Skylla—the danger was unspeakable, so they might stop rowing and cower together in the hold. And then I forgot Kirke's stern command not to arm myself for battle. I strapped on my armor and grabbed two long spears, and went to the foredeck on the ship's bow. There, I guessed, I might be the first one to see this Skylla, this rock thing, a peril to my crew. But I could not make anything out anywhere, and my eyes grew tired as I looked all around, all over the rock, lost in fog.

"We sailed up the channel, moaning. There, on one side, was Skylla, and there, on the other, shiny Kharybdis sucked down the salt water and, awfully, vomited it out, seething and thrashing like a cauldron on a large fire, while high above, the spray descended over the pinnacles of both cliffs. But when she sucked the salt water down, I could see all of her, thrashing about, and all around the rock, there was a horrible roaring, and below, the earth looked black as mud. And pale fear seized the whole crew. We looked over toward her, scared to death.

"Right then, Skylla snatched up six of my men from our hollow ship, the best I had in skill and strength. I turned around to the ship and my crew, just as I saw their hands and feet lifted high above. They cried out, and they called to me by name for the very last time, their hearts in agony.

"Like a fisherman on a jutting rock who tosses out morsels of food as bait for little fish and thrusting his long spear, its point crafted from the horn of a grazing ox, into the sea, and then snags one and jerks it, writhing, out of the water—so my companions were lifted, writhing, up the rocks. At the mouth of the cave, she gorged them down, screaming and stretching out their hands to me in their unspeakable death struggle.

"Of all the things I ever went through, hazarding courses over the sea, that was the most miserable of everything I saw with my own eyes. But very soon after we had escaped the rocks and the horrid Skylla and Kharybdis, we came to the unspoiled island of a god. There were the fine, thick-necked cattle and the many well-fed sheep of Helios Hyperion. Even out at sea in my black ship, I could hear the bellowing of cattle being driven and the bleating of sheep. And in my heart rang the words of the blind seer, Teiresias the Theban, and of Kirke of Aiaia, who very plainly told me to steer clear of the island of the Sun, who brings such joy to us mortals. And so I spoke to my companions, their hearts in anguish.

"'Listen to my words despite your sufferings, comrades, so I can tell you the forewarnings of Teiresias and Kirke of Aiaia. She very plainly told me to steer clear of the island of the Sun, who brings such joy to us mortals. Here, she said, we'll find our most dangerous peril. So row this black ship on beyond this island.'

"That's what I said, but their spirits had been broken, and at once, Eurylokhos answered me with harsh words.

"'You're a hard man, Odysseus. No one can match your heart, and your limbs don't ever grow tired. You must be totally made of iron—you don't allow your fellow sailors, worn out with work and fatigue, to set foot on land, here on this remote island where we might just put together a tasty meal. Instead you tell us to wander on, through the quickly falling night, and be driven away from this island into sea fog. It's out of the night that hard winds come into being, the scourge of ships. How could anyone avoid total destruction if a sudden blast of the wind from the south or the violent west wind arose—those which so often dash ships to pieces, in spite of the power of the gods? No, by all means. let's give in for now to the black night and make our supper but keep close beside our swift ship. And then, at dawn, we'll get on board and put into the open sea.'

"As Eurylokhos was speaking, the rest of the crew agreed. And I knew some god was plotting something terrible. I turned to him and sent these words winging toward him.

"'Eurylokhos, you are utterly forcing this on me because I am alone. But come now, all of you, swear to me this solemn oath. If we happen to come upon a herd of cattle or a great flock of sheep, no one will cruelly or recklessly kill either the cattle or the sheep. We'll content ourselves to eat the food that the deathless Kirke brought us.'

"After I spoke, they all swore to do as I had asked. And when they had sworn and taken the oath in full, we landed our sturdy ship within an open harbor, near a spring of sweet water, and the crew went off, away from the ship, and skillfully prepared their supper. But when they had set aside their craving for food and drink, they remembered their dear companions whom Skylla, from her sunken cave, had taken and eaten, and they wept. And as they were weeping, sweet sleep came over them.

"That night, at the third watch, when the stars had passed over us, Zeus, gathering dark clouds, stirred up a perfect storm of fierce winds and covered land and sea with clouds. And very early, as soon as Dawn's rosy fingers appeared, we hauled in our ship and moored her in an open cave. Inside, it was like a hall with dancing floors for nymphs. I gathered the whole crew together and I said to them, 'My friends, here in our swift ship are food and drink, so let's keep our hands off those cattle, or no doubt we'll pay the price. Because they're the cattle and fat sheep of a god, much to be feared—Helios, who looks down over all of us and hears everything.'

"After I spoke, although their hearts were bold, they agreed. And for a whole month the south wind kept on blowing without a stop, and no other wind arose except the east and south winds. For as long as my men had grain and red wine, they kept their hands off those cattle. They were eager to keep their lives. But when our ship's entire provisions had been exhausted, they felt the urge to venture out, looking for game, fish, and birds, the finest they could catch with their hands, using hooks they had bent into curls, since hunger tore at their bellies.

"And I set off, away from the ship, to pray to the gods, so one of them might show me the way to get back home. As I went over the island to get away from my shipmates, I washed my hands in a place where there was shelter from the wind, and I prayed to the gods that inhabit Olympos. And they covered my eyes with sweet sleep. It was then Eurylokhos talked his fellow sailors into a terrible plan.

"'Mates, you're suffering badly, so listen to my words. All kinds of death are horrible to us miserable mortals, but to come to the end by dying of hunger is the most awful. So come now, let's drive off all the best of Helios' cattle and offer a sacrifice to those who live there in the vast sky and never have to die. And if we ever reach Ithaka, our native land, at once we'll build a splendid temple to Hyperion the Sun, and inside, we'll put many valuable offerings. And if he happens to be a bit angry about his cattle, with their straight horns, and chooses to destroy our ship, and the other gods agree—well, I'd rather lose my life all at once, mouth open, gasping at a wave, than slowly waste away on this desolate island.'

"After Eurylokhos spoke, the other mates agreed. Right away, they drove off the best of Helios' cattle that were close by, since the fine thick-necked cattle were grazing not far from the ship's dark prow. They stood around these cows and prayed to the gods. They plucked off some large leaves from a full, towering oak, since they had no white barley stored under the benches of the ship. And then, after they had prayed and slit the cattle's throats and flayed them, they cut away the thighs, covered them with a double fold of fat, and laid raw flesh on top. They had no wine to pour over the blazing sacrifice, but they poured water instead and roasted all the entrails.

"After the thighs had burned down and they had tasted the inner organs, they cut up all the rest and put it on spits. It was only then that sweet sleep slipped away from my eyelids, and I went down to the swift ship and the seashore. But when I came close to the curve of the ship, the sweet smell of roasting flesh drifted about me. I groaned. I cried out loud to the gods, who never have to die.

"'Zeus, Father, and all you carefree gods who live forever—it was you who must have lulled me into merciless sleep to ruin me. And the shipmates I left behind have now cooked up this awful act.'

"Lampetiē, in his long robes, quickly went to tell Helios Hyperion that we had killed his cattle, and at once, his heart enraged, Helios spoke to the immortals.

"'Zeus, Father, and all you blessed gods who live forever, I am seeking revenge against these companions of Odysseus Laertiádes. They have brazenly killed my cattle. I have always treasured them whenever I climbed into the sky, full of stars, and then again when I turned back toward earth out of the sky—so if they do not repay me a fitting compensation, I'll go down into Hades and shine on the dead.'

"And Zeus, gathering dark clouds, answered him.

"'Helios, keep shining here for those of us who live forever and those who are doomed to die on earth, the source of grain. And I will strike their swift ship quickly with a bolt of lightning and splinter it in a flash, in the middle of the sea, dark as wine.'

"I heard all this from the lovely-haired Kalypso, who had heard it herself from Hermes the runner. So when I went down to the sea and our ship, I rebuked the crew, going around to each in turn, but we could find no recourse. The cattle were dead. And right away, the gods sent omens. The stripped skin began to move, and the flesh, both cooked and raw, bellowed on the spits, like the moaning of cattle. And yet, for six days, my trusty companions continued feasting on Helios' best cattle. But when Zeus, the Son of Kronos, brought on the seventh day, the wind stopped blowing so furiously, and without delay, we went on board, raised the mast, hauled out the white sail, and put out to the open sea.

"And yet, after we had left that island, no other land appeared, only sky and sea. The Son of Kronos sent a black cloud over our hollow ship and the sea darkened under us, and it was not long before a howling west wind came rushing in with a huge storm. A blast of wind snapped both the forestays and the mast fell backward, and all its tackle crashed into the hold. At the stern, the mast struck the helmsman's head and smashed all the bones in his head into a pulp, and like a diver, he fell backward from the afterdeck, and his great heart left his bones. At that moment, Zeus thundered and threw a bolt of lightning down on the ship and the boat trembled all over, jolted by Zeus's blow and filled with a sulfurous stench. All my companions fell out of the ship, and like crows, they were carried away in the waves about the black ship. Zeus himself had taken away their return home.

"But I kept on moving around the ship, back and forth, until a surging wave ripped off the sides of the ship from the keel and carried them away, stripped bare, and broke off the mast right at its base. But there, a backstay, made of leather, had blown down on top of it. With that, I worked them both together, keel and mast, and sitting on top of them, I was carried along by the horrible winds. The west wind stopped blowing so furiously, but the south wind came up swiftly, throwing my heart in anguish that I might have to retrace my course to the horror of Kharybdis.

"All night, I was carried along, and just as the Sun was rising, I came to the cliff of Skylla and horrid Kharybdis. She was at that moment sucking down the sea's salty water, and I jumped up to the tall fig tree and hung on like a bat. But I could not plant my feet firmly or climb it. Its roots were too far away, and its thick, long branches were far too high, casting a shadow down on Kharybdis. So I hung on, stubbornly, in case she might vomit up the mast and keel—and there at last, to my joy, they came.

"At the hour when a man stands up from the assembly to go to supper, after sorting out many disputes between men who have fiercely pleaded their cases—that's when those slabs of wood spewed out of Kharybdis. I pushed off with both my feet and hands. I plunged. I splashed down in the swirling water, next to those long slabs, and I sat on top of them and rowed with my own hands. And the father of men and gods did not allow Skylla to notice me, or else I would not have escaped my utter destruction.

"From there, I was carried along for nine whole days. And then, on the tenth night, the gods brought me to Ogygia. There, she cared for me—Kalypso, with her lovely hair and human voice, yet still a goddess, much to be feared. But why should I tell you this? I already told you and your lovely wife, just yesterday, right here in this very house. And it's tiresome, I think, to say yet again what one has clearly just said."

XIII

Ithaka

After Odysseus had spoken, they were all speechless, awed to silence among the shadows of the great hall. Alkinoos lifted his voice to answer.

"Odysseus, now that you have reached my home, with its bronze floors and high ceilings, I believe that you will not be turned away from your return any more, you have suffered so much. And now I say to all of you men. I urge each one of you who are always drinking the elders' shimmering wine and listening to our singers in these halls. Here in this elegant strongbox already are clothes for the stranger and finely crafted gold and all the other gifts the Phaiakian council brought here. So come now, let us offer him a large tripod and a cauldron, each one of us, and we'll in turn exact some compensation from our people, since it is hard to be munificent without remuneration."

As Alkinoos spoke, they were all pleased with what he said, and each one went home to rest. And very early, as Dawn's rosy fingers appeared, they all hurried to the ship and carried back ingenious bronze gifts, and the towering will of Alkinoos moved throughout the ship, and he himself packed in all the gifts under the benches, so they would not obstruct any of the crew when they were leaning vigorously into their oars. Then they all went back to the palace and prepared a feast.

The towering will of Alkinoos sacrificed a bull for them to the Dark Cloud, Zeus, the Son of Kronos, lord of everything. And after they had roasted all the oxen thighs, they set into the sumptuous feast, and they enjoyed themselves as the heavenly singer, Demodokos, whom everyone idolized, sang among them. But Odysseus kept on turning away his head, toward the blinding sun, yearning for it to set, he was so anxious to return home.

Like a man aching for supper, whose team of oxen, dark as wine, has drawn along the plow he crafted by himself, through the hard ground—all day—and the sunlight as it is going down, looks wonderful to him, because he can now see the way clear to his supper, his knees buckling as he goes. In the same way, the sun, as it was setting, looked wonderful to Odysseus. Right away, he spoke to the Phaiakians, who love the oar, and especially to Alkinoos.

"Lord Alkinoos, eminent above all men, pour your offering of wine and send me away safely, and to all of you, farewell, since everything my heart is yearning for has come to this end—safe conduct and lovely gifts. And may the gods above bless them for me, so that when I return home, I find my blameless wife and all of those I love, safe and sound. Those of you who remain here, may you take pleasure in your wives and children, and may the gods tender you prosperity of every kind, and may nothing evil ever come to your people."

As he spoke, they nodded their approval and called for the guest to be sent on his way for speaking so aptly. The towering will of Alkinoos spoke to his attendant.

"Pontonoos, mix the wine in the bowl and serve it to everyone in the hall, so that after praying to Father Zeus, we may send our guest to the land of his fathers."

After he had spoken, Pontonoos mixed the sweet red wine and served it to each of them in turn. They poured out their offerings to all the peaceable gods, who rule from where they live, there in the vast sky. And radiant, Odysseus stood and placed the double-handed cup in Arete's hands, and as he spoke, his words stirred the air like wings.

"I wish you joy, dear queen, all the way through life—until old age and death come, as they will, to all of us. I am going home. But you, rejoice in your home and your children, your people, and Lord Alkinoos."

After speaking, brilliant Odysseus stepped across the threshold. And powerful Alkinoos sent with him an attendant to lead him to the sleek ship on the shore of the sea. Arete also sent along her slaves with him. One carried a fresh cloak and tunic, and one the sturdy strongbox, and another brought bread and red wine. And when they came down to the sea and their ship, quickly the noble escorts took it all, including the food and drink, and they stored it below in the ship's hull. They spread a rug and linen sheet out on the stern deck for Odysseus, so that he could sleep undisturbed. And he himself went aboard, and lay down in silence. Then they all sat down at their benches, each in order, and released the cable out of the hole bored through the mooring stone. When they leaned back, tossing up the salt spray with their oars, a sweet sleep fell upon his eyelids, the deepest, sweetest sleep, the nearest thing to death itself.

As four stallions, harnessed all together, leap high with the flick of the lash and charge forward as they start to run their course quickly over the plain, the ship's stern leaped up, and behind it a wave coursed and flashed brightly on the boisterous sea, as the ship sailed on, sure and steady. Not even a circling hawk, the quickest of all birds, could have kept up with it as it rushed on, swiftly slicing through the sea waves, carrying a man much like the gods in subtle reckonings—a man who had suffered so many sorrows in his heart before, cutting his way through disheartening waves and battling men. But for now he was quiet, sleeping, having forgotten everything he had been through. And then, when the brightest star rose, signaling the first light of dawn, the ship, having crossed the sea, touched ground.

There, on the island of Ithaka, is an inlet belonging to Phorkys, the old man of the sea, where two headlands jut out—sheer cliffs on one side but on the inside sloping down toward the harbor. On the outside, they offer shelter from gigantic waves, powered by violent winds. Inside, ships with many benches can lie about without any mooring lines, once they have landed. There, at the tip of the inlet, is an olive tree with long leaves, and nearby, there is a dark, enchanting cave that is sacred to the nymphs who are called the Naiads.

Inside the cave are mixing bowls and stone jars where bees store their honey, and there are tall stone looms where the nymphs weave webs, dyed in the purple of shellfish, a wonder to see, and there are also springs, flowing endlessly inside. There are two entrances. One is open to the north wind, by which human beings go down into the cave, but the one that opens to the south wind is sacred. No man may enter there. It is the way for those who never have to die.

It was here they rowed in, having known about it from before. Quickly they landed with fully half of the ship's length on shore, the rowers' arms had driven it in so well. Stepping away from the ship's benches, they first lifted Odysseus out of the hollow ship, leaving the linen and the bright rug where they were, and they placed him down on the sand, still overcome by sleep. Then they lifted out all the goods the gracious Phaiakians had given him to honor benevolent Athena, when he was setting off for home. They placed them together by the trunk of an olive tree, away from the path, so that no one who might be happening by would disturb them before Odysseus awoke. And then they returned home.

But he who makes the earth tremble had not forgotten all the threats that he had sworn against Odysseus from the beginning. He asked Zeus about his plans.

"Zeus, Father, I will no longer be respected by the gods, as humans show me no respect at all—even these Phaiakians, who are my own offspring—because I have only just now said that Odysseus would suffer many awful things, although I did not deny him his return, since you had already promised that and showed me your orders with a nod. And now, while he was sleeping, they have carried him across the sea and laid him down in Ithaka. And they have given him countless gifts—bronze, gold, and piles of finely woven clothes—much more than Odysseus would have carried off from Troy, if he had managed to return unscathed, with his full share of the spoils."

Zeus, gathering dark clouds, answered him.

"Appalling! You, who move the earth itself, whose reach is so vast—the things you say! The gods do not dishonor you. It would be hard to dishonor the oldest, the best of us. And these human beings? If any of them trusts so much in his own strength and power that he shows you disrespect, then revenge is yours—for all time to come. Do as you will, whatever your heart desires."

And Poseidon, who moves the earth, answered him.

"I was about to do what you have said, Dark Cloud, but I always shudder and stand in awe of your fierce heart. Yet now I want to strike at these Phaiakians' pretty ship—as it sails across the misty sea after escorting him, so that they will hold back and give up ushering men to safety—and enclose their city, all around, with a massive mountain."

And Zeus, gathering dark clouds, answered him.

"Old friend, here in my heart is what seems best to me. When all the people are looking out to sea, away from their city, as the ship is speeding home, close to land, turn it into a stone, shaped exactly like a swift ship, so that everyone will wonder, and then close in their city, all around, with a huge mountain."

When Poseidon, who moves the earth, heard this, he went across to Skheria, where the Phaiakians live. There, he waited. And after it had crossed the sea, as the ship raced quickly in, close to shore, he who causes the earth to tremble came near. He turned the ship to stone and jammed it down hard with the flat of his hand. Then he went away. The Phaiakians, well known for their ships and long oars, spoke words that flailed at each other like wings, as each one looked over to the person next to him and said, "Oh my, what made our quickly moving ship stop short, just as it was heading home in full view?"

So one said to another, and no one understood what was to come. But Alkinoos addressed them all.

"My dear friends, all the warnings my father told me so long ago, now they are coming back to me. He'd say how Poseidon was going to get angry at us, for giving safe conduct to everyone. Back then, he said that someday, as one of the Phaiakians' lovely ships was coming back from an escort over the dark sea, Poseidon would strike it down and enclose our city, all around, with a massive mountain. The old man told me this, and now it is all coming to be. But come now, let us all comply with what I say. Let us stop escorting people whenever anyone comes here to our city. And let us pick out and sacrifice twelve bulls to Poseidon, so he will spare us and will not enclose our city, all around, with towering mountains."

After he had spoken, they were terrified and began to prepare the bulls for sacrifice. The leaders and advisors of the Phaiakian people, standing around the altar, prayed to Lord Poseidon, as Odysseus awoke from his sleep in the land of his fathers, but he did not recognize it, since he had been away for so long. All around him, a mist had been spread by the goddess, Pallas Athena, Zeus's daughter, so that she could tell him everything, and he would not be known by his wife, by his loved ones, or by his people, before the suitors had completely paid him back for all their offenses. Yet everything appeared unfamiliar to its ruler—the long, continuous paths, the still harbors, the jagged rocks, the verdant trees. He jumped up and stood there, looking at the land of his fathers. He moaned and smacked the flat of his hands against his thighs. Sorrowfully, he voiced these words.

"Ah, me, whose country and what people have I come to now? Are the people violent, wild, without any sense of justice, or are they friendly to strangers, their minds intent on the gods? Where should I take all these things? Where will I be driven next? I should have stayed with the Phaiakians, and then gone off to some other powerful kings, who would have befriended me and sent me to return home. Now I do not know where to carry all of this wealth, but I will not leave it here to become someone else's takings.

"Appalling, they were neither very smart nor fair—those Phaiakian leaders and advisors who brought me to this alien land. They told me they'd take me to sunny Ithaka, but they didn't see it through to the end. I hope Zeus, the protector of drifters, who watches over all men and punishes anyone who falls short, will give them what is their due. But come now, I'll sort and count all these things, in case they've taken and carried off anything in the hull of their ship."

As he spoke, he started to count the exquisite tripods, the cauldrons, the gold, and finely woven cloth, and he found that nothing was missing. And yet he ached for his own land, and he paced along the shore beside the pounding sea, moaning again and again. Athena approached, in the guise of a young man, a shepherd, but very delicate, like the children of lords. There was a finely crafted cloak in a double fold around her shoulders, and she was wearing sandals on her gleaming feet, and in her hand, she held a spear. Odysseus was glad to see her, and he went to her. He found his voice, and his words carried like wings.

"My friend, since you are the first person I've met here in this land, I wish you well and I hope that you have come to me with no evil intent. Save me—save what's mine! I pray to you as to a god, and I reach out for your precious knees. Tell me truthfully, so I may know—what land is this? What people? What kind of men live here? Is this some island that can be clearly seen from a distance? Or the shore of some fertile mainland, sloping down to the sea?"

Athena, the goddess, spoke to him, her gray eyes gleaming.

"You are a fool, stranger, or you've come from far away, if you have to ask about this land. It's not so little known. Many know about it, both those who live for the dawn and sunlight, and those who live beyond, among shadows and darkness. This is a rugged island, not so good for driving horses about, but it's not so poor, although it's not too spacious. Corn grows here in abundance and grapes too. There's rain, all the time, and luscious dew. It's good for goats and cattle. And there are all kinds of trees and watering holes that last the whole year through. And so, stranger, the name of Ithaka has reached all the way to Troy, which they say is very far away from Akhaia."

As she spoke, brilliant Odysseus, who had suffered so much, was thrilled, and he rejoiced in his own land when he heard those words from Pallas Athena, daughter of Zeus, who carries the aegis. So he spoke to her, his words fluttering like wings, but he did not tell the truth. He held back everything that he was about to say, since he always turned every thought over in his mind.

"I've heard of Ithaka, even in spacious Crete, far over the sea. And now I've come here with these belongings. I fled and left behind much more with my children, after I murdered the beloved son of Idomeneos—Orsilokhos, quick on his feet. He was the best, the fastest on his feet of all men who work for their living. But he wanted to steal all the Trojan plunder I had suffered heartbreaks for, passing through wars with men and horrifying waves, because I had refused to ingratiate myself and serve under his father. Instead, I led my own troops.

"And so I waited near the road with one of my men, and I plunged the bronze tip of my spear into him as he came in from the field. The deep darkness of night filled the sky. No one knew about us, and unseen, I took his life. And after I'd cut him down with sharp bronze, I went straight for the ship and made my plea to the always gracious Phaiakians, and I gave them plenty of stolen goods. I asked them to take me on and set me ashore at Pylos or at bright Elis, where the Epians hold power. But the force of the wind drove them away from there, against their will, since they had no wish to betray me.

"Driven from there, we came to this place during the night. We rowed quickly into the harbor. None of us had a thought of eating, though we were hungry. We disembarked from the ship and lay down. I was worn out, and sweet sleep came over me. They took my goods out of the hollow ship and laid them where I was lying on the sands, and then they went on board and set sail for populous Sidonia. And I was left behind here, my heart in anguish."

As he spoke, the goddess Athena, her eyes gleaming, smiled and stroked him with her hand, now with the body of a woman, tall and beautiful, skilled in exquisite crafts. And as she spoke, her voice stirred the air like wings.

"Shrewd and devious anyone would have to be, to better you in duplicity, even though it was a god who came across you. Hard, shifty in your schemes, unspeakably deceitful—even in your own country, you're not about to stop lying and fabricating stories. But come on, let's talk no more of this. We're both skilled manipulators, as you are the best of all human beings in sharp sense and smooth talk, and I'm well known among all the gods for my cunning and craftiness.

"But you did not recognize Pallas Athena, Zeus's own daughter, who alone has stood by you and watched over you in all your troubles. It was I who made the Phaiakians love you. And now I have come here to fabricate a strategic plan with you and to hide these things the gracious Phaiakians gave you, due to my guidance and consideration, when you set off for home. I will tell you about your full share of the trouble, which you are now about to withstand in your well-made home. But take heart—tell no man or woman, any of them, that you have come back from your wandering. In silence, endure all your troubles and resign yourself to human violence."

Odysseus, always thinking ahead, answered her.

"It's hard, Goddess, for a mortal man to know you when he meets you, no matter how much he thinks he knows, since you can make yourself look like anyone. But I do know this—you were well-disposed to me in the past, as long as we sons of the Akhaians were fighting there at Troy, but after we had burned and looted Priam's towering city and we went away in our ships and some god scattered us Akhaians, I have never seen you since, Daughter of Zeus—I've never known you to come on board my ship, to defend me against trouble. But I have always wandered on—my heart, torn apart inside my chest yet holding on until the gods released me from the very worst—until you inspired me with your words there in the rich land of the Phaiakians and led me yourself to their city. But now, in the name of your father, I ask you—since I don't think I've yet reached the clear air of Ithaka. No, it's some other land I'm wandering through, and you, I think, are taunting me—tormenting me to deceive my heart—so tell me, truthfully, if I've really come to the dear land of my fathers."

Athena, the goddess, her eyes gleaming, answered him.

"This is always the thought you hold in your chest, and this is why I cannot leave you to your sorrow. You are so soft spoken, alert, and careful. Any other man who's returning from his wanderings would have hurried eagerly to see his children and his wife, but it's not your way to seek and find out what you desire, before you've tested your wife, who is, as usual, there inside your halls, as the nights and days fade away, miserable as always, her tears streaming down. But I myself never had a doubt. I knew within my heart that you would return, after you had lost all of your companions.

"But I did not want to fight for you against Poseidon, my father's brother, who holds so much anger inside his heart against you—outraged, ever since you blinded his beloved son. But come now—I will show you the land of Ithaka, so that you can be persuaded. This is the harbor of Phorkys, the old man of the sea, and here at the head of the harbor is the olive tree, with all its long leaves. And nearby is the lovely cave, full of shadows, sacred to the nymphs called Naiads. And this, of course, is the towering cave where you used to give the nymphs huge offerings of many hundreds of oxen, to bring about your aims. And there is Mount Neriton, covered with forests."

As she was speaking, the goddess swept the mist away, and the land appeared. And there, in that moment, brilliant Odysseus, who had endured so much, was thrilled, crying out his joy—to be in his own land—and he kissed the earth, our source of grain. And right away, holding up his arms, he prayed to the nymphs.

"Naiad nymphs, Zeus's children, I had thought I'd never see you, ever again. But now I'm calling out to you with my gentle prayer, and I will give you gifts, as I always have before, if the generous daughter of Zeus will allow me to survive, and lets my dear son grow to maturity."

And Athena, her gray eyes gleaming, answered him.

"Take heart. Don't let these things go to your heart. Let's place your treasures here in the inner depths of this wonderful cave, so they will remain safe for you, and then, let us each think it over—how everything might turn out for the very best."

After she had spoken, the goddess entered the shadows of the cave and searched its most hidden recesses. Odysseus carried everything inside—the gold, the hard bronze, the exquisite fabrics that the Phaiakians had given him. He stored them all deep inside, and Pallas Athena, daughter of Zeus, who holds the aegis, placed a stone into the cave's opening. Then they both sat down by the trunk of the sacred olive tree and plotted out the destruction of the arrogant suitors. Athena, the goddess, her eyes gleaming, spoke first.

"Son of Laertes, spawn of Zeus, Odysseus, always scheming, start thinking now about how to get your hands on those shameless suitors, who for three years have been lording over your estate, courting and tempting your loyal wife with gifts. And she, always aching for your return, keeps giving hope to all of them by sending messages of reassurance to each man while her own mind remains on other things."

Odysseus, always thinking ahead, answered her.

"Appalling, I was about to meet the terrible fate of Agamemnon, Atreus's son, if you, goddess, had not told me this. But come now, fabricate a scheme for me to pay them back and stand by me so that there will be the same iron nerve in me as when we seized the battlements, the blazing crown of Troy. Stand by me, pressing just as hotly as you did back then, your gray eyes gleaming, and with you, I'll fight three hundred men, if you, fierce goddess, help me with all your heart."

The goddess Athena, her eyes gleaming, answered him.

"Of course I'll be with you—do not forget me as we work together on this. I think that some of those suitors eating up your resources will splatter their blood and brains unspeakably on the ground. But come now, I will make you unrecognizable to all mere human beings. I will shrivel the smooth skin on your sinuous limbs and ruin that auburn hair on your head and wrap you in rags too awful to look at. And I will cloud over those eyes that were so radiant before, so that you will appear despicable to all the suitors, as well as to the wife and son you left behind, there in your estate.

"And you, set out first of all for the old man who keeps your pigs and who supports you without fear and loves your son and your constant wife, Penelope. You'll find him staying with the pigs. They are feeding next to Korax Rock, beside Arethousa Creek—gorging themselves on acorns and drinking up the blackened waters that fatten pigs' flesh. Stay there. Sit down beside him and question him about everything, while I go to Sparta, with its beautiful women, to call back Telemakhos, your precious son, Odysseus. He went to vast Lakedaimon to see Menelaos, seeking some word of you, in case you still happen to exist somewhere."

Odysseus, always thinking ahead, answered her.

"Why didn't you tell him, then, since you are able to see everything in your mind. Maybe so that he would go through sorrows too, wandering about the restless sea, as others are using up his resources?"

The goddess Athena, her gray eyes gleaming, answered.

"Don't let him worry you too much. I myself encouraged him to go, to earn himself a fine reputation, and he has not had any hardship. He is sitting in the palace of Atreus's son, just lying around endlessly. True, young men in a black ship are waiting for him, ready to kill him before he reaches his own land. But I do not think this will come about. The earth will sooner cover any of the suitors who are using up his belongings."

After she spoke, Athena touched him with her staff, and shriveled the smooth skin on his sinuous limbs, and ruined the auburn hair on his head, and over all of his limbs, she laid the skin of an old man. And then she clouded over his eyes, which were so brilliant before. And around his rags, she threw a ghastly cloak and tunic, disheveled and soiled and blackened with grimy smoke, and over that a large deer hide, worn bare, and then she gave him a staff and a nasty old, torn rucksack with a twisted strap. And after they had conspired a bit more, they parted ways, and the goddess went to brilliant Lakedaimon, to bring back Odysseus's son.

XIV

The Keeper of Pigs

He went from the harbor up the rocky path and on through the woods to the high ground where Athena had told him he would find the pig keeper, who cared the most for his estate of all the slaves that brilliant Odysseus had taken. He found the man there, sitting beside the house where the courtyard was built, high up in an open space, large and round and beautiful. The brilliant pig keeper had built it all by himself, without the knowledge of the queen or the old man Laertes, for the pigs of his departed master, with huge stones that he had hauled in and bordered with a prickly hedge. All around it, at regular intervals, thick and close, he had pounded in the stakes, split all the way down to their black oak core.

Within this courtyard, he had built twelve closed-in sties for the pigs to lie in. Inside each one, fifty sows were wallowing around, pressing up against each other, females for breeding. The boars lay around outside, and there were far fewer of these. The impertinent suitors had feasted on them and had reduced their numbers, because the pig keeper was constantly sending them the best and most well fed, the fattest and heaviest hogs, three hundred sixty of them.

Near them lay four dogs, like wild animals, raised by the pig keeper, a master among men. He was cutting up a tanned ox hide and fitting sandals about his feet. He had sent three other men away, here and there, with bunches of hogs, and he had sent a fourth to drive a hog to town for the overbearing suitors, so they could slaughter it and slake their souls with meat.

Right then, the dogs spotted Odysseus. They barked and howled and ran at him. Wisely, he sat down, and his staff fell away from his hand. He would have suffered terrible harm, there inside his own stalls, but the pig keeper followed after the dogs with quick steps through the gate, the ox hide falling from his hand. He yelled at them and drove them off with a torrent of rocks. He called out to his master.

"Old man, these dogs would have torn you apart in no time, and you'd have laid the blame on me, and the gods have given me other sorrows and troubles.

I keep on going here, mourning and grieving for a good master, and raise fat hogs for others to eat, while he goes hungry, wandering lands and towns of people who talk in strange tongues—that is, if he's actually alive and still can see the sunlight. But come now, we'll go to my hut, old man, so you can ease your mind with some food and wine and tell me where you've come from and what sorrows you've endured."

As he spoke, the pig keeper led the man over to the hut and brought him inside. He scattered about some twigs and spread out the hide of a wild goat, large and thick with wool—his own bedroll. Odysseus was overjoyed to be made so welcome, and he addressed the pig keeper warmly.

"Stranger, may Zeus and all the other gods who never die grant you whatever it is that you desire the most, for taking me in so warmly."

And Eumaios, keeper of pigs, you answered him.

"Stranger, it's not right to demean a stranger, even if they're worse off than you, because all strangers and beggars are from Zeus, and even a small gift from us is kind. This is the way of slaves, always in dread of domineering masters like those young men, since the gods prevented the return of the one who would have cared so well for me and given me good things—a house, a plot of land, a desirable wife, all the things a thoughtful master gives a slave who has worked so hard and long that the gods have made all his work flourish, as the work I manage flourishes. My master would have helped me so much, if he had grown to old age right here, but . . . he died, just as I wish the ranks of Helen had all been utterly slaughtered, as she weakened the knees of so many men. And he too, went off to Troy, with all its horses, to fight those Trojans, and for Agamemnon's honor."

As he spoke, he abruptly drew his belt in tightly about his tunic and went out to the sties, where the ranks of pigs were lying about. He chose two, brought them inside, and slaughtered them both. He singed all their bristles off, cut them apart, and pierced them with spits. He roasted them and brought everything over and placed it, still hot on the spits, in front of Odysseus. He sprinkled it all with white barley, and in a bowl made of ivy wood, he mixed some wine, sweet as honey, then sat down across from the other man, and urging him on, he spoke.

"Eat now, stranger, what there is to share among slaves. It's piglet, since it's only those suitors who can feast on fattened hogs, without any thought in their heads of compassion or revenge. But the peaceable gods, they don't like coldblooded acts. They honor what's right and the decent things people do. Even hardened, lawless men who invade other lands, whenever Zeus grants them a haul and they load up their ships and head for home—the fear of divine revenge falls on their hearts.

"But these men here—they must have seen something, or heard the voice of some god about his awful death, since they refuse to do their courting fairly or to return among their own, and carelessly, rudely, they use up everything that's ours—and ruthlessly. But every night and day that comes from Zeus, they kill not just one sacrificial victim, or even two, I think, and they waste our wine, swilling it down to the last drop. Our very means to live, once beyond words—none of those heroic men ever had so much, not on the black mainland, and not here in Ithaka. Not twenty men altogether ever had so much.

"I'll lay the whole thing out for you. Twelve herds of cattle, and just as many flocks of sheep, as many ruts of pigs and herds of free-ranging goats as any herdsmen, foreign or local, might set out to pasture. And even here, the goats graze freely, in the remotest part of the island. Trusty men watch over them. Every day, each one leads a flock to *them,* whichever of the fattest goats look best. But me, I keep these pigs. I guard them, and I carefully choose the best to send off to them."

As he spoke, the other man assiduously chewed the meat and drank the wine ravenously, in silence—plotting violence against the suitors. But when he had eaten his meal and fortified his soul with food, the pig keeper filled the cup from which he himself was used to drinking, and gave it to that man, full to the brim with wine, and the other took it, and his heart was so full of happiness, he spoke and his words flew as if with wings in answer.

"My friend, who was the one who purchased you with his wealth—the one who was so rich and powerful as you say? You say he died for the honor of Agamemnon. Tell me, in case I may somehow know who the man may be. Since only Zeus and the other immortal gods know if I may have seen him and could offer you some news, since I have wandered a long way."

And the keeper of pigs, first among men, answered him.

"No wanderer who's come, bringing in rumors of that man, could ever persuade his wife and dear son. Besides, these men who wander around in need of help are liars. They do not even want to tell the truth. Every wanderer who makes it here to the island of Ithaka goes straight to my mistress and tells her a pack of lies. And she receives him kindly and asks about everything. And in her sorrow the tears run down from her eyelids. That's the way a woman is, when her husband is killed, far away. And you too, old man, would at once string together some yarn if someone was to give you a wrap, a tunic and some clothes.

"But as for that man—by now the dogs and birds have stripped the flesh from his bones, and his life breath has left him. Or in the sea, the fish have eaten him up, and his bones lie on the shore, buried deep in sand. So he's perished, somewhere out there, and the future holds only sorrow for his loved ones, especially me, since I will never find another master so kind-hearted, no matter how far I go, even to the home of my own father and mother, back where I was born. And they raised me themselves.

"But it's not for them I'm now grieving, much as I would love to see them with my own eyes and to be on my own home ground. No, it's my longing for Odysseus, who is so far away, that grips me, stranger, and I hesitate to say his name, because he's not here, although he loved me and cared for me, deep in his heart. I only call out 'Ah, dear sir'—he's so far away."

Brilliant Odysseus, who had endured so much, answered.

"My friend, since you are in such total denial and say that man will never come back, and your heart simply can't believe it, I'll lay it out for you, not straight out, but as a vow—Odysseus will return. And when that man gets back and reaches home, give me something for bringing this good news. Wrap me up in a shawl, a tunic, some good clothes. But before he comes, although I am very much in need, I'll take nothing, since any man who would give in to hardship by telling such a bunch of lies is odious as the gates of Hades to me.

"So now, with Zeus, the first among the gods, as witness to the hospitality that I've come to at faultless Odysseus's table and hearth—all of these things will take place just as I am telling you. This very year, Odysseus will return here. Between the waning of this moon and the waxing of the next, he will return home. And he'll take revenge on anyone of those who have dishonored his wife and his beaming son."

And Eumaios, keeper of pigs, you answered him.

"Old man, I won't pay you anything for this news, and Odysseus will never return home. But drink on, at your leisure, and let's turn our minds elsewhere. Just don't remind me of all this, because this heart, here in my chest, aches, when anyone reminds me of my good master. As for your vow—we'll see. I hope Odysseus comes. How I want him to—as do Penelope and Laertes, the old man, and Telemakhos.

"For now, it's the son Odysseus fathered I sorrow for—endlessly. Telemakhos. When the gods made him sprout up like a little shoot, I thought that he'd be no weaker than his dead father, splendid in looks and figure. But one of the gods has wounded his mind, or maybe it was just a man. He went off to Pylos, to find out about his father. Now, those noble suitors are waiting in ambush for him, so that the line of the formidable Arkeisios can be wiped out, nameless, from Ithaka. But let him go—either he'll be taken or the Son of Kronos will reach out his hand and he'll escape.

"But you, old man, tell me all your troubles and tell it to me straight, so I can understand it clearly. Who are you? Where is your city and your parents? What kind of ship brought you here? And how did they bring you to Ithaka? Who did they say they were? Since I hardly think you have traveled here on foot."

Odysseus, always thinking ahead, answered him.

"I'll say all this bluntly—if only the two of us could go on eating this food and this sweet wine quietly for a while, here inside your hut, and let the others do the work! Even then, even in a whole year, I couldn't finish telling you all my troubles—all I've endured in my heart through the will of the gods.

"Let's just say that I come from spacious Krete, the son of a rich man. And many other sons were born and raised in his halls, the legitimate sons of faithful wives. But the mother who gave birth to me was bought and paid for, a kept woman. Yet Kastor Hylakides, whose son I say I am, treated me like an equal to his legitimate sons. He was esteemed as a god for his fine estate, his riches, and his upright sons. But Death's messengers took him to Hades, and his hotheaded sons divided up his property among themselves and cast lots for it. They doled out a small piece of land and a house for me. And through my own backbone, I gained a wife from a prominent family, since I was no fool and was not afraid of a fight. Now, all that's gone.

"And yet, look at the reed and know the seed. So much trouble has had me in its grip. But Ares and Athena have given me the courage and strength to break through the ranks of men, and whenever I've planned out hard times for our enemies, choosing the best men for an ambush, my bold heart never had a worry about death. I was always the first to leap out and jab with my spear whichever of those men who were our enemies had fallen back in front of me. That's the way I was during the fighting, and work was not to my liking, nor taking care of a home, raising nice children. I liked the ships, the oars. The fighting too, the polished spears and the arrows, awful things, that to others are horrible. But I liked them. Some god must have put that inside my heart, since different men relish different kinds of work.

"And so, before the Akhaian sons went off to Troy, already I'd led our men and our sleek sailing ships nine times against foreigners. I picked up a great deal, and I was happy to take it all away. Later I got much more by lot. My household prospered, and I became feared and esteemed among the Kretans. But Zeus, whose voice carries a long way, plotted out that dreadful road that weakened the knees of so many men. They asked me and the famous Idomeneus to lead ships to Ilios. There was no way to refuse. The voice of the people held us tightly in its grip. And for nine years, we sons of the Akhaians waged that war, and in the tenth, we burned Priam's city down, and we headed for home in our ships.

"But some god scattered all of the Akhaians. And so, for me, miserable wretch that I am, Zeus, the manipulator, brought about hard times. Only a month I stayed, enjoying my children, my wife, and my possessions. Then my heart drove me to load my ships and sail for Egypt with my blameless shipmates. I loaded up nine ships, and the people gathered quickly. I offered many animals to sacrifice to the gods and make a feast for them.

"For six days, my trusty shipmates feasted, and on the seventh, we went on board, and we set sail from spacious Krete, and a north wind blew hard and steady and we went on as easily as if we were flowing downstream. And since my ships had suffered no damage, and we sat there, untouched and healthy, the wind and our helmsman held the ships on a straight course. And on the fifth day, we came to the strong currents of the River Egypt, and we moored our boats. I told my trusty mates to stay right there and guard the ships, and I sent out some patrols as lookouts.

"But they gave in to their own bluster and taste for fighting. Right away, they raided the Egyptians' lovely fields and carried off all the women and little children, and killed the rest. The screaming reached the city very quickly, and hearing the outcry, the people came out at dawn. The entire plain was filled with foot soldiers, chariots, gleaming bronze. Zeus himself hurled a horrible panic like lightning among my fellow soldiers. They killed many of us with their sharp bronze blades. And all the rest they led away to their city, alive, to work against their will.

"But Zeus put this idea in my heart—and I wish I'd met my end and died there in Egypt, since sorrow had yet to offer me its welcome. At once, I took the finely sculpted helmet off my head, my shield from my shoulders, and let my spear drop from my hand. I went forward and faced the king's horses. I took his knees and kissed them. He took pity on me and drew me up onto his chariot, and brought me in tears to his home. Many of his soldiers lunged at me with their wooden spears, eager to kill me—they were so utterly enraged—but he held them off. He dreaded the rage of Zeus, the stranger's god, who, the most of all the gods, detests malicious actions.

"I stayed there for seven years. And I gathered considerable wealth among the Egyptian people, because they all gave me gifts. But as the cycle turned into the eighth year, a man arrived from Phoenicia—a cunning, devious character who had already worked his wickedness among men for a long time. He took me into his confidence and led me away to Phoenicia, where he had his house and all his worldly possessions. I remained there for a whole year, but as the days and months drew to a close, and the year turned in its cycle, and the seasons came and went, he put me on a seagoing ship to Libya with the false understanding that I was to transport a cargo with him. Although I fully suspected he'd sell me there at some unspeakable price, I boarded the ship against my will. It sailed before a north wind that blew hard and fair, and midway above Krete, Zeus set in motion his plan to destroy all of them.

"As we left Krete, with no other land to be seen, only the sky and the sea, the Son of Kronos sent a black cloud above the hollow ship, and the sea grew dark beneath it. Then Zeus thundered and launched his thunderbolt down at the ship. Struck by lightning, the whole boat shuddered and was suffused with a sulfurous stench. Everyone on board fell off the ship. Like crows they were carried away on the waves, all around the black ship, and Zeus took away their return home.

"Except for me—my heart was filled with anguish. Zeus himself placed in my hands the huge, lurching mast of the dark-hulled ship, so I might escape harm. I held on to it, cast about by those deadly winds. For nine days I floated about, and during the tenth black night, an enormous curling wave carried me to the land of the Thesprotians. There, the king of the Thesprotians, the famous Pheidon, took me in, because his own beloved son had come upon me, beaten down by cold and exhaustion. He led me to his father's home and put some clothes, a tunic and a cloak around me.

"There it was that I heard about Odysseus. The king stated that he had welcomed him and treated him well as his guest on his way back to his homeland. He showed me all of the treasures Odysseus had collected—bronze, gold and skillfully wrought iron. There was so much wealth that they'd stored for him there in the halls of that king—enough to feed everyone to the tenth generation. The man, he said, had gone off to Dodona to hear the will of Zeus in the high leaves of that oak tree the god has there—how he might return, in the open or in secret, to Ithaka, that fertile land from which he had been away for so long.

"He swore to me myself, while pouring a drink, there in his house, that the ship had been launched and the crew had been in place to carry him back to his beloved homeland. But he sent me away first, since there was a Thesprotian ship that happened to be setting out to Doulikhios, where there is so much wheat. He told them to take me straight there to King Akastos. But they gave in to a terrible pact to bring me to utter ruin.

"When the ship had sailed out, away from the land, they conspired to bring about my day of slavery. They tore off my clothes, my cloak and tunic, and threw around me an awful tattered top—these rags you see before your eyes. In the evening, they reached the fields of Ithaka, which is visible from so far away. They tied me down tightly with braided rope to the ship's solid deck, then disembarked, and grabbed and ate their supper down on the sea shore.

"But the gods themselves loosened my bonds without effort, and I cloaked my rags about my head. I went down the smooth plank and eased my body into the sea. I dog-paddled with both hands, and then I swam, and soon I was out of the water and off, away from them. I went up to a place where there was a thicket, full of leaves. I crouched and stayed there. They all rushed about and moaned and groaned quite a bit. But since there seemed to be no use in searching any more, they went back on board their hollow ship. The gods hid me with no trouble and then guided me and brought me to the lodging of a judicious man. And for now, it seems, it is my lot to go on living."

And then, Eumaios, keeper of pigs, you answered.

"Poor stranger, you have deeply stirred my heart, telling me about all your suffering and wandering. But I think you have told it somewhat out of order, and you're not going to change my mind about Odysseus. Why would anyone in so much trouble as you are lie so thoughtlessly? I know all too well about my master's return. He was so utterly hated by all the gods, they did not bother to bring him down, back when he was among the Trojans, or in the arms of his loved ones, when the war ended. If they had, the Akhaians would have built him a tomb, and he would have won great honor for his son and for all time.

"As it is, the storm winds have swept him away without a name. And me? I have retired here among the pigs and do not go into the city, unless Penelope, thoughtful as always, sends for me, whenever there's any rumors from somewhere. Then they sit around and question whoever comes, both those who mourn for the master and those who cheerfully consume all his worldly goods without compensation.

"But I don't have the heart to ask any questions or grill them, since that time an Aetolian duped me with his story. He had killed a man and now was wandering the world, when he came here to my place. I welcomed him openly. He said he had seen Odysseus in Krete, staying with Idomeneus, where he was patching up his ships, battered by squalls. He said that he'd come here during the summer or by harvest time and bring back a huge cache and his blameless mates. So you, old man, whatever you've endured, as some god must have brought you here to me, don't suck up to me or charm me with your lies. I won't respect you or show you kindness for that, but only out of compassion—in fear of Zeus, the god of strangers."

And Odysseus, always thinking ahead, answered him.

"What a suspicious heart beats inside your chest, since I see that I cannot lead you on or convince you, even when I swear a vow. But come on, let's make this bargain, with the gods as witnesses for us both—when the time comes, if your master returns to this house, give me some clothes, a tunic and a cloak and send me to Dulkhios, where I truly long to be, and if your master doesn't come, as I have said, set your slaves on me and throw me down from the highest rocks, so other beggars will shun duplicity."

The brilliant pig keeper answered him and said, "Stranger, no doubt that would bring both present and future honor and prosperity among men—for me, the one who led you into my hut, showed you hospitality, and then killed you and took your precious life away. How thoughtfully, then, I would pray to Zeus, the Son of Kronos. But for now, it's time for supper. My mates will be here soon, and we'll cook up a tasty meal."

They went on talking like this to each other until the other herdsmen drew near with their pigs. They pressed them all tightly into their usual sties, and an unspeakable pandemonium arose as they were penned in. The brilliant pig keeper called out to his partners.

"Bring in the best of the boars, and I'll kill it for our guest, who has come here from far away. We'll enjoy it ourselves—those of us who have gone through so much work and trouble, for the sake of all these pigs with their white tusks, while others eat up the fruit of our labor with impunity."

As he voiced these words, he began to split up some wood with merciless bronze, and they brought in a large boar, five years old, and held it close to the fire. The pig keeper did not forget the immortals, since he was endowed with a good heart. To begin the sacrifice, he picked the bristles out of the boar's head, with its white tusks, and threw them into the fire. He prayed to all the gods for Odysseus, always so sensible, to return home. Then he stood up. He smacked the boar with a slab of wood left over from the splitting, and its breath passed away. The others slit its throat, singed its skin, and cut it apart. The pig keeper began to place bits of raw flesh from the boar's legs to soak in the fat. He sprinkled them with barley corn and threw them all into the fire.

They cut up the rest, pierced it with spits, roasted it, drew it all off carefully, and threw it in heaps on the cutting board. The pig keeper stood up to dole it out, since he knew in his heart what was fair, and he carved it all up and served it out in seven shares. He set one of them aside for the nymphs and Hermes, son of Maia. He divided all of the rest among the other men. But he honored Odysseus with the long strips off the boar's back, which thrilled the heart of his master. Always thinking ahead, he raised his voice and he spoke these words to the man.

"For all of this, Eumaios, may you come to be as dear to Zeus, our Father, as you are to me, for offering such choice pieces for someone like me."

And Eumaios, keeper of pigs, you answered him.

"Eat, stranger, touched by Zeus. And enjoy what's there before us. It's only Zeus who gives or takes away as he chooses in his heart, since he can do anything."

With that, the pig keeper offered up the first share to the gods, who live forever. And he poured the shimmering wine and placed a cup in the hands of Odysseus, the scourge of cities. The bread was passed around to all of them by Mesaulios, whom the pig keeper had acquired for himself while his master was away, unknown to his mistress or to the old man Laertes, getting him from the Taphians in return for his own goods. And all their hands reached out for the helpings before them. And when they had put away their craving for food and drink, Mesaulios removed the leftovers, and they all hurried to bed, stuffed with bread and meat. Night came on, dark and foul and moonless. Zeus rained down all night, and the west wind, which always brings moisture, blew hard. Odysseus spoke up, testing the pig keeper, to see if he would shrug off his cloak and give it to him in sympathy, or tell one of his companions to do it.

"Listen to me now, Eumaios, and all the rest of you fellows, and I'll tell a tall tale on myself, because this wine's leading me on. It's strange how it inspires even someone who is really serious to sing and snicker softly, or stand up and dance, and even spit out stuff that's better left unspoken, but since I have already started squawking, I won't suppress this.

"If only I was still as young and strong and sure on my feet as I was back then, when we were setting up our ambush under the walls of Troy. Odysseus and Menelaos, Atreus's son, they led us, and I was third in command, since they had said so. When we reached the city and its steep walls, we all lay there in the thick brush among the reeds and marshes around the town, crouching under our arms. Night came on—it was awful when the north wind dropped. It was freezing. Snow came down from above, like frost, ice cold, and crystals set in solid, all around our shields. All the others had tunics and cloaks, their shields sheltering their shoulders.

"They all were sleeping peacefully. But I myself had stupidly ditched my cloak when I had left behind the other soldiers. I had not thought that it would be so cold, and I had come out with only my shield and my shiny belt. And so, about when the third night watch came around, and the stars had run their course across the sky, I spoke up to Odysseus, who was next to me. I jabbed him with my elbow, and at once he listened.

"'Son of Laertes, progeny of Zeus, Odysseus, always planning, I soon won't be among the living. This cold's killing me. I've got no cloak. Some god tricked me into wearing just my tunic and now there's no way out.'

"As I was speaking, he worked out a strategy in his heart—that's how he was, both in scheming and in scrapping—and muttering in a low voice, he said these words to me.

"'Quiet now, so none of the other Akhaians will hear you.'

"He propped his head on his elbow and said these words.

"'Listen, my friends, in my sleep a dream came to me from the gods. We've come out too far from the ships. If only there was someone here to take a message to Agamemnon Atreïdes, shepherd of the people, to send some more men to come up from the ships."

"Thoas, Andraimon's son, jumped up and threw his purple cloak aside, and set off for the ships. Gratefully, I lay back in his clothing until Dawn appeared on her golden throne. If only I was still young and strong and steady on my feet, then one of you herdsmen, here in these digs, might offer me your cloak out of kindness or respect for a good man. As it is, I'm scoffed at for these awful clothes I have."

And Eumaios, keeper of pigs, you gave your answer.

"Old man, you tell a great story for sure, and not a word you've said has been in any way mean or out of place. And so you won't be going without clothing or anything else that a beggar in deep trouble has a right to ask for from someone he meets—at least for now. In the morning, you'll have to wrestle yourself into those rags again. Around here, there aren't too many cloaks or changes of tunics to wear. Each man has only one. But when Odysseus's son returns, he'll give you a cloak and a tunic and some clothes, and then he'll send you anywhere your heart and soul desire to go."

After he had spoken, he stood up and set out some bedding next to the fire, and there on top of it, he flung the skins of sheep and goats. Odysseus lay down. The pig keeper threw a large, thick cloak next to him, and kept it there close by, in case a bad storm arose. There, Odysseus drifted off to sleep. And the younger men slept beside him. But the pig keeper did not want to bed down there or to lie down anywhere away from the hogs, and so he prepared to go outside. Odysseus was pleased that the man had taken such good care of things while he himself was away.

The keeper of pigs slung his sharp sword across his broad shoulders. He tossed a thick cloak around them to keep off the cold and grabbed a heavy goatskin and a spear, to hold off dogs or men, and then he went outside to go to sleep, up close to where the boars were sleeping, under a hollow rock, sheltered from the north wind.

XV

Telemakhos Returns

Pallas Athena went to spacious Lakedaimon to arouse Odysseus's brilliant son and urge him to return. She found Telemakhos lying in the portico of Menelaos's palace with Nestor's splendid son. Nestor's son had been overcome with gentle sleep, but sweet sleep did not enfold Telemakhos. All through the everlasting night, he lay awake, deep in anguish over his father. Athena, her eyes gleaming, stepped close to him and spoke.

"Telemakhos, it's no good for you to be drifting about so far away from home any longer, because you have left your fortune behind you, among unruly men who are living in your home and could divide up and totally consume all your possessions and worldly belongings, and then you will have made a futile journey. Go, as quickly as you can, and urge Menelaos, who is so good at shouting orders, to send you on so you can find your faultless mother.

"Her father and brothers are pressing her to be married to Eurymakhos, who has outdone the other suitors with ingratiating gifts and is now increasing them. Don't let her take anything valuable away from your home against your will, since you know what kind of spirit lies inside a woman's breast. She wants only to enlarge the household of any man who marries her, and then will forget her own husband, once he is dead, and ask no longer about her own children.

"So go yourself and entrust everything that is yours to whichever of the servants seems the best to you, until the gods show you the one you will honor as your wife. And another thing I'll say to you—keep it in your heart. The best of all the suitors, a gang of them, are waiting to ambush you in the strait between Ithaka and the rugged coast of Samos. They are intent to kill you before you reach your native land. But I don't think this is going to happen. The earth will sooner cover many of those courteous men who are using up what belongs to you.

"So keep your sturdy ship well away from the islands. Sail both night and day. And one of the immortals who guards and protects you will send a favorable wind. And when you reach Ithaka's nearest shore, then send your ship and all your mates on to the city. And you yourself, go first to the man who keeps your pigs. He thinks well of you. Pass the night there, and then send him off to town to bring Penelope, who thinks things over deeply, the news that you have come safely back from Pylos."

After she said this, she left for towering Olympos. Telemakhos woke Nester's son from a sweet sleep. Nudging him with his heel, he said these words to him.

"Wake up, Peisistratos. Bring your clopping horses and yoke them to your chariot, so we can get on our way."

And Peisistratos, Nester's son, answered back.

"Telemakhos, there's no way we can make it through this darkness, no matter how much we want to hit the road. Soon it'll be dawn. Let's wait until Menelaos Atreïdes, that heroic lancer, brings us gifts and places them in our chariot and sends us away with nice, good-natured words, since a guest will always remember a kindly host."

As he spoke, Dawn arrived on her golden throne. Menelaos, known for his fine battle cry, came by, after getting up from his bed beside Helen and her lovely hair. Odysseus's beloved son noticed him, and hurriedly drew his shimmering tunic over his skin. He threw his cloak across his broad shoulders and went outside. Telemakhos, the beloved son of the legendary Odysseus, then went to Menelaos and said to him, "Menelaos, Atreïdes, nurtured by Zeus himself, shepherd of the people, send me back now to my own country. My heart is anxious to return home."

Menelaos, in his great loud voice, answered him.

"Telemakhos, I will by no means hold you here for long, when you're so eager to return. I'd reproach any man who, as a host, loves too much or hates too much. Always prefer what's proper. It's equally wrong to speed a guest who's not ready to go and to impede a guest who's raring to go. Best to welcome the willing guest and hasten the hasty. But wait until I bring some lovely gifts and place them in your chariot, so you can see them with your own eyes, and I'll tell the women to prepare a meal from the ample stores we have here in my house. Two for one—honor and opulence—and relief too—to eat one's fill before heading out into the vast world.

"And if you want to travel through Hellas and into Argos, I'll go with you. I'll hook up some horses and lead you off to the cities of men. And no one will send us away with empty hands. They'll give us something to carry away. A bronze tripod or cauldron, a couple of mules, a gold cup."

Telemakhos, drawing a deep breath, answered back.

"Menelaos Atreïdes, nurtured by Zeus himself, shepherd of the people, because I have left behind no one to watch over my possessions, I would prefer to go home at once, before I become lost myself, or some prized treasure vanishes from my home."

When Menelaos heard this, in his usual loud voice, he called out right away to his wife and her slaves to prepare a meal from the ample stores in the house. Eteoneus, Boethos's son, who had only now climbed out of bed, approached, because he did not live far away. Menelaos, in his great loud voice, ordered him to light a fire and roast some meat. The man listened and obeyed. Menelaos himself went down into his scented chamber, not alone, but with Helen and Megapenthes.

When they reached the place where his treasures were stored, Atreïdes picked up a cup with two handles, and he encouraged his son to take a silver mixing bowl. Helen herself stepped over to the chest where lay the embroidered robes that she had worked so hard to make. Helen, this radiant woman, lifted out the most beautifully embroidered and largest of them all, which had been lying under the others. It shimmered like a star. Then they all went back up through the house until they reached Telemakhos. And the blond Menelaos spoke to him.

"Telemakhos, may Zeus, Hera's thundering blustery husband, bring about your return, just as you are longing for. I want to give you the most beautiful and most precious of all the prized gifts that lie about inside my house—this elegantly crafted cup. It is solid silver, and its rims are lined with gold. It is the work of Hephaistos, and Phaidimos, the heroic king of the Sidonians, gave it to me when he offered me safe haven as I was returning homeward. And now I want to pass it on to you."

Atreus's heroic son placed the double-handled cup in his hands. And Megapenthes carried over the silver mixing bowl and set it down before him. Helen with her lovely cheeks then moved close to him, with the robe in her hands. She spoke his name and said, "This gift also I offer you myself, dear child, as a fond remembrance from the arms of Helen, for your bride to wear on the occasion of your wedding to your heart's desire. Until then, leave it in your dear mother's care within your house. And you—I hope you reach your home, there in the land of your parents."

She placed it in his hands, and he received it joyfully. Peisistratos received the gifts and placed them in a chest and gazed at them with wonder in his heart. Menelaos, with his auburn hair, led them back to the house. They sat down in comfortable chairs with armrests. A slave brought an elegant golden pitcher full of water, and she poured it in a stream over a silver basin to wash their hands. She drew a polished table close to them, and the esteemed housekeeper brought bread and lots of meat and set it before them. She generously shared with them everything there was. Beside her, Boethous's son carved up the meat and measured out the helpings. The son of the great man,

Menelaos, poured the wine. And they reached out their hands to the delights in front of them.

But when they had put aside their desire for food and drink, Telemakhos and Nestor's son yoked the horses and climbed up onto their sleek chariot. They drove out through the gate, away from the echoing portico. And Menelaos Atreïdes, with his auburn hair, went with them, holding a golden cup full of wine with a hint of honey in his right hand, so that they could pour libations before setting out. He stood in front of the horses and called out to the others.

"Goodbye, young men, and greetings to Nestor, shepherd of the people. He was like a father to me, when we Akhaian sons were fighting the war at Troy."

Telemakhos took a deep breath and answered back.

"We'll tell him for sure, when we get there—and if I find Odysseus there when I reach Ithaka, I'll tell him how much kindness I've received from you, and how I brought away such beautiful gifts when I left."

As he was speaking, a bird flew by on the right, an eagle, carrying in its talons a goose, pure white and huge. It was tame, straight from the barnyard, and right behind, men and women ran, shouting. The eagle came close to them, then darted to the right in front of the horses. They were delighted to see it, and their hearts leaped with joy inside their breasts. Peisistratos, Nestor's son, was the first one to speak.

"Menelaos, Zeus's protege, leader of the people, do you think God showed this sign for us or for you?"

Menelaos, Ares's favorite, thought hard. He wondered how he might understand this thing for what it was. But Helen, in her long robes, cut in and spoke first.

"Listen to me, and I will tell you what I think is going to happen, as those who never die have thrust it deep inside my heart. Just as this eagle has come down out of the mountains, where he was brought to life among his own kind, to snatch this tame, homebred goose, so Odysseus, after wandering so far and wide and going through so much, will come home and exact his own revenge. Or maybe he's already home, sowing the seeds of trouble to come for all the courtiers."

Telemakhos took a deep breath and answered her.

"May Zeus, Hera's loud, thundering husband, make it so. Then and there, I will pray to you, as a goddess."

After he spoke, he cracked the whip at the horses, and they raced away quickly, charging through the city toward the plain. And all day, the horses shook the yoke about their necks, until the sun set and all the roads grew dark. They came to Pherae and the house of Diokles, the son of Ortilokhos, the child of Alpheos. There, he welcomed them as his guests. They passed the night, and very early, as Dawn showed her rosy fingers, they yoked the horses and climbed into their sleek chariot and drove it through the gate, away from the echoing portico. The whip cracked, and willingly the horses leaped forward. And soon after, they reached the towering fortifications of Pylos. There, Telemakhos spoke to Nestor's son.

"Nestorides, make me a promise and carry it out to the letter. Let's say that we have been friends for a long time, because of our fathers' friendship, and we ourselves are just about the same age. This journey will make us even more likeminded. Don't take me past my ship, my friend. Leave me there. Or else your old man will hold me against my will, there in your house, he is so eager to show me kindness, but I have to reach my home as quickly as possible."

After he had spoken, Nestor's son weighed in his heart how best to make this promise and carry it out. He thought over which way seemed the better way to go. Then he turned the horses toward the quick ship on the shore of the sea. He took out the beautiful gifts and set them in the stern of the ship, the clothes and the gold that Menelaos had given him, and he sent him on, with words that carried like wings.

"Hurry now, go on board and tell all your mates to do the same, before I reach home with the news. I know very well in my heart and mind how fierce his heart is. He won't allow you go. He'll come and call you back to his home, and I don't think he'd go back without you, since for sure he'll be extremely angry."

Then he drove off his horses, their beautiful manes flowing, back to the city of Pylos, and quickly he reached the palace. Telemakhos called to his mates and gave them their orders.

"Get your gear together on the black ship, mates, and then let's go on board ourselves and quickly be on our way."

As he spoke, they obeyed at once. They went on board and sat down at their benches. But while he was busying himself, offering up a sacrifice to Athena in the stern of the ship, a stranger approached him, a sage who was fleeing Argos, where he had killed a man. He was descended from Melampos, who lived long ago in Pylos, the mother of flocks, and was a rich man who had a big house, there among the Pylians. But later, he had gone to live among strangers, fleeing from Neleus the Bold, who was the most eminent of all men then alive, and who for a whole year had forcibly set aside for himself most of the other man's wealth.

But now he lay aching in chains inside the halls of Phylakos, enduring agonizing sorrows, for the sake of Neleus's daughter, and the awful blindness inside his heart that Erinys, the goddess of household disruption, had once inflicted on him. He escaped this burden and drove off the cattle, mooing loudly, from Phylake to Pylos and then took his revenge on Neleus, who was like a god, for his disgraceful act. He brought the woman home to be his brother's wife. And he went off to live among strangers in Argos, where horses graze. It was his destiny to live there and rule the people of Argos. It was there that he married a woman and built a house with high roofs. He fathered two strong sons, Antiphates and Mantios. Antiphates fathered Oikles the Daring, who himself fathered Ampiaraus, the rabble rouser, whom Zeus, who carries the aegis, loved. And Apollo supported him, too, with all kinds of favors.

But he did not reach the threshold of old age. Instead, he died in Thebes, because of a woman's gifts. He fathered two sons, Alkmaion and Aphilokhos, and Mantios himself fathered Polypheides and Kleitos. It was Kleitos who was snatched away by Dawn to her golden throne. But Apollo made Polypheides a sage, since his heart was in the clouds. He was by far the best of all men, after Amphiaraus died. He went away to live in Hyperesia after he had argued with his father. There, he lived and told everyone his visions. It was his son, Theoklymenos by name, who came and stood next to Telemakhos as he was pouring libations, praying in his black ship. The man's words beat like wings.

"My friend, since I've found you burning an offering here in this place, I pray to you, by this offering and by whatever god you pray to, and by your own life and those of your shipmates. Answer truthfully what I ask you and don't conceal anything from me. Who are you, and where among men are you from? Where is your city and where are your parents?"

Telemakhos took a deep breath and answered him.

"Fine, stranger, I will tell you everything openly. I was born in Ithaka, and my father is Odysseus, if he ever existed. But by now he must have died some miserable death. It is for this that I have now taken my companions on this black ship, to seek news of my father, who's been away so long."

Theoklymenos answered him back like a god.

"I am far away from my own country too, because I killed a man, one of my own people. Many of his family and friends rule over the Akhaians there in Argos, where horses love to graze. I am fleeing to escape death and a black end, since it seems to me that my destiny is to wander around among human beings. But take me onto your ship—I ask you as a fugitive—so they won't cut me down, because I think they're about to close in on me."

Telemakhos took a deep breath and answered him.

"As you wish, I won't throw you off this sleek ship. You'll be welcome here to anything we have at hand."

After he spoke, he took the man's bronze spear and laid it flat on the deck of the curved ship. And the man boarded the sea-going ship. Telemakhos sat down and made Theoklymenos sit down next to him. They released the stern lines, and Telemakhos called to his mates to man the rigging, and they sprang to it. They raised the pine mast and stood it within the hollow mast block and held it fast with forestays, and then they hoisted up the white sail with ox hide thongs, tightly twisted. And Athena, her eyes gleaming, sent along a favorable wind, rushing forcefully through the sky, so the ship might run its course most swiftly through the salty sea water. They went on past Krouni and Khalkis, with its beautiful streams. The sun set, and all the ways grew dark. They sailed in close beside Pheae with a wind stirred up by Zeus and on past brilliant Elis, where the Epians rule. From there, he made his way through all the islands, and as they swiftly slipped by, he wondered if he would escape death or be captured.

Odysseus and the brilliant pig keeper were both eating inside the hut, and the other men were eating with them too. But when they had set aside their desire for food and drink, Odysseus spoke up among them, testing the pig keeper once again to find out if the man would go on offering him all this attentive hospitality and encourage him to remain, there in the farm house, or send him off to the city.

"Listen now, Eumaios, and you other fellows. Tomorrow morning, I'm thinking I will head off for the city to beg, so I won't use up everything you and your men have. But give me some good advice and send a good guide with me to lead me there. Once I'm in town, I'll have to wander about on my own, until someone offers me a cup of water or a loaf of bread. And I might go straight to the house of Odysseus himself—who is so much like a god—and take the news to Penelope, who is so thoughtful. I might even intermingle with those arrogant suitors, to see if they will give me dinner, since they enjoy so much. Right away, I'd serve them up well—whatever it is that they might wish for. Because I'll tell you—now pay attention and listen to me—by the grace of Hermes, the messenger, who confers fortune and fame on all the work men do in service, no other living man can match me, splitting up dry wood and building up a fire and carving up and roasting the meat and pouring the wine—all the things us lesser men do for higher-ups."

And Eumaios, keeper of pigs, deeply upset, you spoke to him.

"Stranger, why has such a thought entered your mind? You must totally want to die there, if you're hoping to move into that pack of suitors. Their bluster and brutality reach up to the iron sky. Their servers are not like you. They are young men—those who do the serving—dressed in fine cloaks and tunics. Their fresh faces and heads of hair are always oiled and glowing. And the tables are loaded with bread and meat and wine. No—stay here. No one here is bothered by your presence. Not I, and not these others here with me. And when Odysseus's beloved son arrives, he will himself give you clothes to wear, a tunic and a cloak, and he will send you on, wherever your heart and soul desire."

Radiant, Odysseus who had endured so much, answered him in turn.

"Eumaios, may you be as dear to Father Zeus as you are to me. You have brought my wandering and awful suffering to a close. Nothing is more terrible for living men than being driven about, and yet we keep on going, through misery and trouble, if only for the sake of our damned bellies, when wandering, suffering and hardship come to us. But for now, since you are keeping me here and urging me to wait for that young man, tell me about Odysseus's mother, so like a goddess, and about his father, whom he left behind on the threshold of old age. Are they still alive below the rays of the sun, or have they died, and now are in the house of Hades."

And the keeper of pigs, a leader among men, answered him.

"All right, stranger, I'll tell you plainly. Laertes is still alive, but inside his house, he is endlessly praying to Zeus for his life to pass from his limbs. He grieves terribly for his son who went away and for his wife, that wise woman. Her dying wounded him so much, it dropped old age down on his shoulders. She passed away aching for her famous son, such a miserable death, as I would wish no one to die who lives here as a friend and offers me good will.

"As long as that woman was alive, however much in sorrow, it was always a pleasure to me to ask and inquire after her, since she herself had raised me along with Ktimene, the youngest of all the children she gave birth to—her lovely daughter—in her long robes. I was brought up with her. And the mother regarded me as hardly less than one of her own, but when we had both reached the blushing prime of our youth, they sent her away to Samos, and raised an enormous bride price.

"And me—that woman dressed me in a tunic and cloak, very nice ones, and sent me out to the fields. But in her heart, she loved me all the more. And now I don't even have this. Although, as for myself, the exalted gods have made the work I've managed very successful. And so, I've eaten and drunk and given things to those who deserve it. But from the lady of the house, I've heard nothing to my liking, neither words nor action, because a malevolence has fallen on the house—those arrogant suitors. Still, we slaves long deeply to speak with our lady, face to face, to hear about everything, to eat and drink, and later to carry something away into the fields—those things that always warm the heart of a slave."

Odysseus, always thinking ahead, answered him in turn.

"My God, how young you must have been, Eumaios, when you were taken so far away from your own country and parents. But come, tell me this and tell me openly. Was it a crowded city with wide streets that burned down, where your father and mother lived, or was it when you were alone with your sheep or cattle? Did violent men grab you and take you away on their ships to sell you to the house of this man, who must have paid a good price?"

The pig keeper, a leader among men, answered him frankly.

"Stranger, since you're asking and probing about all this, listen now—in silence—and take your pleasure, drink your wine as you sit here. The night is more immense than even a god can say. There is a time for sleeping and a time for listening and enjoying. No need to lie down before your time. Too much sleep is exhausting too. And as for you others, if your heart tugs, go on out and sleep. And when dawn comes, go ahead and eat and head out with our master's pigs. But the two of us will be drinking and eating here inside the hut, since we enjoy recalling each other's miserable misfortunes, since a man finds joy, even in hardships, after having wandered about, suffering so much.

"But I'll tell you what you're asking and inquiring about. There is an island called Syria—maybe you've heard of it—it's there above Ortygia, where the sun turns about. It's not especially populous, but the land is good. Fine herds and fine flocks, full of wine, and lots of wheat. Hunger never comes to this land, and no other dreadful disease falls upon us miserable mortals. Whenever people grow old there in that city, Apollo arrives with his silver bow, together with Artemis. He attacks them with his painless arrows and kills them. There are two cities there and everything is divided in two. My father—Ktesios Ormenides, a man, but like the immortals—ruled over them both.

"To that place came the Phoenikians, well known for their ships and for being slippery scoundrels, and they brought countless trinkets on their black ship. There, in my father's house, there was a Phoenikian woman—lovely and tall and skilled in brilliant craftsmanship. The sly Phoenikians seduced her. First, while she was washing clothes near the mooring stones beside their empty ship, one of them talked her into making love, because this will loosen a woman's mind, even when she has good intentions. He asked her who she was and where she came from, and right away, she showed him the high roofs of my father's house.

"'I can only tell you I am from Sidon, with its bronze. I am the daughter of Arybas, whose wealth was like a flood. But Taphian thieves took me as I was coming in from the fields. They brought me here and sold me into the house of that man. And he paid a high price for me.'

"And the man who had slept with her answered back.

'Why not go back home with us, so you can see your father and mother's house, with its high roofs, and them too? I hear they are still alive, and rich, too!'

"The woman answered him and said these words.

"'It is possible, if you sailors will pledge an oath that you will take me home, safe and sound.'

"After she spoke, they promised her what she asked for. And after they had sworn their solemn vow to its close, the woman opened up and spoke these words to them.

"'From now on, be silent. None of you should say a word to me, if you run into me on the street, or by the well—or else, someone might go up to the palace and tell the old man so he gets to thinking and locks me up in awful chains and then makes plans to kill you. Keep these words in mind.

"'So hurry up your trade in goods, and when your ship's full of cargo, have a messenger come quickly to the palace, and I will grab whatever gold I can take under my arm, and I will give you something extra for my passage—the child of this great man. I take care of him in the palace, and he runs around with me outside. Such a clever child. I could lead him to the ship. He would bring you a huge price, wherever you might go to sell him among men who speak strange tongues.'

"After saying these words, she went to the lovely palace. They stayed there trading for a whole year and brought a huge cargo onto their hollow ship. But when the ship was full enough to sail home, they sent a messenger to pass the news to this woman. A man came, very shrewd, to my father's house, bringing a golden necklace, strung with amber beads. My dear mother and all her servants were feeling it in their hands and inspecting it with their eyes, about to make an offer. He nodded to the woman in silence. And after nodding, he went back to the ship, and she took me by the hand and led me out of the house.

"On the palace porch, she found the cups and tables left by my father's attendants, who had just eaten and then moved on to the council and the public debate. She quickly hid three of the chalices deep inside the folds covering her breasts, and she carried them away. And without thinking, I followed her. The sun set, and all the roads grew dark. We hurried down and reached that marvelous harbor where the Phoenikians' swift ship was waiting. The men embarked and brought the two of us on board and sailed out on the waters, and Zeus sent a favorable wind.

"We sailed for six days and nights, but when Zeus, the Son of Kronos, brought the seventh day, Artemis, the archer, struck the woman. She fell down with a thud into the hold, plunging like a sea gull. They threw her body overboard, to become the prey of seals and fish. I was left alone, my heart in anguish. And the wind carried them, and the waters brought them to Ithaka, where Laertes bought me with his riches, and so it was that my eyes came to see this land."

Odysseus, Zeus's descendant, answered him in turn with these words.

"Eumaios, you have deeply stirred this heart inside my chest, telling me all the agonies you've suffered in your heart. But clearly Zeus has given you the good along with the bad, since after all these hardships, you have come to the house of this kind man who generously gives you food and drink, and your life is good, while I have come here, after wandering around so many cities."

They went on talking to each other, and then lay down to sleep—not for long, just a short time—since Dawn, on her shining throne, came soon. Drawing close to shore, Telemakhos's crew released the sail, lowered the mast quickly, and rowed the ship to anchorage with their oars. And they threw out the mooring stones and tied down the stern cables. They jumped onto the shore. They prepared their meal, mixed some sparkling wine, and when they had put aside their desire for food and drink, Telemakhos gathering his thoughts, was first to speak.

"Row our black ship to the city. I will make my way to the fields and the herdsmen. And tonight, I will come to the city, after looking the land over. And in the morning, to pay you off, I'll give you a feast with sweet wine."

Theoklymenos then spoke to him like a god.

"Where should I go, my son? To whose house should I go, of all the lords, here in rocky Ithaka? Or should I go straight to your mother's house?"

Telemakhos, gathering his thoughts, answered him.

"If things were different, I'd tell you to go to our place, as there's no lack of hospitality there. But that would be worse for you, since I will be away. And my mother will not see you, since she does not often appear among the suitors inside the house, but is always weaving at her loom in an upper room, away from them. I'll tell you someone else you can go to—Eurymakhos, the son of Polybos, a shrewd man, whom Ithakans now view as a god. Eurymakhos is the best by far and most desires to marry my mother and hold Odysseus's authority. But only Olympian Zeus, who lives high above, knows if he himself, before the wedding, will bring about a terrible day."

As he spoke, on the right a bird flew by—a hawk—Apollo's quick messenger. It held a dove in its talons, plucking the feathers and shedding them on the ground between Telemakhos and the ship. Theoklymenos pulled him aside, and he gripped his hand. He called him by name and said, "Telemakhos, I am sure that this bird just flew by at the will of some god. I knew, when I saw it—it is an omen. No other lineage here in Ithaka is more regal than yours. Your power is for all time!"

Gathering his thoughts, Telemakhos answered in reply.

"Ah, stranger, if only what you're saying might come to be, you'd know my friendship and generosity, so anyone who met you would call you a happy man."

As he spoke, he turned to Peiraios, his trusted companion.

"Peiraios Klytides, you are the most loyal of the men who went with me to Pylos. Take this stranger to your house and show him your hospitality and respect until I come."

And Peiraios, the famous spearsman, answered in reply.

"Telemakhos, however long you stay here, I will make him welcome, and he will lack for nothing any guest should have."

As he spoke, he climbed onto the ship and called out to his mates to come aboard and release the stern cables. They quickly boarded and sat down at their benches. Telemakhos put his lightweight sandals on his feet. He grabbed his thick spear, with its sharp bronze point, out of the ship. And the men released the stern cables. They pushed off and sailed away toward the city, as ordered by Telemakhos, Odysseus's own son. His feet carried him quickly and he walked on and on, until he came to the farmhouse, where all of his innumerable hogs and pigs were sleeping, together with his trusted pig keeper, who was so loyal to his masters.

XVI

Plans

Inside the hut, Odysseus and the brilliant pig keeper had kindled a fire and were preparing their meal at dawn. The herdsmen had been sent out with all the packs of pigs. As Telemakhos came near, the usually snarling dogs wagged their tails about him. Brilliant Odysseus noticed the lively dogs and the tread of approaching footsteps. Right away, his words rushed to Eumaios on the wing.

"Eumaios, it must be a friend of yours who's coming here, or someone you know, at least. The dogs aren't barking. In fact, they're wagging their tails, and I hear the sound of footsteps."

These words were not yet fully spoken when there was his own precious son, standing in the doorway. The pig keeper jumped up in surprise. The bowls he had been tinkering with as he mixed the shimmering wine fell from his hands. He went straight to meet his master. He kissed his head and both his beautiful eyes and both his hands. A large tear welled up and fell. Like a father who lovingly regards and greets his son, who has come home from a distant land, after ten years—his dearly loved, only son, for whom he had suffered so much sorrow—the radiant pig keeper threw his arms around Telemakhos, who looked like a god, and kissed him again and again, like someone who has just escaped death. Through his sobs, he said these words, quivering like wings.

"You've come, Telemakhos, sweetest light of my eyes. I thought I'd never see you, after you went away in your ship to Pylos. But come—come in, dear child, so I can take my heart's delight in seeing you here, after just returning from faraway lands. It's not often you come here to visit the farm and the field hands. You stay in town instead, so I suppose then your heart was delighted to see that plagued pack of courteous men."

Telemakhos took a deep breath and answered back.

"So it will be, Papa. It's for you I came here, to see you with my own eyes and hear what you have to say—if my mother remains in the house, or if some other man has married her, or maybe Odysseus's bed, with no one sleeping on it, is just lying there, full of nasty spiders' webs."

The pig keeper, a leader of men, answered him directly.

"Yes, for sure, she's still right there in your palace, with her stubborn heart, and always deep in sorrow, the nights and days fall away as her tears keep falling."

After saying this, Eumaios took the bronze spear, and Telemakhos stepped over the stone threshold and went in. As he approached, Odysseus, his father, rose from his stool and stepped back. Telemakhos, from where he was standing, held him back and said, "Sit, stranger. We will find a place to sit elsewhere in this hut. This man here will set one up for us."

As he was speaking, Odysseus went back and sat down. The pig keeper spread out some fresh twigs and lay a goat skin over it, and there, Odysseus's own son sat down. The pig keeper then placed before them some dishes full of roasted meat, left over from the day before, and he quickly put out heaps of bread in baskets and mixed up some wine, sweet as honey, in a wooden bowl. Then he himself sat down, across from Odysseus, who sat there like a god, and all of them reached their hands out toward the good things that lay in front of them. But when they had put aside their desire for food and drink, Telemakhos then spoke to the radiant pig keeper.

"Papa, where did this stranger come from? How did the seamen bring him here to Ithaka? And who did they claim to be? Because I hardly think he's traveled here on foot."

And Eumaios, keeper of pigs, you answered in turn.

"Child, I'll tell you the whole truth. He claims he was born in Krete, and he says he's wandered round and about to many cities that people live in. Some god has spun this web for him. But now he has slipped away from a Thresprotian ship and has come here to the farmhouse. I put him in your hands. Do as you wish. He comes to you as someone in need."

Telemakhos, gathering his thoughts, answered back.

"Eumaios, what you've said troubles me deeply. How am I to welcome this stranger into my house? I'm still young and don't really trust my own strength to defend myself against any man when he gets angry, and my mother—her heart keeps wavering, back and forth, whether to stay with me and keep the house, in respect to her husband and the voice of the people, or to go away now, with whoever is the best of the Akhaians courting her in her own halls, or whoever offers the best gifts.

"As for this stranger, since he has come to this house, I will give him some fine clothes, a cloak and a tunic, and also a double-edged sword and some sandals for his feet and I'll send him wherever it is his heart and soul want to go. If you wish, keep him here at the farmhouse and take care of him. And I will send the clothes here, along with all his food, so he won't make it worse for you and the others. But I will not let him go there among the suitors—they are so totally, so unforgivably pigheaded! They'd mock him and I would be deeply upset. To carry out anything against so many is hard, even for a brave man, and they are much stronger."

Odysseus, who had been through so much, answered back.

"My friend, since I'm sure it's only right for me to offer you an answer—it tears my heart apart as I'm listening to you. This shamelessness that you say these suitors are persisting in, there in your halls, in spite of you—tell me, do you subject yourself to this willingly? Or do the people of this land despise you, trusting in the voice of some god? Or is it a lapse among your brothers, whose help a man can always depend on whenever some serious dispute arises?

"I wish I was as young as I feel, here within my heart. I wish I was the son of the flawless Odysseus, or Odysseus himself! Then some total stranger would soon cut off my head, if I failed to show myself to be the curse of all those who have come to the house of Odysseus Laertiádes! Even if they overcame me, all by myself, against all their numbers, I have to say, I'd rather die, murdered inside my own halls, than to see these abominable acts over and over again, knocking guests about and dragging slave women around that beautiful house, and using up all of the wine and eating up all of the bread, without even a thought—endlessly, pointlessly."

Telemakhos, gathering his thoughts, answered back.

"Stranger, I am going to tell you this very frankly. No one among the people here finds fault with me or hates me, and I cannot lay any blame on a brother whose fierce backing a man can always depend on whenever some serious dispute arises, since the Son of Kronos singled out my family to be loners. Arkeidios had one son, and Laertes, Odysseus's father had only one. And Odysseus himself had only one, and he left me alone in his halls, and never was able to see any joy or use in me. And now, there are countless enemies in my house—all the very best of those who hold power in the islands, Dulikhios and Samos, and the forests of Zakynthos, and all those who hold sway here in rugged Ithaka.

"They're now courting my mother and desecrating my house. She neither refuses to make an undesirable marriage nor is she able to put an end to it all, and they are eating me out of house and home. And very soon they will break me down and leave me with nothing. But all these things lie on the knees of the gods. Papa, go quickly and tell Penelope I have come back safely from Pylos. I will stay here. And you come back here too, after you have told the news—only to her. Do not let any of the other Akhaians learn this, or they will plan something terrible for me."

And Eumaios, keeper of pigs, you answered him in return.

"I hear you, and I see all that. You're talking to someone who understands. But come, tell me this and lay it out frankly. Should I go on the same way with the news for Laertes? He is so unfortunate. For a while, though he was mourning so much for Odysseus, he kept his eye on the fields, and he ate and drank with all the servants in the house, as his heart urged him to inside his chest. But now, since you left by ship for Pylos, they say that he no longer eats and drinks as he did before and doesn't watch over the field work. He sits in sorrow, moaning, groaning, and the flesh is shriveling from his bones."

Taking a deep breath, Telemakhos answered him.

"That's very sad, but we'll leave him there alone, even though it troubles us. If only it were somehow possible for living men to have everything they wished for—then we'd choose, first of all, the day of my father's return. So, deliver your message and then come back, and do not go meandering about the fields, looking around for that old man. Just tell my mother to send the housekeeper, her servant, as quickly as possible, but in secret. She can carry the message on to the old man."

And so he hurried the pig keeper on his way. Eumaios picked up his sandals in his hands, strapped them onto his feet, and went off to town. And Athena was by no means unaware of Eumaios, the pig keeper, leaving the farmhouse. She came close by in the guise of a woman, tall, beautiful, and skilled in exquisite crafts. She stood by the door of the hut and showed herself to Odysseus. But Telemakhos did not notice or see her standing before him, because somehow the gods do not make themselves visible to everyone. But Odysseus saw her, and the dogs did too. They did not bark. They whimpered and drew back in fear, to the far side of the hut. She made a gesture with her eyebrows. Odysseus, radiant, noticed, and he went outside the hut and out past the high wall of the courtyard. There he stood in front of her, and Athena spoke to him.

"Laertiádes, descendant of Zeus, Odysseus, you're always working out some scheme, but now, go and tell your son what you have to say, and do not hide it any longer. And after you two have figured out your plans for the suitors' death and doom, go on to that legendary city. I'll not be away from you for long. I am eager for the fight."

And Athena touched him with her golden wand. First, she placed a freshly washed cloak and tunic about his chest and gave him back the fresh figure and bearing of his youth. His skin grew darker once again, and his cheeks grew firm and taut. His beard turned dark as iron about his jaw. And when she had finished doing all of this, she went away. Odysseus entered the hut. His son gazed at him in wonder. He turned his eyes away, trembling, fearing that this might be some god. Then he spoke out, his words quivering like wings.

"You seem different to me, stranger, much younger than before. The clothes you're wearing and even your skin's no longer the same. You must be some god, one of those who live above in the boundless sky. Be gracious, so we may greet you and honor you with some finely crafted golden gifts. Have mercy on us."

Radiant, Odysseus, who had endured so much, answered him in turn.

"A god? No. I'm not a god. Why do you say I am like the gods? No. I am your father—the one you have sighed for and have suffered so much sorrow for, while coming up against the violence of men."

He spoke and kissed his son, and his tears welled up and fell from his cheeks, before he was able to hold them in. Telemakhos still did not believe that this was his father, and again, he spoke, answering in return.

"You are not Odysseus, my father, but some god trying to trick me, so I will moan and sigh even more. There is no way a mere man could think this up in his own mind, unless a god came to him and effortlessly made him young or old at will. Before, you were just an old man, shabbily dressed, and now, suddenly, you look like one of the gods who occupy the vast sky."

Odysseus, always thinking ahead, answered him in turn.

"Telemakhos, it's not right for you to be so utterly amazed and shocked that your father is standing here in front of you. No other Odysseus will ever be coming here. Here I am, just as you see me, after suffering through so many horrible things and wandering around for so long and so far—after twenty years, I have come to my own land. This is the work of Athena, who makes me just as she wishes, because she can—at one time like a beggar, and later, a young man, wearing fine clothes about his skin. It is easy for the gods, who hold the boundless sky, to lift a man to glory, or drive him to desolation."

He voiced these words and sat down. And Telemakhos flung his arms around his beloved father and sobbed and let his tears fall. The urge to cry poured from both their hearts. They cried out loud, bellowing like birds or eagles or vultures with crooked talons, whose chicks the farm workers have taken away before they were able to learn to fly. They openly let their tears fall from their eyes, and the sunlight would have set upon their weeping, if Telemakhos had not suddenly said to his father, "On what kind of ship, dear father, did those sailors bring you here to Ithaka? Who did they say they were? Because I hardly think you reached here on foot."

Odysseus, who had endured so much, answered back.

"And so, son, I will tell you openly. The Phaiakians brought me here. They're famous for their ships and for sending on the people who've come their way. They brought me while I was sleeping in their swift ship, set me down in Ithaka, and gave me some fine gifts, bronze and gold and plenty of woven fabrics. And that is now fully stored in caves by the will of the gods. I have come here on Athena's advice, to discuss our enemies' end. But come now, count the suitors for me and tell me all about them, so I'll know who and how many there are, and so I can figure out in my faultless heart if the two of us can hold our own against them with no one else, or if we need to look for others."

Telemakhos, gathering his thoughts, answered him.

"Father, I've always heard you were a famous spearman, both in tactics and the strength of your hands, but what you are saying is too much. I am amazed. It just cannot be that two men could fight against so many strong men. There are not just ten suitors, or twice that. There are so many more. Here are the numbers. From Doulikhios there are fifty-two select young men, and there are six attendants with them. From Samos, there are twenty-four men. And from Zakynthos, there are twenty young men. And there are twenty from Ithaka itself, all of them elite, and with them is Medon, their messenger, the heavenly singer, and two attendants, skilled at carving. If we faced all of them while inside, our attempt to force them back and exact our revenge would be very bitter, horrific. You have to bear in mind whether you're able to think of any supporter who would back us up with a determined heart."

Odysseus, who had endured so much, answered him.

"All right, I'll tell you. Listen to me and pay attention. Think about whether Athena and Father Zeus will be enough, or whether I should think up another supporter."

Telemakhos took a deep breath and answered him.

"These supporters you suggest are indeed reliable, yet they sit high in the clouds, ruling all the rest of men and the gods who never have to die."

Radiant, Odysseus, who had endured so much, answered him.

"The two of them won't hold back for very long when the force of Ares settles the matter between the suitors and us. But for now, when dawn comes, go home and join in with all those arrogant suitors. The pig keeper will lead me to the city, looking like a repulsive old beggar. And if they demean me in my own house, let your heart keep beating within your chest, even if I am suffering badly. Even if they drag me by the feet through the door or throw things at me, watch them and keep on watching. Or tell them to stop their foolishness or try to persuade them all with soothing words. They won't listen. The day of their ruin is here.

"And I'll say something else—hold it in your heart. When Athena places her thoughtful guidance inside my heart, I'll nod my head to you. And when you notice, take up the weapons of war that lie about in our halls and put them all away in the innermost part of the upper room. When the suitors miss them and begin to ask about them, soothe them with these gentle words.

'I've laid them away, since they're no longer like those Odysseus left behind when he went to Troy. They're tarnished because the fumes from the fires have reached them. Also, the Son of Kronos has placed an even greater fear in my heart. You might get drunk and fight and wound each other, and thus disgrace your feast and courtship. For iron's a magnet to men.'

"Only for us two, leave behind two swords, two spears, and two ox hide shields, so that we can rush them and seize them, and take them up in our hands, while Pallas Athena and Zeus, our guides, distract the others. And another thing I'll say, and hold this too, there inside your heart. If you are truly my own son and of the same blood, let no one know—Odysseus is back. Do not let Laertes know, or the pig keeper, or anyone else inside the household, and not even Penelope. On our own, we'll learn the women's leanings and test the serving men to learn who respects us or who fears us in his heart, and who doesn't care for us or who demeans such a man as you."

Radiant, his son found his voice and answered him in turn.

"Father, I think you'll come to know my heart soon enough. I'm not mindless. And I do not think that this plan will work for us. I suggest that you think again. To go around the fields and farms, testing each man, would be useless and take a long time, while those other men are casually and unsparingly using up all your fortune in your own halls, and with such arrogance. But I strongly urge you to find out which of the women do not respect you and which ones are innocent. I would rather not test out the men out on the farms but do that later, if you have some sign from Zeus, who holds the aegis."

They continued talking to each other in this way as the sturdy ship that had carried Telemakhos and all his mates to Pylos put in to Ithaka. Entering the deep harbor, they dragged the black ship onto the shore. Enthusiastic attendants unloaded their equipment and right away they carried away all the beautiful gifts to the house of Klytios. They sent a messenger on to the house of Odysseus, to take the word to thoughtful Penelope that Telemakhos was in the country and had ordered the ship to sail on toward the city, so that the great queen would not be alarmed in her heart and let her delicate tears fall. And the messenger and the brilliant pig keeper came together on the same mission, to break the news to Odysseus's wife. And when they reached the king's palace, there in front of the women slaves, the messenger said, "Just now, your majesty, your beloved son has returned."

But the pig keeper approached Penelope and told her everything that her beloved son had urged him to say. After he had told her everything he had been ordered to say, he left the palace and the courtyard, and he went back among the pigs. But the suitors were disturbed and troubled in their hearts. They left the palace and went outside, past the courtyard's high wall, and they sat down in front of the gates. Eurumakhos, Polybios' son, was the first to speak among them.

"With this voyage, a great act has certainly been accomplished by Telemakhos, and we had thought that he would never see it through. But come now, let's take out our own black ship, the best there is, and pull together some sailors to serve as rowers, so that they can go and tell those others to return here as quickly as possible."

He had not even finished speaking when Amphinomos turned around and saw a ship in the harbor. They were rolling up the sail, holding their oars in their hands. He laughed out loud and spoke to his companions.

"No need for us to send a message now. Here they are. Either some god told them about this or they saw Telemakhos's ship sail by, but could not overtake it."

After he spoke, they stood up and went down to the sea. Quickly they dragged the black ship onto the shore, and enthusiastic attendants hauled in their equipment. Together, they went to the place of assembly, but they did not allow any of the other people to sit with them, neither the young ones nor the old men. And Antinoos, son of Eupeithes, spoke among them.

"Awful, how the gods have delivered this man away from his worst fear. Every day our lookouts sat out on the windy headlands, one after another, and after sunset we never passed a night ashore. We sailed out quickly in our ship and stayed there until the light of dawn, waiting in ambush for Telemakhos, to take him and kill him. It must be some god that has brought him back. As for us, let's think up a horrible death for Telemakhos, and not allow him to escape out of our hands, since I think this work of ours will not turn out well if this man remains alive. He's too clever at thinking and plotting things out, and the people are no longer showing us any favor at all.

"But come, before he gathers the Akhaians to assembly, and I don't think he will hold back anything. He'll be enraged and stand up and declare before them all, how we blatantly conspired to assassinate him but did not catch him. They will not back us when they hear about our malicious action. They'll work their malice against us and drive us from this country to some land of strangers. Let's act first and seize him in the country far from the city, or out on the road.

"We'll keep his property and assets ourselves and divide them up fairly among ourselves, although we will give the house to his mother to keep for herself and whoever marries her. And if you don't like this plan and you'd rather let him live and keep all his family fortune, let's not keep on using up this wealth of delectable pleasures, as we gather here together. Let's court her, each one of us, from our own homes, court her with our gifts, and she will then marry whoever it is who offers her the most and thus becomes the man of destiny."

After he spoke, all of them were hushed in silence, until Amphinomos, the handsome son of Lord Nisos Aretiádes, faced the assembly. He led the suitors from Doulikhios, rich in wheat and grasses, and Penelope liked him most of all for the way he talked, since he had a courteous heart, when it served him. With good intentions, he addressed them all and said,

"My friends, for myself I'd much prefer not to kill Telemakhos. It's such a dreadful thing to kill someone of royal blood. Instead, let's first elicit the will of the gods. And if the authority of almighty Zeus allows, I myself will execute him and urge all the rest of you to follow. But if the gods turn us away, I'd suggest that we all desist."

As Amphinomos spoke, they found his words agreeable. They all stood at once and went to Odysseus's house. They entered and sat down on the finely polished chairs. Penelope, deep in thought, noticed them and decided to show herself to the suitors, no matter how overbearing their arrogance was, since she had learned of their threats to kill her son in her own home. Medon, the messenger, had told her. He had overheard their meeting, and so she made her way to the great hall, with all her serving women. But when the lovely woman reached the suitors, she stood very still beside the doorpost of the grand hall, holding a shimmering veil in front of her face. She rebuked Antinoos, calling him by name.

"Antinoos, you are plotting arrogantly, maliciously. They say you're the best in planning and eloquence of all those of your age in the land of Ithaka. But you're not. You lunatic! Why are you planning death and destruction for Telemakhos, without a thought of becoming one of those who have to beg for mercy, for whom Zeus himself is both witness and judge? It's horrible to contrive malicious plans against others. Don't you remember when your father came here to this house in fear of the people?

"They were enraged at him because he joined the Taphian cutthroats and tormented the Thesprotians, our allies. They wanted to murder him, to rip out his heart and take away everything he loved so dearly. It was Odysseus who held them back. Heated as they were, he held them back. And it is his household that you are now consuming so dishonorably, and you are courting his wife, and now, here you are seeking to kill his son. You are tormenting me deeply. I'm telling you to stop now and urge these others to stop as well."

Eurymakhos, the son of Polybos, answered back.

"Penelope, Ikarios's daughter, you always think too much. Cheer up. Don't trouble your heart with these things. There's no man alive, or yet to be born, who shall lay his hands on your son Telemakhos, while I am alive and able to look upon this world. I'll say this outright—and it will be carried out—the black blood of that man would quickly run down my spear, since it was me, too, that Odysseus, the scourge of cities, placed on his knees and put roast meat in my hands, and held the red wine to my lips. Telemakhos is the dearest of all men to me. And so I urge him not to fear death from these gentlemen, although no one can escape whatever may come from the gods."

He said all this to cheer her up, while he himself was plotting the man's death. And so she simply went up to her brightly lit upper room, and there she wept for Odysseus, her beloved husband, until Athena, her gray eyes gleaming, shed sweet sleep over her eyelids.

That evening, the brilliant pig keeper came back to Odysseus and his son, who were standing around, preparing their supper, after they had slaughtered a one-year-old boar. Athena herself approached Odysseus Laertiádes and touched him with her wand, turning him back into an old man. She wrapped some nasty clothing around his skin, just in case the pig keeper saw him and knew him and went back to tell the news to faithful Penelope, instead of keeping the secret in his heart. Telemakhos spoke to him first.

"Eumaios, you've come. What's the news in the city? Have those brave gentlemen come back from their ambush yet, or are they still looking to take me on my way home?"

And Eumaios, keeper of pigs, you gave your answer in return.

"It wasn't for me to go around the city, inquiring about all that. My heart told me to come back here after giving my message. But there, a prompt messenger from your mates met me, and he talked first to your mother, but I know this as well. I saw it with my own eyes. Heading along Hermes' Ridge, above the city, I saw a ship, quickly putting into port. There were a lot of men on her, weighed down with shields and double-edged spears. I was thinking it might well be them, but I do not know for sure."

As he spoke, the deep inner strength of Telemakhos smiled, his eyes glancing at his father, but he avoided looking at the pig keeper. And when they had finished the work of preparing the meal, they ate, and no one's heart was found unequal to the feast. But when they put aside their desire for food and drink, they decided to get some rest, and they received the gift of sleep.

XVII

Stranger in the House

Very early, as Dawn's rosy fingers appeared, Telemakhos, Odysseus beloved son bound his excellent sandals under his feet and clutched his thick spear, which perfectly fit his grip, and anxious for the city, he spoke to the pig keeper.

"Papa, I'm going to town so my mother can see me. I don't think she'll ever stop sobbing bitterly or shedding her tears until she actually sees me in the flesh. But let me trouble you with this. Take this pitiful stranger to the city, so that he can beg for his meals there, and whoever is willing can give him bread and a cup of water. But as for me, there's no way I can worry about every person. I have my own troubles, here inside my heart. And if the stranger gets really angry about this, so much the worse for him. I'd rather tell the truth."

Odysseus, always thinking ahead, answered him in turn.

"My friend, I am myself not eager to be left behind here. For a beggar it's better to beg for food in town than in the country. Whoever wishes to will give me something, and I'm no longer the age to stay on a farm, obeying all kinds of orders from some foreman. Go on. This man will show me the way, as you ordered, as soon as I've warmed myself beside the fire and it warms up outside. Because these clothes I have are horribly bad, and the morning frost might bring me down because, as you say, the city's a bit far."

After he spoke, Telemakhos went out through the yard with quick steps, plotting troubled times for the suitors. When he reached his stately home, he leaned his spear against a tall pillar, crossed the stone threshold, and went inside. Eurykleia, his nurse, saw him first, as she was spreading out some fleeces on elegantly crafted chairs. Bursting into tears, she walked straight to him, and the other women slaves of iron-willed Odysseus gathered all around. They greeted him lovingly and kissed his head and shoulders. Penelope, deep in thought, came out of her room, looking like Artemis or golden Aphrodite, and bursting into tears, she threw her arms around her beloved son. She kissed his head and both his beautiful eyes and crying and sobbing, she spoke to him, her words trembling like wings.

"You have come, Telemakhos, sweet light of my eyes. I thought I'd never see you again, after you went away in your ship to Pylos, secretly, against my will, for word about your beloved father. But tell me now, if you have caught sight of him."

Telemakhos took a deep breath and answered her.

"Mother, don't make me cry or trouble the heart inside my chest for having escaped my own death. Go and bathe yourself and put some clean clothes over your skin, and go up to your upper room with all your servants and make a vow to all the gods that you will perform a sacrifice of a hundred oxen, so that Zeus might one day bring about his own acts of reckoning. And I'll head to the assembly, to invite here a stranger who came back with me from Pylos. I've sent him off with my trustworthy friends and urged Peiraios to take him home and show him both honor and generous hospitality, until I come for him."

After he spoke, her own words did not take wing. She went upstairs to bathe, and she put on fresh clothes over her body. She vowed to all the gods that she would perform a sacrifice of a hundred oxen, so Zeus would one day achieve his own acts of justice. Telemakhos left, spear in hand, with two dogs, and the grace Athena shed down upon him was a wonder. All of the people watched in awe as he walked by.

The reckless suitors gathered around him, chattering with respect, although in the depths of their hearts, they brooded maliciously. He eluded the swelling pack of them and went and sat with Mentor, Antiphos and Halitherses, family friends from the beginning. They asked him about everything, and then Peiraios, the famous spearman, approached, leading the stranger through the city to the assembly. Telemakhos did not hold back from the stranger for long. He stood up and faced him, but it was Peiraios who spoke first.

"Telemakhos, send your women to my house quickly, so that I can send you the gifts that Menelaos gave you."

Gathering his thoughts, Telemakhos answered him.

"Peiraios, we don't yet know how all these things will turn out. If these brave gentlemen kill me in secret within my own halls, and divide up all my father's things, I wish you would keep it all and enjoy it for yourself, rather than one of them. But if I manage to sow the seeds of their bloody slaughter and death, then yes, go on and bring it to my house joyfully, and I'll be joyful too."

As he spoke, he led away the stranger, who had faced so many ordeals, back to his house. When the two had reached the stately home, they laid aside their cloaks on the stools and chairs and entered the polished baths to wash themselves. And after the slave women bathed them, anointed them with oil, and threw soft tunics and cloaks about them, they came out of the baths and sat down in chairs. A slave brought out water for their hands in an elegant golden pitcher. She poured it out, over a silver basin, to wash them. And then she drew a polished table nearby.

And the revered housekeeper brought out and set before them bread, and plenty of food, offering freely everything that was available. His mother sat beside the doorpost across from him. She leaned back in the chair, spinning some fine woolen threads. They reached out their hands to the refreshments that lay before them, and when they had all put aside their desire for food and drink, Penelope, deep in thought, was the first to speak.

"Telemakhos, I'm going up to my room to lie in bed, which for me has become a place to weep, always damp with my tears, ever since Odysseus set out for Ilios with the sons of Atreus. But you have not yet bothered to tell me openly, in front of these brave courtiers gathered in this house, about your father's return, if you have heard anything."

Gathering his thoughts, Telemakhos answered her.

"I will of course, Mother, tell you the whole truth. We went to Pylos to see Nestor, the shepherd of his people, and he received me in his towering palace and made me very welcome—just as a father would do for his own son who'd come home from far away, he and his splendid sons cared for me generously. He said he had never heard a thing about unwavering Odysseus, alive or dead, from anyone on earth. But he generously sent me on with a chariot and horses in harness to the famous lancer, Menelaos Atreïdes. There I saw the Argive, Helen, for whose sake the Argives and Trojans struggled so mightily at the will of the gods. And at once, Menelaos, in his usual loud voice, asked me why I'd come to gleaming Lakedaimon. And I laid out the whole truth to him. He answered me in turn and said these words.

"'For shame! Clearly they're eager to slip into the bed of a man with a greater heart than theirs, since they're so spineless. It's like when a doe puts her suckling fawns to sleep in a dense thicket, the lair of a great lion, and goes out to graze on the slopes and passes, until the lion returns and unleashes a pitiless end on them. That's how Odysseus will unleash a pitiless end on those men. Father Zeus, Athena and Apollo, if only he'd rise up, like that time in lovely Lesbos, when he wrestled Philomeleïdes and threw him down so hard, and the Akhaians all cheered. Like that, Odysseus would tangle with those suitors, and all of them would come to face a bitter marriage—a very quick death.

"'But about what you're asking, I won't evade you and speak of other things or mislead you. I will not withhold a word of all that utterly truthful old man of the sea told me. He said he had seen Odysseus on an island, suffering bitterly within the house of the nymph, Kalypso, who is holding him there under duress, so that he is not able to reach his native land, because he has no ships, no oars, no mates to send him on, over the broad back of the sea.'

"That's what Menelaos Atreïdes said. And to finish it, I came home. The immortals gave me a favorable wind and brought me quickly back to my own land."

His words stirred her heart within her chest. And then, Theoklymenos, like a god, spoke among them.

"Honored wife of Odysseus Laertiades, obviously he does not know, but listen to what I have to say. And I will give you my exact prediction, and I will hide nothing. As Zeus, the first among the gods, is my witness, along with this hospitable table and hearth belonging to faultless Odysseus, know Odysseus is already in his own country, whether sitting back or lurking around, finding out all about these awful actions, and he's planting the seeds of troubled times for all the suitors. I saw an obvious bird of omen as I sat on the benches of our ship, and I have made all of this known to Telemakhos."

Penelope, deep in thought, answered him frankly.

"Ah, stranger, if only that might come to be. Then you'd very quickly come to realize our generosity, with many gifts from me, so that anyone who met you then would call you blessed."

And they went on talking to each other in this way, while the suitors went on enjoying themselves in front of Odysseus's house. They were throwing the discus and spears in a cleared area, as recklessly as ever. But when it was time for their meal, and the flocks were coming in from all of the fields, with the men, as usual, leading them in, Medon, the messenger whom they liked most of all, and who was always with them at their feasts, spoke to them.

"Young men, since you've enjoyed yourselves so much at sports, come to the palace and we will prepare a feast, since it's not so bad to take your meal at the right hour."

As he spoke, they obeyed what he said and stood up and went. And when they had come to the stately palace, they threw down all their cloaks on the stools and chairs. They killed some large sheep and goats and slaughtered some fattened sows and a cow taken from the herd. And they began preparing the meal, while Odysseus and the pig keeper urged each other to hurry and make their way from the country to the city. The pig keeper, a leader among men, spoke first.

"Stranger, you're so anxious to go to the city, as my master told you to, though I'd rather leave you here to guard the farm. But I respect and fear him—he might shout at me later, and the scolding of masters can be hard to take, so come, let's go. The day is almost gone, and soon enough, toward evening, it will be getting colder."

Odysseus, always thinking ahead, answered him in turn.

"I hear you and I know. You're talking to someone who understands. So let's go. You can lead the way. But give me a staff to lean on, if you have one cut somewhere, since you said the road is slippery."

He threw his ragged leather pouch, full of holes, with its rope strap, over his shoulder and Eumaios gave him a good staff, and they set off. The herdsman and the dogs remained behind to guard the farm, as Eumaios led his master toward the city, looking like a miserable old beggar, leaning on a staff, and the clothes he wore over his body were awful. They made their way along the rutted road near the city and came to a well-constructed fountain, flowing freely, and people were drawing their water there. Ithakos had built it, together with Neritos and Polyctor. Around it was a grove of poplars, which love the water—in a circle, all the way around, and the cold water flowed down from the stone above, and on top of it an altar had been constructed to the nymphs. There, everyone who passed by would make an offering.

It was there that Melanthius, the son of Dolios, ran into them as he was driving the goats, the best looking ones from the herd, up to the suitor's feast. When he saw them, he called out and rebuked them with rude, terrible words. It stirred Odysseus heart.

"Here now, if it ain't utter filth leading total filth. As always, God's bringing like and like together. Where are you taking this hog, you revolting pig keeper—this begging vermin, to spoil our feast? Standing there, scratching his shoulders against all the doorposts, begging for scraps, instead of swords or cauldrons. Give me this bum to keep my farmhouse, clean out all the pens, and carry out twigs to the kids. Maybe he'd thicken his thighs, drinking whey. But as he's only learned bad habits, he couldn't cope with real work. He'd rather go poking around the country, pleading for food to fill his greedy gut. But I'll tell you this, and it will come to be. If he comes to Odysseus's house, those cheeks of his'll get polished off nicely by all the footstools thrown at his head from the hands of real men."

As he said this, he was passing beside the beggar and in his foolishness, he kicked him in the hip but did not knock him off the road. Odysseus stood there, steady. He pondered whether to jump on top of him and take his life with his staff, or to pick him up by the ears and smash his head against the ground. But he endured it. He held his heart back. The pig keeper looked the man in the face and rebuked him. And he lifted up his hands and prayed out loud.

"Nymphs of this fountain here, daughters of Zeus, if Odysseus ever burned the thighs of lambs and kids for you, all smothered in the richest fat, fulfill this wish for me—that my master will come, guided by some god, and shatter this pompous show you're putting on, always wandering the city, while lousy herdsmen ruin the flocks."

And Melanthios, herder of goats, answered back.

"Ha, the dog can talk, chewing over its hate. But *that* one, one day, I'll take him far from Ithaka on a black ship, full of benches, so he can bring me a huge fortune. If only Apollo with his silver bow would strike down

Telemakhos at home today, or if only he was brought down by the suitors, as sure as Odysseus's day of return is lost, somewhere far away."

With these words, Melanthios left them, as they walked on slowly, and he went ahead and quickly he came to the palace. He went straight in and sat down among the suitors, facing Eurymakhos, since the goatherd liked him best. The slaves came and set out a slab of meat in front of him, and the revered housekeeper brought some bread to eat, and she set it before him. Odysseus and the pig keeper approached, and then stopped. All around them rose the sound of the hollow lyre, as Phemios began to strum the chords in front of them. Odysseus grabbed the pig keeper's hand and spoke.

"This has to be the beautiful house of Odysseus. It's easy to recognize, even if you see it as one among so many others. But the courtyard is enclosed within a wall with cornices, and the double gates nicely framed. No man could sneer at that. I see that inside many men are feasting, since its aroma is pouring out, and the lyre, which the gods have made attendant to the feast, is ringing out."

And Eumaios, keeper of pigs, you answered him in turn.

"You're so sharp. You've seen it easily, but let's think about how to do this. Either you enter the house first and go among the suitors, and I'll stay back here, or if you want, you stay here, and I will go on ahead. But don't hang back for long. Someone might see you and throw something at you or hit you. Think about it."

Brilliant Odysseus, who had endured so much, answered in return.

"I hear you and see the point. You're talking to someone who understands. You go on in before me. I'll hold back, because I'm not unacquainted to being hit or having things thrown at me. I have a steady heart, since I've gone through a lot of awful things in war and on the waves. So let this be yet one more thing on top of those. But no one can hide a raging belly, this damned thing that brings so much trouble to people. It's because of this that ships with many benches are launched upon the restless sea, to bring hard times to our enemies."

As they were talking to each other in this way, a dog that was lying there lifted its head and pricked up its ears. It was Argos, Odysseus's faithful dog, which he himself had bred and raised, but before he had been able to enjoy it, he went away to powerfully built Ilios. In the past, young men had taken the dog out to hunt wild goats, deer, and rabbits. But now he merely lay there—abandoned, his master gone—in heaps of mule and cow muck piled in front of the doors, until Odysseus's slaves took it to fertilize his extensive lands. It was there Argos lay, crawling with ticks. But as he noticed Odysseus close by, he wagged his tail and let his ears drop down, but he no longer had enough strength to move any closer. Odysseus looked away, and he rubbed away a tear. He kept all of this hidden from Eumaios, but he was quick to question him.

"Eumaios, this is strange, this dog that's lying here in the muck. He seems to be in quite good shape, but I can't tell if he's as fast as he looks, or if he's just like one of those house dogs, kept for show."

And then, Eumaios, keeper of pigs, you answered him in return.

"Yes, he is definitely the dog of a man who died, far away. If he had the same build and liveliness that he had when Odysseus left him and went to Troy, you'd be surprised right away to see his speed and drive. No wild animal that he spotted, deep in the thick of the forest, could get away, he was so sharp at tracking. Now he's at his worst. His master has died, far from home and the women are hard-hearted. They just don't care. When masters stop giving their slaves orders, they no longer want to do what they are supposed to do, since Zeus, whose thunder carries so far, takes away half a man's good will whenever the day of slavery comes."

After he spoke, he entered the stately house and went straight to the great hall among the gathered suitors. And the finality of black death took hold of Argos, as soon as he had seen Odysseus after twenty years.

As the keeper of pigs went through the house, Telemakhos, looking like a god, was by far the first to see him and nodding quickly, he called the man close to his side. And the old man looked around the hall as the others were feasting and grabbed a nearby stool, where the server usually sat among the suitors, carving off many slabs of meat. He picked it up and placed it at the table across from Telemakhos. He sat down. One of the servers took up a piece of meat and set it down in front of him, together with a bit of bread from the basket.

Odysseus entered the house close behind him. He looked like a miserable old beggar, leaning on his staff, and the clothes he was wearing about his skin were appalling. He sat down upon the ash threshold in the doorway and leaned back against the old cypress doorpost, which long ago an artisan had planed, polished, and straightened to the plum line. Telemakhos called to the pig keeper, clutched a whole loaf from the elegant basket, and grabbed as much meat as he could possibly hold in his hands. He said, "Take this and give it to the stranger. Tell him to go around to these courteous gentlemen and do his begging, since shame is not much good for a man in need."

When he heard Telemakhos say this, the pig keeper went up to the man, and his words carried like wings.

"Telemakhos offers you this, stranger, and urges you to go around to all these courteous gentlemen and beg. Shame, he said, is never any good for a man in need."

Odysseus, always thinking ahead, answered him in turn.

"Lord Zeus, may Telemakhos be blessed among men, and may he receive everything that his heart desires."

He took the food in both hands and laid it at his feet on his grimy pouch, and he ate for as long as the singer kept on singing. Then, pandemonium broke out among the suitors throughout the hall. And Athena came up close beside Odysseus Laertiádes, and she urged him to go around and gather pieces of bread, to find out which of them would behave properly and which of them were mean-spirited, although she was not willing to hold the very worst back from even one of them. Starting on the right, he went to beg from each man. He reached out his hand in every direction, as if he had been a beggar for a long time. They pitied him and gave him something, and they looked at him, wondering. They asked each other who he might be and where he came from. Melanthios, the goatherd, spoke to them.

"Listen to me, you who have come here to court our illustrious queen. This stranger, I've seen him before. That pig keeper brought him here but I don't really know him, or where he says he was born."

When he said this, Antinoos chided the pig keeper.

"Pig keeper, we know all about you, but why did you bring this man to the city? Don't we have too many drifters and tiresome beggars already spoiling our meals? Don't you hate it that they gather here and eat up all your master's livelihood, and now you invite this one here, too?"

And Eumaios, keeper of pigs, you answered in return.

"Antinoos, honorable as you are, what you're saying isn't fair. Who'd invite a stranger to come here from far away, except one of those public craftsmen, a prophet, a healer of maladies, a wood worker, or a heavenly singer? These men are often called in from all over the measureless earth, but no one would risk bringing himself down by calling in a beggar. But more than any of these courteous gentlemen, you are always so harsh to Odysseus's servants, and to me especially. But I don't really care, as long as Penelope, who is so thoughtful, lives with Telemakhos in this house."

Telemakhos, gathering his thoughts, answered him.

"Silence! Don't waste so many words, reacting to this man. Antinoos is so accustomed to provoking others with hard words, and encouraging others to do the same."

And he flung these words to Antinoos on the wing.

"Antinoos, you must really care for me, like a father for his son, to advise that I drive this stranger away from these halls with threatening words. May no god let this be. Take something. Give it to him. I won't hold it against you. I ask you to. And don't worry about my mother or the other servants, here in Odysseus's house. But that isn't the notion in your chest. You'd rather stuff yourself than give to anyone else."

At once Antinoos answered back and said, "Telemakhos, you patronizing windbag, of all the insufferable nerve—the things you say! If all the other suitors offered him as much as I'm about to, it would keep him far away from this household for three full months!"

After he spoke, he picked up the footstool from where it had been lying under the table, where he liked to rest his gleaming white, well-oiled feet as he ate his fill, and he showed it to everyone. But all the rest gave him something, and they filled up his pouch with pieces of bread and meat. Odysseus was just about to go back to the threshold, without the taste of payback from the Akhaians, but he stopped and stood next to Antinoos and spoke these words.

"How about a gift, my friend? You don't seem to be the worst of the Akhaians, but the very best, because you look so much like a king. So you ought to give me a piece of bread that's even better than the rest, so I can carry your fame across the boundless earth. I too once lived well among men, in a house of my own, a happy man, and I would often give to some wanderer, whoever he was and whatever need he came with. I had slaves too, beyond counting, and all the things with which men live well and are called 'well to do.'

"But Zeus, the Son of Kronos, swept it all away. For some reason he wanted to. He urged me to go on a long voyage to Egypt with nomadic pirates, so I'd come to ruin. I anchored all my curved ships on the River Egyptos. I ordered all my trusty mates, of course, to stand by the ships and guard them, and I sent out scouts to scope out some observation points. But they gave in to their own overconfidence and trusting in their own nerve, right away, they ravaged the beautiful fields of the Egyptians. They led away their women and little children and killed all the men.

"Quickly the outcry reached the city, and when they heard all the screaming, the people appeared at daybreak. The whole plain filled with foot soldiers and chariots, the flash of bronze. And Zeus, who is so fond of lightning bolts, cast a deep panic over my mates. Not one of them was able to stand and face them, since the danger came from everywhere. They killed many of us with their sharp bronze and led away the survivors to work against their will. And they gave me to Dmetor Iasides, who ruled by force over Cyprus. From there I came here, after facing so much trouble."

Antinoos raised his voice and answered him in turn.

"Which of the gods has brought this pest here, to spoil our feast? Go and stand over there, in the middle of the room, away from my table, or you'll very soon come to an equally odious Egypt and Cyprus. What a rash, shameless beggar. You come here and stand next to each one of them, one after another, and they give you something for nothing. There's no holding back or feeling regret in freely giving away the things that belong to someone else. We all have plenty in front of us."

And Odysseus, always thinking ahead, stepped back and spoke to him.

"My, my. It seems you don't quite have the wits to match your looks. You won't give to a beggar even a touch of salt from all you have, while you are sitting at someone else's table. You can't stand to take off even a piece of your bread and give it away, when there's so much lying about in front of you."

Antinoos became even more outraged and glaring under his eyebrows, his words flailed like wings.

"Well, I don't think you can get through this hall and out safely, now that you've uttered such a rant."

As he spoke, Antinoos picked up the stool and threw it. It struck Odysseus on the back, close to the right shoulder blade. He stood there, unshaken, like a rock. He did not flinch from Antinoos's blow. He shook his head in silence, thinking dark thoughts. Then he walked back to the threshold, and he sat down. He laid his full pouch aside and spoke to the suitors.

"Listen to me, those of you who are courting this illustrious queen, while I put into words what this heart inside my chest is driving me to say. There's no heartache or sadness when a man is belted while fighting for his own possessions, his cattle or his white sheep. But Antinoos here has struck me because of my damned belly, this curse that makes life so hard for so many people. So if somewhere there are gods or goddesses of revenge for beggars, may Antinoos come to his own dead end before he comes to marriage."

Antinoos, son of Eupeithes, answered back.

"Take it easy, stranger—either sit down and eat or go away—or else these young men here will drag you through the house by your hands or feet, and they'll skin you alive for what you've said."

After he had spoken, they were all so deeply angered that one of the pretentious young men spoke up.

"Antinoos, it's not at all good that you've struck this miserable wanderer. You're doomed if maybe he is some god who's come down from above. The gods take on all kinds of shapes to look like strangers from far away, visiting city to city, to keep their eyes on people's deference or disrespect."

The other suitors also spoke like this, but Antinoos ignored what they said. Telemakhos, when he saw his father struck, felt the bitterness growing deep inside his heart, but he did not let a tear drop from his eyelids to the ground. He shook his head in silence, thinking dark thoughts. But when she heard that the man had been struck in her own house, Penelope, deep in thought, spoke in the presence of her slaves.

"And even so, may the famous archer, Apollo, strike you yourself down in the very same way."

And Eurynome, her housekeeper, said these words to her.

"If only such an end might answer your prayers, so none of these men would reach the throne of Dawn."

Penelope, deep in thought, answered back.

"Nurse, they are all vile, plotting their evil schemes. But Antinoos, most of all, is like black death. There's some unfortunate stranger wandering about the house, driven by his need, begging the men for scraps, and all the others gave him something to fill his pouch. Antinoos, though, threw his stool and hit him in the back."

Brilliant Odysseus went on eating as she talked with her slaves. She called to the brilliant pig keeper, "Eumaios, go and tell the stranger to come here, so I can meet him and ask him if he has ever heard of our unwavering Odysseus, or seen him with his own eyes, because he looks like he has wandered long and far."

And Eumaios, keeper of pigs, you answered in return.

"If only these Akhaians would just keep quiet, because what he says would charm your dear heart. I had him with me for three nights. For three days I kept him in my hut. He came to me first, after he had slipped away from a ship, but then he never finished the worst of his story. It's like when you're gazing at a singer, who's crooning songs of passion learned from the gods to all of us ordinary people, and your desire grows deeper and deeper to keep on hearing him as he sings.

"That's how much he enthralled me while he was sitting in front of me in my house. The stranger says that he is an old family friend of Odysseus, and he lives in Krete, there among the descendants of Minos. From there he came here, after suffering hard times, wandering all around in circles, and he claims he's heard about Odysseus, nearby in the fertile land of the Thresprotian people. He's alive, and he'll bring home lots of riches."

Penelope, deep in thought, answered back.

"Go, call him here, so he himself can tell me to my face. Let these others sit by the doors or here inside the house and play their games, since they are so full of spirit. Because their own things are lying untouched, back in their own houses—the bread and sweet wine, tasted only by their servants. But every day they swarm into our house, and they kill our cattle and our sheep and fat goats, and they stuff themselves and idly drink our shimmering wine. So much waste, because there is no one like Odysseus to watch over the house. But if Odysseus ever comes back to his native land, very quickly he and his son will make these men pay for their brutality."

As she spoke, Telemakhos sneezed forcefully. It echoed ominously throughout the room. Penelope laughed and the words she spoke to Eumaios beat like wings.

"Go—please—call the stranger here before me. You see how my son sneezed at all my words? So it is to be. Death will not go unconsummated for these courteous gentlemen, all of them. None of them will manage to escape death and its messengers. And I'll tell you something else. Hide it deep in your heart. If I find out he's telling us the truth, I will give him some good clothes, a cloak and a tunic."

After she spoke, the pig keeper came close to Odysseus and his words whispered like wings.

"Stranger, Penelope, Telemakhos's mother, is deep in thought and she is calling for you. Her heart's pressing her to inquire about her husband. She's suffered so much. If she finds that everything you tell her is true, she'll offer you a cloak and tunic, or whatever it is that you may need the most, and you'll be able to beg for your bread throughout the land and feed your belly, and whoever wishes to will give it to you."

Radiant, Odysseus, who had endured so much, answered back.

"Very soon, Eumaios. I'm going to tell Penelope, Ikarios's very thoughtful daughter, the whole truth. I know a lot about that man. We've both gone through the same misfortunes. But I am afraid of this pack of hard-hearted suitors, whose arrogance and cruelty reach as high as the iron sky. Just now, as I was going through the house, doing no harm, someone hit me, causing me pain, and not even Telemakhos nor anyone else could prevent it. So ask Penelope to wait for me within her rooms, anxious as she is, until sunset. Then she can ask me about her husband and his return, as she allows me to sit close to the fire. You yourself know, since I first came to you in need, how awful my clothes are."

As soon as he had heard these words, the pig keeper went, and as he crossed the threshold, Penelope said, "You are not bringing him, Eumaios. What is he thinking, this drifter? Is he too afraid of someone more than he needs to be, or is he for some reason too wary? Because a bashful beggar is bad off."

And Eumaios, keeper of pigs, you answered her in turn.

"What he said is right, as anyone who seeks to avoid the arrogance of those overbearing men would think. He asks you to wait until sunset, and for you too, your highness, it's better to speak to the stranger alone, and hear what he has to say."

Deep in thought, Penelope answered him.

"The stranger's not witless. He sees how it is, since how could there ever be anyone, of those of us who must face death, who plan their malevolence with such blatant futility as these overbearing men."

After they finished talking, the brilliant pig keeper went back right away into the crowd of suitors. The words he spoke to Telemakhos whispered like wings, since he held his head close, so the others would not hear.

"My friend, I'm heading off to guard the pigs and the other things we both value. You take care of everything here. Above all, keep safe and keep your mind alert, so nothing happens to you. Many of these Akhaians are planning horrible things for you. May Zeus wipe them out before we come to harm."

Gathering his thoughts, Telemakhos answered back.

"So it will be, Papa. Go your way, after you've had your evening meal. In the morning, come again and bring back some more fine animals to sacrifice. Leave everything here to me—and to the gods."

After he had spoken, the pig keeper sat down once again on a polished chair. But as soon as he had satisfied his heart with food and drink, he went his own way, back to the pigs, leaving behind the court and the great hall, full of people, still feeding themselves, full of high spirits, singing and dancing. The end of their day had come.

XVIII

Almost Home

A beggar arrived. He was well known to everyone for begging all around the city, for his raging belly and for eating and drinking endlessly. He had no real strength or drive, but he was large and bulky. His name was Arnaios. That is, his esteemed mother gave him that name at birth, but all the young men called him Iros, since he would run messages whenever anyone told him to. He came over to Odysseus to chase him away from his own home, and began uttering abusive words that flit about like wings.

"Get away from the door, old man, right now, or get dragged away by the foot. Don't you see? Everyone's constantly winking at me, goading me on to drag you off. So get up, or our differences will be quickly settled by fists."

Looking up at him from under his eyebrows, always thinking ahead, Odysseus spoke.

"Madman, I haven't said or done you any wrong, and I wouldn't hold a grudge, even if someone gave you a lot. This doorway will hold us both. There's no need for you to resent what others have. You look like a drifter, just like me. And prosperity? That's for the gods to give. Don't taunt me with your fists or you're going to get me angry and though I'm old, I will spatter your lips and chest with blood, and it'll be much more calm for me tomorrow, since I don't think you'll ever return again to the house of Odysseus Laertiádes."

Iros, the beggar, was enraged and said to the other,

"Ah now, how the bum runs at the mouth, like an old kitchen maid. But I'll cook up some trouble for him, pound him left and right, and knock all his teeth out of his jaws and onto the ground, just like a pig rooting in the crops. Get up, so everyone can see how we fight—but how could the likes of you fight a younger man?"

They quarreled fiercely, there on the polished threshold before the tall doors. Antinoos, with divine disdain, burst into shrill laughter and made his voice heard among the other suitors.

"Friends, there's never been anything like this before. Some god or another has brought inside this house such rare amusement—the stranger and Iros fighting each other, hand to hand. Let's egg them on!"

As he spoke, they all jumped up, laughing and circling the scruffy beggars. Antinoos, son of Eupeitheos spoke to them.

"Listen to what I have to say, my lordly gentlemen. Here on the fire lie the goat stomachs, which we placed there for our supper, after filling them with fat and blood. Whichever one of the two is victorious and shows himself to be the stronger, let him stand up and choose whichever of these he wants. And from then on, he'll always feast along with us and we won't allow any other beggar to mingle here together with us or beg from us."

As Antinoos spoke, what he said pleased them all. Odysseus, always thinking ahead, spoke craftily.

"My friends, there's no way for an old man who's beaten down with trouble to stand and fight a younger man. But my belly's a hard driver, and it spurs me on to be knocked down by his blows. But come now, all of you, swear to me your firm promise, that no one here will help Iros, or strike out at me with blunt force and overpower me before him."

They all promised not to strike him, as he had asked. But after they had uttered their oath to the last word, the inner strength of Telemakhos spoke among them.

"Stranger, if your proud heart and spirit oblige you to defend yourself against this man, have no fear of the other Akhaians, because whoever strikes you will have to face much more than you. I am your host. And these princes have endorsed the oath, Antinoos and Eurymakhos, and both of them are cautious men."

After he had spoken, they all expressed their approval. So Odysseus tied his rags around his waist, exposing his fine, sturdy thighs, his broad shoulders, his chest and strong arms. And Athena drew near, and she filled out the limbs of the shepherd of the people. The suitors were all maliciously amazed, and one of them would say, glancing at the man next to him, "Soon enough, we'll see Iros erased by the trouble he's brought upon himself. What a set of thighs the old man's showing underneath those rags."

Iros's heart was seriously shaken. But the attendants tied up his clothes and urged him on, full of fear. The flesh was trembling on his limbs. Antinoos heckled him, calling him down with these words.

"Well, now, you great ox, it would have been better if you'd never existed and had never been born, if you're trembling and so afraid of this old man, who's been beaten down by all the troubles that have come to him. But I'm telling you now, and this will happen—if this man beats you and shows himself stronger, I'm going to throw you onto a black ship and send you to the mainland, to King Ekhetos, the scourge of all men, and he will cut off your nose and ears with sharp bronze, and tear out your genitals and give them to the dogs to eat raw."

As he spoke, an even greater fit of trembling seized the beggar's limbs. They all led him into the middle ground, and both of them held up their hands. And brilliant Odysseus, who had endured so much, wondered whether to strike him so that his breath would leave him at once as he fell, or simply to give him a light blow and stretch him out flat on the ground. As he thought about it, the second idea seemed to be better—to hit him lightly, so the Akhaians would not take it quite so seriously. They both raised their hands, and Iros threw a punch at Odysseus's right shoulder. Odysseus struck Iros in the neck below the ear, jamming the bones underneath. And red blood streamed down his mouth. He fell in the dust with a moan. He ground his teeth and kicked at the ground with his feet. The lordly suitors raised their hands and almost died of laughter. Odysseus seized Iros by the foot and dragged him through the doorway into the courtyard, over to the gates of the portico. He leaned him up against the wall of the courtyard. He thrust the man's staff into his hand, and then he found his voice, his words whispering like wings.

"Sit here for now. Keep away the dogs and pigs, and stop trying to lord it over strangers and beggars, you wretch, or you'll bring on something even worse."

He tossed back over his shoulder his grimy pouch, full of holes, hanging from a twisted cord, and he went to the threshold and sat down. And all the others went inside and greeted him with high-pitched laughter.

"Stranger, may Zeus and the other immortal gods give you whatever you want most and is dear to your heart, since you've stopped this gluttonous bum from begging in this land. We'll take him away soon to the mainland, to King Ekhetos, the scourge of all human beings."

Radiant, Odysseus was delighted at their prophetic words. And Antinoos placed a large goat gut, stuffed with fat and blood, in front of him. Amphinomos grabbed two loaves from the basket and set them before him, and he raised his voice and toasted him with a golden cup.

"Cheers, father, stranger—may good fortune come to you some day, although now you're having so many troubles."

And Odysseus, always thinking ahead, answered him.

"Amphinomos, you seem to be a thoughtful man, and so, too, was your father, since I've heard of his great reputation—Nisios of Doulikhios, a good and prosperous man. They say you are of his blood, and you seem a courteous man. So I'll tell you. Listen and hear me out. Nothing the earth nurtures is more questionable than human beings, of all the things that breathe and move on earth. No one thinks that he'll ever have to face hardship in the time to come, as long as the gods keep giving him health, spirit, and limber knees. But later, when the carefree gods bring misery to bear, he puts up with this too, halfheartedly, because the minds of people who live on earth are much like the days that Zeus the father of both men and gods brings to them.

"I, too, was once successful among men and carried out many thoughtless acts, relying on my own power and cruelty or trusting in my father and brothers. So no man should ever neglect what's right, but hold on, in silence, to whatever gifts the gods offer. I see the thoughtless acts these courteous gentlemen here are carrying out, wasting the worldly goods and dishonoring the wife of a man who, I'm telling you, will not be away for very long from his loved ones and his native land. He's very close. But you—let some god lead you back home, so you won't meet him face to face, when he returns to his own native land, since I really don't think that man and these gentlemen will ever separate from each other without bloodshed, once he has returned to his own household."

After he spoke, he poured out his offering and drank the wine, sweet as honey, and then he handed the cup back to the lord, who stood up and walked around the room with a troubled heart, his head held down, because his heart was anticipating something terrible. Yet he could not avoid his own heart, his own death. Athena held him back, to be brutally killed by a spear at the hand of Telemakhos. He sat down on the chair he had risen from. And at that moment, the goddess Athena, her eyes gleaming, put it into the heart of Ikarios' daughter, Penelope, deep in thought, to show herself to the suitors and set their hearts to fluttering, and thus win even greater honor from her son and husband than she had had before. She let out a forced laugh and she spoke to her housekeeper, calling her by name.

"Eurynome, my heart is longing, as never before, to show myself to the suitors, hateful as they are. I also want to say a word to my son, because I think it's better for him not to mingle so much with those arrogant courtiers, who speak politely to his face, but plan to do him harm in the near future."

Eurynome, the housekeeper, had these words to say.

"Yes, my child, everything you've said is fitting and proper. So go, reveal your thoughts to your son—don't hide them—as soon as you have washed your body and anointed your cheeks with oil. But don't go yet with your face still marked with tears. It's no good to cry forever. Your child is now at the age that you have begged the gods for, grown up, beard and all."

Deep in thought, Penelope answered her again.

"Eurynome, as much as you love me, don't distract me with all this—to wash my body and anoint myself with oil. The gods who occupy Olympos have ruined whatever beauty I once had, when *he* went away in his hollow ship. Have Autonoe and Hippodameia come, so they can stand beside me in the hall. I will not go among the men alone. I'd be ashamed."

After she spoke, the old woman went through the hall to alert the women and tell them to come. And Athena, her gray eyes gleaming, had yet another thought. She shed sweet sleep over Ikarios's daughter, and Penelope leaned back and fell asleep on her couch. All her joints relaxed, and during that time, the brilliant goddess was giving her exquisite gifts, so the Akhaians would look at her with amazement. First of all, she cleansed her lovely face in divine beauty, like that with which Kythereia in her shining crown anoints herself, when she goes into the hypnotic dance with the Graces. Athena made her taller and more elegant to see, and whiter than freshly cut ivory. After she had done all this, the brilliant goddess left. The women, with their white arms bare, came out of the hall and approached her, talking among themselves, and sweet sleep released Penelope. She rubbed her cheeks with her hands and spoke.

"In my utter despair, a deep, gentle sleep enclosed me. If only blameless Artemis would offer me a death so gentle that I'd no longer waste my whole life away, mourning for my dear husband's talents, which far exceeded those of the other Akhaians."

She said this and then went out of the bright upper room, but not alone. The two slaves accompanied her. And when this radiant woman arrived among the suitors, she stood beside the doorpost of the well-built hall, with a loyal woman slave on each side of her, and she held her shimmering veil before her face. The suitors' knees gave way, their hearts enthralled with desire, all of them craving to lie in bed with her, but she spoke only to her beloved son, Telemakhos.

"Telemakhos, your heart and mind are no longer steady. Even when you were still a child you were more sensible, but now that you're tall and have reached a measure of maturity, anyone from far away who saw you here so big and handsome, would say you would have to be the son of a very prosperous man. But your heart and mind are no longer in the right place. What is this spectacle that has taken place in this room? That you would let this stranger be so poorly treated! What if he'd been harmed while being so roughly handled in our house? The shame and disgrace among men would be on you!"

Gathering his thoughts, Telemakhos answered her.

"Mother, I don't at all blame you for getting angry. In my heart, I know and understand it all, the good and the bad. Before I was still only a child, but now I'm not able to think everything out reasonably, and these other men, sitting around me, thinking up trouble. They distract me, and there's no one here to help me out. Anyway, the scuffle between Iros and the stranger didn't turn out quite as these courteous gentlemen had planned. *He* was stronger.

"Ah, Father Zeus and Athena and Apollo, if only the suitors would now hang their heads, beaten down, here in our house, some in the courtyard and some in the great hall, and each one's limbs were hanging as limp as Iros himself is right now, sitting over there by the courtyard gate, unable to stand up straight on his feet or to go back home, wherever it is he might call home, because his own limbs are so slack."

They continued talking, but then Eurymakhos spoke up.

"Daughter of Ikarios, brooding Penelope, if every Akhaian in Iasian Argos could see you now, even more suitors would be feasting in your halls from tomorrow on, because you surpass all women in your beauty, your figure, and your inmost heart."

Penelope, deep in thought, answered him.

"Eurymakhos, any endowments I may have had, either in beauty or figure, the ones who never die devastated when the Argives embarked for Ilios, carrying along with them my husband Odysseus. And if he ever does come back and fulfill this life of mine, all the greater and finer my reputation will be. But now I am in mourning, since some god has brought me so much hardship. When Odysseus left his own land and went away, didn't he grasp my right hand and say these words to me?

'Woman, I don't think that all of the Akhaians, however well equipped, will return from Troy unharmed. They say the Trojans are men of war, lancers and archers and riders of fast horses, who can quickly decide the fight in a balanced battle. So I don't know if the gods will bring me home or if I'll be killed at Troy. Take care of everything here and take care of my father and mother in this house, as you are now, but even more while I am away. But when you see my son growing a beard, marry anyone you will and leave this house behind.'

"That's what he said. And now it is all coming to be. A night is drawing near when a bitter marriage will come to me, only in sorrow, my happiness having been taken away by Zeus. In this situation, a bleak grief has clutched my heart and soul. This is not the fitting way that suitors have always acted before. Those who desire to compete with one another in courting a woman of value, who is the daughter of a wealthy man, they themselves bring their own cattle and fattened sheep and they offer her lovely gifts, a feast for her friends, and they don't use up someone else's livelihood without any compensation."

As she spoke, Odysseus, who had endured so much, was radiant, since she was charming presents out of them and luring their hearts with gentle words while her mind was on other things.

Eupeithes' son, Antinoos then spoke.

"Daughter of Ikarios, thoughtful Penelope, as for gifts, if any Akhaian would like to bring them here, then take them, since it's not a good thing to refuse a gift. But as for us, we will not go back to our own lands or anywhere else, till you marry whoever is the best of the Akhaians."

Antinoos's words pleased them all, and each of them sent off a messenger to bring back gifts. One brought Antinoos a long, beautiful robe, exquisitely embroidered, and in it, twelve golden brooches, fitted with nicely curled clasps. And another brought Eurymakhos an intricately crafted golden chain, strung with amber, beaming like the sun. Eurydamas's attendants brought him a pair of earrings, each with three dark pearls, gleaming elegantly. The attendant from the house of Lord Peisander, the son of Polyktor, brought a necklace, an especially beautiful piece. And so one of the Akhaians brought one lovely thing, and another brought another.

Radiant, the woman went to her upper room, and her slaves carried up the lovely gifts. The suitors returned to their dancing and uproarious singing, and they enjoyed themselves, waiting for evening to come. And as they went on enjoying themselves, the dark evening arrived. Right away, they set three braziers inside the great hall for light, and all around them they placed some dried-up firewood, seasoned especially hard and brittle and freshly split with a bronze axe. In the space between they set up torches, and one by one, Odysseus's women slaves lit the fires. In that moment, Zeus's descendant, Odysseus, always thinking ahead, spoke to them.

"Servants of Odysseus, your master who's been away so long, go to the rooms where her majesty, the queen, is now and spin some yarn beside her and cheer her up as you sit there in the room, or comb the wool with your hands. I'll keep the light going for all these men. Even if they want to wait for Dawn's lovely throne, they won't outlast me. For I can endure an awful lot."

When he spoke, the women looked at each other and laughed. Melantho, with her pale cheeks, scolded him insultingly. She had been born to Dolios, but Penelope raised her, cared for her as her own child, and gave her delightful playthings, and yet she felt no empathy for Penelope but even slept with Eurymakhos and was in love with him. Now she belittled Odysseus with contemptuous words.

"Stupid stranger, you're out of your mind if you choose not to go to some blacksmith's floor to sleep or to some local tavern, but keep on jabbering away so bluntly with no fear in your heart, here among so many real men. This wine's taken over your brains, for sure, or else you always think like this, blathering on so aimlessly. Is your mind wandering because you've just stretched out that vagrant Iros? Watch out or certainly someone else, with stronger hands than Iros, will soon smack you about the head and chase you out of this house, smeared with blood."

And Odysseus, always thinking ahead, looked at her from under his eyebrows and spoke these words to her.

"Soon I'll go to Telemakhos, bitch, and tell him what you've said. He'll slash you limb from limb on the spot."

As he spoke, his words shocked and scattered the women. They went away through the house, and the limbs of each one sagged, because they sensed he was telling the truth. He stood there by the burning braziers to tend the light, and he watched all the others. But his heart was stirred with thoughts of other things, not to be left undone. Athena did not for a moment allow the proud suitors to hold back from harsh insults, so that the pain would sink deeper in the heart of Odysseus Laertiádes. Eurymakhos, son of Polybos, to make his friends laugh, jeered at him.

"Listen to me, suitors of this illustrious queen, so I can say what my heart compels me to. It's not without the will of the gods that this man has come here to the house of Odysseus. Look how the radiance of fire emanates from his head, as there's not even a lick of hair on top."

Then he called over to Odysseus, the scourge of cities.

"Hey, stranger, would you be willing to work for pay, if I picked you up to work for me, gathering thorn bushes or planting some tall trees, out on some isolated farm? The pay would be good enough for you. I'd provide you with bread there, for the whole year, and put some clothes around you and give you some sandals for your feet. But no, because you've never learned to do anything. You wouldn't want to work. You'd rather go on begging everywhere, to feed your bottomless belly."

And Odysseus, always thinking ahead, answered him.

"Eurymakhos, if only we could have a contest, working in springtime, when the days get long, out in a field of wheat, me with a curved scythe in my hands, and you with one too, and the grass all around us, so that we could test out our work without eating until it gets totally dark. Or if there were oxen to drive, the best, large and tawny, both well fed with grass, equal both in age and pulling power, tireless in strength, and there was a four-acre field, with soil malleable to the plow, then you would see if I could cut a straight furrow, all the way to the end.

"Or if the Son of Kronos would bring on a war today, out of nowhere, and I had a shield and two spears and a helmet, totally bronze, that fit close about my head, then you'd see me in the mix with the leading fighters—instead of all this talk, blaming me for my hunger. You are so arrogant. Your mind is so cruel. You think you're someone great and powerful, simply because you dally around with these others, who are weak and of no account. If only Odysseus would finally come back to the land of his fathers, right away those doors over there, wide as they are, would grow too narrow for all of you to flee through."

When he said this, Eurymakhos was even more heartily enraged, and he spoke words that trembled like wings.

"Idiot, I'll bring you down soon. You keep on chattering away so brashly here, with no fear in your heart among so many real men. I'm sure the wine has seized your brains, or maybe you always think like this, yammering on so aimlessly. Is your mind wandering because you've just stretched out that tramp, Iros?"

As he spoke, he grabbed a footstool. But Odysseus sat down in alarm by the knees of Amphinomos of Doulikhios, and Eurymakhos struck the right hand of a wine steward, and his pitcher fell to the ground with a loud ringing. The steward groaned and fell backward into the dust. The suitors roared, and it echoed throughout the halls. And one of them glanced at another and said, "If only this stranger had died somewhere while he was wandering about, before he came here. He wouldn't have brought in all this turmoil. Now we're quarreling over rabbits. This great feast will be no fun, if these lowlifes keep getting the better of us."

The inner strength of Telemakhos spoke among them.

"You madmen, driven by some god. You're raving and are no longer able to hide inside your hearts all your eating and drinking. One of the gods must be urging you on. But now that you have eaten your fill, go on back to your homes and lie down, whenever your hearts lead you. I won't send anyone away."

As he spoke, they all bit their lips and looked at him in wonder, he spoke so boldly. But Amphinomos, the son of the striking Lord Nisos Aretiades, addressed them all.

"My friends, there's no one who'd take offense at what's been spoken so fairly and argue back with harsh words. Don't mistreat this stranger or any of the servants here in the house of the great Odysseus. But come now—let the wine steward pour some drops into all of our cups, so we can pour out our offerings and go on home to bed. And let's leave this stranger here in Odysseus's halls for Telemakhos to care for, since it was to his own house that the man has come."

He spoke, and what he said was agreeable to them all. A bowl was mixed by Mulios, that heroic messenger from Doulikhios, an attendant to Amphinomos. He went around and stood in front of each one of them and served it out, and after pouring out their offerings to the carefree gods, they drank the wine, sweet as honey, to their hearts' content. Then they went back home, each one to his own house, to lie down and rest.

XIX

Face to Face

Left behind in the great hall, brilliant Odysseus made plans with Athena for the killing of the suitors. He cast his words on the wing to Telemakhos.

"Telemakhos, take away all the battle weapons, and when the suitors miss them and ask about them, turn them away with these soothing words.

'I have put them away, out of the smoke, because they are no longer like those Odysseus once left behind, when he went off to Troy. They're soiled, because the fumes from the fire have reached them. And also, some god has put this thought in my heart—that you might get drunk and start fighting among yourselves and you might injure each other and bring your feast and your courtship to shame, since iron's a magnet among men.'

After he said this, Telemakhos obeyed his beloved father. He called over to Eurykleia, the nurse.

"Nurse, come. Draw the women into their rooms while I put into storage my father's fine weapons. The smoke throughout the hall has soiled them. They've been so neglected, ever since my father went away when I was only a child. But now I'd like to put them away, so the fumes won't reach them."

Eurykleia, his dear nurse, answered him.

"Yes, child, I only wish that you'd think more often of caring for the house and guarding all these good things. But come now, who will take a light and hold it for you, since you won't allow the servants to go before you and light the way?"

Gathering his thoughts, Telemakhos answered her.

"This stranger here. I will not let any man who grabs a share of my food to be idle, even if he's come from far away."

After he spoke, her words did not take wing, and she locked all the doors of the magnificent hall. They both jumped up, Odysseus and his splendid son. They carried in the helmets, the studded shields, and the spears with their sharpened points. In front of them, Athena, holding a golden lamp, cast a dazzling light. At length Telemakhos spoke to his father.

"Father, this is a great wonder, what I'm seeing with my own eyes. It's as if the walls of the room and its niches and the fir crossbeams and the pillars that reach up so high are glowing from a blazing fire. Surely, one of those who live in the vast heavens must be in here."

Always thinking ahead, Odysseus answered him in turn.

"Silence. Hold your thoughts. Don't ask questions. This is the way of the gods who live on Olympos. Now go and lie down, and I myself am going to stay behind here, to unsettle the servants and your mother even more, so she will feel upset and ask me about everything in turn."

After he spoke, Telemakhos made his way through the hall, its torches glimmering, to his own room to lie down. But while in the past, sweet sleep usually came over him, now he simply lay down, waiting for brilliant Dawn. But brilliant Odysseus, left behind in the great hall with Athena, went on planning, plotting the slaughter of the suitors. Penelope, deep in thought, came out of her chamber, looking like Artemis or golden Aphrodite.

They set out a chair for her by the fire, where she liked to sit. Ikmalios, the artisan, had crafted it, turned with ivory and silver, and attached underneath it was a footstool. A large fleece was placed on top. Here, Penelope sat, deep in thought, and the slave women with their white arms came out of their rooms and took away all of the food, tables, and cups from which the lords had been drinking. They threw the ashes from the lampstands onto the floor, and they piled on new logs to offer some light and cheer. But at once Melantho scolded Odysseus for the second time.

"Stranger, are you going to bother us here all night, wandering about the house, leering at the women? Get out, you bum, and be glad for your supper, or you'll be getting out fast, prodded by a torch."

With a dark look, always thinking, Odysseus spoke to her.

"Crazed woman, why are you laying into me with such an angry heart? Because I'm so dirty, with awful clothes on my body, and I go begging all around the country? Well, I'm driven by need. Beggars and wanderers are like this. But I too once lived happily within a fine house, and I was always generous to any wanderer, whoever he was and with whatever need he came. And I had servants, too, so many, and all the other things with which men live well and are called 'well to do.' But Zeus, the Son of Kronos, swept it all away. I guess he just wanted to.

"So now, woman, take care that you don't one day lose all this charm with which you now outshine the other servants, or your mistress storms and rages at you, or Odysseus returns, since there's always a trace of hope. But even if he's lost and never to return, his son, by the grace of Apollo, is like he was—Telemakhos! He is no longer too young to overlook it, if any of the women in his house are doing wrong."

Deep in thought, Penelope heard him saying this. She rebuked the slave and called her by name.

"Brazen, shameless bitch, this disgraceful conduct is not lost on me! You'll wipe it away with your own head, because you knew very well—you heard it straight from me—how I wanted to question the stranger about my husband—I am deeply upset!"

And she spoke these words to the housekeeper, Eurynome.

"Eurynome, bring a chair with a fleece on it, so the stranger may say what he has to say and then listen to me. I want to hear him out."

When she said this, Eurynome quickly brought a chair and set it down and threw a fleece over it. Radiant, Odysseus, who had endured so much, sat down. Deep in thought, Penelope spoke first.

"Stranger, I'll ask you this first. Who are you among men? Where are your city and your parents?"

Always thinking ahead, Odysseus answered her in turn.

"Woman, not one of us mortals on this immeasurable earth could find any fault with you. Your fame reaches to the vast heavens, like that of some blameless king who rules righteously over many fine men and upholds justice, and the black earth bears wheat and barley and the trees heavy with fruit, the sheep give birth often, and the sea gives up its fish, and so his people thrive under him, because of his benevolent leadership.

"So ask me, here in your house, about anything else, but not about my own people or my native land, or you will fill my heart with even more pain as I think about it, because I am full of sorrow. And it's no good to sit around, moaning and groaning in someone else's house. It's no good mourning all the time. I don't want any of your servants, or you yourself, to get mad at me or say I'm swimming in tears, because my heart is loaded down with wine."

Deep in thought, Penelope answered him in turn.

"Stranger, any distinction of mine, either in beauty or figure, the gods destroyed that day the Argives embarked for Ilios, and with them my husband, Odysseus. If that man would come and take care of my life, my fame would be so much greater and lovelier. But now I am upset. Some god has brought me so much wrong, because of the lords who rule the islands, Doulikhios and Samos, and Zakynthos with its forests, and those who live around here in open Ithaka. They are courting me, against my will, and ruining my home.

"And so I pay no attention to strangers or beggars, nor to messengers, who work in the public interest. It is in longing for Odysseus that I waste my heart away. They hurry me to get married. I entwine them in deceit. Some god first breathed it into my heart to set up a large loom within my chamber, to weave a shroud, very long and fine, and right away I spoke among them.

'Young men, my suitors, since Odysseus is dead, anxious as I am for my wedding, wait till I finish this shroud—I wouldn't want what I'm spinning to come to nothing. It's for the great champion, Laertes, for that time when the shattering fate of unforgiving death strikes him down. Or in case some of those Akhaian women throughout this land might become outraged with me because he, who had gained so much, should lie without a shroud.'

"I said this and their swaggering hearts were persuaded. And so, day after day, I'd weave at the huge loom, and at night, once I had the torches placed beside me, I unraveled it. And so for three years I made the Akhaians believe it, and they didn't notice, but when the fourth year came, and the seasons rolled around and the months passed, and so many days came to their end, then, because of my own servants, the careless bitches, they surprised and caught me, and they all shouted at me.

"And so, by force, against my will, I finished. And now I'm unable to avoid the marriage or to find some other deception. My parents are pushing me to marry, while these men eat up all my provisions, and my son is beside himself, as he himself well knows. Because he is a man now, able to manage a household, as Zeus honors. But tell me about your background, and where you are from, since you have hardly sprung from the oak of old stories, or from a rock."

Always thinking ahead, Odysseus answered her in return.

"Esteemed wife of Odysseus Laertiádes, will you ever stop asking about my background? Well, I'll tell you. Though you'll trouble me with even more anguish than I already have. That's the way it is, when a man's been away from his home country as long as I have now, wandering about the many cities of us mortals and suffering hardship. Yet even so, I'll tell you what you're asking.

"There is a land called Krete in the middle of a sea that's dark as wine. It's beautiful, lush, with water all around it. There are many men, beyond number, and ninety cities, with a jumble of languages, utterly different from each other. There are the Akhaians, and the passionate Kretans, the Kidonians, the elegant Dorians, and the aristocratic Pelasgians. There's a great city, Knossos, where Minos, the king from the age of nine, a man close to the mighty Zeus himself—the father of my father, the fearless Deukalion. Deukalion fathered me and Lord Idomeneus, who went to Ilios in his rounded ships along with the sons of Atreus.

"My name is Aithon. I was the younger by birth, and he was my elder and my better. I saw Odysseus there, and offered him accommodation, since the force of the wind had brought him to Krete on his way to Troy and driven him far off course by way of Malea. Struggling to skirt the winds, he set in at Amnisos, next to the cave of Eileithos, in a harbor hard to reach. Right away he went up to the city and asked for Idomeneus. He said he was a friend, a very close, respected friend. But already the tenth or eleventh dawn had passed since they had left for Ilios in their curved ships.

"So I took him home and offered him amusement. I welcomed him in, as is only fit, with everything we had in the house. To his shipmates, I gave some barley from our storehouse and to fill their hearts, I gathered bulls for sacrifice. For twelve days those fine Akhaians stayed, since a strong north wind forced them to stand by ashore. It was some hardnosed god that had roused it. Then, the thirteenth day, the wind dropped, and they set off."

He made all of these lies in his story seem so real and truthful. As she was listening, her tears flowed and her face melted away—just as the snow melts on towering mountains, the east wind melting it as the west wind makes it flow downward, and as it is melting, the streams and rivers are filled. Her lovely cheeks melted as she wept and grieved for her man. Odysseus, in his heart, was sorry for his sobbing wife. But under his eyelids, his eyes held steady, hard as horn or iron. He hid his tears shrewdly. And when she had had enough of all her tears and crying, she again spoke to him.

"Now, stranger, I really feel that I have to test you—whether you actually entertained my husband and his worthy crew, there in your palace as you are telling me. So tell me what kind of clothes he wore on his body and what he was like himself and the crew who had come with him?"

Always thinking ahead, Odysseus answered her in return.

"Madam, it's hard for someone who's been away for so long to tell you all this, because by now it is already twenty years since he went away from there, leaving my country. But I will tell you how it looks to me in my heart—Odysseus, brilliant in his purple wool cloak, doubled over, but its clasp made of gold with two eyelets. And in front the clasp was intricately molded—a dog, gripping a spotted fawn in its front paws and gazing at it as it struggled. Everyone was amazed at how, though made of gold, the dog gazed at the fawn that it was strangling, and how the fawn struggled desperately with its feet to get away.

"And I saw how the tunic about his body shined like the skin of a dried onion, as soft and brilliant as the sun itself. Many women admired it, and I'll tell you something else. Hold it within your heart. I do not know whether Odysseus wore such things at home, or if a friend, or maybe a stranger, gave it to him when he went on board his ship, because Odysseus was a friend to many, as few Akhaians were his equal.

"I myself gave him a bronze sword and a cloak with double folds that shimmered when it moved in the light and a tunic lined with fringe, and I sent him off with due respect in a ship with many benches—ah, and there was an aide with him, a bit older than he. I'll tell you about him too, what he was like. Round shoulders, dark skinned, and curly haired. His name was Eurybates, and Odysseus respected him more than his other mates, because they thought alike."

As he was speaking, the urge to weep surged inside her even more, as she recognized the sure signs that Odysseus had mentioned. And when she had enough of all her tears and crying, she spoke these words to him in turn.

"Stranger, although you were pitied before, now you will be welcomed and respected in my halls. I was the one who gave him these clothes, exactly as you have described. I folded them. I brought them out of the storeroom, and I added the bright clasp, as something to enjoy. But I'll never get him back. And he will never return to the native land he loved. And so it was a terrible misfortune for him to go off in his empty ship, to see unspeakable Evilios."

Always thinking ahead, Odysseus answered her in return.

"Honored wife of Odysseus Laertiádes, don't distort your lovely face any more and don't let your heart waste away, weeping for your husband. I don't blame you, not at all. Any woman would mourn when she has lost the man she married, the one to whom she's borne her children after mingling together in the act of making love—even if he's not like Odysseus, who, they say, is like a god himself. But stop crying and listen to what I have to say. I'll tell you for sure and I won't hide a thing—just recently I heard that Odysseus is returning.

"He's close at hand, in the fertile land of the Thesprotians. He's alive and he's bringing many valuable gifts, collecting them from place to place. But he's lost his loyal shipmates and his open ship, out on the sea, dark as wine, while they were sailing past the island of Thrinakia. Odious he was to Zeus and also to Helios, whose cattle his shipmates slaughtered. All were lost in the crashing sea. But holding onto his ship's keel, he was thrown by the waves onto the shore in the land of the Phaiakians, who are near and dear to the gods. They honored him with open hearts, like a god, and they were glad to send him home unharmed.

"Odysseus would have been here long ago, but in his heart it seemed to him much better to gather what he could by roaming this vast world. More than any other man who's doomed to die, Odysseus knows a good thing, and there isn't any other man who could match him. Or so Pheidon, the king of the Thesprotians, told me. Right in front of me he swore, as he was pouring wine, there in his home, that the ship was launched and the crew at hand, those who were to take him to his own native land.

"But first he sent me on, because a Thesprotian ship was about to set out for Doulikhios, with all its wheat. He showed me all of the treasures Odysseus had collected. There was so much lying there in the king's halls that it would feed all of his descendants for ten generations. But he himself had moved on to Dodona, to listen to the will of Zeus, high in the leaves of his own oak tree, about how to return to his cherished native land—openly or in secret—having been away for so long.

"And so he's safe. He'll return soon. He's very close. He won't be away for much longer from his own country and his loved ones. But I'll swear this, right now, before Zeus, the highest and greatest of all the gods, and before blameless Odysseus's hearth, right here where I've arrived at last. All of these things will come to be as I've said. Odysseus will return here, in the course of this very month, between the waning of this moon and the waxing of the next."

Penelope, deep in thought, answered him right away.

"I wish, stranger, what you say would take place. You'd quickly see my kindness, as well as many gifts from me, so that anyone who met you would call you a happy man. But this is how I feel, here in my heart, how it's going to be. Odysseus is never going to come back, and you won't find any transport, since there are no leaders in my house as Odysseus, if he ever existed, was among men—to welcome and send away strangers with respect. But forget it. Servants, pour him a bath and make his bed—a real bed, with real blankets and colorful throws, so that he'll be warm when he reaches Dawn's golden throne. And early in the morning, bathe him and anoint him, so he can think about a good meal here in our house beside Telemakhos.

"It will be all the worse for anyone who torments him. There'll be nothing here, no matter how hard their anger becomes—because how, stranger, can you find out if I might outshine other women in thoughtful presence of mind, if you sit here at my table in disheveled clothing. Men don't last long. And any man who lets himself grow hard and look hard—all of us who face death will call hard times on him for life, and mock him when he dies. But any man who is and shows himself to be faultless—strangers will carry his name far and wide among all people and they'll speak highly of his charm."

Always thinking ahead, Odysseus answered her in turn.

"Esteemed wife of Odysseus Laertiádes, to me, blankets and colorful throws have been a burden since I left behind the snow-covered peaks of Krete, cruising in my ship with its long oars. I'll lie down as I've rested through sleepless nights before. So many nights I've passed the time in a rough bed, waiting for Dawn's bright throne, and washing my feet does not put my heart at ease. No woman shall touch my feet, of all the servants here in your home, unless there is some old woman, with a caring heart, who has suffered as much as I have. I wouldn't mind if someone like that touched my feet."

Penelope, deep in thought, spoke to him again.

"My dear stranger, of all the very welcome strangers who've come to my house from far away, no one has been so thoughtful. Everything you say is sharp and clear. I have an old woman with a deep, understanding heart, who brought up and treasured that unfortunate man with care and gathered him up in her arms, right after his mother first bore him. She will wash your feet, although she's very weak. Come, stand here, thoughtful Eurykleia, and wash someone who's the equal of your master. No doubt, the feet and hands of Odysseus are just like his, because mortal men who are in terrible misfortune quickly sink into old age."

As she spoke, the old woman hid her face in her hands and warm tears fell as she spoke words full of sorrow.

"Oh my, child, I am so hopeless. Zeus must have hated you much more than other men, even though you have a reverent heart. No one has ever burned so many meaty thighs or offer up so many choice sacrifices as you have offered up to thunder-loving Zeus, in your appeals to reach an easy old age and to raise your splendid son. But now he's taken away the day of your return. No doubt the women mocked him too, when he came to some great house in some strange place far away, just as these bitches here mock you. It is to keep away from all this spite and insult that you will not allow them to wash your feet. But Penelope, Ikarios' daughter, has so thoughtfully asked me, and I am not unwilling. I will wash your feet for Penelope herself and also for you, because my heart is all stirred up with sorrows. But come now, listen to these words I have to say. So many troubled, worn-out strangers have come here, but I have to say, so far I've seen no one, in build or voice, or in his feet, who is so much like Odysseus."

Always thinking ahead, Odysseus answered her in return.

"Old woman, so it is—everyone whose eyes have seen us both, says that we are just alike, as you in fact have recognized and said yourself."

As he spoke, the old woman picked up a gleaming basin for washing his feet and poured plenty of cold water, and then she added the hot. Odysseus sat beside the fireplace, and quickly turned away toward the darkness. He had a sudden premonition that when she touched him, she might recognize his scar, and everything would be revealed. She approached and began to wash his feet. And right away, she knew the scar, where a wild boar had once gored him with its white tusk, back when Odysseus had gone over to Parnassos to be with his uncles and Autolykos, his mother's peerless father, who surpassed all men in cheating and swearing. A god gave him this talent, Hermes himself, to whom he had aptly burned the thighs of lambs and kids, so the god was willingly attentive. When Autolykos had come to the lush land of Ithaka, he had found his daughter with a newborn child. And Eurykleia laid it on his knees as he was finishing his meal. She called him by name and said these words to him.

"Autolykos, find a name now for this child of your own child, since he has been prayed for, for so long."

Autolykos spoke up and answered her in return.

"My son-in-law, and you, my daughter, give him the name I tell you. Since I have come here as someone who has been as utterly odious as I am to so many men and women, all across this teeming earth, so call him by the name 'Odysseus.' And when he reaches his prime and comes over to the great house of his mother's kinfolk in Parnassos, where all my possessions are, then I will give him a share of it and send him off with a great heart."

It was for this reason that Odysseus had come, so Autolykos would give him wonderful gifts. And Autolykos and all the sons of Autolykos welcomed him with handshakes and nice words. Amphithea, his mother's mother, threw her arms around Odysseus and kissed his head and both of his beautiful eyes. And then, Autolykos called out to all his boisterous sons to get the meal ready, and they answered his call.

Right away, they led in a five-year old bull and flayed and dressed it, and they cut off all its limbs. They sliced them up expertly and pierced them with spits. They roasted them adeptly and set out the portions. Then they feasted, all day long, until the sun set, and their hearts found nothing lacking as the meal was dished out equally. But when the sun set and darkness arrived, they all lay down and received the gift of sleep.

Very early, as Dawn spread her rosy fingers, they rose and set out on the hunt—Autolykos's sons and their dogs—and with them went Odysseus. They climbed up a steep mountain, Parnassos itself, blanketed with forest, and soon they all reached the wind-swept chasms. Just when the sun was beginning to fall across the fields, just as it rose over the gentle currents of the deep flowing sea, the hunters came to a clearing. The dogs went on ahead, sniffing out the tracks, and behind them, Autolykos's sons, and there among them, close behind the dogs, brilliant Odysseus moved ahead, waving his spear with its long shadow. A wild boar was lying close by, in a thicket so dense, the force of the damp winds did not blow through. The brilliant rays of the sun did not fall there, and the rain never penetrated, because it was so thick and packed with fallen leaves. Now, all around it, the crunching feet of men and dogs approached as they pressed forward.

It burst out of his lair against them, back bristling, fire flashing in its eyes. It stood there, right in front of them. Odysseus rushed in first, lifting his long spear high in his sturdy hand, eager to thrust forward. The boar was too quick for him. It dodged and charged in from the side, and its tusk tore a deep gash in his flesh, but it did not reach the bone. Odysseus aimed true and struck the boar in the right shoulder. The brilliant point of his spear went right through. The boar fell down in the dust with a yowl, and its life flew away. Autolykos's devoted sons tended to it and expertly bound the wound of Odysseus, who looked faultless as a god. And with an chant, they stopped the black blood and went back to their dear father's home.

After Autolykos and his sons had healed him and brought him glorious gifts, they sent him right away, back to his own land, to Ithaka. His father and his esteemed mother rejoiced when he returned and asked him about everything—how he had suffered the wound. He laid it all out to them—how, when he had gone to Parnassos with Autolykos and his sons, while they were out hunting, a boar struck him with its white tusk.

The old woman took his foot in the flat of her hands, and she grasped what it was she was feeling. She dropped the foot. The leg fell into the basin. The bronze rang out as it turned over and the water spilled on the floor. All at once, joy and sorrow clutched at her heart, and her eyes filled with tears. Her voice was thick and heavy as she held back. She touched Odysseus's chin and she said to him,

"You are Odysseus himself, dear child, and I didn't even know you until I grasped my master in the flesh."

With her eyes, she glanced over at Penelope. She wanted to reveal her beloved husband was there, but she could not return the look or understand. Athena had turned her thoughts away. Odysseus felt for her throat and held it in his right hand and with the other hand he drew her close and spoke to her.

"Mother, why do you want to destroy me? You once nursed me yourself at your own breast and now, after going through so many sorrows, I've come in the twentieth year to my own land. But since some god has cast it into your heart and you have seen me—silence—or else someone here in these halls might hear. And I'll tell you this, and it will surely come to be, that if some god allows me to overcome these noble courtiers, although you are my nurse, I will not spare you when I kill the other servants here in these rooms."

Thinking deeply, Eurykleia answered back.

"My child, what words escape the barrier of your teeth. You know how steady and loyal my spirit is. I'll be as stubborn as a rock, or iron, and I'll tell you another thing—plunge it into your heart. If Zeus allows you to overcome these noble suitors, I'll tell you which of the women dishonored you and which are innocent."

Always thinking ahead, Odysseus answered her in return.

"Mother, why should you even speak of them? There's no need for you to do anything. I myself will look them over now and get to know each one. Keep your voice silent, and leave it to the gods."

After he spoke, the old woman went away, through the halls, to bring more water for his feet, since the first quantity had completely spilled. After she had washed him and anointed him freely with oil, Odysseus drew his chair closer to the fire, to get warm, and he covered his scar with his rags. Penelope, deep in thought, was then the first to speak.

"Stranger, this one little thing I want to ask you for myself. Very soon, it's going be the hour for soothing rest, at least for someone to whom sweet sleep may come in spite of all of his troubles. But some god has brought me endless sorrow. Day after day, I keep yearning only to weep and wail as I look to the servants' and to my own household tasks, and as night comes and sleep takes hold of everyone, sharp worries swarm all around my heart and upset me as I weep.

"Like Pandareus's daughter, the pale green nightingale, who sings so beautifully as spring arrives, and perches up among the trees' thick leaves and pours out her voice with echoing trills for her child, dear Itylos, Lord Zethos's son, whom she killed by mistake with her sword—my heart is goaded by doubt, back and forth, whether to stay close by my son and keep everything as it is—everything I own, my servants, this large house with its high ceilings—to honor my own bed and the voice of the people or to go away with whoever's the best of the Akhaians now courting me with countless gifts here within these halls. And also my son, while he was only a thoughtless child, would not let me marry and move away from my husband's household. But now that he has grown and reached his prime of life, he prays that I'll withdraw from these halls, because he's so worried about all this property that the Akhaians are eating up. But come now, listen to this dream of mine and interpret it for me.

"There are twenty geese that come out of the water to the house and begin to eat wheat. I am filled with joy as I watch them. And then, down from the mountain came a huge eagle with a crooked beak. It broke their necks and killed all of them. They lay strewn about in heaps, all over these halls, as it soared away into the brilliant sky. And I cried and wept, even though it was only a dream and my servants, with their lovely hair, drew around as I cried disconsolately over how the eagle had killed my geese. Then it came back and perched upon a projecting roof beam. With a human voice it consoled me and spoke.

'Take heart, daughter of the renowned Ikarios. This is not a dream. It is a real vision of something good that is going to come about. The geese are your courtiers and I, who was the eagle before, am now your husband, returning to inflict a horrible death against these courtiers.'

"After he spoke, sweet sleep released me and looking all around the hall, I saw the geese pecking at the wheat near the feeding trough, as they had been before."

Always thinking, Odysseus answered her in turn.

"Woman, there's no way to interpret this dream any other way, since Odysseus himself has said how it will come about. It's obvious—the destruction of the suitors, all of them. There's not one of them who will escape his own destiny, his own death."

And Penelope, deep in thought, answered back.

"Stranger, dreams are indecipherable and rambling and don't always come out as people think they will. Dreams are elusive, with double gates. One's made of horn, and the other ivory. The ones that pass through sculpted ivory are deceptive, their messages unfulfilled. But those that pass through the gate of polished horn bring real things whenever someone sees them. However, it seems to me, that's not where my strange dream came from. That would have been welcome to me and my son.

"But I'll tell you this—and you should drive this deep inside your heart. It is very near, the looming dawn that will tear me away from the house of Odysseus. Because now, I am going to put together a contest, using those axes, twelve in all, that he used to set in a straight line, like a keel hold, and he'd stand far back and shoot an arrow through them. I'll set up this contest for the suitors, and whoever strings and stretches the bow most easily in his hands, and then shoots an arrow through all twelve, I'll go with him, and I'll leave behind this marriage house, which is so beautiful, so full of life, and which I know I will always remember, even in my dreams."

Odysseus, always thinking ahead, answered her in turn.

"Esteemed wife of Odysseus Laertiádes, hold off for now on this contest in your house. Odysseus is sharp, and he'll come back to you here before the likes of these will take his polished bow, and string it, and shoot an arrow through the iron."

But Penelope, deep in thought, answered back.

"If you wanted, stranger, to linger and give me joy, here in my halls, sleep would never pass over my eyes. But it's not really possible for human beings to go without sleep for very long, because those who never die have set down for those of us who have to die their exact share for each and every thing, here on earth, the source of grain. And so, for your sake, I will go up now to my upper room and lie on my bed, which for me has turned into a bed of mourning, dampened by my tears, since Odysseus went off to see unspeakable Evilios. I'll lie down up there. But you—you can spread something on the floor and lie down here inside the house, or I'll have the servants set up a cot for you."

After she had said this, she went up to her bright, upper room, but not alone. Her women went with her, and when she had ascended to her upper room with them, she wept for Odysseus her beloved husband until Athena, her eyes gleaming, cast sweet sleep over her eyes.

XX

Hard Words

Brilliant Odysseus lay down in the front hall. He spread a rough ox hide on the floor and on top of that, many fleeces from the sheep that the Akhaians had slaughtered. After he lay down, Eurynome threw a cloak over him. Odysseus lay there, wide awake, thinking dark thoughts about the suitors. The women who were always sleeping with the suitors came out of their rooms, sharing their joy and laughter with each other. His heart grew agitated deep inside his chest, and he mulled over in his mind and heart whether to rush and kill every one or let them intermingle with the arrogant courtiers for the latest and very last time. Like a hound standing over her young pups, snarling at an unknown man, ready to fight—inside, his own heart was snarling, enraged at their disgraceful actions. But he beat his own chest and rebuked his own heart with these words.

"Hold on, my heart. You once endured much worse than this, that day when the Kyklops, whose strength was so overpowering, ate your daring companions. But you held on, until your cunning led you out of that cave where you thought you were going to die."

As he was speaking, chiding the heart in his own chest, his heart obeyed him and kept on beating stubbornly. But he himself tossed and turned, back and forth. Like a man who is turning a sausage, full of fat and blood, back and forth, over a flickering fire, anxious to roast it quickly, Odysseus tossed and turned, again and again, wondering how he, just one against so many, might get his hands upon the arrogant suitors. Athena came down from the sky and drew near to him, in the body of a woman. She stood above his head and said these words to him.

"Why are you still awake? Are you a man who is unluckier than any other? This is your own house, and here inside your house are your wife and such a son as anyone would wish to have as his own son."

Odysseus, always thinking ahead, answered her in return.

"True, goddess, everything you're saying is true, but here in my chest, my heart keeps murmuring—how to lay my hands on those patronizing suitors by myself. They are always together in here, and in my mind, I keep murmuring this other, harder thought. Even if I kill them, by your grace and by Zeus's will, where can I run to? Think of that—I ask you."

And the goddess Athena, her eyes gleaming, spoke to him again.

"So stubborn—well, there are many who put their faith in someone worse than I, some ordinary man who knows fewer ways and means than I do. I am a goddess, and I am going to protect you through all of your troubles. I will tell you openly. Even if fifty mortal troops surrounded us, ready to kill us in combat, you would take away their cattle and sheep. So let sleep come over you. Nothing but exhaustion comes from staying awake, keeping watch all night, and soon your life is not to be so odious as before."

After she spoke, she spread sleep over his eyelids, and then the goddess went back to Olympos. But as sleep came over him, slackening his limbs and releasing the cares within his heart, his wife woke up, her heart open. She wept as she sat in her soft bed. But when she grew tired of crying, the woman prayed first to Artemis.

"Artemis, venerated goddess, daughter of Zeus, if only you would send your arrow into my breast and take my life away right now, or if a storm would catch me up and carry me away, flying through the darkness, and throw me down into the ebb and flow of ocean currents, as the storm winds long ago carried away Pandareus's daughters. The gods killed their parents, and they were left behind as orphans in their home. Aphrodite provided them with cheese, sweet honey, and light wine. Hera gave them more beauty and sensitivity than any other women. Unblemished Artemis made them tall, and Athena taught them to create fine crafts. But as brilliant Aphrodite was ascending into the heights of Mount Olympos, to seek the fruition of marriage for them from Zeus, who delights in lightning and knows everything, both the inexorable and the unexpected ends we humans face, the harpies snatched the young girls and gave them to the hideous Furies to be their slaves.

"If only those who make their homes on Olympos would obliterate me, or if Artemis with her lovely hair would strike me down, so I could go down below the bitter earth to be there with Odysseus, and never have to please the mind of a lesser man. It is a tolerable horror when one weeps all day with a heart that is deeply distressed, but then one sleeps all night. Sleep wipes away everything, good and bad, when it covers our eyes. But some god is sending me terrible dreams. Tonight, once again, someone like him was lying beside me. Someone who was just like he was, back when he went off with the army. And my heart was happy, because I did not think it was only a dream but, at last, real."

While she spoke, Dawn appeared on her golden throne. And as Penelope wept, brilliant Odysseus heard her. He wondered about it and deep in his heart it seemed that she was standing beside his head and recognized him. He gathered up the cloak and the fleeces on which he had been lying. He placed them on a chair, there in the hall, and carried the ox hide outside, and he put it down. Then he raised his hands and prayed to Zeus.

"Father Zeus, if it is your will to have led me over the lands and waters to my own land, let one of those who are waking up inside say something momentous, and also show me a sign out here."

As he prayed, Zeus the Deliberator heard him. From gleaming Olympos, high above the clouds, he thundered. And brilliant Odysseus took heart. From inside a house nearby, where the millstones of the shepherd of the people were set, a woman was grinding away. Twelve women in all worked there, preparing barley and wheat, the human staple. The others slept, since they had ground their wheat already. She alone had not yet finished, since she was the weakest at this grind. But now she stopped the mill and said these words—a sign for her master.

"Father Zeus, ruler of gods and men. How loudly you've thundered in a sky full of stars. There's not a cloud anywhere. You are showing somebody a sign. Make what I am about to say come true, for poor me. May those suitors gulp down their marvelous feast for the very last time inside the halls of Odysseus. They've spread my knees apart with hard labor, as I've fixed their barley. Now let them eat their last."

As she was speaking, Odysseus brightened at her telling words and at the thundering of Zeus, and he thought about getting revenge against the wrongdoers. By now the other women slaves had gathered inside Odysseus's beautiful house. They were adding kindling to the restless fire and Telemakhos, looking like a god, rose from his bed and put on his clothes. He slung his sharpened sword over his shoulder and tied his sandals on his freshly oiled feet. He grabbed his thick spear with its sharp bronze point and went to stand on the threshold. He spoke to Eurykleia,

"Nurse, did you show the stranger respect with a bed and some food or is he lying about uncared for? My mother is like that, as deeply understanding as she is. She'll honor a lesser man by chance and sends away a better man without respect."

Deep in thought, Eurykleia answered back.

"Now, my child, you should never blame someone who's not to blame. The man sat right there and drank wine for as long as he wanted to. She asked him about food, but he said he was not hungry. And then, just as he was thinking about rest and sleep, she told the slaves to spread out his bedding. But he, like someone who is utterly miserable and without any luck, did not want to lie down on a bed under blankets. Instead, he slept there in the front hall on an untanned ox hide and some fleeces of sheep. And we threw a cloak over him."

After she had spoken, Telemakhos went out through the hall, carrying his spear, and two dogs quickly followed him. He went straight to the agora to sit among the well-dressed Akhaians. And brilliant Eurykleia, the daughter of Ops Peisenorida, called out right away to all the women.

"Come on, get moving—sweep out the house and sprinkle it over. And toss all those purple throws over the crafted chairs. And you, wipe down all the tables with sponges and clean the mixing bowls and those carved, two-handled cups. And you others, go down to the spring for water and bring it here quickly. Those courtiers won't be away from the hall for long. They'll be back soon, since it's a feast day for everyone."

As she spoke, they listened and obeyed. Twenty of them went down to the spring with its dark waters, and all the others busied themselves expertly about the house. The Akhaians' male slaves arrived and split the wood with expert skill. The women returned from the spring, and after them, the pig keeper came, driving three boars, the best of them all. He let them feed in the lovely courtyard. And he himself spoke to Odysseus with honeyed words.

"Stranger, are the Akhaians viewing you any better, or are they disrespecting you in these halls as they did before?"

Odysseus, always thinking ahead, answered him in turn.

"Ah, Eumaios, if only the gods would avenge the disgrace these men in their arrogance are inflicting, viciously and without any shame, here in someone else's house."

As they were speaking to each other, the goatherd Melanthios came, leading the best of all the goats for the suitors' feast, and two other goatherds followed along. He tied them down underneath the echoing portico, and he spoke to Odysseus with mocking words.

"Stranger, are you going to keep bothering us with your begging, here in this house? Go outside, or just go away. I don't think we are going to part before tasting each other's fists. You don't beg properly, and besides, there are other Akhaian feasts to go to."

After he said this, Odysseus, always thinking ahead, gave no answer. In silence, he shook his head, thinking hard thoughts. In addition to these, a third man arrived, Philoitios, a leader of men, driving a barren cow and some fat goats, brought over by ferrymen, who carry other men as well, whoever comes to them. He tied them up under the echoing portico and stood close to the pig keeper and questioned him.

"Who is this stranger, pig keeper, who has just come here to our house? Whose people does he come from? Where is his family and his father's fields? He's unlucky, but in his build he's like a king or lord. Of course, the gods plunge men who've been driven far and wide into misery, even if they're kings, when they spin their tough thread."

He drew close to Odysseus and held out his right hand. He spoke to him, and his words soared like wings.

"Cheers, father, stranger, may good luck be yours in times to come, though now you are having such hard times. Father Zeus, no god's more brutal than you! You have no feeling at all for those you yourself have brought to life. You screw them all with the most awful, the bleakest troubles. When I saw you, sir, I broke into a sweat and my eyes filled up with tears, thinking about Odysseus, since I think that he too is in such rags as he wanders around among men, if somehow he's alive and still can see the sunlight, unless he's dead and in Hades' dominion. Oh—Odysseus, without a fault—he put me over these cows when I was but a boy in the land of the Kephallenians. Now they've grown, too many to count, and there's no way any other strain of cow, with such broad heads, could bring a better yield. But now these others have ordered me to drive in the herd so they can eat them up.

"They don't care at all about the son of this house and don't tremble at the gods' anger, they're so determined to divide up the spoils of our master, who's been away so long. But as for me, my heart, here inside my chest, keeps on turning around, because it's bad, with his son still alive, to go off with my cows to some other land with strange people, but what's even worse is to stay right here and go through hard times with cows that are handed over to other folks. I'd have left and gone away a long time ago to some other high and mighty king, since I just can't stand it any longer, but I keep thinking—that unfortunate man just might come back from somewhere or other and make these courteous men here in his house scatter."

Always thinking ahead, Odysseus answered him in turn.

"Herdsman, it's clear you're neither evil nor dull, and I see myself you have a thoughtful heart, and so I'll speak out and announce a great promise. By Zeus, the first of the gods, and this generous table and faultless Odysseus's hearth, to which I've now come—while you are here, Odysseus will return home, and you will see with your own eyes, if you want, the killing of the suitors who presume to run this place."

The man who took care of the cattle spoke back to him.

"Ah, stranger, if only the Son of Kronos would bring about exactly what you're saying. Then I'd know my own strength and how my hands are to obey it."

In the same way, Eumaios prayed to all the gods for Odysseus to return home. And while they went on talking to each other, the suitors were busy plotting Telemakhos's terrible doom and death, but then a bird came down upon them, passing from right to left, an eagle flying from high above, clutching a frightened dove. Amphinomos spoke out loud before them all.

"My friends, I do not think this plan to murder Telemakhos will go very well for us. Let's think about our feast."

Amphinomos said this, and they liked what he said. They entered Odysseus's house. They laid their cloaks on the various chairs, and the male slaves began to slaughter some large sheep, fat goats, stuffed pigs, and cattle from the herd. They roasted and served up the inner organs and stirred up the wine in bowls. The pig keeper handed out the cups, and Philoitios, a leader among men, passed the bread out to them in beautiful baskets, and Melanthios poured the wine. They all stretched out their hands to the fare that lay within reach before them. But thinking shrewdly, Telemakhos had Odysseus sit close to the stone threshold inside the elegant hall. And he placed a broken-down stool and a small table and laid out a share of the roasted organs, and he poured some wine into a golden cup. He spoke these words.

"Now sit here among these men and drink your wine, and I myself will hold off all the suitors' insults and prodding, since this is no public space but the house of Odysseus. It was for me that he acquired it. And you courtiers, hold your hearts back from laying blame and prodding, so no conflict or quarrel will be stirred up."

As he said this, they all bit their lips and wondered at Telemakhos, who was speaking out so bluntly. Antinoos, Eupeithes's son, spoke out among them.

"Hard as it is, Akhaians, let's go along with what Telemakhos says, much as he blusters away at us. Zeus, the Son of Kronos, would not have allowed it, or we would have shut him up already, loud as he talks."

Telemakhos paid no attention to what Antinoos said. The heralds were at that moment leading through the city a hundred sacrificial cattle for the gods. The Akhaians, with their long hair, gathered together in the shadow of the sacred grove belonging to Apollo, the archer god. And as soon as they had roasted the outer flesh and pulled it off the carcass, they divided up the portions and treated themselves to a magnificent feast, and the servers placed beside Odysseus the same portion as the suitors themselves received, as Telemakhos, the beloved son of godlike Odysseus, had ordered. But Athena did not allow the rash suitors to hold back from their cutting insults, so that the hurt would sink even deeper into the heart of Odysseus Laertiádes. There was a man among the suitors, a disorderly man—Ktesippos was his name. He made his home in Samos. Trusting in his great wealth, he was courting the wife of Odysseus, who had been away for such a long time. It was he who then spoke to the overbearing suitors.

"Listen to me, proud courtiers, while I say something. For a long time, this stranger here has had a portion, an equal one, as is fitting, since it's not right to deprive Telemakhos's guests of their fair share, whoever comes to this house. Listen, though, I'll also give him what a stranger deserves, so he himself can give it to the washing woman or another servant here in the house of Lord Odysseus."

As he spoke, he grabbed the hoof of an ox from the basket where it had been lying, and with all his force, he threw it. Odysseus dodged it with a quick shift of his head and smiled with bitter scorn in his heart. The hoof hit the solid wall. And Telemakhos rebuked Ktesippos with these words.

"Ktesippos, it's better for you the way this turned out. You did not strike the stranger. He dodged your throw. Or else I would have driven the point of my spear into your gut, and instead of a wedding, your father would have busied himself with a funeral. Show no rudeness, here in my house, none of you! Although I was just a child before, now I'm watching, and I understand everything you do—the good and the ugly. And so, we will keep on watching all these things for now, as the sheep are slaughtered and the wine is drunk and the bread swallowed, because it's hard for one man to hold back so many. But come now, don't do these awful things anymore, simply out of spite. If you really want to kill me with your bronze, I'd prefer that. It would be far, far better to die, than to observe these impertinent acts all the time—knocking about strangers and dragging servant girls around through this beautiful house without any shame."

As he was speaking, they were speechless, awed to silence. Agelaos Damastorides spoke at last among them.

"My friends, no one should become angry and answer back with heated words to what's been said in fairness. Don't mistreat the stranger or any of the slaves any longer, here in the house of Lord Odysseus. And I would say these calm words to Telemakhos and his mother, in the hope that it will be agreeable to both of you. For as long as the hearts inside your breasts hoped that clever Odysseus would return to his home, you were not at fault for waiting or for fending off us courtiers in your house. It was better, just in case Odysseus had come back home. But it's clear by now that there is to be no return. So come now, sit here beside your mother and lay it out for her. She has to marry the best man, the one who brings her the most, so that you may fully enjoy your legacy, eating and drinking, and she can take on another man's house."

Gathering his thoughts, Telemakhos answered him.

"By Zeus, Agelaos, and by the sufferings of my father, who has died or is still wandering far from Ithaka, I'm not delaying my mother's wedding in any way. I call on her to marry whom she will, and I'll offer her countless gifts. But in due respect, I'm reluctant to send her away from her home against her will with forceful words. May no god ever make this happen."

As Telemakhos spoke, Pallas Athena aroused the suitors to helpless laughter, and turned their minds elsewhere. They laughed as if their jaws were not their own. The meat they chewed was flecked with blood. Their eyes filled with tears, and even within their own minds, they seemed to be weeping. Theoklymenos then spoke to them like a god.

"You fools, what madness is this that you're suffering from? Your heads and your faces are covered up below your knees. Your cheeks are burning with tears and sobbing, and the walls and lovely niches are splattered with blood. And the front hall and the courtyard are filled with shadows, flitting down to Erebos into darkness, and the sun is blotted out entirely, clouded in an awful mist."

As he spoke, all of them went on laughing loudly at him. Eurymakhos, Polybos's son, was the first to find his voice.

"He's insane, this stranger who just arrived from far away! Quick, you young men, let's send him outside the house and off to the assembly, since he thinks it's like night here inside."

Theoklymenos spoke right back, just like a god.

"Eurymakhos, I do not need your guides to lead me on my way. I have both eyes and ears and two feet and a mind, here inside, that's not so badly made. With these I'm going to make my way outside, since I see a hard time is about to come to you, and none of you suitors are going to escape or dodge it—not one of you who are contriving cruelties and overstepping yourselves with other men here in the house of godlike Odysseus."

After saying this, he went out of those elegant halls, and he made his way to the house of Peiraios, who welcomed him graciously. But all the suitors were glancing at each other, and they mocked and goaded Telemakhos, and they kept on laughing at his guests. And one of these arrogant young men would say:

"Telemakhos, no one has worse guests than you, seeing how you let in such a dirty drifter who's always begging for bread and wine, with no skills for work or war. He's no more than a burden to the earth itself. And then this other one stood up to spout his prophecy. It would be a lot better if you listened to me. Let's toss these strangers onto a galley with lots of benches and send them off to the Sicilians. That'd bring you a seemly sum."

The suitors kept on talking. Telemakhos did not care what they said. He looked over at his father in silence, all the time anticipating the moment to lay his hands on the mindless suitors. And Ikarios's daughter, Penelope, deep in thought, placed her beautiful chair opposite them, and she listened to what each man in the hall had to say. And as they continued laughing, they made their preparations for a sweet, delicious dinner, for which they had slaughtered so many animals. But no dinner was less appealing than what a goddess and a forceful man were soon about to set before them, since they had been the first to put in play their malicious actions.

XXI

The Contest

The goddess Athena, her gray eyes gleaming, placed it in the heart of Ikarios's daughter Penelope, deep in thought, to set up the bow and the gray iron as a contest—the commencement of death for the suitors in Odysseus's halls. She climbed the high stairway to her rooms, and she held firmly in her hand a coiled key, a beautiful bronze key with an ivory handle. And then she went together with her women to an isolated storeroom. There lay her husband's things, made of bronze, gold and iron, intricately wrought. There the bow, bent backwards, was lying, along with the quiver that held so many arrows, the source of groaning. They were gifts that a friend had once given to Odysseus when they had happened to meet in Lakedaimon—Iphitos Eurytides, a man like those who never die. They had come upon each other in Messene at the house of Ortilokhos, a hot-blooded man.

Odysseus had come to collect a debt, which the people there all owed him. The men of Messene had taken three hundred sheep and their shepherds from Ithaka in their huge ships. It was all because of these that Odysseus had made this long journey as a mission, when he was still very young, since his father and the other elders had sent him. Iphitos had come, searching for twelve mares and some work mules that he had lost. Later he encountered his destiny and death when he came upon Herakles, Zeus's powerful son, who was used to extreme actions and who brutally killed Iphitos while he was a guest in his house, without regard for the anger of the gods or for the table that he himself had set before the man. He killed Iphitos and kept the mares all for himself in his own halls.

It was while seeking these horses that he encountered Odysseus, and he gave him the bow that the great Eurytos had once carried, before he left it behind for his son in his enormous home when he died, and Odysseus in return gave Iphitos a sharpened sword and a hefty spear in warm friendship. But they never got to know each other at table. Before they had a chance, Zeus's son killed Iphitos Eurytides, a man like those who never die.

He had given the bow to Odysseus, who did not take it with him when he went to war in the black ships. Instead, it lay within his halls in memory of a close friend, although he would carry it around at home. Now, when the radiant woman had reached the storeroom and stepped on the oak threshold, which a carpenter had once expertly planed, true to the line, and placed within the doorposts and set into the bright doors, quickly she released the thong and put in the key, and the bolts shot right back in front of her.

Like a bull, moaning as it grazes in a meadow, the beautiful doors moaned when struck by the key, and they flew open quickly before her. She went straight to the raised platform where stood some chests in which some scented clothing lay. Reaching up from there, she took the bow, wrapped in its bright case, down from its peg. She sat down and laid it across her knees. She sobbed out loud as she unwrapped her husband's bow. But when she had her fill of tears and moaning, she went back to the great hall to the lordly courtiers, carrying in her hands the backward-bent bow and the quiver for the arrows, and in it were many arrows, the source of groaning. At her side, her slaves carried a chest full of iron and bronze, her husband's trophies.

When the radiant woman reached the courtiers, she stood by the doorpost of the sturdily built structure, and she held up a glistening veil before her face. A loyal slave came and stood on each side of her. And at once, she spoke these words among the courtiers.

"Listen to me, you self-assured courtiers, you have commandeered this house to eat and drink continually, since its master has been away for such a long time. And you could find no other way to justify this, except your desire to marry me and take me as your woman. But come now, courtiers, here is your test. I show you the legendary Odysseus's great bow. Whoever can take in his hands and string this bow most easily and shoot an arrow through all twelve axes, I will go with him and renounce the house of my marriage, which is so utterly beautiful and full of wealth, I think I will always remember it, even in my dreams."

As she spoke, she asked Eumaios, the keeper of pigs, to set the bow and the gray iron in front of the courtiers. In tears, Eumaios accepted them and laid them down, and the cattle herder also wept when he saw his master's bow. Antinoos rebuked them.

"Stupid field hands, you think only of today. You idiots, why are you shedding tears and troubling this lady's heart, now slumped back in pain, since losing her husband? Sit back and eat in silence or go weep outside and leave the bow in here. It's an an onerous test for us to settle the matter, for I don't think it's going to be easy to string this polished bow, since among all of us who are here, there's no one like Odysseus. I remember him myself, though I was just a child."

As he spoke, the heart inside his chest held hope that he himself would string the bow and shoot an arrow through the iron—but he would be the very first to taste an arrow from the hands of faultless Odysseus whom, even there and then in his own household, he was dishonoring and urging all his companions on. The deep inner strength of Telemakhos then spoke among them.

"Ah now—Zeus, Son of Kronos, has made me utterly thoughtless! My own dear mother, wise as she is, is saying she will go away and leave behind this, her marriage house, and yet I am laughing and cheerful in my mindlessness. But come on, you courtiers, since this is your prize, a woman unlike any other now in the land of the Akhaians—not in powerful Pylos, nor in Argos or Mykenae, and not in Ithaka itself, nor on the dark mainland. You yourselves see this. Do I need to praise my mother? Come on now, don't put this off with excuses or turn away from stringing the bow, and we will see. I myself will try the bow, and if I string it and shoot through the iron, it won't trouble me if my esteemed mother leaves this house with someone else, because I'll be left behind as a man now able to take up his father's weapons."

He stood up, erect, and shrugged his red cloak off his shoulders. He took the sharp sword from his shoulder. First, he set up the axes, after digging a trench, a long one for all of them, and he set it all up true to the line and stamped the earth all around the axes. Amazement seized everyone who saw him, since he had set them up in perfect order, although he had never seen them before. Then he went and stood next to the threshold, and he tried out the bow. As he strained to draw it back, he made it quiver three times. Three times his strength gave out, as much as he had hoped, deep in his heart, to stretch the string and shoot an arrow through the iron. Now, at last, drawing it tight for the fourth time, he would have strung the bow by using all his force, but as eager as he was, Odysseus shook his chin to hold him back, and the deep inner strength of Telemakhos spoke again among them.

"Ah now—and so I'll always be, worthless and weak, or else I'm just too young and can't trust my own hands to defend myself against any man who gets angry over nothing. But come on now, you're all so much better and stronger than I. Try the bow. Let's run this contest through to the end."

As he said this, he put the bow down beside him on the ground, leaning it up against the polished, hinged door, and there he leaned his sleek arrow against the lovely door hook. Then he sat down once again in the chair from which he had stood. And Antinoos, Eupeithes's son, spoke among them.

"Get up then, all of you companions, in proper order, starting right from the place where the wine is now being poured and moving along toward the right."

Antinoos said this, and they all liked what he said. Leiodes, Oinopos's son, was the first to stand up. He was their sage, who always sat away from them, deep in a corner near the gleaming mixing bowl. Their recklessness was repugnant to him alone, and he was outraged by all of the suitors. Now he became the first to take the bow and the sleek arrow. He went and stood at the threshold. He tried the bow but could not string it. His soft, tender hands tired as he pulled the bow back, and he spoke among the suitors.

"Friends, I cannot string it. Someone else take it, because this bow is going to rob many of the best of their hearts and souls, and it's much better to die than go on living after failing at what we all gathered here for, in anticipation, all these days. There are many, even now, who are hoping in your hearts, yearning to marry Penelope, Odysseus's wife. But after you try it and see for yourself, then go off and court some other Akhaian women in fine robes. She should take the lucky one who comes along, bringing her the most."

As he said this, he put the bow down beside him on the ground, leaning it up against the polished, hinged door, and there he leaned his sleek arrow against the lovely door hook. Then he sat down once again in the chair from which he had stood. Antinoos called him by name and rebuked him.

"Leiodes, what words escape the barrier of your teeth! It's despicable, hard to tolerate! It angers me to hear it—that this bow will rob the best of us of our hearts and souls simply because you yourself are not able to string it. Your honorable mother did not give birth to the likes of you to become the kind of man who is able to draw back a bow and shoot arrows. But there are others here among us lordly courtiers who soon will string it."

Saying this, he called to Melanthios, the goat keeper.

"Come on already, light up a fire here in these halls, Melanthios, and beside it, set down a large chair with sheep skins on it, and bring out a large wheel of that hardened fat that lies within, so we young men can warm up the bow and rub it down with grease, then try it out and finish up this match."

As he spoke, Melanthios rekindled the unflagging fire. He carried over and placed beside it a large chair, covered with sheep skin, and then he brought out the large wheel of hardened fat that had been within. With this fat, the young men warmed up the bow and tried it out, but they were not able to string it, because they were so utterly lacking in strength. Antinoos and the godly Eurymakhos, the leaders and the most skilled among the suitors, kept at it. But the cattle man and Odysseus's pig keeper went outside, and after them brilliant Odysseus himself left the house.

As soon as they were outside the courtyard gates, he addressed them, speaking with gentle words.

"Cattle man, and you, pig keeper, should I say it or keep it to myself? Ah, my heart urges me to say it. What would you do to defend Odysseus, if he came out of nowhere suddenly, or if some god were to bring him here before your eyes? Would you defend the suitors or Odysseus? Speak up, as your heart and soul urge you to."

And the man who herded the cattle answered him.

"Father Zeus, bring about this wish, so that man will come or some god bring him. Then you'll know my strength and how my hands follow through."

In the same manner, Eumaios prayed to all the gods for shrewd Odysseus to return to his own home. Now that he knew, without a doubt, how they both thought, he hurried to answer them with these words.

"Here I am right now, myself, right here in front of you. After suffering so many troubles, I've come in the twentieth year to my own land. And I know of all my slaves, you are the only ones who wish for my arrival. I've not heard even one of the others praying for me to come back home again.

"And so, I'll tell you two the truth—how it's going to be. If a god will bring down these grand suitors for me, I will bring wives to each of you and I'll give you property and build you a house near mine, and from then on, for me, you will be like the friends and brothers of Telemakhos. Look, I'll show you a clear sign, so you'll know me well and have confidence in your heart—this scar a boar once gave me with his white tusk, back when I went to Parnassos with the sons of Autolykos."

After he spoke, he pulled back his old rags, away from the large scar. And after they had both looked it over and commented on it to each other, they both threw their arms around skillful Odysseus, and they wept. They kissed his head and shoulders, and they heartily welcomed him. And in the same way, Odysseus kissed their heads and hands, and the sun would have set on this oddest scene of sorrow, if Odysseus himself had not held them back and spoken.

"Stop crying and groaning, or someone might come out of the hall and see, and then tell those who are inside. Go on inside, one after the other. Not together. First, me—then, you. And this can be our sign. All the others—those grand suitors, will not allow the bow and quiver to be given to me. But you, Eumaios, as you carry the bow through the hall, place it in my hands and then tell the women to bar the room's close-set doors. And if any of them hears the groans and uproar of the men, here inside our walls, do not let them go outside. Keep them quietly at their work. I'm giving you, brilliant Philoitios, the order to lock the courtyard gate by its bolt and quickly bind a strap around it."

After he spoke, he went into the crowded house, and he sat in the same chair from which he had arisen. Then Odysseus's two slaves went inside. Eurymakhos was now holding the bow. He warmed it, here and there, in the firelight. But even then, he was not able to string it. In his heart, eager for glory, he groaned. Overcome with anger, he called out to the others.

"Ah now—I'm upset, for myself and for everyone. It's not only for some marriage that I feel miserable, upset as I am, since there are many other Akhaian women, some here in Ithaka, surrounded by the sea, and some in other cities. But if we're so much weaker than Odysseus that we are not able to string his bow, that's a disgrace that those to come will hear about."

At that point, Antinoos, Eupeithes's son, answered him.

"Eurymakhos, it's not so, and you know it yourself. Today is *that* god's sacred feast, so who would draw a bow? Just set it aside. Why don't we let the axes all stand where they are? No one, I think, is going to come to the hall of Odysseus Laertiádes and somehow carry them away. So come on, let the wine bearer fill our cups so we can pour our offerings, and lay this crooked bow aside. And in the morning tell Melanthios, the keeper of goats, to bring along some goats, the very best of all the herds, so we can place their thighs before Apollo, the glorious archer, and try out the bow once again and finish the contest."

As Antinoos spoke, they found what he had to say pleasing to them. So their attendants poured water over their hands, and young men filled up their bowls to the brim with drink and served it out in cups to all of them. And when they had poured out their offerings and drunk to their hearts' content, Odysseus, always thinking ahead, spoke craftily.

"Listen to me, you suitors of this glorious queen, so I can put into words what this heart inside my chest compels me to say. I'm asking Eurymakhos, most of all, and godlike Antinoos, too, since what he said was right, to hold off for now from trying out the bow, and leave it to the gods. And in the morning the gods will give the power to whomever it is they wish. But come, give me that polished bow, so I can test out my hands and strength among you—whether I still have the strength I once had in my agile limbs—or if, by now, wandering and hunger have taken it away."

As he spoke, they all became totally incensed, fearing that he might string the polished bow, and Antinoos spoke up and called him down and rebuked him.

"You miserable stranger, you do not have even the least bit of sense. Aren't you content to feast in comfort, here with the best of us, and not miss any of it as you listen to all our words and talk? No other stranger or beggar hears what we say. This sweet, honeyed wine is impairing you, as it harms others who gulp it down so greedily and don't drink wisely.

"Wine also made an ass of that famous centaur, Eurytrion, in great-hearted Peirithoos's hall, back when he went to the Lapithae, and when the wine had blurred his mind into madness, he did horrible things in Peirithoos's house and anguish took hold of those brave men, and they jumped up and after cutting off his ears and nostrils with merciless bronze, dragged him out through the gate, and stupefied, he went off, aching with the blunder in his foolish heart. The quarrel between centaurs and men came out of that, but he first found the trouble for himself, when loaded down with wine.

"And so I'm letting you know—there will be a lot of trouble for you too, if you string the bow, because you'll find no mercy in our land. We'll send you off straight away in a black ship to King Ekhetos, the scourge of all who have to die, and there'll be no way to save yourself. So be quiet and drink up. Don't compete with younger men."

Penelope, deep in thought, answered him.

"Antinoos, it is neither good nor just to deny Telemakhos's guests, whoever comes to this house. Do you expect that if this stranger, trusting in his hands and strength, strings Odysseus's bow, that he will lead me to his home and make me his wife? There is no way he is hoping for this in his heart. And none of you should feast here, aching within his heart because of this. That would be tasteless."

Eurymakhos, Polybos's son, answered her.

"Penelope, thoughtful daughter of Ikarios, none of us think that he might lead you off to his home. It's unthinkable. But we would feel ashamed at men and women's talk, if later on, some worse than despicable Akhaian might say, 'These must be weaker men who are courting the wife of a man without blame, and yet they cannot string his polished bow, while some other man, some beggar who's come here in his wanderings, has easily strung the bow and shot through the iron.'

"That's what they'd say, and so, for all of us, this talk would become the source of our disgrace."

Deep in thought, Penelope then answered him.

"Eurymakhos, there is no way that there can be high regard in this country for men who misuse and consume the household of the best of men, so why do you take this as an insult? This stranger is very tall and well-built and he claims to be the son of a good father. So give him the polished bow so we can see for ourselves. I'll say this much, and I'll follow it through—if Apollo gives him glory, and he strings it, I will fit him with a cloak and tunic, and fine clothes, and I will give him a sharp javelin to keep off dogs and men, and a double-edged sword. And I will give him sandals for his feet, and then I will send him wherever his heart and soul may call him."

Gathering his thoughts, Telemakhos spoke to her.

"Mother, no one has a better right than I do to grant or refuse the bow to whomever I wish—not those who are lording over rocky Ithaka, nor those from the islands out toward Elis, where they breed horses. Not one of these will hold me back against my will, even if I want to give this bow to our guest to take away, once and for all. But go up to your chamber and keep yourself busy with your own tasks, the loom and the spindle, and tell your servants to engage themselves in their work. This bow is for the likes of men, for everyone, but most of all, for me. The power in this house is mine."

Struck with wonder, she went back up to her room, aroused in her heart by the inspired words her son had spoken. She went to the upper room with her women slaves, and she wept for Odysseus, the husband she loved, until Athena, her eyes gleaming, shed sweet sleep over her eyelids. Just then, the brilliant pig keeper grabbed the curved bow and was taking it away when all the suitors in the hall shouted at once, and one of the overbearing young men spoke.

"So where are you taking that curved bow, you crazy, miserable keeper of pigs? Soon the playful dogs you yourself raised will eat you up, alone and away from people, if Apollo and the other gods are willing."

As they spoke, the pig keeper set down the bow, exactly where he was, in fear of so many shouting in the hall at once. Across the room, Telemakhos called out a threat.

"Papa, take the bow away. Soon you'll not listen to them all, afraid that I, though younger than you, would drive you out into the country, throwing rocks because I'm stronger than you. If only I were stronger in my hands and use of force than all the suitors in this house—I would soon send one or two of them out of this house bitterly, to go back home, since they keep on thinking up so much trouble."

As he spoke, all the suitors laughed gleefully at him and abandoned the harshness of their anger at Telemakhos. The pig keeper carried the bow through the room and stood by Odysseus, fuming. He placed it in his hands. Then he beckoned to the nurse Eurykleia.

"Telemakhos is asking you, vigilant Eurykleia, to bar the room's firmly set doors. And if anyone hears the groans and uproar of the men inside these walls, do not let them go outside, but keep them where they are, quietly at their work."

After he had spoken, not a word from her took wing, and she barred the doors to those crowded halls. In silence Philoitios rushed out of the house and barred the gates to the walls around the courtyard. Under the portico there was a papyrus rope from a rounded ship. He tied the gates with it and went inside. There, he went and sat down in the chair from which he had risen. He watched Odysseus, who was already holding the bow, turning it over and over again, trying it out here and there, in case worms had eaten the horn while its master was away. And one suitor would glance at another next to him and say, "He's got to be some kind of fanatic, a dealer in bows. Either he already has one like this, lying somewhere at home, or he's stirred up to design one for himself, the way he is brandishing it, this way and that in his hands—like a drifter knowledgeable in evil."

And another of the arrogant young men would say, "He's as likely to turn a profit from those odds as he will ever be able to bend and string this bow."

The suitors kept on talking. But Odysseus himself, always thinking ahead, raised the huge bow and looked it over. As a man who is knowledgeable in lyre and song casually stretches the string about a new peg and tightens the twisted sheep gut at both ends, Odysseus strung the enormous bow without effort. He grasped it firmly in his right hand and tried the string. It sang like the voice of a swallow under his touch. A great uneasiness came over the suitors. Their skin turned pale. Zeus thundered loudly as a sign, and radiant, Odysseus, who had endured so much, was heartened that the son of that crooked deceiver, Kronos, had sent him an omen.

He picked up a sleek arrow that was lying exposed on the table beside him, while all the others were stored inside the hollow quiver—the others about to be tried out on the Akhaians. He picked it up and laid it at the bow's center, and he drew back the string with the notch in the arrow, and while he was still sitting on his stool and aiming straight ahead, he let the arrow go—and it did not miss any of the axes' holes. From first to last, the sleek arrow weighted with bronze took flight, passing all the way through and out the other side.

And then the man called over to Telemakhos.

"Telemakhos, the stranger sitting here in your great hall has brought you no shame. I did not miss my target nor take too much time stringing the bow. My strength is still unshaken, although these suitors have insulted and ridiculed me. But the hour has now arrived to set the Akhaians' table, while it's still light, and then on to another song and dance to accompany such a feast."

He nodded his brow. And Telemakhos, Odysseus's beloved son, threw his sword belt over his shoulders and grabbed his own spear with both hands, and he stood beside the stool, next to the man, armed with gleaming bronze.

XXII

Slaughterhouse

Always thinking ahead, Odysseus stripped away his rags and leaped up onto the large threshold with his bow and quiver full of arrows. He emptied the arrows quickly at his feet and spoke among the suitors.

"This onerous game has reached its end, and now we will go for another target that no one has yet to hit, if Apollo answers my prayer and I can make it."

As he spoke, he aimed a sharp arrow at Antinoos, who was holding a shiny, double-handled gold cup in his hands, about to raise it up to sip the wine, without a thought of death. Since what man dining among others would think that he—one man among so many, however strong he is—would bring such a horrible death and black desolation upon himself? Odysseus aimed and shot an arrow into his throat. The point went all the way through his tender neck, and as it struck, he slumped to one side.

The cup fell from his hand. A jet of thick human blood came out of his nostrils. He gave a quick kick with his foot, and shoved the table away. All the food spilled onto the floor, and the bread and roasted meat were spoiled. When they saw the fallen man, the suitors filled the great hall with their uproar. They jumped up from their chairs, and they glanced about in agitation at the thick walls on all sides, but there was not a shield or a thick spear for them to grab anywhere. They all castigated Odysseus with angry words.

"Stranger, it's outrageous for you to aim your bow at men. You'll never take part in any other contest ever again. Your total destruction is now a sure thing, because you've killed the best of all the young men in Ithaka. For this, vultures will devour you here."

So each man would say, because they all were thinking that he had not meant to kill the man, and foolishly they did not see how the noose of their annihilation had been tied. Peering at them from under his brows, always thinking ahead, Odysseus said to them, "You dogs, you thought I would never reach home from the land of the Trojans, and so you ravaged my home and forced yourselves on the women servants and while I was still alive, you flagrantly courted my wife without fear either of the gods who retain the vast skies or of human outrage in the time to come. But now the noose of your utter annihilation has been tied."

As he was speaking, pale fear gripped them all. Each one of them peered around to see how he might escape his own utter destruction. Only Eurymakhos spoke up and answered him.

"If you're in fact Odysseus of Ithaka who has returned, everything you're saying is right about everything the Akhaians have done—many indignities both in these halls and out in the countryside. But now the one to blame for everything is lying there, Antinoos. He was the one who instigated these actions, not out of need or the desire for marriage, but for something else—that he might ambush your son and then kill him and become king himself in the orderly land of Ithaka, which the Son of Kronos has not brought about. Now he's been killed, which is what he deserves, but spare your own people. From now on, we will make amends throughout this land for everything that's been drunk and eaten inside these halls, and we will bring you justice, each of us, the value of twenty oxen, and pay you back with bronze and gold, until your heart is pacified. Till then, no one could blame you for your indignation."

And peering up from under his eyebrows, always thinking ahead, Odysseus called over to the man.

"Eurymakhos, not even if you give me your entire inheritance, everything you have now and whatever you might add to it from somewhere else, I won't keep my hands back from killing, until all of you have paid me back for your offenses. But now, what lies before you is to fight, face to face, or flee, if anyone can manage to escape death and destruction, but I don't think any of you are going to escape your utter annihilation."

As he spoke, their knees gave way right where they stood, and their hearts beat faster. Eurymakhos spoke again.

"Friends, this man will not restrain his stubborn hands, and now that he has seized his polished bow and quiver, he'll shoot from the sculpted threshold until he kills all of us, so let's turn to the fight. Draw your swords! Hold the tables in front of us against the arrows and their quick death. Everyone, have at him, together! We can drive him away from the threshold and doorway and go through the city and raise the alarm quickly! Soon this man will shoot his bow for the last time!"

He shouted and drew out his bronze sword, sharpened on both sides. Yelling horribly, he leaped at the man. At that moment, brilliant Odysseus shot an arrow. It flew into the man's chest, next to his nipple and quickly the shaft stuck firmly in his liver. The sword dropped to the floor away from his hand and tumbling over the table, he doubled over and fell. All the food and the double-handled cup spilled on the floor. His heart in agony, he beat the earth with his forehead. With both feet, he kicked out and shook the chair, and a dark mist passed over his eyes.

Antinomos then went for glorious Odysseus. He rushed straight at him, his sharp sword drawn, so that he would give way from the doorway, but Telemakhos was too quick. He threw his bronze-tipped spear from behind the man and struck him between the shoulders. He drove it through his chest. The man fell with a thud, smacking the ground with his forehead. Telemakhos jumped back and left the spear, with its long shadow, there inside Antinomos, in case one of the Akhaians might come rushing in and attack him with a sword and strike at him as he was leaning over. He started to run and quickly reached his dear father. Standing next to him, he sent these words on the wing,

"Father, I'll bring you a shield and two spears and a helmet, all bronze and fitted to your temples. As soon as I get back, I'll throw on some armor and give some to the pig keeper and the cattle herder."

Always thinking ahead, Odysseus answered him.

"Run and get them while I still have some arrows to defend myself or they might be able to drive me away from the door, since I'm all alone for now."

As soon as he spoke, Telemakhos obeyed his dear father and headed for the storeroom, where all the legendary old arms were stored. There, he took four shields, eight spears and four bronze helmets with thick horsehair plumes. He carried them out and went very quickly to his beloved father. First, he hitched the bronze around his own flesh and similarly the two slaves put on the beautiful armor and stood next to where quick-witted Odysseus was standing, with fire in his heart. But for as long as he had arrows to defend himself, he kept aiming and shooting the suitors, one by one. They fell in tangled heaps throughout the hall.

But when the master's arrows ran out as he was shooting, he leaned the bow by the door of that sturdily built hall and stood it against the bright entrance walls. He set a four-fold shield around his shoulders and placed a well-crafted helmet with a horsehair plume securely over his head, and the crest waved chillingly above him. He grabbed two thick spears, tipped with bronze. Set in the wall's solid construction, there was a kind of hidden doorway and close to the very top of the threshold was a passageway with tightly fitted door frames. Odysseus ordered the brilliant pig keeper to stand close by and keep an eye on it. There was space for only one man to rush through. And Ageleos spoke up and told everyone about it.

"Someone climb up by that hidden door and raise the alarm and tell all the people. Quick as possible! Soon this man will shoot his bow for the last time."

Melanthios, the goat keeper, answered him.

"No, the courtyard door is too close, Ageleos, and the mouth of the passage is too narrow. One man can hold back all of us, if he's brave enough. But I'll bring some weapons so you can arm yourselves—from the storeroom, because I think Odysseus and his pale son have put them away in there and nowhere else."

As he spoke, Melanthios the goat keeper climbed the steps toward Odysseus's storeroom. He grabbed twelve shields and as many spears and bronze helmets with thick horsehair plumes, and then he went back. Very quickly, he brought them and gave them to the suitors. Odysseus's knees gave way. His heart beat faster when he saw them throwing on armor and brandishing long spears in their hands. The challenge before him seemed enormous. Right away, he called these words on the wing to Telemakhos.

"Telemakhos, one of the women in these halls must be raising a hard battle for us, or else it's Melanthios."

Gathering his thoughts, Telemakhos answered him.

"Father, I myself made this mistake—no one else is to blame. I left the tight doors of the storeroom ajar. Their lookout was better than I am. Go, Eumaios, close the storeroom door. And see if one of those women did this—or Melanthios. I bet it's him."

As they spoke, Melanthios the goat keeper went to the storeroom yet again to bring back more armor, but the brilliant pig keeper noticed him and right away, he called over to Odysseus, who was nearby.

"Son of Laertes, Zeus's descendant, there's that destructive man again, who we believe was going to the storeroom. Tell me straight—should I kill him, if I prove to be better, or bring him back to you, so he can repay you for so many wrongs that he has thought up here in your house?"

Always thinking ahead, Odysseus answered him.

"Yes, Telemakhos, and I'll keep these proud suitors inside the hall, hot-headed as they are. You two, bend his feet back behind him, with his arms up and back, and then throw him into the storeroom. Tie some boards behind him and wrap a twisted rope all around him and hoist him up on that high pillar post. Then pull him up near the roof beams, so that he'll live for a long time suffering harsh pains."

As he spoke, they listened closely and obeyed. They went to the storeroom, unseen by the man inside. He was rummaging around for weapons, deep in the innermost recesses of the storeroom. The two waited, each standing on one side of the doorpost. Then Melanthios the goat keeper came out across the threshold, holding a beautiful helmet in one hand and in the other, a wide old shield, spotted with rust—Laertes' shield, which he had once carried as a young man, but long ago laid aside, its straps now loose.

The two jumped out at him, grabbed him and dragged him inside by the hair. They threw him down on the floor, his heart in anguish, and they bound together both his feet and hands with a painful binding, tying them tightly behind his back, exactly as Laertes's son, brilliant Odysseus, who had endured so much, had told them to. They wrapped a twisted rope around him, hoisted him up the high pillar post, and pulled him up near the roof beams.

Then Eumaios, keeper of pigs, you mocked him.

"Now for sure you're going to keep close watch for the whole night, Melanthios, lying on a nice soft bed, as is only right, and you won't miss Dawn, rising early out of the undercurrents of Okeanos on her golden throne, right when you usually herd your goats to the house to prepare the feast for the suitors."

They left him like that, racked in his awful bindings. The two put on their armor and shut the bright door. And they went back to Odysseus, the shrewd man with fire in his heart. They stood there, breathing fiercely, four of them on the threshold, while those in the hall were many and skilled at fighting. Athena, Zeus's daughter, approached, looking like Mentor in body and voice. Odysseus saw her, and he was glad. He said these words.

"Mentor, watch over me in this fight and remember me, your true friend who did some good for you, my age mate."

He said this, thinking it was Athena, who inspires the people, but on the other side of the hall, the suitors shouted out, and Agelaos Damastorides rebuked her.

"Mentor, don't let Odysseus persuade you with all his talk to fight against the suitors and protect him, because I think our plan will be carried out. When we kill these men, both father and son, you yourself will be killed along with all of them. No matter what you may want to achieve here within these halls, you'll pay with your own head, and when we've taken away your power with our bronze, all the possessions that you own, both inside and outside, we'll throw together with Odysseus's things, and we will neither let your sons go on living in your halls, nor let your daughters or your dear little wife go about unconfined through the city of Ithaka."

As he spoke, Athena grew more furious in her heart, and she reproached Odysseus with fuming words.

"No longer, Odysseus, is your nerve so steady as that courage you showed Helen, with her white arms, fighting the Trojans continually for nine years. You killed so many men in deadly fighting, and it was with your advice that Priam's city, with its wide streets, was taken. So why, now that you have returned to your own home and possessions, do you only whimper about showing all your strength to these suitors? Come, my friend. Stand here next to me and watch the things that I can do, and you will see what kind of man Mentor Alkimides is, to pay you back for the good things you've done, here in the face of threatening men."

Yet she did not give him enough power for a decisive victory. She was still testing the strength and courage of both Odysseus and his splendid son. She herself alighted to the hall's roof beam, and she sat there, looking like a swallow. Agelaos Damastorides now urged on the suitors, along with, Euronomos, Amphimedon, Demoptolemos, Peisander Polyktorides, and Polybos, a man with fire in his heart, since these were the best by far of all the suitors left alive. They fought for their lives. The bow and the cascade of arrows had brought all the others down. Agelaos spoke up, shouting his words out to them all.

"Friends, already this man's holding back his stubborn hands. Mentor has gone, after making empty boasts, and they're left alone there at the outer doors. So don't throw your long spears all at once, but come on—six of you throw first, so Zeus will let us strike Odysseus down, and we will win our glory. There'll be no trouble with the rest, once he's fallen."

After he spoke, they all threw their spears eagerly as he had ordered, but Athena made it all for nothing. One of them hit the doorpost of the well-built hall. Another hit the fitted doors. Another's ash spear, with its heavy bronze, stuck in the wall. And when the others had dodged all of the suitors' spears, brilliant Odysseus, who had endured so much, was the first to speak.

"Friends, now at last I tell you, hurl your spears together into this crowd of suitors, who are so eager to kill us on top of all the other wrongs they've done before."

After he spoke, they all aimed straight and threw their sharp spears. And Odysseus hit Demoptolemos. Telemakhos hit Euryades. The pig keeper hit Elatos. And the man who herded the cattle killed Peisander. At once, all of them clinched at the boundless earth with their teeth. And the other suitors drew back into the furthest recesses of the great hall, and then they leaped forward and pulled the spears out of the dead bodies. Again, the suitors eagerly hurled their sharp spears, but Athena made most of them come to nothing. One man struck the doorpost of the well-built hall. Another hit the fitted doors. Another's ash spear with its heavy bronze stuck into the wall.

But Amphimedon struck Telemakhos above the hand along the wrist—a glancing blow, and the bronze tip only broke the skin's surface. Ktesippos's long spear grazed Eumaios's shoulder above his shield, but it flew over his head and dropped onto the ground. Once again, Odysseus, thinking craftily with fire in his heart, and those around him threw their sharp spears into the crowd of suitors. Odysseus, scourge of cities, struck Eurydamas. Telemakhos hit Amphimedon. The pig keeper struck Polybos, and then finally the man who kept the cattle struck Ktesippos in the chest. He boasted over him.

"Son of Polytherses, you lover of wrongdoing, you'll never again talk so big while giving in to foolishness, but leave the last word to the gods, since they are much more powerful. Here's a present from your host, in return for that hoof you once presented to Odysseus, back when he was begging, here in his own home."

As the keeper of the spiral-horned cattle was speaking, Odysseus stabbed Damastorides with his long spear in a close fight. Telemakhos stabbed Leiokritos Euenorides with his spear, thrust deep in the gut, and he drove the bronze through, and the man crashed to the ground on his forehead. At that moment, Athena held up her deadly shield from high above, near the ceiling, and the suitors lost their nerve. They fled through the great hall like a herd of cattle that darting flies fall upon and drive along at springtime as the days get longer.

Like vultures with crooked talons and curved beaks that come down from the mountains to dive at little birds, flying low under the clouds over the plain, they spring upon them and kill them, because there is no defense, no escape, and men enjoy watching the chase. That is how the others fell upon the suitors and cut them down, one after another, throughout the hall. An awful groaning arose from them as their heads were cut down. And the floor swam with blood.

But Leiodes fell in front of Odysseus and grabbed his knees. And begging him, he spoke these words on the wing.

"At your knees, Odysseus, I beg you. I tell you I've never wronged any of the women in your halls in word or action. I tried to stop the other suitors when they were doing these things. They wouldn't listen to me or hold back from doing wrong, and through their own malice have met their awful doom. And so—will I, their oracle, after doing no wrong, be killed, as there's no thanks later for good that's been done?"

Looking at him from under his eyebrows, always thinking ahead, Odysseus answered him.

"If you claim to be their oracle, you must have often prayed, right here in these halls, that the final moment of my sweet return would be kept away from me, and my dear wife would go off with you and bear you children. For this, you'll not escape a terrible death."

As he spoke, in his thickset hand he picked up a sword lying close by. Agelaos had let it fall to the ground when he was killed. With it, he struck him in the neck and even while he was still speaking, his head mingled with dust.

Phemios Terpiades, the singer, who had sung for the suitors against his will, in the hope of avoiding a black doom, stood there with his inimitable lyre in his hands, close to the hidden door. His mind was torn—whether to slip out from the hall and sit outside on the step of the well-built altar to mighty Zeus, lord of the courtyard, where Laertes and Odysseus had burned many oxen thighs in offering, or to throw himself forward at the knees of Odysseus and beg. He thought it over and it seemed better to grab the knees of Odysseus, son of Laertes. He laid the hollow lyre down on the ground between a mixing bowl and a silver-studded chair, and he rushed forward and grabbed Odysseus's knees, and he begged, speaking these words on the wing.

"At your knees, Odysseus, pity me and have mercy, or later you'll be sorry you killed a singer, who plays for both gods and men. I'm self-taught, because some god has planted so many melodies in my heart. I'm good enough to sing for you as for any god. So don't be anxious to cut my throat. Telemakhos, your own son, will tell you. Unwillingly, without wanting to, I'd come to your house to sing to the suitors at their feasts. There were so many of them, so much stronger than I am, and they brought me here against my will."

As he spoke, the deep inner strength of Telemakhos heard him, and he quickly spoke to his father, who was nearby.

"Hold back. Don't stab him with your bronze. He's not to blame. Let's also spare Medon the attendant, who used to care for me at home when I was a child. Unless maybe Philoitios has killed him or the pig keeper, or he came up against you, storming through the house."

As he spoke, Medon, breathing heavily, lay cowering under a chair, after throwing an ox hide, freshly flayed, around himself to escape a black doom. Right away, he rose from under the chair and threw the ox hide aside. He rushed forward and grabbed Telemakhos by the knees with pleading words sent on the wing.

"My friend, here I am. Restrain your hand and tell your father to, so he won't, in a flood of strength, hurt me with his sharp bronze, in rage against those men, those suitors, who, here in these halls, used up his possessions and, the fools, disrespected you."

Odysseus, always thinking, smiled and spoke to him.

"Cheer up—he has pulled you out and saved you, so you will know in your heart and then tell others that doing good is far better than doing wrong. But go now, outside the hall, and sit in the courtyard, away from the slaughter, you and this singer of many melodies, until I've finished everything I have to do in this house."

As he spoke, the two left the great hall and sat down by the altar of almighty Zeus. They both kept looking all around, constantly anticipating death. Odysseus looked around throughout the house as well, in case any of the men were still alive, hiding to avoid their black doom. He found all of them, every one of them, fallen amidst the blood and dust—so many, like fish that fishermen have pulled up in the mesh of their nets on the beach of an inlet, all of them poured on the sands, gasping for the waves of the sea, and the blazing sun takes away their life. That is how the suitors were heaped upon each other. Odysseus, always thinking ahead, spoke to Telemakhos.

"Telemakhos, go and call the nurse, Eurykleia, so I can tell her the thought that's in my mind."

After he spoke, Telemakhos obeyed his beloved father. He shook at the door and said to the nurse Eurykleia, "Get up and come here, old woman. You have watched over the women servants in these halls. So come. My father's calling you to tell you something."

After he had spoken, her words lacked wings. She opened the doors of the stately hall and came out. Telemakhos led the way before her. She found Odysseus among the bodies of the dead, soiled with blood, gore and filth, like a lion that comes from feeding on an ox in a farmyard—his chest and cheeks on both sides all covered with blood, awful for the eye to view. That is how Odysseus was soiled, from his feet and hands upward. When she saw the bodies and the copious blood, she was about to cry out at the sight of this monumental action. But Odysseus restrained her and calmed her eagerness, and he sent her these words on the wing.

"In your heart, old woman, take heart but hold back. Don't cry out loud. It's not right to boast over men who have just been killed. The measure of the gods and their own reckless acts brought these men down, because they did not respect any human being who lives on this earth and who came among them, neither the bad nor the good, and so, by their own wrongdoing, they brought upon themselves a disgraceful death. But now, tell me about the women in these halls, those who dishonored me and those who are innocent."

The beloved old nurse Eurykleia answered back.

"As you say, my child, I'll tell you the whole truth. You have fifty women servants inside these halls. We've showed them how to do their work, and how to comb wool and bear up under the drudgery. Of these, twelve in all have pursued the path of insolence. They've shown respect neither to me nor to Penelope herself. Telemakhos has newly grown to maturity, and his mother would not let him manage the women servants. But come, let me go up to the bright upper room and tell your wife. Some god has sent her sleep."

Odysseus, always thinking ahead, answered her in turn.

"Don't wake her up yet. But tell those women to come here—the ones who were insolent before."

After he spoke, the old woman went throughout the hall to tell the women what had taken place, and she send them down. Odysseus called Telemakhos, the pig keeper, and the cow herder over to him, and his words carried, beating like wings.

"Start carrying out all the bodies now and order the women to help. Clean up these lovely chairs and tables with sponges and water. When you've set the whole house in order, lead those women servants out of this sturdy hall, there, between the roundhouse and the enclosed courtyard wall. Strike them down with your sharp swords, until you've taken away each one's last breath and they have forgotten what they procured from Aphrodite and the suitors, by screwing each other behind the scenes."

As he was speaking, the women arrived in a cluster, weeping, their hot tears welling and streaming down. First they carried out the dead bodies and set them down, under the portico of the secure, walled-in courtyard, and they shoved them in, up against each other, and Odysseus himself directed them and urged them on. Against their will, they carried all the bodies outside. Then they cleaned up the beautiful chairs and tables with sponges and water. At the same time, Telemakhos, the cow herder, and the pig keeper scraped down every surface of the well-built house with shovels.

The women slaves picked up the scrapings and threw it all outside. When they had set the whole house in order, they led the women out of the well-built hall, out between the round house and the secure courtyard walls. And they pushed them all into a cramped space, from which there was no way to escape. Gathering his thoughts, Telemakhos was the first to speak.

"Let it not be by a clean death that I take the lives of these women, who have poured abuse on my head and on my mother's, while sleeping with her suitors."

As he spoke, he tied the rope from a dark-prowed ship to a huge pillar and threw it about the round house. He stretched it up high, so none of them would be able to touch the ground with their feet—as doves or thrushes with long wings, trying to reach their nest, go rushing into a trap set in a thicket, and the bed that welcomes them is bitter. That's how the women held their heads—close to each other, in a row—and nooses were placed around their necks so they would die in the most miserable manner. Their feet fidgeted for a while, but not for long.

They led Melanthios out the door to the courtyard and they cut off his ears and nose with pitiless bronze. They tore out his genitals for the dogs to eat raw, and they cut off his hands and feet, their hearts enraged. And after that, they all washed their own hands and feet and went into the home of Odysseus. The work was done. He spoke again to his beloved nurse, Eurykleia.

"Bring some sulfur, old woman, to cure against this filth, and bring me fire, to fumigate the hall, and urge Penelope to come down here with her servants. And tell all the servants in the house—come."

Again, his dear nurse Eurykleia answered him.

"All this, my child, you have said rightly. But come, let me bring you a cloak and a tunic, some clothes, so you won't be standing here with your broad shoulders wrapped all in rags. That would be disgraceful."

Always thinking ahead, Odysseus answered her in turn.

"First of all, build a fire for me here in these halls."

When he spoke, his dear nurse Eurykleia did not disobey. She brought fire and sulfur, and Odysseus thoroughly fumigated the hall and the house and the courtyard. And then the old woman went off, through Odysseus's beautiful house, to inform the women and tell them to come. They came out through the hall with torches in their hands. They gathered around Odysseus and embraced him. Lovingly, they touched and kissed his head and shoulders and hands, and a sweet urge arose in him to break down and cry, because deep within his heart, he recognized them all.

XXIII

Give and Take

The old woman went up to the upper rooms, laughing aloud, to tell her mistress that her husband was home. Her knees pained her, and her feet stumbled in her haste, but she stood above the woman's head and spoke to her.

"Wake up, Penelope, so you can see with your own eyes what you've longed for, all this time. Odysseus has come. He's come home! Late as his coming is. He has killed those high and mighty suitors who troubled this house, consumed all his livelihood, and pushed around his son."

Penelope, deep in thought, answered her in return.

"Dear nurse, the gods have driven you to raving. They can drive someone who's very thoughtful to mindlessness and set the mindless on the road to reason. Now they've driven you off track, though you were sensible enough before. Why are you mocking me, when my heart is full of sorrow, by telling me this drivel and arousing me from sleep—such a sweet sleep that held me and covered over my eyelids? And I've never before slept so deeply, not since the day when Odysseus himself went off to see unspeakable Evilios. But come now, go back down to the great hall. If any one of my other women had come and told me this and roused me from sleep, I would have quickly sent her back to the hall again in the most spiteful manner, but for you, old age will be to your advantage."

The dear old nurse Eurykleia then answered her.

"I am not mocking you, dear child. It's true! Odysseus has come! He's really come home, just as I'm telling you! He is the guest—the stranger they all kept demeaning here in these halls. Telemakhos knew that he was here, long ago, but with good sense, he hid his father's plans until he could take revenge against those overbearing men."

After she spoke, Penelope took heart. She jumped up from her bed and threw her arms around the old woman. As she allowed the tears to stream down from her eyelids, she answered her and sent these words on the wing.

"So come now, already, dear mother, tell me the truth. If he has really come home, as you are now saying, how did he lay his hands on those shameless suitors, alone as he was? They were always together in here."

The beloved old nurse Eurykleia answered her.

"I didn't see. I didn't ask. I only heard the groans of those who were being killed. We sat in the innermost corner of our secure rooms, terrified. The secure doors held us inside, until your son came from the great hall and called for me. And I found Odysseus standing among the bodies of the killed, lying upon each other all around him, with both his feet firmly on the floor. Seeing him there, covered in blood and gore like a lion, would have warmed your heart.

"Now they have all been piled together at the gates of the courtyard. And he is burning a large fire to fumigate this beautiful house. He sent me to call you. Come on, so both your loving hearts may enter into ecstasy, because you both have suffered so many wrongs. But now, at last your heart's desire has reached its destination. He has himself come home, alive, and he's found both you and his son in these halls. But those who did him so much wrong, those suitors, he has paid back all of them, here in his own house."

Penelope, deep in thought, answered her again.

"Dear nurse, don't boast so much, not yet, laughing out loud like that. Because you know how welcome the sight of him would be to everyone here in these halls, but most of all to me and my son—our child. This cannot be true as you are telling it. No. It's one of those who never have to die who's killed all those self-important suitors, indignant at their disturbing excess and wrong doings, since they did not respect any living human being on this earth who came among them, neither the bad nor the good. But Odysseus, far away, has lost his return to the land of Akhaia. He himself is lost."

Her beloved nurse Eurykleia answered her in turn.

"My child, what a word has escaped the barrier of your teeth—to say that your husband, who's already here at his own fireplace, will never return home. Your heart's always so skeptical. Come, I'll tell you another clear sign—the scar, where long ago a wild boar caught him with its white tusk. I noticed it while I was washing him. I wanted to tell you but he held his hand over my mouth and in the shrewdness of his mind, he wouldn't let me tell you. But come, I'll put my own life on the line, if I am deceiving you. Kill me with the most awful death."

Deep in thought, Penelope answered her in return.

"Dear nurse, it's difficult for you to fathom the guidance of the gods who exist forever, as clever as you are. Still, let's go to my son, so I can see these men, these dead suitors, as well as the one who's killed them."

After she spoke, they descended from the upper room. And her heart brooded a long time whether to hold back and question her beloved husband or to go to him and take hold of his head and hands and kiss them. When she had made her entrance, passing over the stone threshold, she sat down by the opposite wall, in the firelight, facing Odysseus.

He was sitting by a tall pillar, looking downward, waiting to see if his courageous wife would speak to him when she saw him with her own eyes. But she only sat there for a long time in silence, and wonder came over her heart. Now, with her own eyes, she was able to look at him, face to face, but she could not recognize him in his soiled clothes. Telemakhos reproached her, calling her by name.

"Mother, my cruel mother, your heart is so stubborn. Why do you hold back from Father this way and not sit beside him, questioning him, prodding him? No other woman would stand so much in her heart and yet hold back from her man, who after suffering so many hardships for twenty years, has come back to his native land. Your heart is always harder than stone."

Deep in thought, Penelope answered back.

"My child, this heart in my breast is filled with wonder. I'm not able to speak or ask him even a word or look at him, face to face. If he is really Odysseus, and he has come home, surely we both will know each other even better than before, since we have signs, hidden from others, that only the two of us recognize."

Radiant, Odysseus, who had endured so much, smiled. He spoke to Telemakhos.

"Telemakhos, let your mother test me, here and now, inside these halls, and soon she'll see more clearly. But now, because I'm dirty, with these awful clothes on my body, she despises me and won't admit who I am. But let's think how to make the best of this, because in this land, whoever has killed even one man, even if few are left behind to seek revenge, runs away and leaves behind his kin and his own country. But we have killed off the elite of this city, the most aristocratic young men in Ithaka. I urge you to think this over."

Telemakhos gathered his thoughts and answered him.

"You see to those things yourself, my dear father, since your shrewdness about people is unsurpassed, and no one else among us mortal human beings could ever match you. We'll gladly follow you, and I don't believe that we'll be inadequate in your defense, as long as we have our strength."

Always thinking ahead, Odysseus answered him in turn.

"Then I will tell you what seems to be best to me. First, wash yourselves and throw on your tunics and tell the servants here in these halls to choose their clothing well. And let that wonderful singer with his clear-voiced lyre lead us in playful singing and dancing, so that anyone who is passing by on the road or living nearby and hears us outside will think it's a wedding, and the rumor of this killing won't spread through the city, before we go into the countryside among the trees. There, we can figure out what advantage the Olympian may place in our hands."

As he spoke, they all listened closely and obeyed. First, they washed themselves and put on their tunics. The women dressed. The wonderful singer picked up his hollow lyre and aroused their desire for a sweet song and an innocent dance. And the great hall echoed with the footsteps of dancing men and beautifully attired women. And anyone who might have heard it outside the house, would have said, "Ah, someone's married the queen. Cruel, she did not bother to hold onto the great house until he came."

They would say such things but would not know what was really happening.

Eurynome the housekeeper bathed the great-hearted Odysseus in his own house. And she anointed him with oil and threw a beautiful cloak and tunic around him and over his head, and Athena shed a generous radiance that made him look taller and stronger. And she made his hair flow down in curls from his head like hyacinths. As when a skilled artisan whom Hephaistos and Pallas Athena have inspired to learn all kinds of crafts, overlays silver with gold, and his work is full of grace—that is how Athena shed grace over his head and shoulders. He stepped out of the bath, looking like one of the immortals, and he sat down again on the chair from which he had risen, facing his wife, and he spoke these words to her.

"You have been touched by the gods. In you of all nurturing women, those who live there on Olympos have placed a heart that cannot be moved. No other woman would harden her heart as you do and stand back from her man who, after going through so many hardships, has come back to his own land and back to her. But come now, nurse, spread out a bed for me, so I can lie down by myself, since the heart inside her breast is made of iron."

Deep in thought, Penelope answered him in kind.

"You yourself are touched by the gods. I'm neither setting myself apart nor spurning you. Nor am I much in awe. I know very well how you looked when you left Ithaka on your ship with all its long oars. But come, lay out that sturdy bed frame for him, Eurykleia, outside the superbly made bedroom that he himself constructed. Just bring that sturdy bed out there for him and throw on some bedding, sheepskins and cloaks, and some bright blankets."

She spoke like this to test her husband, and Odysseus lost his temper, and raised his voice at his cautious-minded wife.

"Woman, what you're saying is utterly heartbreaking. Who put my bed somewhere else? It would be hard, even for someone who knows what he's doing, unless a god has come and on his own, easily set it down in another place. But here among men, there's no one alive, no matter how young, who could pry it out of place without difficulty, because there's a great feature that is built into the bed's construction, and I built it and no one else.

"An olive bush with long leaves was growing there in the courtyard, strong and hardy and thick as a pillar post. I built the bedroom around it, and I finished it with closely set stones and roofed it over well, and I put in close-fitting doors with joints. Then I cut away the foliage of the olive tree, with its long leaves, and trimmed the trunk, and I smoothed it down well and skillfully with bronze, set it true to the line, and built up the bedposts and bored in holes all over it with a hand drill.

"Starting from there I sanded down the bedframe till I'd finished it, engraving it artfully in gold, silver, and ivory. And I stretched some bright purple ox hide straps all over it. So now I've spoken openly about this piece, but I don't know, woman, whether the bed is still in place, or if someone has placed it somewhere else by chopping through the trunk of the olive tree."

As he was speaking, her knees relaxed and her heart fluttered, recognizing the features that were still in place and that Odysseus had disclosed. She burst into tears, and she ran straight to him. She threw her arms around Odysseus's neck, kissed his face, and then she spoke.

"Odysseus, don't be angry with me. You've always been the most understanding of men. It was the gods who brought us sorrow and objected to our staying together to enjoy our youth and come to the threshold of old age. Don't be angry at me for this or turn away because I didn't welcome you when I first saw you, as I do now. In my own breast, my heart's always shuddered that some man might come and charm me with his words.

"There are so many who offer bad advice for profit. Even the Argive, Helen, daughter of Zeus, wouldn't have fallen in love and gone to bed with a stranger if she had known that the hot-blooded sons of the Akhaians were going to bring her back to her own native land. Yet it was a goddess who aroused her to commit that despicable act. But it was not until later that it occurred to her how awful would be the suffering that has reached even us.

"But now you've clearly laid out the features of our bed, which no other person has ever seen but you and me and one of my servants, the daughter of Aktor, whom my father gave to me before I ever came here, and she guarded the doors of our secure bedroom. But you have utterly won over my heart now, no matter how callous it has become."

Her words aroused in him an even greater desire to cry. He wept, holding his wife, and he felt her heart, close to his own.

The sight of land is welcome to swimmers, after Poseidon has smashed their well-built ship out on the sea, as it was driven about by the wind and heavy waves, and only a few ever escape the gray sea by swimming ashore, their bodies thickly crusted with salt. But when they escape the most horrible agony, they make it to shore, full of joy. That is how welcome her husband was as she looked at him, and she never loosened her white arms around his neck. And Dawn, with her rosy fingers would have risen on their tears, if Athena, her eyes gleaming, had not thought otherwise. She held back the long night on the horizon, and she drew back Dawn, on her golden throne, at Okeanos, and would not let her yoke those fast horses, Lampos and Phaethos, the colts who lead Dawn's chariot and bring light to human beings. But Odysseus, always thinking ahead, spoke to his wife.

"Woman, we've by no means come to the end of all our trials. There's going to be more trouble ahead, long and hard and unfathomable, which I will have to follow through to the end, as the spirit of Teiresias foretold that day when I went down to the house of Hades to ask about my shipmates' and my own return. But come, let's go to bed now, and loll about in sweet sleep and get some rest."

Deep in thought, Penelope answered him in kind.

"Your bed will be there for you whenever your heart desires, since the gods have made it possible for you to return to the house that you built so well and your own native land. But since you've thought of this or some god thrust it into your heart, come—tell me about this trial, since I'm bound to learn about it, and it's no worse to find out right away."

Always thinking ahead, Odysseus answered her in turn.

"You've been touched by the gods. Why are you so stirred up that you're now asking me to tell you? Fine, then, I'll describe it, and I won't hide anything. Your heart won't enjoy it, since I myself can find no joy in it. He urged me to go to many cities with a fine oar in my hands, until I find myself among people who do not know about the sea, who eat their food unmixed with salt, and who know nothing about ships with purple sides or well-crafted oars like a ship's wings. He told me about this clear sign that I won't keep from you. When some other drifter, odd as he is, comes to me and asks me why I have a winnowing shovel on my shoulder, he said, then drive the oar into the earth and offer lavish sacrifices to Poseidon—a ram, a bull, and a boar used to mate with sows—and head home and offer a hundred head of cattle to each and every one of the gods who occupy the vast heavens and never die. My own death will come to me out of the sea and take me away very gently, overcome with comfortable old age, and all the people around me will thrive. All of this, he told me, I must follow through to the very end."

Deep in thought, Penelope answered back.

"If the gods at last will bring you to a happier old age, there's hope that you'll be able to escape from hardship."

While they were talking to each other about these things, Eurynome and the nurse, by the light of blazing torches, prepared their bed with silky throws. After they had busied themselves with spreading the sturdy bed, the old woman went to lie down, while Eurynome, the bedroom maid, led them away, holding a torch in her hands, to bed. She led them to their room, and then withdrew, and they entered, full of joy, into the refuge of their old bed.

And Telemakhos, the cattle herder, and the pig keeper stopped their feet in the middle of their dance, and made the women stop, and they too lay down to sleep in the shadowy halls.

After the two fulfilled their joy, making love, they went on to revel in each other's stories, talking to each other—the radiant woman herself about everything she had gone through there inside their halls, watching that obnoxious crowd of men, those suitors who, all because of her, killed so many of their cattle and their plump sheep, and an enormous amount of wine had been drawn out from the earthen jars, and Odysseus, the descendant of Zeus, laid out all the trouble that he had brought on other men and all the sufferings that he himself had gone through, and she herself took pleasure in hearing it, and sleep did not fall over her eyelids before he had told it all.

He began with how he first overcame the Kikones and came to the fertile land of the lotus eaters and what the Kyklops had done and how it was made to pay the price for devouring some of his courageous companions without mercy and how he had come to Aiolos, who had received him generously and had sent him away but it was not yet his destiny to reach his native land because a squall snatched him up again and carried him across the fish infested sea, groaning deeply, and how he came to Telepylos, among the Laistrygonians, who destroyed his ships and all his well-equipped men and Odysseus alone got away in his own black ship, and then he described Kirke's tricks and intricate deceit and how he traveled in a ship with many benches to the house of Hades in need of Teiresias, the Theban, and had seen all his companions and the mother who had given birth to him and nursed him as a child and how he heard the incessant voices of the Sirens and how he came to the rocks of Plagkas and to ghastly Kharybdis and Skylla, from whom no man had ever escaped unscathed before, and how his shipmates had killed Helios' cattle and how Zeus, who thunders from above, had hurled against his swift ship a flash of lightning and his good mates, all of them, perished, and only he escaped that terrible end, and how he came to the island of Ogygia and the nymph, Kalypso, who longed for him to become her own husband and held him there inside her hollow caves and cared for him and told him that she would make him immortal and ageless, for all his days, but she was never able to convince the heart inside his chest and how, after many troubles, he came to the Phaiakians, who honored him so lavishly like a god and sent him away by ship to his own native land, after giving him plenty of bronze and gold and clothing and this was, at last, the end of the story he told, when sweet, limb-loosening sleep swept over him and released the cares from his heart. The goddess Athena, her gray eyes gleaming, had another thought. As soon as she felt that Odysseus had thoroughly enjoyed, to his heart's content, his wife and his sleep, right away, she stirred Dawn to rise early from

Okeanos on her golden throne, to bring light to human beings. Odysseus rose from the soft bed and urged his wife forward with these words.

"Woman, we've both had more than enough of trials—you here, weeping for my return, full of sorrow, while Zeus and the other gods have held me back, as eager as I was, far from my native land. But now that we've both come to the bed of our deepest desire, you must take care of the wealth I have in these halls, and as for the herds those arrogant suitors devastated, I will myself steal back many, and the Akhaians will give back more, until they fill up all my pens.

"But now I'll head out to that farm, surrounded by trees, to see my good father, who is suffering deeply on my account. The rest I leave to you, woman, since you are so understanding. And as soon as the sun comes up, the word is going to get around about those courteous men that I have killed here in these halls. Go back up to the upper room with the servant women and sit there. And don't look out at anyone or ask them any questions."

He wrapped about his shoulders his beautiful armor. He roused Telemakhos and the cattle herder and, of course, the pig keeper, and he urged them to take up their battle weapons in their hands. They did not disobey. They armed themselves with bronze, opened the doors, and went out. Odysseus led the way. Light was already falling on the earth, but Athena covered them over with darkness, and quickly led them out of the city.

XXIV

Ends and Means

Hermes of Kyllenia called up the suitors' souls. In his hands he held the beautiful golden wand with which he glazed the eyes of anyone he wanted or led them out of sleep again. With it, he aroused those souls, and they followed, nattering like bats, twittering as they all flit about in the innermost recesses of a deep cave when one has fallen off the rock from the cluster where they were holding onto each other. The suitors, nattering, went along with him. Hermes the deliverer led them down along the clammy pathways. They passed along beside the currents of Okeanos and by Leukas Rock and on, past the Sun's gates and the land of dreams.

Quickly they descended into a meadow full of asphodel, inhabited by souls—the shadows of those whose work is done. There they came upon the soul of Akhilleus Peleïádes, Patroklos, the flawless Autolokhos and Aïas, the finest in appearance and physique of all the Danaans, next to the inimitable son of Peleus. They crowded around him and the soul of Agamemnon Atreïdes drew close to them, deep in sorrow. Around him, others began to gather, all those who had died and met their doom along with him there in the house of Aigisthos. And the ghost of Peleus's son spoke first.

"Atreïdes, we had thought that you, above all other heroic men, were loved by Zeus, who adores lightning, since you ruled over so many exemplary soldiers in the land of Troy, where we Akhaians suffered so much hardship. But it was first to come to you, that deadly end that no one who's ever been born can avoid. How much better it would have been if you had met your death and destiny and fulfilled the honor you then held in the land of the Trojans. All of the Akhaians would have built you a tomb, and there would be immense glory for you and your son in days to come. But now it seems it was merely your fate to be cut down in a contemptible death."

And the soul of Atreus's son answered him in return.

"Ah, the lucky son of Peleus, so like the gods, you who died at Troy, so far from Argos, and all around you, others were being killed, fighting over your body, the finest sons of both the Trojans and Akhaians, and in that whirlwind of dust, magnificent in your magnificence, you lay there, your horsemanship forgotten. We fought on for the whole day, and we would never have stopped battling, if Zeus had not stopped us with a furious storm. But then, after we had carried you back to the ships, far from the fighting, we laid you out on the bedsheets and washed your beautiful skin with warm water and oil. The Danaans around you shed many hot tears, and they cut their hair.

"When she heard what happened, your mother came out of the sea with the sea nymphs who never die, and an awe-inspiring outcry soared up over the sea, and it seized every one of the Akhaians with trembling. All of them would have jumped up right away and headed back for our empty ships, if that man, so old and so profound, had not held them back—Nestor, whose advice had always seemed so excellent before, addressed the men thoughtfully and spoke with them.

'Hold back, Argives. Don't run away, Akhaian young men. His mother has come here out of the sea, along with her immortal sea nymphs, to view the face of her dead child.'

"When he spoke, the hearty Akhaians stopped fleeing. Around you stood the daughters of the old man of the sea, and they wailed bitterly. They clothed you in utterly divine attire. Then the Muses, all nine of them, accompanied each other beautifully, singing a dirge. And there, you would not have seen even one of those Argives without tears, the clear voices of the Muses had aroused them so deeply. For seventeen nights and days we all wept over you, both the gods who never die and we men who have to die. And on the eighteenth, we consigned you to the fire, and we slaughtered many fattened sheep and spiral-horned cattle. You burned—in the attire of gods with lots of oil and sweet honey—and so many Akhaians, splendid in their armor, both the foot soldiers and the horsemen, surged around the great fire as you were burning. And there arose an enormous roar.

"But when Hephaistos's blaze at last had fully consumed you, in the morning we gathered up your white bones, Akhilles, and put them all in unmixed wine and oil. Your mother provided a golden urn with two handles. She said it was a gift from Dionysos, the work of the renowned Hephaistos. In it your bones now lie, illustrious Akhilleus, intermixed with the bones of Patroklos, Menoitios's dead son. Placed separately are the bones of Antilokhos, whom you respected most of all your fellow soldiers, save the dead Patroklos.

"And afterwards, all around them, we, the grand army of Argive warriors, piled up a huge, flawless tomb on a jutting headland near the wide Hellespont, so it would be seen from far away over the sea, both by those now alive and by those who are yet to be. And your mother entreated the gods for beautiful gifts and set them in the middle of the contest ground for the very best of the Akhaians. You yourself have witnessed the awesome funeral games of many heroic men when a king dies and the young men arm and equip themselves to win the prizes.

"But if you'd seen that one, there, you would have wondered in your heart even more, as the goddess Thetis, in her silver slippers, set out such beautiful prizes in your honor. You were loved so much by the gods. So you did not lose your name, even in death. You will always have great fame among men, Akhilleus. But what good is it for me that I finished the war? On my return Zeus prepared a bitter death for me at the hands of Aigisthos and my abominable wife."

They were speaking to each other like this when Argeïphontes the messenger approached them, leading down the souls of the suitors killed by Odysseus. When they noticed them, the two were overcome with wonder, and they went straight toward them. The soul of Agamemnon, son of Atreus, recognized the handsome Amphimedon, the beloved son of Melaneos, because he had been the man's guest when he stayed in Ithaka. The soul of Atreïdes was the first to speak.

"Amphimedon, what has happened to make you enter the dark earth, all of you elite men about the same age? One could make no other choice if one were to select the city's finest men. Did Poseidon raise hard winds and high waves and bring you down aboard your ships? Or have violent men killed you on land while you were cutting away their cattle and fine flocks of sheep or as they were fighting for their city and their women?

"Answer me what I am asking. I tell you that I was your guest. Don't you remember when I came there to your house with godlike Menelaos to encourage Odysseus to go along with us on our ships, with their many benches, to Ilios? A whole month crossing over the wide sea, because it was hard to persuade Odysseus, the scourge of cities."

And Amphimedon's soul answered him in return.

"Most illustrious Atreïdes, Agamemnon, Lord of men, born of Zeus, I recall everything you're saying. I'll tell you the whole truth about our horrible end, about our death, and how it all happened. We were courting the wife of Odysseus, who had been gone for so long. She would neither repudiate the marriage as something disagreeable to her, nor follow it through to the end as she connived our black fate, our death. She contrived this other scheme inside her heart. She set up an enormous loom inside her halls and started weaving something extremely large with very fine thread. And then she spoke to us.

'Young men, my suitors, since brilliant Odysseus is dead, though you are eager to marry me, wait till I finish up this robe, so what I am weaving won't be for nothing. It is a shroud for the great Laertes, for the time when that horrible end, pitiless death, strikes him down, since the Akhaian women in this land will be outraged that he, who had won so much, lies without a shroud.'

"So she said, and our generous hearts agreed. But then, every day, she'd weave there at her loom, and at night, with torches placed beside her, she would unravel it. For three years, with her art, she kept the Akhaians from noticing and had them all convinced. But as the fourth year came, as the seasons went by and the months faded away, and so many, many days came to an end, at last, one of the women who knew about it all told us, and we surprised her, unraveling her splendid web. And so, against her will, she finished.

"Right after she had shown us the robe, right after she had woven that enormous web and washed it bright as the sun or moon, some evil god brought Odysseus from somewhere near the country's coast, over where the pig keeper had made his home. The great Odysseus's beloved son came there too, after he had arrived from sandy Pylos. And they prepared a horrible death for us courtiers. The son came first to the famous city, and Odysseus later, but Telemakhos led the way before him. And the pig keeper brought the other, wearing awful clothes on his body and looking like a miserable old beggar, his clothes were so filthy. Not one of us could have known who he was, not even the older ones among us, he showed up so suddenly before us.

"And so we all ridiculed him with hard words and threw things at him. For a while, there in his own halls, he took our taunting and throwing calmly in his heart, but when at last the mind of Zeus, who holds the shield that stirs the winds, aroused him, he took those beautiful weapons and put them down in the storeroom, and shot the bolts home. And then, very cunningly he told his wife to set out his bow and his gray iron axes in front of us courtiers as a contest—it was the beginning of the end for us doomed men.

"None of us could stretch the string on that powerful bow. We all failed by a long shot. But when the great bow reached Odysseus's hands, we all shouted together not to give him the bow, no matter what he said, but Telemakhos urged him on and told him to, and then brilliant Odysseus, who had endured so much, took the bow within his hands, strung it easily, and shot through the iron. Then he went over and stood at the threshold. He poured out the quick arrows. And with a deadly look, he shot King Antinoos. Then he took aim straight at the others, and he shot his arrows, which brought on groaning, as they all fell on top of each other.

"It became very clear that one of the gods was their helper, because right then, in a rage, they ran throughout the house and killed us all, one after another. A horrible groaning arose as our heads were struck down. The whole floor swam with blood. We all perished, Agamemnon. Even now, our bodies lie uncared for, there in Odysseus's halls, since back in each of our homes, our loved ones do not yet know, those who might wash away the black blood from our wounds and lay us out for mourning, since that is what is due the dead."

And then the soul of Atreus's son answered him.

"Lucky son of Laertes, always thinking ahead, Odysseus—no doubt the wife you took is of the highest worth. How good her mind was—Penelope, Ikarios' daughter—without a fault. How well she remembered Odysseus, the man she married. For this, the renown of her distinction will never die, and the immortals will produce for all those who live upon the face of the earth a song in praise of Penelope for her steady mind. Unlike this, the daughter of Tyndareus contrived her awful actions and killed the husband she married. Bitter will be her song among all people. She brings a bad name to all women, even those who do good."

This was the way the two spoke to each other, standing there in the house of Hades, deep below in the depths of the earth.

But when the others had departed from the city, they quickly came to Laertes' beautifully kept farm, which Laertes had won for himself long ago, and he had worked very hard on it. His house was there, and all around it stood the huts where the bonded slaves who did whatever he wanted ate, rested and slept. Inside was the old Sicilian woman who tenderly cared for him at the farm, far from town. Odysseus spoke these words to the slaves and his son.

"Now, go into that well-built house and kill the best of the pigs. I'll test my father to see if he recognizes me with his own eyes, or if I've been away so long, he doesn't know me."

After he spoke, he gave the slaves his weapons. They went to the house quickly, while Odysseus approached the thriving vineyard to make the test. He did not find Dolios as he went down into the large orchard, nor any of his sons or slaves. They had gone to gather some brush to make a hedge around the vineyard, and the old man had led the way. He found his father alone in the orderly vineyard, digging around a tree. He was dressed in a dirty tunic with grimy patches and had strapped around his shins some stitched-up ox hide leggings to guard against scratches, with gloves on his hands because of thorns and a goatskin hat on his head to cultivate his sorrow.

When he saw the man, worn down by old age, with profound sorrow in his heart, brilliant Odysseus, who had endured so much, stood a moment under a tall pear tree and let the tears run down. He wondered in his heart whether to go kiss and hug his father then and tell him all about everything—how he had returned and come back to his own land—or first to question him and test him out about everything. And as he thought it over, the latter seemed to be better. With this intent, brilliant Odysseus went straight to him. The man had his head down as he dug around the tree. Radiant, his son came up to him and spoke.

"Old man, you clearly have no lack of knowledge in taking care of orchards. You care for it well. Nothing at all in your fields lacks any care, neither plant nor fig tree, nor vine, olive nor pear, nor your garden. But I'll tell you something else, and don't hold any anger in your heart. You yourself lack good care. But then, you're old and sad and badly dried up and what you're wearing is revolting. Clearly, it's not because of laziness that your master does not take care of you. When I look at you, you don't look like a slave in appearance or height. In fact, you're like a king. You look like someone who, when he's washed and eaten, can sleep easily, since that's the way old men are. But come on now, tell me this and say it truthfully—whose slave are you? Whose orchard are you cultivating?

"Tell me the truth, so I'll know if this is really Ithaka we have reached, as that man I just met told me as I was coming here, and he was not at all helpful, as he'd hardly tell me anything or listen to what I said when I asked him about my friend, to see if he's still alive or has died and lives in the house of Hades, since I'll tell you this, and you may listen to me and think it over. I once had as a guest a man who came to my place back in my own land and there never was any other man more welcome, of all the strangers from far away who came to my house. He claimed to be from Ithaka by birth and said Laertes Arkeisiádes was his father.

"So I led him to my house and offered him plenty of hospitality, and I made him properly welcome with all that there was in the house, and I brought him the gifts that one gives to a guest, as is only fitting. I gave him seven talents of gold, and a mixing bowl, all silver, with a floral design, and twelve single cloaks and as many throws, beautiful large cloaks, and tunics too, and on top of that, women, with flawless skill in crafts, four of them, with beautiful figures, that he had chosen for himself."

His father answered him then, his tears falling.

"Stranger, you have reached the land you ask about, but arrogant, reckless men are now holding it, and all those gifts you offered—you offered them for nothing. If you had found him alive, here in the land of Ithaka, he would have sent you away with an ample exchange of gifts and great hospitality, because that is the right thing to do for one who has given first. But come, tell me this and tell me truthfully—how many years ago did you host that man, that unfortunate stranger, my son, if he ever lived, my unlucky son?

"Somewhere in the sea, far from his loved ones and his native land, the fish have eaten him, or on the shore he's become the pickings for birds and worms. His mother never wrapped him for burial or wept over him, nor his father—we who gave him birth—and his wife, the steady Penelope, though offered so many gifts, never cried out for him over his bier, after closing his eyes, as is only fitting. And tell me this truthfully, so I will know—among men, who are you? Where are your city and your parents? And where did you anchor the swift ship that brought you here with your good mates? Or did you come as a passenger on someone else's boat, and did they leave after putting you ashore?"

Always thinking ahead, Odysseus answered him in turn.

"I will lay it all out openly. I am from Alybas, where I live in a well-known house. I am the son of Apheidos, the son of Lord Polypemon, and my name's Eperitos. But some god drove me to come here against my will, and my ship stands off the open land, far from the city. As for Odysseus, this is the fifth year since he left there, and went away from my own country. Unlucky man! But he had good birds, flying to the right, and I was heartened as I sent him off, and he was happy to go. And our hearts hoped that we would meet yet again as host and guest and give each other wonderful gifts."

As he spoke, a black cloud of grief enveloped Laertes. With both hands, he grabbed some grimy dust and poured it over his gray head, groaning and groaning. Odysseus's heart was shaken. A stinging pang rushed up through his nostrils as he looked at his father. He leaped forward and hugged and kissed him, and he spoke.

"Father, I am myself that man you're asking about. Here, I have come, after twenty years, to my own land. Hold back your grief, your weeping, all your tears—and I will tell you, although we really have to hurry. I killed the suitors, there in our halls. I have punished their heartbreaking outrage and horrible actions."

Laertes voiced his answer in return.

"If you've really come back, Odysseus, my son, tell me a clear sign, so I can believe it."

Always thinking ahead, Odysseus answered him.

"First, let your eyes examine this scar, where a wild boar caught me with his white tusk on Mount Parnassos, back when I went there. You and my esteemed mother had sent me there to Autolykos, so I might receive those gifts he offered to give me whenever he came here.

"But come, I'll tell you about the trees that you once gave me in this well-kept garden, as I, a mere child, followed you around, begging for everything. We passed among these right here, and you named them and told me about each one. You gave me thirteen pear trees and ten apple trees and forty fig trees. You promised you would give me fifty rows of vines with all kinds of grape clusters on them, which would bear fruit, each in succession, whenever the seasons of Zeus made them heavy."

As he spoke, his father's knees gave way. His heart melted, recognizing the unmistakable evidence that Odysseus had showed him. He threw his arms around his beloved son, and brilliant Odysseus, who had endured so much, held him as he fainted. But when he came to, and his spirit reentered his chest, he again found the words to answer in his turn.

"Father Zeus, surely the gods still exist up there on high Olympos, if the suitors have paid for all their reckless arrogance. But now I'm dreadfully afraid that all the men of Ithaka are going to come against us and send out messages everywhere to all the cities of the Kephallenians."

But always thinking ahead, Odysseus answered him.

"Take heart—don't let these things trouble your thoughts. Let's go back to the house that lies near this orchard, where I sent Telemakhos, the cattle herder, and the pig keeper, so that they would prepare our meal as soon as possible."

And so they went on talking as they made their way toward the beautiful house and as soon as they reached the splendid home, they found Telemakhos, the cattle herder, and the pig keeper, carving up a lot of meat and mixing up some shimmering wine. And the Sicilian slave washed the great-hearted Laertes, anointed him with oil, and threw a fine cloak around him. Then Athena stood beside him, and she thickened the legs of the shepherd of the people. She made him look both taller than before and stronger to look at. And as he came out of the bath, his beloved son observed him in wonder, because he looked exactly like one of the immortal gods. He found his voice, and his words beat like wings.

"Father, there's no doubt one of the gods who live forever has made you greater in both appearance and height."

Laertes, gathering his thoughts, answered him.

"Ah, Father Zeus, Athena, and Apollo, if only it were the same as when I seized Nerikos, that well-fortified stronghold there on the coast of the mainland, back when I was the leader of the Kephallenians, with so much strength I would have stood next to you yesterday, there in our home, my armor all around my shoulders, to defend against the suitors. I would have made the knees of many of them quiver in those halls. Your heart would have been aroused within you."

They went on talking to each other in this way, but when they had stopped working and preparing the meal, they sat down on the stools and chairs. There, they reached out their hands for the food, just as old man Dolios approached with his sons, worn out from work, since their mother, the old Sicilian woman, had gone out and called them in. It was she who saw to them and who gently took care of the old man, now that old age had taken hold. And when they saw Odysseus and recognized him within their hearts, they stood there in the room, astonished. But Odysseus accosted them with words of warning.

"Old man, sit down to eat, and you others, cast aside your surprise, because we have all waited endlessly for you to come, anxious as we were to grab our food."

As he spoke, Dolios ran to him with both arms stretched. He grabbed hold of Odysseus's hand, and he kissed it on the wrist, and the sound of his voice quavered like wings.

"My dear friend—you have come back to us—we who longed so much for you, although we never thought . . . but the gods themselves have brought you . . . Welcome! May the gods bless you! But tell me this—truthfully—so I can be sure—Penelope—she worried so much—does she know yet? You've returned! Let's send a messenger!"

Always thinking ahead, Odysseus answered him in turn.

"Old man, she already knows. No need trouble yourself."

As he spoke, Dolios sat down abruptly on a polished chair. His sons also gathered around the famous Odysseus and welcomed him and shook his hand. And then, in order, they sat down by Dolios, their father, and went to work on their meal, there inside that room.

At that moment, Rumor the messenger was moving quickly throughout the whole city, telling all about the suitors' bitter death and doom. All at once, they heard it as they gathered from here and there, with moaning and crying, in front of Odysseus's home. They each carried their own dead out of the house and buried them, and they sent each of those from other cities homeward, putting them on swift ships for sailors to carry back. But they themselves, sick at heart, went as a crowd to the agora, and when they had gathered together to meet as an assembly, Eupeithes stood up and spoke among them, because an unbearable grief lay over his heart for his son, Antinoos, the first one that brilliant Odysseus had killed. His tears streaming down, he spoke out to the assembly.

"My friends, what an extreme action this man plotted against the Akhaians! He carried away many of our finest in his hollow ships, and then he lost those ships, and he lost all those men. And then, when he returned, he killed even more—by far the best of the Kephallenians. So come, before he rushes away, either to Pylos or gleaming Elis, where the Epians hold power. Let's go right now, or later on, we'll always be ashamed, and it will be a disgrace when those who are yet to be come to hear about all this, if we don't avenge the deaths of our sons and brothers. I for one could not bear to go on living. I'd rather die quickly and dwell among the dead. So let's go, before they expect us and escape across the sea."

As he spoke, his tears streaming down, the Akhaians pitied him. Right then, Medon and the marvelous singer came out of Odysseus' halls and approached, because sleep had finally let go of them. They stood in the midst of the crowd and a sense of wonder took hold of every man. And Medon, gathering his thoughts, spoke to them.

"Listen now to me, fellow Ithakans. Certainly, it was not without the will of the immortal gods that Odysseus conceived these actions. I myself saw a god, not a human, who stood close to Odysseus and seemed like Mentor in every way. He looked just like a god when he first appeared before Odysseus to encourage him, and then storming through the hall, stirring up the suitors, and they all fell down in heaps on top of each other."

As he was speaking, pale fear seized them all. Then the heroic old Halitherses, the son of Mastor, spoke to them. He alone could grasp what had gone before and what was yet to come. Thinking for the best, he addressed the assembly.

"Listen to me, Ithakans, to what I am about to say. It is because of your own cowardice, my friends, that these actions have taken place—because you would not listen to me or to Mentor, shepherd of the people, to make your sons hold back from their foolishness. They all committed an enormous error through their reckless malice, by wasting the wealth and dishonoring the wife of a noble man who, they said, would never return. Now, all this is happening. Listen to what I am telling you. Don't go. Or you might face a catastrophe that you have brought on yourself."

After he spoke, some of them remained where they were, but more than half leaped up with a loud uproar, since they did not like what he had said. Instead, they listened to Eupeithes. They went straight for their weapons, and after they had covered their bodies in gleaming bronze, they all gathered together in a crowd, before the sprawling city. Unwisely, Eupeithes led them. He thought he would avenge his son's death, but he was not to return. He would meet his end.

It was then that Athena spoke to Zeus, the Son of Kronos.

"Our Father, Son of Kronos, higher than all lords, I am asking you to tell me—what are you now hiding in your mind? Will you make more of this hateful fighting possible, this awful battle noise, or will you impose good will between the two sides?"

Zeus, gathering dark clouds, answered her in turn.

"My child, why are you questioning and querying me about all this? Didn't you yourself advise this plan, so Odysseus would take his revenge on those men whenever he returned? Do whatever it is you want. But I'll tell you what makes good sense. Now that brilliant Odysseus has taken his revenge on the suitors, have these people swear a solemn oath and make him king for life. And let us make them forget the killing of their sons and brothers. Let them be amicable with each other, as they were before. Let there be plenty and peace in abundance."

As he spoke, he inspired Athena, who was already more than willing, and so she flew down from the heights of Olympos. And when they had put aside their desire for the delicious meal, brilliant Odysseus, who had endured so much, was the first to speak to the others.

"Someone go out and see if they are approaching."

After he spoke, one of Dolios's sons went out and stood at the threshold. And he saw all the others coming and sent these words to Odysseus on the wing.

"They're already getting close. Let's arm ourselves."

As he spoke, they stood up and put on their armor. Odysseus and all those with him were four, and there were six sons of Dolios, and Laertes and Dolios too, although their hair was gray, also pulled on their armor, warriors by necessity. They covered their bodies in gleaming bronze and opened the doors and went out. Odysseus led the way. Athena, Zeus's daughter, looking like Mentor in body and voice, approached, and brilliant Odysseus was glad to see her. And right then, he spoke to Telemakhos, his beloved son.

"Telemakhos, now you yourself are about to learn all this, as you come up against men, fighting to decide who's the best and to avoid disgrace for the lineage of their fathers, who in the past were so exemplary in strength and courage throughout the whole world."

Telemakhos took a deep breath and answered back.

"You'll see, if you wish, my dear father, how this heart will not bring disgrace to your lineage, just as you say."

As he said this, Laertes was elated, and he spoke these words.

"What is this day you have brought me, beloved gods? I'm so full of joy! Here are my son and his son, arguing over who is the best in facing a challenge!"

Athena, her eyes gleaming, came close to him and spoke.

"Son of Arkeisios, dearest of all my friends by far, pray to the young woman with the gleaming gray eyes and to her father, Zeus. Then very quickly, raise your spear with its long shadow and draw it back and throw it."

As she was speaking, Pallas Athena breathed into him enormous strength. He prayed to the daughter of almighty Zeus and quickly, he raised up his spear with its long shadow and he drew it back and threw it, striking Eupeithes through the cheek guards of his helmet. They did not deflect the spear. The bronze passed all the way through. He fell with a thud, and his armor clattered around him. Odysseus and his splendid son fell upon the fighters in the front and struck at them with their swords and spears, sharpened on both sides. They would have killed them all and given them no chance to fall back, but then Athena, daughter of Zeus, who holds the aegis, shouted out in a piercing voice and held back all the people.

"Stop all this fighting, Ithakans, so you can quickly think through all this discord without more bloodshed."

As Athena spoke, pale fear seized them. In panic, as the goddess raised her voice, their weapons flew from their hands and fell to the ground. They turned back toward the city, anxious for their lives. But brilliant Odysseus, who had endured so much, cried out horribly. He pulled himself together and swooped down upon them like an eagle flying from high above, but at the same exact moment, Kronos's son hurled a flash of lightning. It fell right in front of the flashing eyes of the almighty father's daughter. Her eyes gleaming, Athena called out to Odysseus.

"Son of Laertes, offspring of Zeus, Odysseus—you're always thinking ahead of yourself. Stand back! Stop this tedious brawling and fighting, or else Zeus, Kronos' son, might become angry at you."

As Athena spoke, he obeyed, and his heart was filled with joy. And looking like Mentor in body and voice, Pallas Athena, daughter of Zeus, who holds the aegis, laid out a pact between both sides for the time to come.

About the Translator

Charles Underwood is an anthropologist who has conducted field research in Brazil, India, Scotland, and the United States. From 1996 until his retirement in 2020, he directed various University of California initiatives engaging university faculty and students with young people and their families in innovative learning programs and activities at schools and community-based organizations throughout California. Since 1998, he has also collaborated with university and community educators in research and programmatic efforts to provide inclusive learning opportunities for socially displaced young people in São Paulo, Brazil. He has also been active in collaborative relief efforts providing educational and social resources for young people and their families displaced by Hurricane Katrina. His research interests include: the socio-cultural context of learning; social displacement, learning, and social agency; and inter-institutional collaboration as a sociocultural process. He has discussed twenty-five years of this collaborative work in *A Cultural Approach to Social Displacement and University-Community Engagement: Emerging Research and Opportunities*. Also a classical scholar, he recently authored *Mythos and Voice: Displacement, Learning, and Agency in Odysseus' World*. In retirement, he continues both to conduct research and to collaborate with university and community colleagues throughout the world.